Learn Blue Teaming and Threat Management

Proactive defense, threat hunting, and incident response strategies

Akash Hedaoo

bpb

www.bpbonline.com

First Edition 2026

Copyright © BPB Publications, India

ISBN: 978-93-65890-679

LIMITS OF LIABILITY AND DISCLAIMER OF WARRANTY

To View Complete
BPB Publications Catalogue
Scan the QR Code:

Dedicated to

My mom, my wife, and my daughters (Smeira and Saanvikaa)

About the Author

Akash Hedaoo is the manager of cybersecurity operations at Owens and Minor and an accomplished cyber defense professional with over 14 years of combined experience in IT infrastructure and cybersecurity. Before his current role, he held multiple positions at Allscripts, honing his skills across a wide range of security domains.His deep passion for defensive security is not just a profession but a calling, which led him to build **Security Operations Centers (SOCs)** from the ground up and consult numerous small and mid-sized organizations to establish their own security capabilities.

Akash holds a post graduate diploma in cyber security from Amity University and possesses numerous industry certifications, including **Certified Ethical Hacker (CEH)** and **EC Council Certified Incident Handler (ECIH)**, ISO 27001 Lead Auditor, etc. He believes that cybersecurity is a fundamental societal need and is dedicated to helping both businesses and individuals protect themselves from online threats. This commitment extends beyond his corporate role; he actively participates in cybersecurity groups to learn from and mentor others and is developing a project to train parents on keeping their children safe online. Driven by his passion for making the internet a safer place for everyone, Akash is particularly focused on ensuring online safety for kids. He is deeply involved in a project dedicated to providing parents with the tools and knowledge necessary to protect their children from cyber risks. You can find him talking about cyber safety over a coffee.

About the Reviewers

❖ **Tamilarasan Pandithurai** is a cybersecurity professional with over nine years of experience specializing in security operations, threat hunting, incident response, and vulnerability management. He has contributed to the development of advanced SOC strategies and the implementation of proactive threat detection across critical infrastructure and high-security environments.

His expertise includes aligning cybersecurity operations with global standards and frameworks such as ISO 27001, CIS Controls, and MITRE ATT&CK. With hands-on experience in a wide array of tools, including SIEM, SOAR, EDR, and threat intelligence platforms, Tamilarasan brings both strategic insight and technical depth to cybersecurity operations.

Beyond his core responsibilities, he is deeply passionate about cybersecurity education and community engagement. He actively trains and mentors aspiring professionals, conducts knowledge-sharing workshops, and contributes to skill development initiatives. He has also delivered talks at international conferences, sharing insights on emerging threats and practical defense strategies.

Tamilarasan is committed to strengthening the cybersecurity landscape through continuous innovation, mentorship, and a collaborative approach to knowledge building.

❖ **Deepanshu** is a dynamic cybersecurity leader with over a decade of experience driving enterprise-grade security, designing cloud security architecture, networks, and DevSecOps integration. Proven track record in managing complex end-to-end incident response and executing high-impact digital forensics, threat hunting, malware analysis, etc. Recognized by the Government of India and the Ministry of Home Affairs for outstanding contributions to national cybersecurity. Accomplished author of two books and 18 globally presented research papers, including at DEFCON, ToorCon, and OWASP. He has also demonstrated success in reducing security incidents through proactive threat intelligence, strategic planning, and advanced technical execution.

Acknowledgement

I would like to express my sincere gratitude to all those who have been instrumental in the completion of this book. This project would not have been possible without the guidance, support, and encouragement of many individuals.

I am deeply grateful to my mentors who have shaped my professional journey. A special note of thanks goes to Unni Vishwanathan, Prateek Dixit, and Scott Stanton for their invaluable wisdom and guidance. I also want to extend my heartfelt appreciation to Snehashish Sarkar and Ronald Brown, who instilled in me the passion and drive to pursue excellence in all my endeavors.

First and foremost, I extend my deepest appreciation to my family. Their unwavering support and encouragement have been the bedrock of this endeavor. I am especially grateful for their patience and understanding. As I dedicated my weekdays to building my team and my weekends to writing this book, they stood by me without a single complaint. This book would not have been possible without their immense sacrifice and support.

My sincere thanks also go out to my entire team. I am fortunate to work in an environment where I learn just as much from my seniors as I do from my juniors. Your collective insights and collaborative spirit have been a constant source of inspiration.

I am immensely grateful to the entire team at BPB Publications. Their professionalism, guidance, and support throughout the publishing process have been exceptional and made this journey smooth and rewarding.

Finally, to my readers, thank you for investing your time in this book. I hope it serves as a valuable resource in your professional journey.

Preface

If you are reading this, you know that the digital world can feel like a battlefield. Every day, unseen adversaries launch sophisticated attacks, and the line between a secure organization and a major breach is defended by skilled, vigilant professionals. That is the world of the Blue Teamer, and it is where you come in. My goal with Learn Blue Teaming and Threat Management is to take you from enthusiast to practitioner, to equip you with the skills to become a successful incident responder and a sharp threat management professional who can confidently identify, assess, and shut down intrusions. Consider this book your guide to joining that critical first line of defense.

The book is designed to quickly move the readers from theory to action. This is not just about reading; it is about doing. We will work with the tools of the trade, as we discuss a lot of tools in this book. Together, we will look into packet analysis, learn to centralize logs, and hunt for threats on endpoints. Every chapter is built around practical, real-world use cases, so you are not just learning concepts, but rather you are building muscle memory for the job.

I wrote this book for anyone ready to step into the defender's shoes. Whether you are just starting in information security, you are an experienced SOC analyst looking to sharpen your skills, or you are an IT pro aiming to specialize in security, you will find your path here. A basic grasp of networking and security concepts will certainly help, as will some familiarity with Windows or Linux. But what you need most is a curious mind and the drive to understand how to protect our digital world.

I hope that by the end of this journey, you will feel more than just knowledgeable - you will feel empowered. The world of cyber defense is challenging, but it is also incredibly rewarding. After working through this book, you will have the practical skills and the confidence to step onto a blue team and make a real difference, protecting your organization's most critical assets from the threats of today and tomorrow.

Chapter 1: Introduction to Blue Teaming- This chapter sets the stage by explaining what blue teaming really means and why it is a crucial part of modern cybersecurity. It introduces the role of a blue teamer and how defenders work tirelessly to protect an organization's systems, data, and networks. The chapter emphasizes the importance of proactive defense and explains how blue teams collaborate with red teams to strengthen security posture. You will also explore the types of attacks defenders face and the core mission of blue teaming. By the end, you will have a solid understanding of the goals, mindset, and responsibilities of a cybersecurity defender.

Chapter 2: Advancing Security Fundamentals and Risk Assessment- Here, we will look into the foundational knowledge every blue teamer must master. From basic networking concepts to encryption, access control, and cloud security, this chapter builds the technical groundwork needed for defensive operations. You will also learn about key cybersecurity principles like incident response and risk management. These are not just theories; they directly impact your ability to spot, prevent, and respond to threats. Whether you are analyzing logs or setting up controls, these concepts are your day-to-day tools. Think of this chapter as your cybersecurity 101 crash course.

Chapter 3: Exploring Security Frameworks- This chapter explores the security playbooks that help organizations stay structured and prepared. It breaks down important frameworks like NIST, ISO 27001, and MITRE ATT&CK™, explaining how each one helps you build a mature, defensible security posture. You will learn how these frameworks guide decision-making, streamline incident response, and ensure compliance with global standards. They are more than documents; they are essential tools for any blue teamer aiming to operate effectively in a high-pressure environment. Understanding them will help you prioritize, plan, and communicate security goals clearly.

Chapter 4: Explore Blue Teaming Strengthening Techniques- This chapter focuses on tools and techniques blue teams use daily to identify and stop threats. You will learn about SIEMs, EDR tools, phishing analysis, data loss prevention, and more. The chapter also introduces modern techniques like deception technology and threat hunting, showing how blue teams actively hunt down risks instead of waiting for alerts. By exploring hands-on approaches and automation strategies, you will see how defenders gain visibility and control over complex environments. It is the how behind effective cyber defense.

Chapter 5: Defensive Strategic Methodology- In this chapter, we go behind the scenes of a modern SOC. You will learn how SOCs are structured, how they operate, and why they are the backbone of enterprise cybersecurity. The focus is on people, process, and technology—three pillars that make or break security operations. From alert handling to compliance reporting and automation, we cover how SOCs keep businesses secure in a fast-moving threat landscape. You will also see the evolution of SOCs from reactive units to proactive, risk-driven command centers.

Chapter 6: Incident Response Management- This chapter walks you through the complete incident response lifecycle: preparation, detection, containment, eradication, and recovery. You will learn how to make decisions under pressure, perform digital forensics, and minimize business impact. Real-world case studies help bring the concepts to life. The chapter also stresses continuous improvement—learning from past incidents to strengthen your response strategy. With proper planning and execution, incident response becomes a powerful weapon, not just a safety net.

Chapter 7: Effective Threat Management for Enterprises- This chapter looks into the threats organizations face—malware, phishing, insider threats, ransomware, and nation-state attacks. You will learn how attackers operate and what signs they leave behind. With real examples and hands-on analysis, you will explore how to spot, evaluate, and defend against advanced threats. The goal is to develop a proactive mindset so you are not just reacting—you are anticipating. This chapter makes threat management feel less overwhelming and more strategic.

Chapter 8: Threat Hunting Exploration- Threat hunting is where intuition meets skill. This chapter shifts focus from passive defense to actively seeking out threats. You will learn how to form hypotheses, analyze logs, use threat intelligence, and identify stealthy intrusions that have not triggered alerts. It is a high-skill, high-reward discipline that brings together experience, tools, and a deep understanding of attacker behavior. Whether it is using deception technology or building your own hunting workflows, this chapter will sharpen your instincts and help you find what others miss.

Chapter 9: Deploying and Analyzing Threat Vectors- This chapter introduces **cyber threat intelligence** (**CTI**) and how it helps defenders think like attackers. You will explore different types of intelligence—strategic, tactical, and operational, and how to use them to map attack surfaces and anticipate threats. Tools like OSINT, IOCs, and dark web monitoring are covered in detail. You will also learn how to deploy CTI in real environments, giving your defense the edge it needs. This is where you shift from responding to threats to predicting them.

Chapter 10: Threat and Vulnerability Management- Here, the focus turns to building a security-first culture and infrastructure. You will explore policies, governance frameworks, risk assessments, and awareness training—all vital to maintaining long-term resilience. The chapter also covers how to implement controls using the CIS framework and navigate evolving data privacy laws. By blending policy, people, and technology, this chapter helps you build a mature, well-rounded threat management program. It is not just about tools—it is about strategy, consistency, and communication.

Chapter 11: Future of Blue Team and Threat Management- Cybersecurity is evolving—and so should you. This chapter looks at what is next: AI-driven detection, automation through SOAR, the shift to Zero Trust, and the growing role of cloud-native defenses. You will also explore the future skill sets defenders will need, from scripting to cloud security and behavioral analytics. It is a forward-looking guide to help you stay ahead of attackers and relevant in your career. The battlefield is changing, and this chapter helps you gear up for it.

Chapter 12: Case Studies- There is no better teacher than experience, and this chapter delivers it through real-world breach analyses. From the SolarWinds hack to the Colonial Pipeline attack, each case study walks you through what happened, how the attackers got in, and what defenders did in response. These stories offer valuable lessons on common gaps, attack techniques, and missed opportunities. They help connect theory to practice and prepare you for similar scenarios in your own environment. Think of this as learning from others' mistakes—before they become your own.

Chapter 13: Sites, Tools, and References- This chapter is your go-to resource hub. It lists key cybersecurity platforms, tools for OSINT, malware analysis, phishing response, and hands-on practice through CTFs and labs. Whether you are a beginner looking to learn or a seasoned pro brushing up your skills, you will find curated links to stay sharp and current. It is not a chapter you will read once, it is one you will keep returning to. Cybersecurity never stands still, and this toolkit helps ensure you do not either.

Chapter 14: Building Your Career in Blue Teaming- In this chapter, you will be able to identify various blue team career paths and their requirements, construct a hands-on home lab for practical skill development, and recognize the crucial role of soft skills in professional success. You will also learn how to create a strategic plan for pursuing relevant certifications and prepare effectively for technical interviews, enabling you to translate the knowledge gained throughout this book into tangible career opportunities.

Coloured Images

Please follow the link to download the
Coloured Images of the book:

https://rebrand.ly/5ccbab

We have code bundles from our rich catalogue of books and videos available at https://github.com/bpbpublications. Check them out!

Errata

We take immense pride in our work at BPB Publications and follow best practices to ensure the accuracy of our content to provide an indulging reading experience to our subscribers. Our readers are our mirrors, and we use their inputs to reflect and improve upon human errors, if any, that may have occurred during the publishing processes involved. To let us maintain the quality and help us reach out to any readers who might be having difficulties due to any unforeseen errors, please write to us at:

errata@bpbonline.com

Your support, suggestions and feedback are highly appreciated by the BPB Publications' Family.

At www.bpbonline.com, you can also read a collection of free technical articles, sign up for a range of free newsletters, and receive exclusive discounts and offers on BPB books and eBooks. You can check our social media handles below:

Instagram

Facebook

Linkedin

YouTube

Get in touch with us at: business@bpbonline.com for more details.

Piracy

If you come across any illegal copies of our works in any form on the internet, we would be grateful if you would provide us with the location address or website name. Please contact us at business@bpbonline.com with a link to the material.

If you are interested in becoming an author

If there is a topic that you have expertise in, and you are interested in either writing or contributing to a book, please visit www.bpbonline.com. We have worked with thousands of developers and tech professionals, just like you, to help them share their insights with the global tech community. You can make a general application, apply for a specific hot topic that we are recruiting an author for, or submit your own idea.

Reviews

Please leave a review. Once you have read and used this book, why not leave a review on the site that you purchased it from? Potential readers can then see and use your unbiased opinion to make purchase decisions. We at BPB can understand what you think about our products, and our authors can see your feedback on their book. Thank you!

For more information about BPB, please visit www.bpbonline.com.

Join our Discord space

Join our Discord workspace for latest updates, offers, tech happenings around the world, new releases, and sessions with the authors:

https://discord.bpbonline.com

Table of Contents

CHAPTER 1
Introduction to Blue Teaming

Introduction

Welcome to this comprehensive guide on the fascinating and critical discipline of defensive cybersecurity. This book is designed to equip you with the knowledge and skills required for a successful career in blue teaming.

This first chapter will introduce the foundational concepts of blue teaming, establishing the core principles that will be explored in greater detail throughout the book. We will explore why proactive defense is essential in today's threat landscape and outline the key areas that define the blue team's mission.

Technical know-how and strategic considerations are necessary for efficient blue teaming. Members of the blue team should be well-versed in cybersecurity theories and methodologies and possess the capacity to conduct data analysis and make choices under time constraints. Members of the blue team must also have excellent communication and teamwork skills to effectively collaborate with other teams within the firm, which we will get to learn from in this book.

Structure

In this chapter, we will cover the following topics:

- Definition of blue teaming and threat management

- Role of a blue teamer

- Teams working under blue teaming

- Understanding the threat landscape

- Blue team vs. red team

Objectives

Blue teaming is a proactive cybersecurity approach that defends an organization's systems, networks, and data from cyberattacks. Blue teaming is also often referred to as defensive security. Blue teaming is to strengthen an organization's cybersecurity posture by proactively evaluating and enhancing its defensive capabilities. This is accomplished through the process of blue teaming. The term blue teaming refers to the practice of defending an organization's systems, processes, and data against real-world and simulated attacks. In a common security exercise, a 'red team' will simulate attacks to test the organization's defenses, while the 'blue team' is responsible for detecting and responding to both real-world attacks and these simulations, thereby improving the overall security posture. The key goals of blue teaming are as follows: detection and prevention of threats, management and reaction to incidents, security evaluation and improvement, management of vulnerabilities, and security awareness and training.

Definition of blue teaming and threat management

Blue teaming is the practice of defending an organization's information systems against cyber threats and attacks.. The blue team, acting as defenders, focuses on identifying, neutralizing, and responding to simulated attacks. They collaborate with the **Security Operations Center** (**SOC**) and incident response teams to improve the overall security posture. Blue team activities are often validated through penetration testing and red team-blue team exercises, and they leverage the outputs of vulnerability assessments to prioritize defensive actions.

Threat management is an effective and organized way to find, evaluate, and stop possible threats to an organization's IT systems and information assets. It is the process of constantly keeping an eye on, analyzing, and reacting to security events and situations to lessen the damage they can do. Threat management includes many different tasks, such as getting information about threats, assessing risks, managing vulnerabilities, planning how to respond to an event, and keeping an eye on things all the time. By handling threats well, organizations can make themselves more resistant to attacks, find and stop them faster, and lower the total risk of cyber incidents.

Blue teaming

Blue teaming, also known as defensive security, is the comprehensive practice of protecting an organization's information systems through continuous monitoring and active defense. The primary objective of a blue team is to maintain the **confidentiality**, **integrity**, **and availability** (**CIA**) of an organization's data and infrastructure. This is achieved through a suite of proactive and reactive measures designed to guard against, detect, and respond to cyber threats.

To accomplish this, blue teams utilize a variety of security tools, including **security information and event management** (**SIEM**) systems for log correlation, **intrusion detection and prevention systems** (**IDS/IPS**) for network surveillance, and **endpoint detection and response** (**EDR**) solutions. Beyond relying on automated alerts, a key function is proactive **threat hunting**, where defenders actively search for covert adversaries who have bypassed initial security controls. These defensive activities are often tested and refined through collaborative exercises with a red team, which simulates attacks to validate the blue team's effectiveness.

These activities are guided by the strategy of **threat management**, the structured process of identifying, assessing, and mitigating potential cyber threats. This involves gathering and analyzing threat intelligence to understand adversary tactics, conducting vulnerability assessments to find and remediate weaknesses, and executing a robust incident response plan to contain and eradicate threats when they occur. Ultimately, effective blue teaming integrates technical defense with strategic threat management to create a resilient and adaptive security posture.

Threat management

Threat management is a critical aspect of the blue team's responsibilities. It is the structured process of identifying, assessing, and mitigating potential cyber threats. They must be able to identify potential threats and respond to them accordingly. This includes monitoring suspicious activity, conducting threat-hunting exercises, and deploying countermeasures to prevent attacks. They must also stay current with the latest threat intelligence to ensure the organization's defenses are effective against the latest threats.

In addition to these tasks, the blue team is also responsible for incident response. In a security breach, the blue team is responsible for containing the incident, mitigating the damage, and restoring normal operations. They must also conduct a post-incident review to identify weaknesses in the organization's defenses and address them accordingly.

To effectively carry out their responsibilities, the blue team must thoroughly understand the organization's IT infrastructure and the latest cybersecurity trends and technologies. They must also have strong communication and collaboration skills, as they often work with other teams within the organization, such as the red team and IT support.

To protect an organization's digital assets, the blue team must be vigilant, proactive, and adaptable to stay ahead of the evolving threat landscape.

The blue team plays a crucial role in maintaining the organization's security posture through regular vulnerability assessments, penetration testing, and deploying security measures like firewalls, intrusion detection and prevention systems, antivirus software, and SIEM tools. This ensures confidentiality, integrity, and availability of the organization's data and systems.

It is worth noting that the blue team comprises professionals from various backgrounds, including network security, incident response, threat intelligence, and forensics. They work together to ensure the organization's security posture is up-to-date and effective against the latest threats.

It protects an organization's digital assets from cyber threats. Their efforts ensure that the organization's operations remain uninterrupted and that sensitive information remains confidential.

They must also adapt quickly to new threats and technologies. They must stay current with cybersecurity trends and technologies and have strong communication and collaboration skills. They often work with other teams, such as the red team and IT support. Overall, the blue team is critical in maintaining the organization's security posture and protecting it from cyber threats.

The military coined *blue teaming* to describe friendly forces' defense against hostile forces during war simulations and military drills. In military simulations, the blue team represents the defending force. It utilizes defensive tactics to safeguard its resources, while the red team stands in for the opposing force and employs offensive tactics to strike and take advantage of weaknesses.

The blue team in cybersecurity represents an organization's internal security team or defenders. They aim to defend the organization's assets from online threats and assaults, including data, networks, and systems. By putting security measures in place, keeping an eye on network traffic, and responding to problems, the blue team tries to stop and identify cyberattacks.

The red team, in contrast, stands in for external threat actors like hackers and cybercriminals who employ offensive strategies to break into an organization's systems and data. The red team tests the efficiency of an organization's security defenses by simulating actual assault scenarios.

Cybersecurity blue teams perform various tasks, including vulnerability analyses, security monitoring, and incident response. To provide a coordinated and successful response to cyber threats and assaults, the blue team closely collaborates with other teams, including the red team, the **incident response team** (**IRT**), and the SOC.

In cybersecurity, fending off online threats and assaults by utilizing defensive tactics, security measures, and incident response protocols is known as blue teaming.

Scope and workflow

The scope of blue teaming is vast and ever evolving, covering a wide range of activities and responsibilities aimed at defending an organization's digital assets.

Here is a breakdown of the key areas that fall under the purview of blue teams:

- **Threat intelligence:**
  - o Gathering and analyzing threat intelligence from various sources (open-source, commercial feeds, internal data) to understand the latest threats, vulnerabilities, and attack techniques.
  - o Proactively identifying and assessing potential threats to the organization.
  - o Developing threat profiles and attack scenarios to guide defensive strategies.

- **Vulnerability management:**
  - o Regularly scanning and assessing systems and applications for vulnerabilities.
  - o Prioritizing and remediating vulnerabilities based on risk.
  - o Implementing security controls and hardening systems to prevent exploitation.

- **Security monitoring:**
  - o Continuously monitoring security tools and systems (e.g., SIEM, IDS/IPS, EDR) for suspicious activity.
  - o Analyzing security events and alerts to identify potential attacks.
  - o Investigating and responding to security incidents.

- **Incident response:**
  - o Developing and implementing incident response plans.
  - o Containing and mitigating security incidents.
  - o Eradicating threats and recovering affected systems.
  - o Conducting post-incident analysis and reporting.

- **Digital forensics:**
  - o Collecting and analyzing digital evidence to support investigations.
  - o Reconstructing attack timelines and identifying attackers.
  - o Preserving evidence for legal proceedings.

The scope of blue teaming is constantly expanding as new technologies emerge and the threat landscape evolves. Blue teams need to be adaptable and continuously learn new skills to stay ahead of the curve.

Their operational workflow typically involves a continuous cycle of monitoring, detection, analysis, response, and improvement. Here is a breakdown of the key stages:

- **Monitor and detect:**
  - o **Continuous security monitoring**: The team constantly monitors security tools and systems (e.g., SIEM, IDS/IPS, EDR) for any signs of suspicious activity or security events.
  - o **Threat intelligence**: They leverage threat intelligence feeds to stay informed about the latest threats, vulnerabilities, and attack techniques.
  - o **Anomaly detection**: They use various techniques (e.g., statistical analysis, machine learning) to identify unusual patterns or behaviors that may indicate an attack.

- **Triage and analyze:**
  - o **Alert triage**: When alerts are triggered, the team triages them to assess their severity and potential impact.
  - o **Incident analysis**: If an alert warrants further investigation, the team conducts in-depth analysis to determine the nature and scope of the incident. This may involve:
    - ▪ Examining logs and network traffic.
    - ▪ Analyzing malware samples.
    - ▪ Conducting forensic investigations.

- **Respond and contain:**
  - o **Incident response**: Based on the analysis, the team takes appropriate actions to contain the incident and mitigate its impact. This may include:
    - ▪ Isolating affected systems.
    - ▪ Blocking malicious traffic.
    - ▪ Removing malware.
    - ▪ Restoring data from backups.
  - o **Escalation**: If necessary, the team escalates the incident to senior management or external incident response teams.

- **Recover and remediate:**
  - o **System recovery**: The team works to restore affected systems and data to their pre-incident state.
  - o **Vulnerability remediation**: They identify and address any vulnerabilities that may have been exploited in the attack. This may involve patching systems, updating configurations, or implementing new security controls.

- **Document and learn:**

  o **Documentation**: The team documents the entire incident response process, including the details of the attack, the actions taken, and the lessons learned.

  o **Knowledge sharing**: They share their findings and insights with the broader security team and other stakeholders to improve the overall security posture.

  o **Continuous improvement**: They use the lessons learned to refine their processes, tools, and techniques for future incident response efforts.

The following figure depicts the key stages of a blue team workflow, emphasizing the continuous improvement loop:

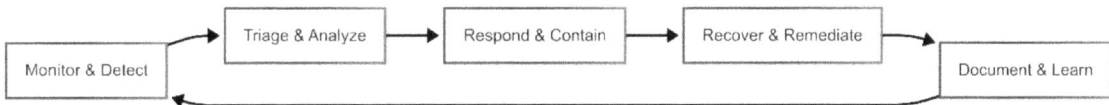

Figure 1.1: *Workflow of a blue teamer*

Role of a blue teamer

Blue teamers are the defenders of an organization's digital assets. They are the cybersecurity professionals who work tirelessly to protect critical systems and data from cyber threats. Their role is multifaceted, requiring a combination of technical expertise, analytical thinking, and communication skills.

To succeed, a blue teamer must possess a diverse set of skills and a proactive mindset. These can be broken down into two key areas:

Technical skills

A strong technical foundation is essential. This includes:

- **Knowledge of security technologies:** Deep familiarity with core defensive tools such as SIEM, EDR, firewalls, IDS/IPS, and vulnerability scanners.

- **Network security:** A solid understanding of network protocols, topologies, and fundamental security concepts.

- **Operating system security:** In-depth knowledge of operating system hardening and secure configuration for systems like Windows and Linux.

- **Cloud security:** As organizations move to the cloud, familiarity with cloud security principles for platforms like AWS, Azure, or GCP is critical.

- **Programming and scripting:** The ability to write scripts (e.g., in Python or PowerShell) to automate analysis and response tasks is a significant advantage.

Analytical and soft skills

Technology alone is not enough. The most effective blue teamers also excel in non-technical areas:

- **Analytical thinking:** The ability to analyze large datasets, identify patterns, and draw logical conclusions to uncover hidden threats.

- **Problem-solving:** The capability to troubleshoot complex security challenges under pressure and develop effective solutions.

- **Communication:** The skill to clearly communicate technical information to both technical peers and non-technical stakeholders, such as management or legal teams.

- **Collaboration:** The ability to work effectively as part of a team, sharing information and coordinating actions with other security professionals and IT teams.

- **Continuous learning:** A commitment to staying updated on the latest threats, vulnerabilities, and security technologies is non-negotiable in this rapidly changing field.

Professional qualification

While a strong foundation in technology is often associated with cybersecurity, the truth is that the field thrives on diversity. *Anyone* with the right mindset, a relentless drive to learn, and the essential skills can excel as a blue teamer or cybersecurity professional. It is more about passion, dedication, and a knack for problem-solving than adhering to a specific background. We see professionals with backgrounds in arts, history, finance, and various other disciplines seamlessly integrating into the security fraternity. Their unique perspectives and experiences often bring fresh insights and approaches to tackling cybersecurity challenges.

There are many certifications that can be taken to learn the skills required for being a Blue teamer. Foundational certifications for a blue teamer include CompTIA Security+ and **CompTIA CySA+ (Cybersecurity Analyst)**. For more specialized roles, certifications like the **GIAC Certified Intrusion Analyst (GCIA)**, **GIAC Certified Incident Handler (GCIH)**, or **Computer Hacking Forensic Investigato**r **(CHFI)** are highly valued.

Beyond the certifications, the following is also important:

- **Continuous learning**: Cybersecurity is a constantly evolving field. Blue Teamers must stay updated on the latest threats, vulnerabilities, and technologies through continuous learning, attending conferences, participating in online communities, and pursuing further education.

- **Practical experience**: Hands-on experience is invaluable for Blue Teamers. Participating in **Capture the Flag (CTF)** competitions, building home labs, and contributing to open-source security projects can provide valuable practical experience.

- **Networking**: Building a strong network with other security professionals can provide opportunities for learning, collaboration, and career advancement.

Teams working under blue teaming

Although many teams comprise blue teams, let us discuss a few, like SOC, IR, etc. We shall discuss all the different teams in the future chapters of this book.

Security Operations Center and the incident response team

A modern defensive strategy relies on two core components: the SOC and the **incident response (IR) team**. The SOC acts as the central command hub, where analysts continuously monitor the organization's networks and systems, analyzing data from various security tools to detect potential threats in real-time. When a significant security event is confirmed, the specialized IR team takes the lead, executing a structured plan to contain, eradicate, and recover from the breach. The detailed architecture and operations of the SOC will be explored in *Chapter 5, Defensive Strategic Methodology,* while the complete methodology for incident response management will be covered in *Chapter 6, Incident Response Management.*

Computer Security Incident Response Team

Computer Security Incident Response Teams (CSIRTs) are responsible for responding to high-level security incidents that can significantly impact an organization. They work closely with the IR team to coordinate responses to these incidents.

CSIRT members are typically highly skilled and possess deep technical knowledge of various technologies and systems. They may also have specialized expertise in malware analysis, network forensics, and threat intelligence.

Overall, CSIRTs play a critical role in maintaining the security of an organization's network and systems, minimizing the impact of security incidents, and helping to prevent future incidents from occurring.

Computer Emergency Response Teams

Computer Emergency Response Teams (CERTs) are responsible for responding to cyber threats at the national or international level. They work closely with other government agencies and organizations to coordinate responses to these threats.

Several national and international CERTs collaborate and share information on cyber threats and incident response best practices. These include the **United States Computer Emergency Readiness Team (US-CERT)**, the **Indian Computer Emergency Response Team (CERT-In)**, the **European Union Agency for Cybersecurity (ENISA)**, and the **Asia-Pacific Computer Emergency Response Team (APCERT)**.

These teams work together to ensure that the organization's digital assets are protected from cyber threats. By working together and sharing information, one can maintain the organization's security posture and respond to security incidents quickly and effectively.

The blue team and its sub-teams play a key role in protecting an organization's digital assets from cyber threats. They work together to ensure that your organization's security posture is up-to-date and effective against the latest threats. The role and scope of these teams may differ in different organizations, considering which protocol and framework they follow. The detailed architecture and operations of the SOC will be explored in *Chapter 5, Defensive Strategic Methodology,* while the complete methodology for incident response management will be covered in *Chapter 6, Incident Response Management.*

Understanding the threat landscape

When it comes to properly protecting oneself against cybersecurity threats, it is essential for enterprises to have a solid understanding of the threat landscape. The term threat landscape refers to the whole of the types and breadth of the possible dangers that are present in the digital world. It considers a wide range of aspects, including the various sorts of threats, the origins of such threats, attack routes, and the goals of threat actors.

A blue team's effectiveness is directly tied to its understanding of the adversary. To build a resilient defense, one must first comprehend the vast and varied threats that organizations face in the digital realm. A deep dive into the specific tactics, techniques, and procedures used by malicious actors is essential for any cybersecurity professional. Key threats, including malware, social engineering, ransomware, and advanced persistent threats, will be covered in detail in *Chapter 7, Effective Threat Management for Enterprises.*

Blue team vs. red team

Initially, the term red team and blue team were coined in the military. The term red team refers to a group of individuals who were tasked with testing the defensive capabilities of a military unit or organization. In this context, the red team was responsible for simulating the tactics and techniques used by an enemy force in order to identify weaknesses and vulnerabilities in the unit's defenses. The red team was also called the red cell. Red cell members demonstrated the vulnerabilities of military bases and would regularly use false IDs, dismantle fences, barricade buildings, take hostages, and kidnap high-ranking personnel. Similarly, the blue team was responsible for defending against the simulated attacks from the red team.

The concept of the red team has evolved to encompass a broader range of activities beyond just penetration testing. Today, red teams are often used to simulate a variety of different types of attacks, including social engineering attacks, phishing attacks, and other forms of cybercrime. In addition to penetration testing, red teams are also used to help organizations improve their overall security posture by identifying weaknesses in their security policies, procedures, and processes. Red team exercises can be used to test the effectiveness of security controls, evaluate the response of security teams to a simulated attack, and identify areas where security training and education may be needed.

A blue team consists of security professionals who have an inside-out view of the organization. Their task is to protect the organization's critical assets against any kind of threat. They are aware of the business objectives and the organization's security strategy. Therefore, their task is to strengthen the castle walls so no intruder can compromise the defenses.

The following figure contrasts the actions of a Red Team (offensive) and a Blue Team (defensive) during a security engagement. Here is a breakdown of the roles and interactions between attackers and defenders in a simulated cyberattack.

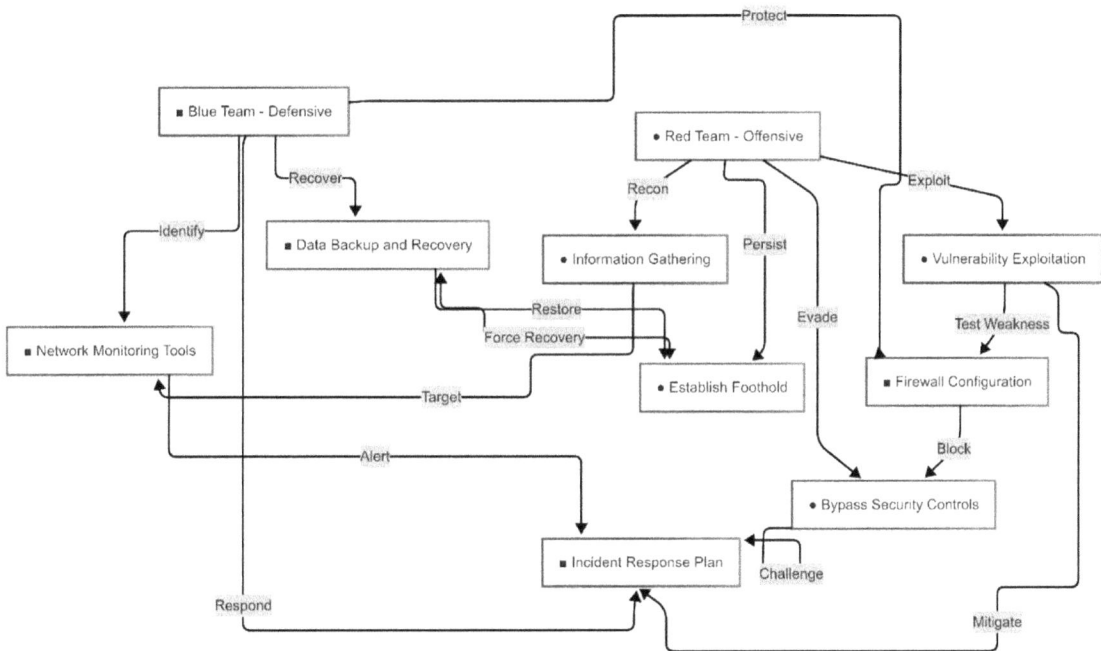

Figure 1.2: Workflow between red vs. blue team

Red team

The primary function of a red team is to simulate a real-world cyberattack on a network or system in order to identify weaknesses and vulnerabilities that could be exploited by a real attacker. By performing a thorough and realistic simulation, the red team can help an organization better understand its security posture and identify areas where improvements are needed.

In addition to penetration testing, which is a core function of a red team, there are several other functions that a red team may perform, including:

- **Physical security testing**: A red team may also test an organization's physical security controls, such as access controls, surveillance systems, and security personnel. This can help identify weaknesses in the organization's physical security posture.

- **Identifying security gaps in any organization**: Red team services are used to evaluate and improve defensive layers. The red team explores attack vectors and routes to get into the system and succeed in breaching the organization's assets. In this way, they can detect breaches and weaknesses that have gone unnoticed by the blue team and other cybersecurity services.

- **Exploiting vulnerabilities to simulate real attacks**: By exploiting weaknesses, the red team can complete the phases of a real attack, studying the routes that malicious actors might take and extracting valuable information from them. This is where the blue team's ability to detect and respond to the red team's actions comes into play. For the blue team to improve, the red team must be able to push it to the best of its abilities and teach it about the various attack options it faces.

- **Optimizing blue team detection and response capabilities**: The red team enables the blue team to improve its detection and response procedures in the face of real attacks by finding the gaps and highlighting them before a real attack can happen, hence optimizing the overall security posture of an organization. This is normally done by penetration testing.

Blue team

The primary function of a blue team is to defend a network or system against cyberattacks. The blue team is responsible for monitoring the network or system for any signs of suspicious activity and responding to any detected threats or vulnerabilities.

The functions of a blue team include:

- **Defensive security**: The blue team carries out defensive security tasks using different models or teams; hence, there are multiple teams under the umbrella of the blue team, such as SOC, incident response, threat detection, vulnerability management and remediation, risk management, security compliance, and threat intelligence.

- **Detection, response, and remediation**: The blue team is responsible for detecting potential threats to the network or system. This includes monitoring network traffic, system logs, and other data sources for any signs of suspicious activity. Once a potential threat is detected, the blue team responds quickly to mitigate the impact of the threat. After the incident is contained, the blue team must work to remediate the issue and restore normal operations. This may include applying security patches, removing malware or other malicious code, and resetting passwords or access controls. The blue team must also conduct a post-incident review to identify any gaps in their security posture and develop plans to prevent similar incidents from occurring in the future.

- **Threat detection and hunting**: These are critical components of the blue team's responsibility to protect a network or system from cyberattacks. By proactively monitoring the network for potential threats and conducting regular threat-hunting exercises, the blue team can identify and mitigate security risks before they result in a major incident.

- **Digital forensics and incident response**: These are critical components of the blue team's responsibilities in protecting a network or system from cyberattacks. By conducting digital forensics investigations and implementing effective incident response processes, the blue team can quickly detect and respond to security incidents, minimize the impact of the incident, and prevent future incidents from occurring.

- **Security patch management and system hardening**: Maintaining the security of a network or system is a top priority for the blue team. To accomplish this, security patch management and system hardening are two crucial aspects of their responsibilities. By ensuring that all software and systems are up to date with the latest security patches, the blue team can effectively address potential vulnerabilities and reduce the risk of successful cyberattacks. Additionally, system hardening plays a significant role in securing a network or system by implementing secure configurations, disabling unnecessary services and ports, and limiting user privileges. Overall, these efforts help to reduce the attack surface and protect sensitive information and critical infrastructure from cyber threats.

While the red team and blue team have different roles and responsibilities, they both play an important part in the overall security of an organization. Collaboration between the two teams is essential for identifying weaknesses, testing security controls, and responding to security incidents in a timely and effective manner.

The importance of the red and blue teams in cyber lies in the fact that they provide a comprehensive approach to security. The combination of the red team's ability to identify vulnerabilities and the blue team's ability to detect, respond to, and remediate security incidents is essential to protecting sensitive information and critical infrastructure from cyber threats.

Conclusion

In this chapter, we discussed the ideas of blue teaming and threat management, as well as the relevance that each of these concepts has in the subject of cybersecurity. Organizations may increase their capacity to identify and avoid cyberattacks, evaluate security policies, and improve incident response skills by participating in blue team exercises. It encourages collaboration, raises the level of security awareness among users, and delivers vital threat intelligence so that users may keep one step ahead of new hazards. In addition, this chapter explored a variety of different kinds of assaults, and subsequent chapters will go into further depth regarding each of these kinds of attacks.

In a nutshell, efficient cybersecurity requires blue teaming, threat management, and in-depth familiarity with the whole threat ecosystem. Organizations may improve their capacity to identify, avoid, and respond to cyberattacks by applying these practices and using the knowledge of multiple teams. This will eventually protect their important assets and ensure that they have a robust security posture.

We shall learn a lot of concepts required in blue teaming in the next chapter. This will be a refresher for everyone reading this book who already has some experience in cybersecurity and will build the core concepts for readers who are new to the field or wish to enter this amazing field.

Join our Discord space

Join our Discord workspace for latest updates, offers, tech happenings around the world, new releases, and sessions with the authors:

https://discord.bpbonline.com

CHAPTER 2
Advancing Security Fundamentals and Risk Assessment

Introduction

In this chapter, we will explore the foundational concepts that are essential for a successful career in blue teaming and defensive security. We will delve into the intricacies of IP addressing, network protocols, routing, and switching, which lay the groundwork for understanding network infrastructure and communication. We will also discuss the principles of network security, monitoring, and management, which are crucial for maintaining a secure and operational network. Additionally, we will examine the importance of security governance and compliance, access control, authentication, encryption, firewalls, intrusion detection systems, and incident response and management. These concepts are interconnected and play vital roles in protecting networks and data. By mastering these fundamental concepts, you will be well-equipped to tackle the challenges of blue teaming and defensive security.

Structure

In this chapter, we will cover the following topics:

- Network basics
- Network security
- Cybersecurity concepts

- Encryption and cryptography

- Incident response

- Risk and compliance

- Cloud security

Objectives

In this chapter, we will understand the concepts of cybersecurity is intended to foster a comprehensive and strategic approach to protecting digital systems and data. These concepts provide the intellectual framework for professionals to comprehend the complex interplay between technology, human behavior, and threats. By understanding these fundamental concepts, individuals can effectively analyze vulnerabilities, foresee emergent threats, and design bespoke security solutions. In addition, comprehending concepts facilitates the growth of critical thinking and problem-solving skills, which are essential for defending against sophisticated cyberattacks. With this foundational knowledge, professionals can design secure systems proactively, respond rapidly to incidents, and collaborate with multidisciplinary teams. The ultimate goal is to equip cybersecurity practitioners with the ability to mitigate threats, safeguard assets, and meaningfully contribute to a safer digital environment.

We shall learn all these concepts that will be required to excel in your career on the Blue Teaming side.

Network basics

A solid grasp of network principles is not only beneficial but essential in the field of cybersecurity. Since the network is the foundation of contemporary digital infrastructure, it serves as the main battlefield for security experts. One must first understand how the network functions in order to guard against advanced cyberthreats. Starting with the fundamental idea of IP addressing, the language of network communication, this section explores the essential elements of network fundamentals. To have a firm grasp of how data moves throughout the network, we will analyze IP packets, deconstruct the IP header, and investigate IP address classes. We will also look at network protocols, the laws that control this communication, and the crucial operations of switching and routing that control traffic flow. By identifying vulnerabilities, analyzing traffic patterns, and putting effective defense measures into practice, security practitioners are empowered to protect the digital landscape.

IP addressing

A solid grasp of **internet protocol (IP)** addressing is essential for any blue teamer. An IP address is a unique numerical label assigned to each device on a network, which is fundamental for analyzing network traffic, identifying threats, and configuring security controls like firewalls.

Key concepts in this area include understanding the differences between IPv4 and IPv6, the purpose of public vs. private IPs, the use of subnetting for network segmentation, and the function of static vs. dynamic addressing. Mastery of these concepts is required to effectively monitor and protect a network.

Since there are many aspects that are different in IPv4 and IPv6, let us look at the following table to understand the difference:

Aspect	IPv4	IPv6
Address length	32 bits (4 octets)	128 bits (16 octets)
Address notation	Dotted decimal format (e.g., 192.168.1.1)	Hexadecimal colon-separated format (e.g., 2001:0db8:85a3:0000:0000:8a 2e:0370:7334)
Address space	Limited to approximately 4.3 billion addresses	Vast address space, allowing for billions of times more addresses
Address exhaustion	Depletion of addresses due to growing internet usage	Significantly larger address pool, mitigating concerns of depletion
Network configuration	Often requires manual configuration (DHCP may be used)	Facilitates automatic configuration through **Stateless Address Autoconfiguration (SLAAC)**
Network address translation (NAT)	Frequently used to conserve IPv4 addresses	Less dependence on NAT due to ample address availability
Subnetting	Common for efficient IP address allocation	Still relevant, but the large address space reduces the need
Header length	Minimum header size of 20 bytes, can be up to 60 bytes with options	Fixed 40-byte base header, with optional extension headers for added flexibility
Security features	Limited built-in security (IPsec is optional)	Built-in support for IPsec, enhancing security
Quality of service (QoS)	Lacks native QoS support	Native support for QoS and traffic prioritization
Mobile and IoT support	Supports mobile and IoT devices, but limitations due to address scarcity	Well-suited for mobile and IoT with ample address space and efficiency
Multicast	Supports multicast, but not as efficiently	Better support for multicast traffic
Fragmentation	Routers handle packet fragmentation	Hosts are responsible for packet fragmentation

Aspect	IPv4	IPv6
DNS records	Limited support for DNS records (e.g., A and PTR records)	Expanded DNS records (e.g., AAAA records for IPv6 addresses)
Internet adoption	Predominant in current internet infrastructure	Increasing adoption, particularly as IPv4 addresses become scarcer
Backward compatibility	Devices may need to support both IPv4 and IPv6	IPv6 supports transition mechanisms for backward compatibility
Migration challenges	Transition mechanisms required for coexistence	Requires careful planning for a smooth transition
Current standard	Historically the standard	Becoming the prevalent standard for new deployments

Table 2.1: IPv4 and IPv6

IP packets

IP packets are the fundamental building blocks of network communication. They encapsulate data and provide the necessary addressing and routing information for its delivery across networks.

For a blue teamer, this is not just a theoretical concept; it is a practical skill used daily to triage alerts and investigate threats. For instance, during an alert triage, an analyst examines the IP packet header. By looking at the **source IP**, they can immediately check threat intelligence feeds to see if the traffic originates from a malicious location. By checking the **destination port** and **protocol**, they can determine if it is targeting a web server (TCP/443) or a sensitive database (TCP/1433), which is essential for both traffic analysis and configuring firewall rules. This initial analysis, derived directly from the packet, is a crucial first step in incident response, helping to reconstruct the attack path and differentiate a benign event from a potential attack.

IP header understanding

The IP header is a critical component of IP packets, serving as a roadmap for data delivery across networks. It contains essential information such as source and destination IP addresses, protocol type, and packet length, enabling network devices to properly route and process data. For security professionals, in-depth knowledge of IP headers is paramount for effective network monitoring and threat analysis.

By understanding the structure and fields within IP headers, security professionals can identify malicious activity, such as spoofed IP addresses or suspicious packet fragmentation. Analyzing IP headers helps in filtering network traffic, implementing access controls, and detecting potential attacks. Additionally, familiarity with IP headers aids in troubleshooting network issues, optimizing performance, and ensuring secure communication channels.

Furthermore, as organizations transition to IPv6, security professionals must adapt their skills to interpret the updated header format and address the evolving security challenges associated with the new protocol.

Mastery of IP header knowledge empowers security professionals to proactively defend networks, protect sensitive data, and maintain the integrity of digital infrastructure.

Network security

The foundation of a strong cybersecurity posture is network security, which includes a variety of strategies for safeguarding sensitive information and important assets in a networked setting. This section explores the fundamentals of network security, providing the framework for comprehending risks, weaknesses, and efficient defenses. The significance of proactive surveillance and control will be emphasized as we examine network monitoring and management strategies. In-depth network traffic analysis is part of this, using techniques like packet capture and NetFlow collectors to obtain fine-grained insight into network activities. We will look at each method's advantages and disadvantages, emphasizing the advantages of integrating packet capture with NetFlow for thorough analysis. Lastly, we will explore the tools and methods that enable security experts to efficiently monitor, assess, and safeguard their networks as we dig into the realm of packet capture software.

Network security fundamentals

Network security is the practice of protecting an organization's data, devices, and communication channels within a networked environment. In today's interconnected world, this requires a proactive defense against a wide range of cyber threats, from sophisticated malware to clever social engineering tactics. The ultimate goal is to build robust barriers against unauthorized access and data breaches, ensuring the **confidentiality, integrity, and availability** (**CIA**) of critical assets. Understanding these principles is not just theoretical; it empowers professionals to anticipate vulnerabilities, identify attack vectors, and make informed decisions to mitigate risk.

Achieving this protection involves mastering several essential components. Foundational controls like strong authentication protocols and access control mechanisms ensure that only authorized users can access sensitive systems. Data is further protected, both in transit and at rest, through encryption techniques like public-key and symmetric-key cryptography. Beyond these barriers, security professionals must proactively identify and mitigate risks using tools like **intrusion detection and prevention systems** (**IDS/IPS**) and regular vulnerability assessments, while also deploying strategies to ensure system availability against attacks like **Distributed Denial of Service** (**DDoS**).

Effective network security also extends to governance and adaptation. Professionals must navigate a complex web of compliance requirements, adhering to regulatory frameworks and industry standards like the **General Data Protection Regulation** (**GDPR**), the **Health**

Insurance Portability and Accountability Act (HIPAA), and the **Payment Card Industry Data Security Standard (PCI DSS)** to operate within legal and ethical bounds. As technology evolves, these principles must be applied to new frontiers, including the **Internet of Things (IoT)** and cloud computing, which introduce unique security challenges. A mastery of these concepts allows an organization to create a holistic, resilient, and dependable security posture fit for the modern digital world.

Networks critical to cyber defense

Network security is a central concept in the field of cybersecurity, playing a crucial role in safeguarding network communication and data. In an interconnected world where data traverses intricate digital highways, network security is of paramount importance. This discipline focuses on implementing safeguards against unauthorized network access, data intrusions, and cyberattacks.

Understanding **Transmission Control Protocol (TCP)** and **User Datagram Protocol (UDP)** protocols, ports, **Secure Sockets Layer (SSL)** encryption, the **Open Systems Interconnection (OSI)** model, the **Address Resolution Protocol (ARP)** table, and **virtual local area networks (VLANs)** is essential for effective networking in cybersecurity. The TCP and UDP govern the transmission of data packets, with TCP providing reliability through its three-way handshake mechanism and UDP operating in a connectionless manner, which is frequently preferred for streaming applications. Ports, on the other hand, function as virtual gateways through which data enters or departs a system, making them essential for efficiently routing traffic.

By establishing secure connections between clients and servers, SSL encryption increases network security. This, along with the seven layers of the OSI model, helps to dissect network functions and resolve vulnerabilities at various levels. The ARP table associates IP addresses with physical devices, thereby improving network performance. VLANs, on the other hand, generate secure enclaves within local networks, thereby enhancing data isolation and privacy.

Understanding prevalent ports is not only advantageous for job interviews but also essential for success in the cybersecurity industry. It demonstrates a candidate's understanding of network fundamentals and their ability to implement this knowledge in practical situations.

The transport layer is responsible for end-to-end communication. Protocols like TCP provide reliable, error-checked data delivery, while others like UDP (User Datagram Protocol) prioritize speed over reliability, offering a connectionless, best-effort delivery. This layer's function is exemplified by the SSL and **Transport Layer Security (TLS)** protocols, which encrypt communications to protect sensitive data from potential threats during transmission.

The network layer is responsible for logical addressing (IP addresses) and routing data packets between different networks. To deliver packets on a local network segment, the **Address Resolution Protocol (ARP)** is used to map these Layer 3 IP addresses to Layer 2 physical (MAC) addresses. This stratum serves as the foundation of continuous connectivity, allowing for efficient data routing.

Professionals frequently utilize *Nmap*, an indispensable utility for network discovery and vulnerability assessment, to enhance network security. Other applications, such as *Wireshark* and *Net Scan*, permit in-depth network analysis, thereby facilitating the identification of anomalies and vulnerabilities.

The concepts underlying network security serve as the pillars of effective cybersecurity strategies. From comprehending protocols and encryption to dissecting the OSI model and utilizing tools, these concepts comprise the arsenal of professionals attempting to secure network communication and data. A thorough understanding of these principles not only fortifies digital landscapes but also empowers individuals in an ever-changing and dynamic cybersecurity environment.

Demilitarized zone

A **demilitarized zone** (**DMZ**) is a fundamental network security architecture that creates a perimeter network, or subnetwork, positioned between an organization's secure internal network and the untrusted, external internet. The DMZ is designed to house external-facing services that need to be accessible to the public, such as web servers, email servers, and DNS servers.

Its primary function is to provide layered security. If an attacker compromises a server in the DMZ, they are still isolated from the internal network by a second firewall. For a blue teamer, understanding the DMZ is critical for configuring firewall rules, placing network sensors like an IDS, and prioritizing alerts. An intrusion into the DMZ is a serious event, but traffic moving from the DMZ to the internal network is a critical, high-priority incident.

Network monitoring and management

Network monitoring and management are the two pillars that ensure a network's security, performance, and operational health.

Network monitoring is the practice of proactive surveillance, using tools to gain real-time insights into network performance, trace bandwidth utilization, identify bottlenecks, and detect anomalous activities that could indicate a security breach.

Network management complements this by focusing on the network's design, configuration, and maintenance. It involves managing changes, optimizing resource allocation, and ensuring the network infrastructure is consistently aligned with organizational goals and security policies. Together, these disciplines allow security teams to move from reactive problem-solving to proactive threat detection and resolution.

Monitoring network traffic

One key objective lies in the mastery of monitoring network traffic using packet capture software and NetFlow collectors. Packet capture tools, exemplified by Wireshark, enable the detailed examination of individual data packets traversing a network. This proficiency allows network administrators to inspect the contents of packets, identifying potential threats, anomalies, or performance issues. NetFlow collectors, on the other hand, provide aggregate data about network traffic, offering insights into patterns, trends, and utilization. By grasping these tools, professionals can swiftly identify unauthorized activities, diagnose performance bottlenecks, and enhance network resource allocation.

Packet capture

Packet capture, also known as **packet sniffing**, involves capturing and analyzing individual network packets as they traverse the network. This granular level of inspection provides detailed insights into network communication, allowing security professionals to identify potential threats, anomalies, and performance issues.

Tools for packet capture

Wireshark is a popular open-source packet capture and analysis tool. It provides a user-friendly interface to capture, filter, and analyze network traffic, allowing security professionals to inspect packet headers, payloads, and protocols. Other tools for packet capture include **tcpdump**, **WinDump**, and **Omnipeek**.

The following are the benefits of packet capture:

- **Identify malicious activity**: Packet capture helps detect malware, intrusions, and suspicious network behavior by inspecting packet contents and patterns.

- **Diagnose network issues**: Analyzing packet captures helps identify network bottlenecks, latency issues, and other performance problems.

- **Troubleshoot application problems**: Packet capture aids in identifying application-level issues, such as slow response times or communication errors.

- **Verify security controls**: Packet capture can be used to verify the effectiveness of security controls, such as firewalls and intrusion detection systems.

NetFlow collectors

NetFlow is a network protocol that collects and aggregates network traffic data. NetFlow collectors gather this data, providing insights into network traffic patterns, trends, and utilization. This information is valuable for network monitoring, capacity planning, and security analysis.

Tools for NetFlow collection

Several tools are available for collecting and analyzing NetFlow data, including:

- **SolarWinds NetFlow Traffic Analyzer**: A commercial tool that provides real-time traffic analysis, network forensics, and reporting capabilities.

- **ManageEngine NetFlow Analyzer**: Another commercial tool that offers comprehensive network traffic analysis and bandwidth monitoring features.

- **nfdump**: An open-source command-line tool for collecting and analyzing NetFlow data.

The following are the benefits of NetFlow collection:

- **Network visibility**: NetFlow provides a high-level view of network traffic, allowing administrators to identify top talkers, applications, and protocols.

- **Bandwidth monitoring**: NetFlow helps monitor bandwidth usage, identify bandwidth hogs, and optimize network resource allocation.

- **Security analysis**: NetFlow data can be used to detect DDoS attacks, network anomalies, and other security threats.

- **Capacity planning**: NetFlow data helps predict future bandwidth needs and plan for network capacity upgrades.

Combining packet capture and NetFlow

Packet capture and NetFlow collection provide complementary approaches to network traffic monitoring. Packet capture provides detailed information about individual packets, while NetFlow offers a broader view of network traffic patterns. Combining these two techniques provides a comprehensive understanding of network activity, enabling security professionals to effectively monitor, analyze, and secure their networks. Beyond packet capture and NetFlow collectors, several other tools and techniques play a crucial role in network traffic monitoring, like IDPS, SIEM, network performance monitoring tools, etc., which are covered in future chapters.

Simple Network Management Protocol

Understanding the **Simple Network Management Protocol** (**SNMP**) is pivotal in network monitoring and management. SNMP facilitates the monitoring and control of network devices, allowing administrators to collect data about device performance and configuration. Proficiency in SNMP empowers professionals to manage network elements, monitor the health of devices, and promptly respond to critical events or errors. By grasping SNMP, experts can proactively maintain network devices, ensuring their optimal functionality and mitigating potential vulnerabilities.

The following are the SNMP key components:

- **SNMP manager**: This is the central management system responsible for monitoring and controlling network devices.

- **SNMP agent**: This software runs on network devices and collects data about their performance and configuration.

- **Management Information Base (MIB)**: This database stores information about network devices and their parameters.

The following figure illustrates the architecture of an SNMP system, demonstrating how a manager application communicates with devices in a network to monitor and manage them using SNMP operations:

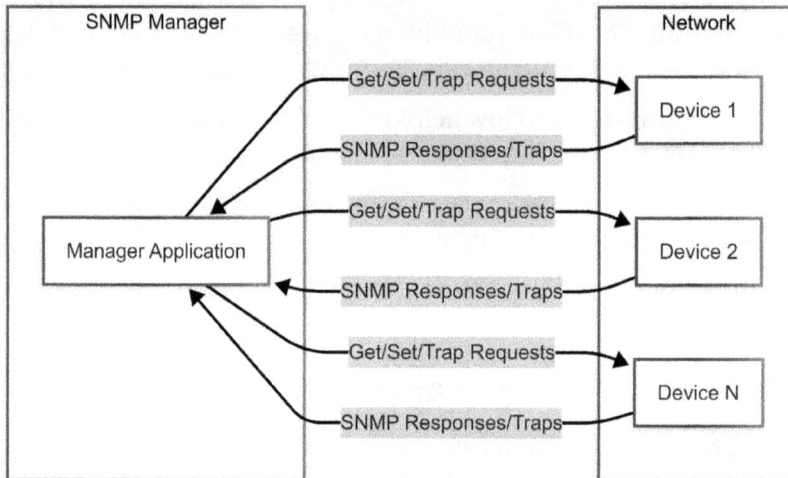

Figure 2.1: SNMP manager-Device communication

VPN traffic protection protocols

An integral part of network monitoring and management is the comprehension of protocols for safeguarding traffic within **virtual private networks** (**VPNs**). Different protocols, such as IPSec, SSL/TLS, and L2TP, are used to establish secure encrypted tunnels over potentially untrusted networks. Understanding these protocols enables professionals to design and implement secure VPN connections, ensuring the confidentiality and integrity of data transmitted between remote locations or users and the central network.

Packet capture software

Mastery of packet capture software, like Wireshark, is crucial for comprehensive network analysis. Wireshark enables the inspection and analysis of individual data packets, offering insights into protocol behavior, communication patterns, and potential security vulnerabilities. By skillfully utilizing packet capture tools, cybersecurity professionals can identify malicious activities, diagnose network issues, and optimize network performance. This proficiency ensures that network administrators can promptly address emerging threats and maintain optimal network operation. There are many other tools, like *TCPdump, Nmap, Fiddler,* and *Ettercap,* which are used by cybersecurity professionals and can add a feather in your cap if you have these skills.

The following figure showcases a Wireshark interface displaying the analysis of a captured network packet trace file. It highlights details such as TCP segments, protocol hierarchy, and detailed packet information, aiding in troubleshooting and analyzing network traffic:

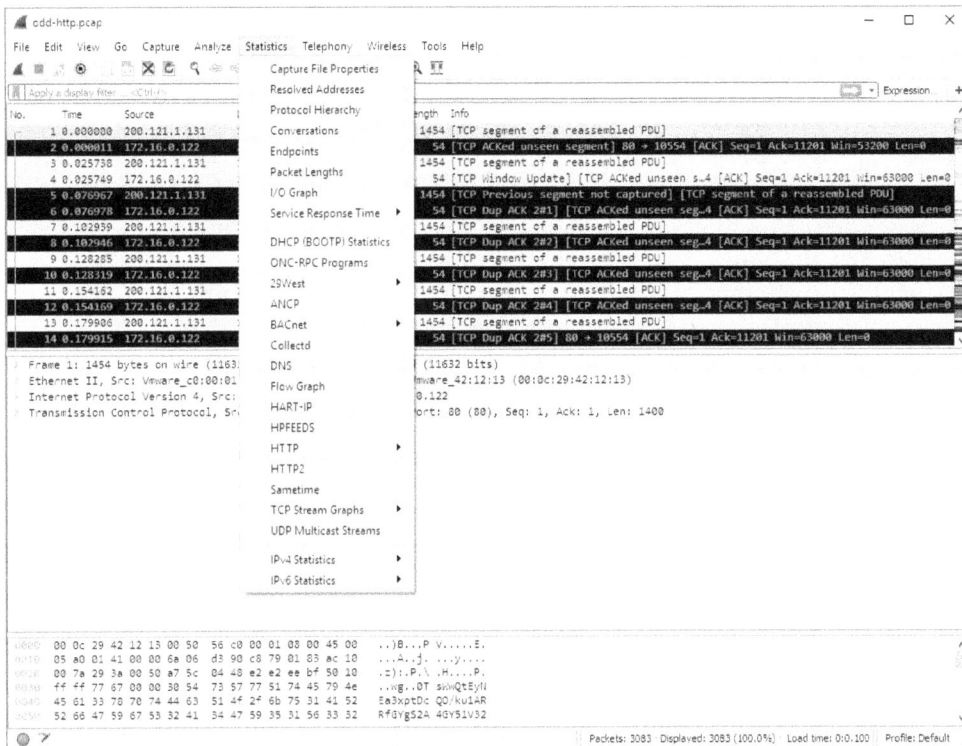

Figure 2.2: Wireshark packet analysis

In conclusion, the objective of understanding network monitoring and management encompasses a range of critical practices and technologies. Proficiency in monitoring network traffic through packet capture and NetFlow collectors, mastery of the SNMP protocol, comprehension of VPN traffic protection protocols, and utilization of packet capture software like Wireshark collectively empower cybersecurity experts to ensure network security, performance, and resilience. By attaining these objectives, professionals stand poised to navigate the complexities of modern network environments and effectively mitigate emerging cyber threats.

The goal of understanding network monitoring and management is multifaceted, seeking to ensure the dependable, secure, and effective operation of computer networks. This includes real-time performance analytics, proactive threat detection, customized network design, configuration control, change management, and resource optimization. By comprehending these concepts, cybersecurity professionals assume the role of vigilant stewards, orchestrating networks that meet organizational requirements while upholding the highest standards of security, performance, and resiliency.

Cybersecurity concepts

It is crucial to have a solid understanding of basic cybersecurity concepts in order to navigate the complicated world of digital dangers. Beginning with the fundamentals of security, this section examines the essential ideas that support a strong security posture. We will explore the always-changing world of threats, attacks, and vulnerabilities in order to comprehend the strategies used by bad actors. We will also look at authentication and access control systems, which protect private information and systems from unwanted access. We will stress the significance of security awareness and training since we acknowledge the human factor in security. After that, we will explore the fundamentals of network security, strengthening the digital framework that binds us all together. Lastly, we will look at endpoint security, which safeguards the gadgets that act as entry points to the internet. Individuals and companies can proactively protect against cyber dangers and guarantee the confidentiality, integrity, and availability of vital assets by comprehending these fundamental ideas.

Security fundamentals

Understanding the concepts of security fundamentals in the context of *Blue Teaming* aims to establish a solid foundation of knowledge and guiding principles that underpin the protection of digital assets, information, and systems from a broad variety of threats and risks. Based on these security fundamentals, effective cybersecurity strategies and practices can be developed, allowing individuals and organizations to construct resilient defenses and maintain the confidentiality, integrity, and availability of their digital resources.

By understanding security fundamentals, individuals can comprehend the fundamental principles that regulate cybersecurity, including threat landscape analysis, risk assessment, and mitigation strategies. This knowledge enables them to identify potential vulnerabilities, assess the associated risks, and implement the necessary countermeasures to prevent or mitigate potential breaches.

In addition, security fundamentals include an understanding of a variety of attack vectors and threat actors, from pernicious software (malware) and phishing attacks to more sophisticated forms of cyber warfare. With this information, cybersecurity professionals are able to anticipate potential attack vectors and design proactive defense mechanisms.

Understanding security fundamentals requires familiarity with cryptographic, authentication, and access control fundamentals. This knowledge enables individuals to establish secure communication channels, verify the authenticity of users, and enforce stringent permissions so that only authorized entities have access to sensitive data and resources.

In addition, security fundamentals emphasize the importance of continuous monitoring and incident response. In a threat landscape that is becoming increasingly dynamic, the ability to detect anomalies and respond quickly to security incidents is crucial. By comprehending these principles, individuals can create effective incident response plans, mitigate the effects of security breaches, and recover from disruptions quickly.

The ultimate goal of grasping security fundamentals is to provide individuals with a comprehensive comprehension of cybersecurity's fundamental principles. This knowledge enables them to make informed decisions, implement best practices, and continuously adapt to ever-changing security threats. Individuals can play a pivotal role in enhancing the overall security posture of organizations and contributing to a secure digital environment by establishing a solid foundation of security fundamentals.

We have covered the practical implementation of Blue Teaming and Threat Management in this book, as it is essential for everyone to learn the basics beforehand. We shall touch base on all these aspects listed in the further chapters.

Threats, attacks, and vulnerabilities

To build a strong security posture, it is essential to understand the ever-changing world of digital dangers, including the strategies employed by malicious actors. A foundational understanding of the threat landscape, including various attack vectors and threat actors from malware and phishing to more sophisticated cyber warfare, is necessary to design proactive defense mechanisms. This knowledge enables security professionals to identify potential vulnerabilities, assess the associated risks, and implement countermeasures to prevent or mitigate potential breaches. We shall be discussing different types of threats, attacks, and vulnerabilities in multiple future chapters.

Access control and authentication

Access control ensures that system entry is restricted to authorized users, while authentication validates the identities of those users. Together, these systems serve as digital gatekeepers to protect private information and systems from unwanted access. Acquiring knowledge in these areas is crucial as it facilitates the development of secure access mechanisms and the effective administration of user privileges. By understanding these fundamentals, cybersecurity professionals can enforce stringent permissions to ensure that only authorized entities have access to sensitive data and resources.

Security awareness and training

Promoting security awareness among users is essential for any organization. Understanding the significance of training aids in imparting knowledge about potential threats and best practices for avoiding them.

Beyond technical safeguards, human behavior plays a pivotal role in cybersecurity. In the upcoming chapters, we will explore the key concepts related to security awareness and training, empowering cybersecurity professionals to become the first line of defense.

Network security essentials

Network security is the practice of protecting sensitive data, systems, and networks from any unauthorized access, use, disclosure, disruption, modification, or destruction. This field encompasses a wide range of essential components that work together to create a robust defense. Key elements include the deployment of firewalls and intrusion detection systems, the use of encryption and cryptography to protect data, and the implementation of secure network designs. Other crucial components involve managing secure access through VPNs and network access control, alongside consistent network monitoring and logging to detect and respond to threats; all these will be covered in future chapters.

Endpoint security

The practice of protecting individual devices, such as computers, laptops, smartphones, and tablets, from cyber threats. These devices are often the entry points for attackers to infiltrate networks and access sensitive data.

Incident response and handling

Incident response is a coordinated set of actions to identify, contain, eradicate, and recover from a security breach or other adverse event. It is essential to have a well-defined incident response plan in place to minimize the impact of incidents and ensure a swift recovery.

We shall learn more in *Chapter 6, Incident Response Management,* in this book about IR and handling incidents:

Security governance and compliance

Security governance and compliance are essential components of a robust security framework. They provide a structure for managing and overseeing security activities, ensuring that organizations meet regulatory requirements and industry standards.

Ethical and legal aspects of cybersecurity

Cybersecurity, while essential for protecting digital assets, raises significant ethical and legal concerns. These issues often intersect, creating complex challenges for individuals, organizations, and governments.

Security risk mitigation

Security risk mitigation is the process of identifying, assessing, and addressing potential threats to a system or organization. It is a proactive approach that helps minimize the impact of security incidents and protect valuable assets.

Encryption and cryptography

For a blue teamer, **cryptography** is the fundamental science behind securing data, and **encryption** is its most critical tool. Its primary function is to protect the confidentiality and integrity of an organization's most valuable assets. This is achieved by converting readable data (plaintext) into an unreadable format (ciphertext), ensuring that information is protected both **at rest** (stored on servers and devices) and **in transit** (as it moves across the network).

In practice, you will encounter two main types of encryption. **Symmetric encryption** uses a single shared key for both encryption and decryption, making it fast and ideal for protecting large volumes of data, like entire hard drives. **Asymmetric encryption**, or public-key cryptography, uses a key pair—a public key to encrypt and a private key to decrypt. While slower, this method is the backbone of secure communication online, enabling core technologies like digital signatures and the TLS protocol that secures **Hypertext Transfer Protocol Secure** (**HTTPS**) web traffic. A blue team's focus is less on designing these algorithms and more on ensuring their correct implementation, such as validating TLS certificates, managing encryption keys, and analyzing traffic to ensure data remains protected.

Incident response

Effective incident response and threat management are paramount. This section explores the critical processes and technologies involved in detecting, responding to, and recovering from security incidents. We will explore the stages of incident response, from initial preparation and identification to containment, eradication, and recovery. Further, we will examine the role of firewalls and intrusion detection systems in proactively defending against threats. We will discuss different types of firewalls, including packet filtering and stateful inspection, and explore intrusion detection techniques like anomaly-based and signature-based detection. By understanding these concepts, organizations can build resilience against cyberattacks and minimize the impact of security breaches.

Understanding incident response

IR is the process of methodically coordinating a sequence of actions with the goal of locating, mitigating, and recovering from security issues as quickly as possible. These instances span a broad spectrum, encompassing anything from malware infiltrations and data breaches to denial-of-service assaults and more. The adherence of IR to a well-choreographed plan that includes specific processes to identify, evaluate, contain, eliminate, recover from, and reflect upon occurrences is one of the distinguishing characteristics of IR. The objective is to rapidly return things to normal while minimizing the disruption to business operations, reputation, and the integrity of data.

In-depth analysis of incident management

Unlike IR, which focuses on the more technical components of responding to occurrences, IM takes a more holistic approach, which includes coordination, communication, and overall strategy. The logistical and procedural components of an event are dealt with by IM, which also oversees the allocation of resources, engages stakeholders, and makes certain that a unified response is carried out. IM extends beyond the domain of technical concerns to include public relations, prospective legal proceedings, and even compliance duties and legal issues.

There are several stages that make up an incident's lifetime, and each one contributes to the efficiency of incident response and incident management as a whole. The first step in the process is known as **detection**, and it is during this stage that highly developed technologies like IDS, IPS, and platforms for **security information and event management** (**SIEM**) play an essential part. The subsequent stages consist of Analysis, which examines the nature and scope of the incident; containment, which is aimed at halting the spread of the incident; Eradication, which is the process of eliminating the root cause; recovery, which focuses on the restoration of the system; and finally, the lessons learned phase, in which the organization draws insights to strengthen its defenses.

Classifying events is essential for effectively prioritizing actions since occurrences differ in both their nature and the potential impact they might have. The severity of an incident might range from a minor anomaly to a full-blown security breach. This categorization assists blue teams in allocating resources according to the severity of the event and the potential implications that might arise as a result of it.

An **incident response plan** (**IRP**) that has been carefully designed is essential to the success of both IR and IM. The roles, duties, communication protocols, escalation processes, and technological specifics are all outlined in this blueprint. It acts as a playbook that directs the organization's response to incidents that have occurred. An IRP that is well-structured will ensure that every member of the team is aware of their responsibilities, hence reducing the likelihood of misunderstanding and improving reaction times.

Triage and prioritization of an event are of the utmost importance to quickly determine the severity of an event when one is underway. The practice of categorizing and prioritizing occurrences based on their potential effect may be accomplished through a procedure that is known as incident triage. Blue teams are able to efficiently deploy resources and carry out focused actions to successfully prevent attacks when they can identify key occurrences and use this information.

Incident response and management

The practices of IR and **incident management** (**IM**) are the procedures that stand as the vanguard against possible disasters in the ever-changing environment of cybersecurity, which is characterized by the proliferation of both threats and assaults. This book will lead you through the complex world of information retrieval and information management, illuminating their complexities, approaches, and the role they play in bolstering digital environments.

The field of cybersecurity is riddled with difficulties since its attackers are always looking for ways to bypass defenses and take advantage of flaws. Consequently, IR and IM have emerged as the linchpins of proactive defense and recovery in this context. In the unfortunate event that a security breach does occur, a well-structured strategy may help reduce the damage and speed the recovery process. Their planned execution guarantees that an organization's digital assets are guarded against looming threats.

Tactics for containment and eradication

Once an incident has been recognized, containment tactics are implemented to halt its further spread and prepare for its eventual eradication. This involves isolating systems that have been compromised, putting an end to any harmful actions, and restricting the spread of the assault as much as possible laterally. The next phase, eradication, entails determining the underlying source of the occurrence and taking measures to ensure that it is eliminated entirely from the surrounding environment. The tactics for eradication are adapted to the unique characteristics of the occurrence, with a primary emphasis on comprehensive remediation.

Facilitating and remediation recovery

This serves as the link between the successful containment of an event and the successful restoration of normality. It includes the process of gradually restoring impacted systems, validating the data's integrity, and deploying fixes or upgrades to avoid further breaches in the future. In this phase, it is necessary for technical teams and business divisions to coordinate their efforts in order to ensure that operations can be resumed without interruption.

The climax of an event does not mark the finish; rather, it presents a chance for development. Post-event analysis, also known as the **lessons learned phase**, entails doing research into the timing of the incident, the efficiency of responses, and the weaknesses that were taken advantage of. This reflective approach makes it easier to identify gaps in the organization's defenses, which paves the way for more preventative actions to be taken in the case of similar occurrences in the future.

Firewalls and intrusion detection systems

Firewalls and IDS/IPS are foundation technologies for network defense, each serving a distinct but complementary role. A **firewall** acts as the primary gatekeeper for a network, filtering incoming and outgoing traffic based on a strict set of rules. It makes decisions based on factors like IP address, port, and protocol, effectively blocking known-bad connections at the perimeter. For a blue teamer, firewall logs are a crucial source of information, showing what threats were blocked and revealing patterns of malicious attempts to access the network.

While firewalls enforce the rules, an IDS acts as a vigilant security guard, monitoring all network traffic for suspicious behavior that might indicate an attack in progress. It looks for known attack signatures or anomalous activity that deviates from the norm. An IPS takes this a step further by not only detecting a threat but also actively blocking it in real-time. The synergy is critical: a firewall might allow web traffic on port 443, but an IDS/IPS will analyze that traffic to detect and block a SQL injection attack attempting to exploit the web server. For a blue team, IDS/IPS alerts are high-priority signals that a threat may have bypassed perimeter defenses and requires immediate investigation. Modern defenses often combine these functions in **Next-Generation Firewalls** (**NGFWs**), providing a unified platform for network control and threat detection

Relationship between firewall and IDS

The relationship between firewalls and an IDS creates a multi-layered security strategy, much like a fortress with layered defenses. A firewall acts as the outer wall, preventing the majority of unauthorized access from external threats. An IDS, in turn, functions like a sentinel stationed inside the walls, monitoring any suspicious behavior or threats that manage to circumvent the firewall. This integration provides a more comprehensive safety net, as the firewall limits traffic while the IDS analyzes allowed activity for potential intrusions, protecting digital assets from a wider range of attacks.

The following figure illustrates the combined roles of firewalls and IDS in achieving the goal of protecting internal networks from external threats. It highlights how these security layers work in tandem to filter incoming traffic, detect suspicious activity, and safeguard the internal network.

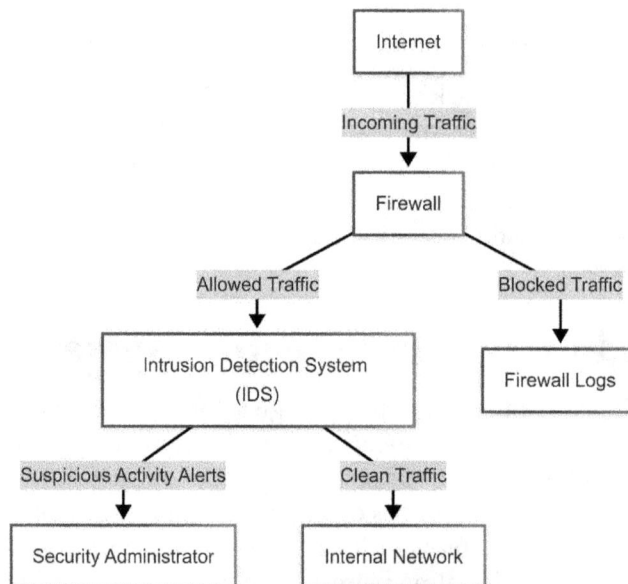

Figure 2.3: Collaborative operation of a firewall and an IDS in network security

Teamwork across functional lines

Teamwork is an essential component. As IR and IM cross over into other technological domains, effective coordination across all departments is required. It is imperative that the IT, legal, communication, and business groups all work effectively together in order to guarantee a complete and efficient reaction to crises.

Analysis and attribution of forensic evidence

The process of digital forensics, which is an essential part of incident response, entails the collection and examination of digital evidence with the purpose of comprehending the nature of the assault and, if possible, attributing it to particular threat actors. The attack vector, the magnitude of the breach, and the tactics used by the perpetrators of the breach may all be determined with the assistance of forensic analysis.

Reporting and documenting incidents

Reporting and documenting incidents in a manner that is both comprehensive and accurate serves a variety of functions. It helps firms comply with legal and regulatory duties, makes it easier for organizations to fine-tune their IRPs, and may be used as evidence in any legal proceedings stemming from the event.

Automation and orchestration

In this era of automation, increasing productivity in IR and IM procedures may be accomplished by integrating automation and orchestration solutions. These technologies make regular processes go more quickly, freeing up team members to concentrate on more difficult forms of analysis and decision-making. Automation helps to assure uniform answers, decreases the risk of human mistakes, and speeds up the resolution of incidents.

Importance of tabletop exercises

When evaluating the performance of an organization's IRP, simulated event scenarios, often known as **tabletop exercises**, are quite helpful. These exercises provide teams the opportunity to put their response plans to the test in a safe setting, allowing them to identify any process flaws and make improvements.

The art of navigating legal and regulatory waters is a vital yet sensitive component of investor relations and investment management. The requirements for notifying authorities of a breach in data security, compliance with industry standards, and the possibility of legal action are all aspects that need to be addressed carefully.

Risk and compliance

To build an effective defense, a blue teamer must understand not only technical threats but also the business context of risk and the legal landscape of compliance. These two areas provide the "why" behind many security controls and procedures.

Risk management is the formal process of identifying, assessing, and mitigating threats to an organization's digital assets and operations. It involves evaluating potential vulnerabilities to determine their likelihood and potential business impact, allowing the organization to make informed decisions. The goal is to treat the risk, whether by mitigating it with new security controls, transferring it (e.g., through cyber insurance), or formally accepting it. Frameworks like the **National Institute of Standards and Technology (NIST) Risk Management Framework (RMF)** provide a structured methodology for this process, which we will explore in-depth in *Chapter 10, Implementing Threat and Vulnerability Management on Business Houses*.

Compliance and regulations refer to the mandatory adherence to laws, industry standards, and policies governing data security and privacy. These requirements dictate the minimum security posture for handling specific types of sensitive information. Key examples include the GDPR in Europe, the HIPAA for patient data, and the PCI DSS. For a blue team, compliance often defines the baseline for required security controls and establishes the legal obligations for data breach reporting.

Cloud security

As organizations increasingly move their data and applications to the cloud, understanding the fundamentals of cloud security is essential for any blue teamer. Cloud security involves protecting data, applications, and infrastructure hosted in cloud environments like **Amazon Web Services (AWS)**, Microsoft Azure, or **Google Cloud Platform (GCP)**.

A core concept in cloud security is the **shared responsibility model**. In this model, the cloud provider (e.g., AWS) is responsible for the security *of* the cloud, which includes the physical data centers and the core network infrastructure. The customer, in turn, is responsible for security *in* the cloud. This includes securing their data, configuring access controls, managing user identities, and ensuring their applications are secure.

Key security practices in the cloud include robust **identity and access management (IAM)** to control who can access resources, proper **network security configurations** like **virtual private clouds (VPCs)** and security groups to segment traffic, and continuous monitoring of cloud environments for threats. We will cover cloud-specific security strategies and tools in a dedicated chapter later in the book.

Conclusion

In this chapter, we explored the fundamental concepts that form the bedrock of a successful career in blue teaming and defensive security. A solid understanding of these concepts is essential for effectively defending networks and systems from cyber threats.

We explored the intricacies of IP addressing, network protocols, routing, and switching, which lay the groundwork for understanding network infrastructure and communication. We also listed the principles of network security, monitoring, and management, which are crucial for maintaining a secure and operational network.

Furthermore, we discussed the importance of security governance and compliance, access control, authentication, encryption, firewalls, intrusion detection systems, and incident response and management. These concepts are interconnected and play vital roles in protecting networks and data.

By mastering these fundamental concepts, you will be well-equipped to tackle the challenges of blue teaming and defensive security. Remember, cybersecurity is a constantly evolving field, and staying updated with the latest trends and technologies is crucial for success. Continuous learning and practice are key to building a rewarding and fulfilling career in this exciting domain, and learning the basic concepts is very crucial.

In the next chapter, we shall explore and learn about the frameworks used in cybersecurity.

Join our Discord space

Join our Discord workspace for latest updates, offers, tech happenings around the world, new releases, and sessions with the authors:

https://discord.bpbonline.com

CHAPTER 3
Exploring Security Frameworks

Introduction

In the field of cybersecurity, a solid foundation is more vital than ever to build effective protection tactics. As we learn more about cybersecurity, the complexity and variety of threats continue to grow, making it difficult for individuals, organizations, and nations. A well-defined and flexible structure is needed to solve these difficulties and secure our digital world. This chapter introduces us to cybersecurity frameworks and discusses why mastering them is essential for a successful career.

This chapter introduces cybersecurity frameworks and their role in protecting us from a variety of digital threats. We will examine how these frameworks help cybersecurity professionals navigate the complicated world of cyber threats, vulnerabilities, and countermeasures. Aspiring cybersecurity practitioners can learn how to manage the ever-changing cybersecurity landscape by understanding these concepts.

Moreover, the chapter will also illustrate why professionals must understand cybersecurity frameworks to make informed decisions, implement strong security measures, and proactively identify and mitigate threats. The concepts in this chapter will lay the groundwork for the chapters that follow, whether you are a beginner cybersecurity professional or an experienced practitioner looking to improve. These cybersecurity frameworks will help you defend the digital domain, protect sensitive data, and defend the digital world.

Structure

In this chapter, we will cover the following topics:

- NIST
- ISO/IEC 27001
- COBIT
- SOC2
- HITRUST
- MITRE ATT&CK™ and MITRE D3FEND
- Cyber kill chain
- Essential frameworks
- Other standards and laws

Objectives

The main goal of this chapter is to give a comprehensive understanding of the crucial function cybersecurity frameworks play in safeguarding our digital environment to convey a thorough understanding of the definition, construction, and applications of cybersecurity frameworks in the field of cybersecurity.

Through the study of cybersecurity frameworks, students will be able to recognize potential weaknesses, understand attack vectors, and evaluate the possible impact of cyberattacks on individuals and organizations. to give experts the skills and information they need to manage cyber risks properly. This entails understanding how to assign resources, allocate resources, and implement countermeasures in compliance with the guidelines provided by recognized frameworks.

This chapter dives deep into cybersecurity frameworks. We will break down why they are so crucial and how they work in practice.

By the end, you will be well-versed in the world of cybersecurity frameworks—a must-have for anyone considering a career in cybersecurity.

NIST

The **National Institute of Standards and Technology's (NIST)** Cybersecurity Framework is one of the most important and widely used cybersecurity models in the world. This framework has become especially useful for businesses of all types and industries that want to increase their cyber resilience because it takes a comprehensive approach to managing cybersecurity risks.

At a time when hacks are common, the NIST Cybersecurity Framework gives businesses a structured but adaptable road map that helps them not only protect their digital assets but also deal with new risks. To find, protect, track, handle, and recover from cybersecurity events, it gives companies a consistent set of words and directions.

This structure shows that NIST wants to help with high-quality cybersecurity. It fits the needs and risk profiles of many businesses because it is scalable and flexible. The NIST Cybersecurity Framework gives all types of businesses, from small ones to large ones, the tools and best practices they need to improve their cybersecurity and deal with threats that are always changing.

We can look at this framework's basic parts, driving ideas, and ways of using it more closely if we dig deeper into it. This study will give you the knowledge and skills you need to use the NIST Cybersecurity Framework correctly. This will assist you in safeguarding digital assets and ensuring your company's digital future.

The NIST framework is becoming an important tool for managing cybersecurity risks. This method gives businesses a structured and adaptable way to boost their cyber resistance. Identify, Protect, Detect, Respond, and Recover are five tasks that work together but are different. It has a shared language and set of rules for how to handle the always-changing cyberspace. It is useful for companies of all types and in all industries. In this in-depth study, we will look at how complicated the NIST Cybersecurity Framework is. We will focus on its main parts, on how to apply them, and how important it is to take things slowly and build on project success:

- **Identify**: The first function lays the foundation for good risk control in cybersecurity. Organizations need to be aware of their own cybersecurity needs and challenges before they can sufficiently protect themselves. This calls for compiling basic organizational knowledge, including goals, important data, business plans, systems and assets supporting operations of the company. Knowing this helps companies to spot possible weaknesses, assess the prompt of cybersecurity threats, and find their risk tolerance.

- **Protect**: Highlighting the creation and execution of protections to reduce cybersecurity risks, the *Protect* function draws on the knowledge acquired during the *Identify* phase. Part of this includes setting security rules, procedures, and controls to guard valuable assets. It addresses a wide range of preventive activities, including access control, staff education, data encryption, and safe configuration management. By vigorously implementing these safeguards, organizations can significantly reduce their attack surface and increase their defenses against a variety of cyber threats.

- **Detect**: Knowing that no defense is flawless, the *Detect* tool emphasizes quick identification of cybersecurity incidents. This encompasses the application of systems for continuous monitoring, anomaly detection, and security incident analysis. Early detection of suspicious behavior and suspected security holes enables businesses to respond fast, therefore reducing the prospective damage and the consequences of cyberattacks.

- **Respond**: Not with standing all the comprehensive security procedures, organizations will undoubtedly have cybersecurity events. Users of the *Respond* tool have the tools and techniques they need to appropriately manage these situations. It entails the creation and implementation of an incident response strategy with regard to roles, responsibilities, and communication strategies. Limiting the incidence, reducing its effects, and allowing rehabilitation is the goal. Organizations should also, where pertinent, include law enforcement and incident response teams among other stakeholders.

- **Recover**: The last, *Recover*, emphasizes the need of continuity and resiliency. Following a cybersecurity event, companies must have plans in place to rebuild and retrieve critical data and operations. Along with technical recovery, this covers correspondence with consumers, regulators, and others. The aim of the recovery period is to minimize disturbance and fast-start regular activities. Now, let us examine the pragmatics of implementing the NIST Cybersecurity Framework within an organization:

The following figure shows the NIST Cybersecurity Framework, which provides a comprehensive roadmap for organizations to manage and mitigate cybersecurity risks. This framework, depicted in the following diagram, outlines five key functions: Identify, Protect, Detect, Respond, and Recover. These functions represent a cyclical process, guiding organizations through the essential steps of understanding their risks, implementing protective measures, detecting threats, responding to incidents, and recovering from attacks.

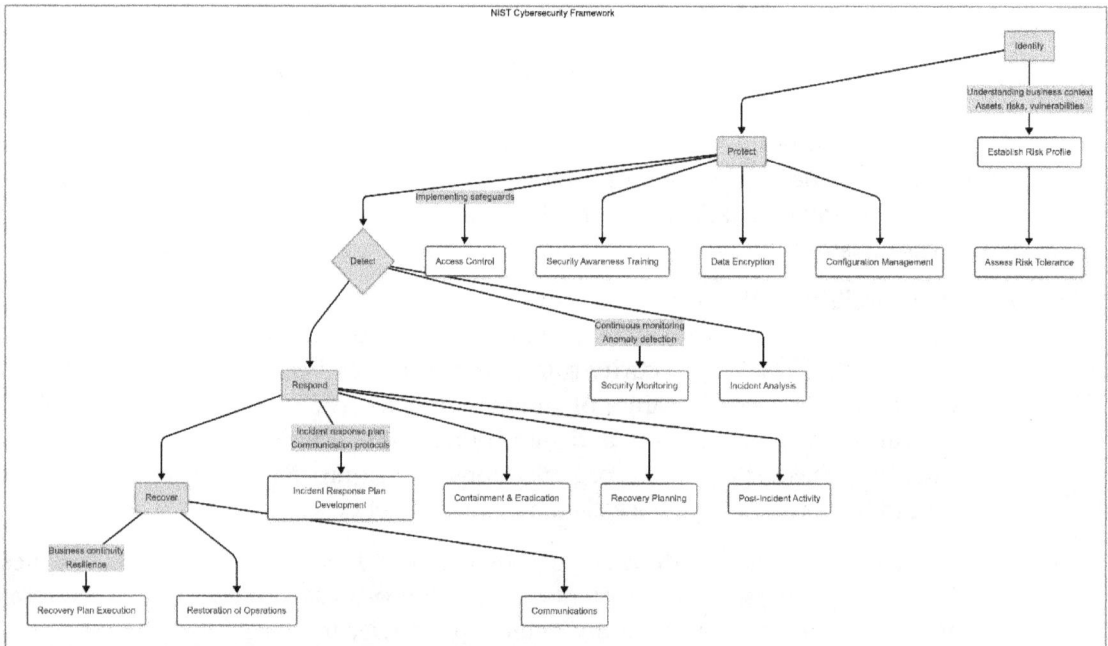

Figure 3.1: NIST Cybersecurity Framework

Implementation of the NIST Cybersecurity Framework

The NIST **Cybersecurity Framework (CSF)** is a dynamic process that helps organizations improve their security posture rather than only being a static blueprint. There are seven essential steps in this process:

1. **Prioritize and scope**:

    a. **Find out what your crown jewels are**: *Which procedures and resources are the most important to your company? What possible effects might they have if they are compromised?*

    b. **Describe your scope**: *Which individuals, systems, and data are covered by your cybersecurity initiatives?*

2. **Orient**:

    a. **Recognize the cybersecurity environment you are in right now**: *What security procedures and controls do you currently have in place? What are your strong points and areas for improvement?*

3. **Create a current profile**:

    a. **Evaluate your security position as it stands now**: Determine which NIST CSF subcategories your present controls are addressing.

    b. **Keep a record of your findings**: Make a *current profile* that shows how the framework is currently being used at your company.

4. **Conduct a risk assessment**:

    a. **Determine possible dangers and weak points**: Examine the risks that your company confronts, taking into account both external and internal variables.

    b. **Evaluate these risks' impact and likelihood**: Assess the possible repercussions of a successful cyberattack.

5. **Create a target profile**:

    a. **Specify the security posture you want to adopt**: Choose which NIST CSF subcategories to prioritize in order to get the security level you want based on your risk assessment.

    b. **Write down your objectives**: Make a target profile that describes the cybersecurity goals of your company.

6. **Determine, analyze, and prioritize gap**:

    a. **Examine the profiles of your target and current self**: Determine the differences between your intended security posture and your existing one.

b. **Make your actions a priority**: Identify the gaps that need to be filled first, since they are the most dangerous.

7. **Put the action plan into practice**:

    a. **Create a plan for improvement**: Make a plan that outlines precise steps, deadlines, and roles to fill in the holes that have been found.

    b. **Continue to observe and enhance**: Review your progress on a regular basis, make necessary adjustments to your plan, and aim for ongoing advancement.

Organizations can use the NIST CSF to create a strong and flexible cybersecurity program that efficiently controls risk and safeguards vital assets by completing these seven steps.

To conclude, the NIST Cybersecurity Framework is a comprehensive and adaptable instrument that enables organizations to systematically manage and reduce cybersecurity risks. Its five capabilities, which are Identify, Protect, Detect, Respond, and Recover, provide an all-encompassing approach to cybersecurity risk management. Organizations can modify the framework to their specific requirements and risk profiles by following a structured implementation process that includes scoping, profiling, risk assessments, and action plans. Also, adopting an incremental approach and expanding on project successes enables organizations to remain resilient and adaptable in the face of evolving cyber threats. As cybersecurity continues to be a paramount concern in the digital age, the NIST Cybersecurity Framework stands as a critical resource for organizations seeking to safeguard their digital assets and secure their future in an increasingly interconnected world.

https://www.nist.gov/cyberframework

Case study

Let us look at some practical case studies that will give us a good insight into the NIST framework.

- **Case study 1: Healthcare provider**:

    o **Organization**: A1 Healthcare

    o **Background**: Prominent healthcare provider A1 Healthcare faced the twin difficulties of preserving private patient data and guaranteeing regulatory compliance with HIPAA and healthcare privacy rules. They wanted a complete cybersecurity system to properly handle these challenging needs.

    o **Implementation and benefits**: Complying with the *Identify* role of the NIST CSF, A1 Healthcare started their path by carefully determining their important assets, including **Electronic Health Records (EHRs)**, and evaluating the related risks. They entered the *Protect* stage with this foundation in place, adding robust access restrictions, patient data encryption, and frequent staff data privacy and security training.

To find possible hazards to patient data, A1 Healthcare used intrusion detection systems and continuous monitoring enabled by the *Detect* capability. Early discovery of a malware attack aimed at their EHR system came from this proactive strategy.

Their readiness paid off in the *respond* phase. A1 Healthcare's NIST CSF-aligned incident response strategy helped them to quickly isolate and contain the malware, therefore stopping a widespread breach. Following legal guidelines, they reported the incident, therefore preventing possible penalties and legal consequences.

A1 Healthcare concentrated on rebuilding the compromised EHR system and improving their general cybersecurity posture in the *Recover* phase. Consistent with NIST CSF guidelines, regular risk assessments guaranteed that their cybersecurity systems changed with the dynamic threat environment. Along with safeguarding private patient information and regulatory compliance, A1 Healthcare showed by using the NIST CSF a dedication to patient privacy.

- **Case study 2: Financial institution**:

  o **Organization**: Royal Bank

  o **Background**: A banking institution, Royal Bank, was dealing with a growing flood of cyber threats. Given their enormous clientele and wealth of private financial data, safeguarding their digital assets became absolutely vital. One complete answer came from the NIST Cybersecurity Framework.

  o **Implementation benefits**: Starting the implementation process, Royal Bank performed a thorough risk assessment in line with the NIST Cybersecurity Framework's *Identify* goal. They noted key assets, evaluated flaws, and calculated possible hazards. Armed with this basic understanding, they then developed a cybersecurity profile fit for their particular needs and risk tolerance.

  Royal Bank tightened security measures during the *Protect* phase, including regular staff cybersecurity training, multi-factor authentication for online banking, and encryption for private client data. Mechanisms for constant monitoring and threat detection were included in the *Detect* feature.

  Designed in line with the *Respond* function, the incident response strategy of the company helped it to react quickly and successfully to a cybersecurity event, including an attempted data compromise. The episode was rapidly confined, lessened, and notified to the relevant authorities, so reducing any possible damage.

  Royal Bank showed their fortitude in the face of hardship during the *Recover* phase by fast bringing client confidence and regular operations back to order. Later risk analyses and response strategies guaranteed ongoing adaptability to fresh challenges. The NIST CSF gave Royal Bank a methodical approach that not only improved its cybersecurity resilience but also ingrained proactive cybersecurity awareness across the company, so safeguarding consumer assets and reputation.

- **Case study 3: Manufacturing company**:

  o **Organization**: D Manufacturing

  o **Background**: D Manufacturing, a company that is known worldwide for manufacturing industrial equipment, faced a growing number of threats that targeted their **Intellectual Property (IP)** and proprietary manufacturing processes. It was important for them to protect their innovations in order to maintain their competitive advantage.

  o **Implementation benefit**: In the manufacturing industry, they started by following the *Identify* function of the NIST CSF. They first identified their most important intellectual property assets, which included proprietary designs and manufacturing processes. They carefully analysed the potential consequences of intellectual property theft and determined the risks involved with cyberattacks by conducting a thorough risk assessment.

  During the *Protect* phase, D Manufacturing took steps to enhance its security measures. This included implementing access controls, encrypting sensitive documents, and providing IP protection training to its employees. Also, they made investments in secure supply chain practices in order to safeguard their designs during the production process.

  The *Detect* function was really helpful for D Manufacturing because it allowed them to keep an eye out for any unusual activities or attempts to access their systems without permission. This came in handy when they discovered an internal threat trying to steal important intellectual property. Thanks to their quick response and following an incident response plan that aligns with the NIST CSF, they were able to prevent any major damage.

  After the incident, D Manufacturing successfully recovered its stolen IP and took the opportunity to improve its IP protection measures. We made sure to regularly assess risks in order to continuously adapt to new threats and weaknesses. The NIST CSF played a crucial role in protecting their valuable intellectual property, maintaining their competitive edge, and demonstrating their commitment to ensuring secure innovation.

These case studies showcase how different organizations, such as those in finance, healthcare, and manufacturing, were able to effectively manage and reduce cybersecurity risks by implementing the NIST CSF. These organizations improved their cybersecurity posture, safeguarded vital assets, and responded robustly to cyber incidents by following the framework's five functions and using a structured approach. The NIST CSF is a versatile and indispensable tool for cybersecurity risk management. It can be applied to organizations of varying sizes and industries, as demonstrated by these real-world examples. This shows its adaptability and applicability in different scenarios.

ISO/IEC 27001

International Organization for Standardization (ISO) and **International Electrotechnical Commission** (IEC) together make up the specialized system for standardization all over the world. Technical committees are created by each organization to deal with specific areas of technical activity. National organizations that are members of ISO or IEC engage in the creation of international standards through these committees. Technical committees from both ISO and IEC work together in areas that are of mutual interest. Also, to ISO and IEC, the work is carried out with the participation of several other international organizations, both governmental and non-governmental.

The ISO 27001 standard, also known as the **information security management systems** (ISMS) international standard, is a crucial framework that businesses worldwide should seriously consider implementing. This standard outlines the specifications and criteria that need to be followed to develop, maintain, and enhance an effective strategy for protecting against cyber-attacks and data breaches. ISO 27001 is designed to help businesses protect and manage their information assets by using a systematic and organized approach to risk management and is one of the critical frameworks.

ISO 27001 places a strong emphasis on complying with various rules. Some of the requirements that need to be considered are the **General Data Protection Regulation** (GDPR), and industry standards like the ISO 27001 standard. One of the most important components of ISO 27001 is this. Ensuring that these requirements are followed is extremely important to guarantee the privacy of information and comply with the law. The GDPR requires businesses to follow specific data protection methods and practices in order to safeguard the privacy and security of personal and sensitive data. ISO 27001 enhances these requirements by offering a more detailed framework for managing information security.

The information security posture of a business may be significantly improved by implementing ISO 27001, which also helps the firm become more resistant to assaults. It accomplishes this by providing exhaustive rules and recommendations for effective practices pertaining to information security management. These recommendations are designed with technology as their primary focus; however, they also consider organizational procedures and human aspects. This is done in recognition of the reality that information security is a multifaceted task.

One of the most important aspects of ISO 27001 is the design of an efficient ISMS. This is a comprehensive strategy that protects sensitive information by combining rules, procedures, and controls. It creates a structure that allows for the methodical identification, evaluation, and elimination of threats to information security. Organizations may guarantee that information security becomes an important part of their everyday business activities by adopting an ISMS that is based on ISO 27001. This transforms information security from a reactive effort into a proactive and continuing endeavor rather of the former.

The measures outlined in ISO 27001 address a comprehensive range of issues pertaining to information security. These measures are intended to mitigate certain dangers and exposures that businesses and other organizations may be exposed to. They include both technical and non-technical measures, such as security awareness training and incident response planning, among others. Network security and encryption are two examples of technological measures that are included in this category. By adhering to these regulations, businesses may develop a strong defense against a range of dangers, both internal and external. This defense can be strengthened.

The protection of data in all its forms, including its availability, integrity, and confidentiality, is ISO 27001's core objective. An ISMS that is based on ISO 27001 will contain a variety of rules, procedures, and controls to accomplish this objective.

Let us go a little more into how firms may better secure these vital facets of data security by implementing ISO 27001:

- **Confidentiality**: It is one of the main goals of ISO 27001, which underlines the need to keep private and sensitive data safe. To reach this goal, controls like access control systems, encryption, and data categorization are used. Access control makes sure that only those with permission can see certain data, while encryption keeps data from being read or intercepted by people who are not supposed to, while it is being sent or preserved. Companies can use data classification to put information into groups based on how sensitive it is. This lets the companies take the right security steps based on the groups.

- **Integrity**: To make sure the information you use is right and reliable, you must keep the data's integrity. This problem is dealt with by ISO 27001, which requires controls like audit trails, data validation, and change management methods to be put in place. Checks for data validity make sure that the data is correct and consistent, and change management methods keep track of and write down any changes that are made to the data. It is helpful to know who viewed or changed data because audit trails keep track of who did it. This is also useful for forensic investigations in case of a security breach.

- **Availability**: Ensuring that information is always accessible, whenever it may be required, is another critical component of ISO 27001. Controls like redundancy, backup and recovery processes, and incident response plans are incorporated into it so that it may accomplish this goal. The presence of redundant components in essential systems or services helps to ensure that there will be as little downtime as possible. Backup and recovery processes provide companies with the ability to swiftly restore data and services if they experience interruptions. Incident response planning, on the other hand, describes activities that may be taken to reduce the effect of security events and quickly restore normal operations.

Given the circumstances, the ISMS sector has adopted the globally accepted ISO 27001. It provides businesses with a whole framework for safeguarding their private data, following required guidelines, and enhancing their defense against cyberattacks. ISO 27001 helps companies create policies, procedures, and necessary controls. This is achieved by giving confidentiality, availability, and data integrity a priority. Implementing ISO 27001 is not simply a best practice, but also a strategic decision for companies seeking to ensure the safety and reliability of their information assets.

https://www.iso.org/standard/27001

COBIT

Designed by the **Information Systems Audit and Control Association (ISACA)**, **Control Objectives for Information and Related Technologies (COBIT)** is a comprehensive framework meant to enable companies to regulate and control their IT environments more successfully. Building on the versions that preceded it and including other improvements, the revised COBIT 2019 framework is *Globally*. This adaptable framework is utilized for numerous purposes, including ensuring that rules are obeyed, that IT objectives complement corporate goals, and that overall IT governance is enhanced.

We will examine the most crucial aspects of COBIT 2019, including its ideas, domains, and objectives:

- **Adaptability and integration**: COBIT 2019 is designed to be flexible and to integrate with other IT frameworks and standards without difficulty. This adaptability permits organizations to tailor their IT governance and management practices to their demands and specifications. It recognizes that in the complex world of information technology, one size does not suit all, making it a valuable tool for organizations with diverse IT environments.

- **SOX compliance**: Following the rules of the **Sarbanes-Oxley Act (SOX)** in the United States, COBIT has become very famous, especially among businesses that have to follow SOX rules. SOX requires public companies to have strict financial and IT controls. These controls make sure that financial reporting is accurate and trustworthy. COBIT brings together financial control and IT control, which makes it easier for businesses to meet SOX standards.

- **Six governance principles**: There are six governance principles in COBIT 2019. These principles serve as the framework's foundation, guiding organizations towards their IT governance goals. The six fundamentals are:

  o **Meeting stakeholder needs**: Organizations must line up their IT strategy and operations with the needs and expectations of their stakeholders, which may include customers, regulators, shareholders, and employees.

  o **Covering the enterprise end-to-end**: COBIT 2019 emphasizes the importance of managing IT holistically across the entire organization, considering all processes, functions, and activities that impact IT.

  o **Applying a single integrated framework**: This principle promotes the use of a single, integrated framework for governance and management of enterprise IT. It discourages the fragmentation of governance practices.

o **Enabling a holistic approach**: COBIT encourages organizations to adopt a holistic approach to governance, ensuring that IT activities are integrated with the overall business strategy and objectives.

o **Separating governance from management**: It is crucial to differentiate between governance, which involves decision-making and oversight, and management, which involves the execution of decisions. This separation helps maintain accountability and transparency.

o **Tailoring to enterprise needs**: COBIT recognizes that every organization is unique and encourages customization of the framework to meet specific enterprise needs, taking into account its size, industry, and regulatory requirements.

- **Five domains of COBIT 2019**: COBIT 2019 defines five domains, each addressing a specific area of IT governance and management. Collectively, these domains encompass a vast spectrum of IT-related activities and processes within an organization. The five categories are:

  o **Evaluate, Direct, and Monitor (EDM)**:

    ▪ This domain focuses on governance processes. It is about ensuring that IT governance is effective and aligned with business goals.

    ▪ It involves setting strategic directions, monitoring performance, and ensuring compliance.

  o **Align, Plan, and Organize (APO)**:

    ▪ This domain deals with management processes related to aligning IT with business strategy.

    ▪ It covers planning, organizing resources, and establishing IT strategies.

  o **Build, Acquire, and Implement (BAI)**:

    ▪ This domain focuses on management processes for developing or acquiring IT solutions.

    ▪ It includes activities like project management, system development, and implementation.

  o **Deliver, Service, and Support (DSS)**:

    ▪ This domain covers management processes related to delivering IT services and support.

    ▪ It involves service management, operations, and user support.

  o **Monitor, Evaluate, and Assess (MEA)**:

    ▪ This domain focuses on management processes for monitoring and evaluating IT performance and compliance.

- It includes activities like performance measurement, risk assessment, and compliance monitoring.

COBIT 2019 provides a comprehensive framework for enterprise governance and management of information and technology. The following figure illustrates the core domains that structure its guidance, separating governance objectives from management objectives:

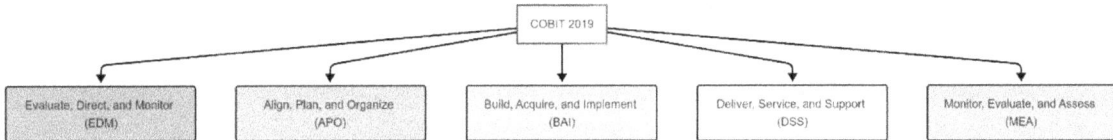

Figure 3.2: *COBIT 2019 and its domains*

To sum up, ISACA's COBIT 2019 is a flexible and widely used framework for IT management and control. It is flexible, works with regulations like SOX, has six governance principles, is organized into five domains, and uses a capability maturity model. All of these things make it a powerful tool for companies that want to improve their IT governance and management. The all-around method of COBIT 2019 makes sure that IT is closely linked to business goals. This helps modern businesses succeed and stay strong in a world that is becoming more and more digital.

https://www.isaca.org/resources/cobit#1

SOC2

Widely accepted compliance framework **System and Organization measures 2 (SOC 2)** helps assess the security and privacy measures followed by service providers. It is a fundamental cybersecurity architecture. Its main goal is to assess and explain how well an organization's security, availability, processing integrity, confidentiality, privacy of consumer data, and sensitive information policies work. Independent auditors who assess an organization's practices against SOC 2 criteria and standards conduct this examination. The **American Institute of CPAs (AICPA)** developed it to evaluate the control effectiveness of a company.

In the present digital scene, when data breaches and cyber threats are common, SOC 2 is of great relevance. It offers service companies a consistent and trustworthy way to show their partners and clients their dedication to privacy and data protection. SOC 2 is a vital assurance tool that guarantees third-party service providers follow strict cybersecurity criteria, as companies depend more on them to manage sensitive data.

SOC 2 is meant to provide consumers and stakeholders with confidence that a service provider has set and followed the required procedures to protect private information and follow legal criteria. By obtaining a SOC 2 report, service providers can show their will to preserving safe and reliable surroundings.

SOC 2 focuses on the following five trust service principles:

- **Security**: This principle evaluates the effectiveness of the organization's controls in preventing physical and logical unauthorized access to the system and data. It assesses measures such as access controls, encryption, system monitoring, and incident response procedures.

- **Availability**: The availability principle evaluates the steps taken by the service provider to ensure that its systems, services, and data satisfy the requirements of its users. This includes evaluating the resilience of the infrastructure, planning for disaster recovery, and establishing incident response procedures.

- **Processing integrity**: This principle examines the integrity and precision of the service provider's processing activities. It examines controls associated with data validation, system processing, and error resolution to ensure that processing is complete, accurate, authorized, and timely.

- **Confidentiality**: The confidentiality principle relates to the prevention of unauthorized disclosure of sensitive information. It assesses controls pertaining to data classification, encryption, access controls, and information security policies.

- **Privacy**: In line with relevant privacy laws and regulations, the privacy principle assesses the organization's restrictions on the gathering, use, retention, and disclosure of personally identifiable information. It guarantees open privacy policies of the company and suitable handling of personal data. A service provider engages an independent auditor to assess their control environment to obtain a SOC 2 report. The auditor examines and evaluates the controls in accordance with the trust service principles and then provides a comprehensive report of their findings. This report can be shared with clients, stakeholders, and other interested parties to demonstrate the service provider's dedication to maintaining a secure and privacy-focused environment.

Compliance with SOC 2 is not a one-time accomplishment, but rather an ongoing process. Service providers must perpetually monitor and evaluate their controls to ensure that they continue to be effective and in line with evolving threats and regulatory requirements.

https://www.aicpa-cima.com/topic/audit-assurance/audit-and-assurance-greater-than-soc-2

HITRUST

The healthcare sector increasingly depends on digital technologies to improve patient care, simplify processes, and handle medical information. These developments expose healthcare companies to an increasing number of security risks, even if they offer many advantages. Preserving the integrity of healthcare systems and safeguarding private patient data now takes first priority. Here, the **Health Information Trust Alliance Common Security Framework (HITRUST CSF)** finds application as a complete solution for cybersecurity, particularly in the healthcare sector.

HITRUST CSF will be thoroughly discussed in this section, together with its objectives, elements, certification procedure, advantages, drawbacks, and practical uses. This training will help you to clearly grasp the purpose of HITRUST CSF in safeguarding healthcare data and the necessary actions to apply it successfully.

Founded in 2007, the non-profit Health Information Trust Alliance, sometimes referred to as **HITRUST**. It was developed to meet the pressing need for a uniform framework that healthcare institutions may apply to control and assess their cybersecurity posture. Over time, HITRUST has emerged as a respected expert in healthcare information security.

The main foundation of the company, HITRUST CSF, is meant to help healthcare companies, including hospitals, insurance companies, and healthcare technology providers, properly controlling and reducing cybersecurity threats. It provides a whole range of controls and best practices catered to the particular difficulties of the sector.

https://hitrustalliance.net/

CSF

The **Common Security Framework** (**CSF**) is fundamental to HITRUST CSF. This framework serves as the basis for all HITRUST certifications and assessments. It comprises a vast array of constraints and requirements that are organized into distinct domains. These controls are based on internationally recognized standards, such as ISO 27001, NIST Cybersecurity Framework, and HIPAA.

The CSF is designed to be adaptable, allowing organizations to customize their security programs to their unique requirements while adhering to industry's best practices and regulatory requirements.

Understanding the objectives

HITRUST defines specific control objectives within the CSF. These objectives define the objectives that organizations should endeavor to achieve to strengthen their cybersecurity posture. The range of control objectives includes data protection, access control, threat detection, and incident response, among others.

Each control objective is connected to one or more specific controls, which provide detailed guidance on how to attain the objective. These controls serve as measures organizations can take to satisfy the CSF's requirements.

Use of HITRUST CSF

Given the volume of private patient data the healthcare sector owns, hackers target it frequently. Comprising a thorough framework, HITRUST CSF helps companies find and fix vulnerabilities, thereby safeguarding sensitive healthcare data confidentiality, integrity, and availability.

Healthcare entities must abide by several rules, including HIPAA and HITECH. Through a compliance road map, HITRUST CSF helps companies follow these rules. By controlling and lowering cybersecurity risk, it also lessens the possibility of expensive data breaches and fines from regulations.

Typically, the HITRUST CSF certification procedure includes the following steps:

1. **Scoping**: Define the scope of the evaluation by designating the systems, processes, and data that fall under the certification's purview.

2. **Control evaluation**: Conduct a thorough evaluation of the controls within the CSF. This involves evaluating the policies, procedures, and technical safeguards of the organization.

3. **Remediation**: Address any identified control gaps or deficiencies. This may entail modifying policies, implementing new security measures, or enhancing existing security measures.

4. **Assessment**: Engage an HITRUST-certified assessor to evaluate the organization's controls and assess their alignment with the CSF requirements.

5. **Reporting**: The assessor provides a report that details the organization's HITRUST CSF compliance.

6. **Certification**: Upon satisfactory completion of the assessment and any required remediation, HITRUST issues a certification, which demonstrates the organization's commitment to cybersecurity and compliance with healthcare industry standards.

7. **Ongoing monitoring**: To maintain HITRUST CSF certification, organizations must continuously monitor and update their controls to adapt to shifting threats and regulatory requirements. Also, periodic assessments are required to ensure ongoing compliance.

MITRE ATT&CK™ and MITRE D3FEND

Adversarial Tactics, Techniques, and Common Knowledge (MITRE ATT&CK™) is a globally recognized cybersecurity framework designed to provide a broad understanding of cyber adversary tactics, techniques, and procedures. It offers a structured approach to analyzing and responding to cyber hazards. On the other hand, MITRE D3FEND is a platform designed to defend organizations against cyber-attacks by providing real-time threat intelligence, threat detection, and incident response capabilities. By combining these two resources, cybersecurity professionals can improve their situational awareness, enhance their incident response, and better defend their organizations from cyber threats.

https://attack.mitre.org/

https://d3fend.mitre.org/

Understanding MITRE ATT&CK™

MITRE ATT&CK™ is a broad understanding base developed by MITRE Corporation. It was originally designed to assist organizations in comprehending the techniques and strategies employed by cyber adversaries. It has grown over time into a community-driven framework that provides plenty of information on threat intelligence, allowing organizations to strengthen their cybersecurity defenses.

To illustrate the structured approach of the MITRE ATT&CK™ framework, the following figure shows a portion of its Enterprise matrix, focusing on the initial stages of a cyberattack.

Note: **As it is not possible to add a screenshot of the entire view of MITRE ATT&CK™, a small snippet is added below. You can access the entire layout on the MITRE website.**

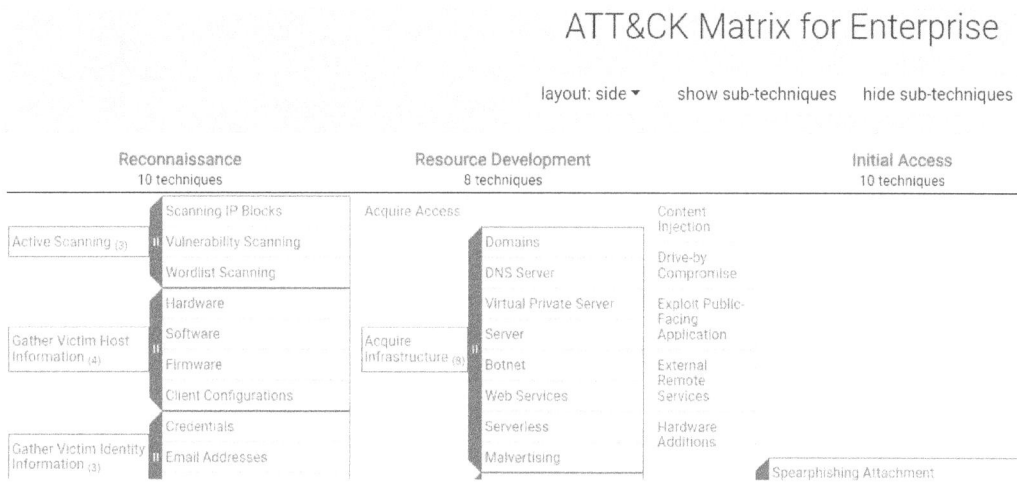

Figure 3.3: MITRE ATT&CK™ matrix

Objectives and goals of MITRE ATT&CK™

MITRE ATT&CK™'s main goal is to be a useful tool for grasping adversary behavior. It offers a disciplined framework for organizing threat actor methods, approaches, and methodologies. MITRE ATT&CK™ lets companies improve their threat detection, incident response, and general cybersecurity posture by charting these behaviors.

Maintaining knowledge of enemies is a continuous difficulty in the always shifting cybersecurity scene. For those in cybersecurity all around, MITRE ATT&CK is a powerful and essential tool. Fundamentally, MITRE ATT&CK is a road map showing the enemy cyberattack behaviors, tactics, and techniques. It offers a shared vocabulary that helps security analysts and teams across communication gaps, therefore providing a consistent framework for understanding, evaluating, and mitigating cyber threats. MITRE ATT&CK offers cybersecurity experts a wealth of knowledge and a shared lexicon by grouping and structuring these strategies and procedures into a structured matrix, thereby improving the security posture of a business and lowering friction across teams.

MITRE ATT&CK is founded on a basis of complete categorization and minute attention to accuracy. The main component of its Enterprise Matrix, a framework, is a wealth of knowledge organized into fourteen general tactics (e.g., Initial Access, Execution, Persistence). These tactics encompass hundreds of specific adversary techniques and sub-techniques, offering granular detail on adversary behaviors. From first access to execution, persistence, privilege escalation, defense evasion, credential access, detection, lateral movement, collection, exfiltration, and impact, even adversary-controlled command-and-control—these approaches span a wide spectrum of cyber threat operations. Within every approach, MITRE ATT&CK painstakingly details the methods used by enemies, offering actual case studies and exhaustive analyses.

MITRE ATT&CK depends critically on the classification of shared adversaries. These groups reflect different threat actors together with their corresponding methods, approaches, and techniques (TTPs). Cybersecurity experts can learn about the enemies, particularly those aiming at their company, by spotting and tracking these organizations. Threat intelligence depends on this kind of understanding since it helps companies to properly plan for and fight against recognized enemies. It also helps to attribute cyberattacks and evaluate how these enemies might compromise the security posture of a company.

One unique quality of MITRE ATT&CK is its focus on accuracy. This paper emphasizes the degrees of every approach and technique rather than offering general explanations of cyber dangers. This roughness gives cybersecurity experts an exact understanding of how enemies work, which is quite important. This thorough understanding allows security experts to evaluate the weaknesses of their company and build strong defenses in line. Within the *Execution* approach, for example, MITRE ATT&CK offers specifics on particular techniques like *command-line interface* and *scripting*, therefore clarifying the ways adversaries employ to run harmful malware on victim systems.

One of the ongoing difficulties in cybersecurity is the need for efficient cooperation across several security teams inside a company. Specialized expertise is possessed by security analysts, incident responders, danger searchers, and network defenders. With its shared vocabulary, which all of these teams can use, MITRE ATT&CK acts as a uniting tool. This common knowledge helps to greatly ease conflict and misinterpretation. Security teams may quickly refer to the MITRE ATT&CK structure to make sure everyone is on the same page, speaking the same language, and working toward the same goal, whether an event happens or a possible threat is found. This raises the general efficacy of cybersecurity activities as well as the efficiency of incident response.

Case studies for MITRE ATT&CK

To comprehend the significance of MITRE ATT&CK in the real world, it is instructive to examine a few case studies that illustrate its practical application. Imagine a financial institution that has incorporated MITRE ATT&CK as a fundamental part of its cybersecurity strategy. When an alert indicating a potential security compromise is triggered, the incident response team immediately consults the MITRE ATT&CK matrix to determine the specific tactics and techniques associated with the detected threat. By referencing the framework, they rapidly discern that the adversary is attempting to execute malicious code using a well-known technique known as **PowerShell**. With this knowledge, they can promptly implement countermeasures to stop the attack and prevent further damage. This is just one example of how MITRE ATT&CK enables organizations to effectively respond in real-time to cyber threats.

- **Case study 1: A retail giant combating point-of-sale malware:**
  - o **Background**: A major retail chain experienced a significant data breach due to malware infecting their **point-of-sale (POS)** systems. Customer credit card information was stolen, resulting in financial losses and reputational damage. They turned to MITRE ATT&CK to improve their defenses and prevent future attacks.
  - o **Solution:** Using the ATT&CK framework, the company mapped the previous attack, identifying the tactics and techniques used by the attackers (e.g., Spearphishing Attachment [T1566.001], Process Injection [T1055], Data Exfiltration [T1041]). This allowed them to:
    - ▪ **Strengthen endpoint security**: They implemented advanced malware detection and prevention solutions on POS terminals, focusing on the specific techniques observed in the previous attack.
    - ▪ **Improve network segmentation**: They isolated POS systems from the rest of the network, limiting the lateral movement of malware in case of a breach.
    - ▪ **Enhance security monitoring**: They deployed SIEM tools to monitor for suspicious activity related to known POS malware techniques.
  - o **Result:** By leveraging ATT&CK, the retail giant significantly enhanced its security posture. They successfully detected and prevented subsequent attempts to compromise their POS systems, protecting customer data and preserving their brand reputation.
- **Case study 2: A government agency defending against APTs**
  - o **Background**: A government agency faced persistent cyberattacks from a sophisticated threat actor. The attackers were using advanced techniques to infiltrate their network, steal sensitive information, and maintain a persistent presence. The agency adopted MITRE ATT&CK to better understand and defend against these APTs.
  - o **Solution**: The agency used ATT&CK to:
    - ▪ **Profile the threat actor**: They analyzed past attacks and mapped them to ATT&CK techniques, gaining insights into the attacker's **tactics, tools, and procedures (TTPs)**.

- **Develop proactive defenses**: Based on the identified TTPs, they implemented targeted security controls to disrupt the attacker's kill chain. This included strengthening their defenses against spearphishing, enhancing network monitoring for command-and-control traffic, and implementing stricter access controls to sensitive data.

- **Conduct threat hunting**: They proactively searched for **indicators of compromise (IOCs)** associated with the threat actor's TTPs, enabling early detection and response to potential intrusions.

o **Result**: By applying ATT&CK, the government agency gained a deeper understanding of the APT they were facing. This allowed them to develop more effective defenses, proactively hunt for threats, and ultimately disrupt the attacker's operations. They significantly reduced the risk of successful intrusions and protected their sensitive information.

MITRE D3FEND

MITRE D3FEND is a strong weapon used to guard against cyberattacks. In the field of cybersecurity, knowledge of opponent tactics and strategies is not enough; companies also must use strong security policies to protect their resources. D3FEND fills in between knowledge and behavior. It guarantees that defensive strategies complement the offensive tactics and approaches described in ATT&CK by means of a smooth coordination with the MITRE ATT&CK Navigator and Matrix. By means of information on attacker techniques and tactics, D3FEND helps companies to develop effective security controls, mitigating agents, and countermeasures, so strengthening their defenses against a wide spectrum of threats.

One very necessary component is the *detect* element. Though prevention is crucial, equally important is having strong systems in place to identify possible threats. D3FEND stresses the need to establish a baseline of regular network activity and of network traffic analysis. Under this proactive approach, network traffic patterns are continuously monitored and deviations from the baseline are found. This helps companies to quickly identify unusual or suspicious behavior, thereby allowing them to react appropriately before a possible security breach. Modern cybersecurity is mostly based on network traffic analysis; hence, D3FEND promotes early application as part of a comprehensive protection plan.

Although MITRE D3FEND is a useful instrument for strengthening cybersecurity defenses, it has certain limits that must be admitted. Its focus on proactive defense strategies is limited significantly. D3FEND mostly helps companies doing system hardening and threat planning. It might not be as good, meantime, at identifying already-occurring breaches. Often, detecting continuous or previous security breaches calls for forensic research and certain tools. Organizations should thus see D3FEND as a proactive defensive tool that enhances incident detection and response capacity.

In the field of cybersecurity, knowledge is power; thus, MITRE ATT&CK Navigator is a great tool for companies trying to understand and prepare for possible risks. This tool lets users explore the minute elements of adversary TTPs, therefore offering a graphic picture of the MITRE ATT&CK Matrix. Users may find certain threat actors and learn about their methods and actions. Assisting companies in threat intelligence, risk assessment, and the development of defensive strategies, the MITRE ATT&CK Navigator helps to deepen knowledge of the threat environment.

To illustrate the structured approach to cybersecurity defense, the following figure presents a section of the D3FEND™ framework, highlighting various hardening techniques and analysis methods.

Note: As it is not possible to add a screenshot of the entire view of MITRE D3FEND, a small snippet is added below. You can access the entire layout on the MITRE website.

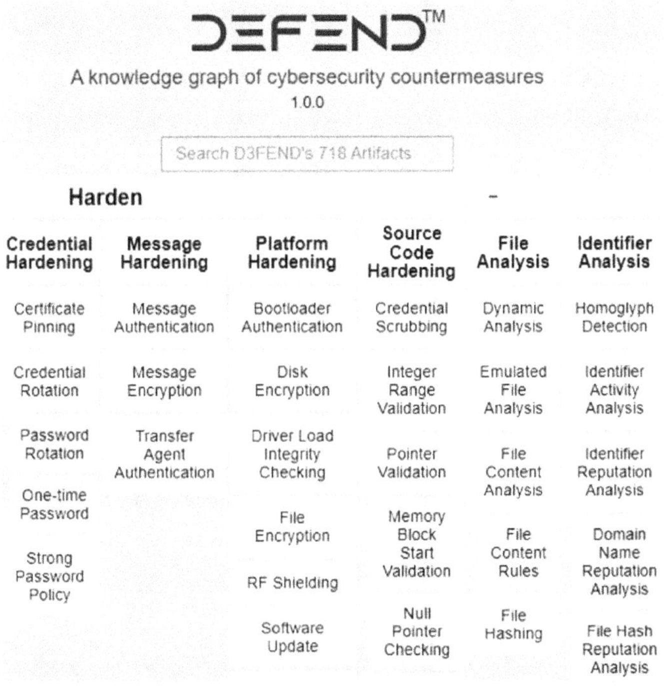

⊃Ξ϶ΞΝ϶™

A knowledge graph of cybersecurity countermeasures
1.0.0

Search D3FEND's 718 Artifacts

Harden   —

Credential Hardening	Message Hardening	Platform Hardening	Source Code Hardening	File Analysis	Identifier Analysis
Certificate Pinning	Message Authentication	Bootloader Authentication	Credential Scrubbing	Dynamic Analysis	Homoglyph Detection
Credential Rotation	Message Encryption	Disk Encryption	Integer Range Validation	Emulated File Analysis	Identifier Activity Analysis
Password Rotation	Transfer Agent Authentication	Driver Load Integrity Checking	Pointer Validation	File Content Analysis	Identifier Reputation Analysis
One-time Password		File Encryption	Memory Block Start Validation	File Content Rules	Domain Name Reputation Analysis
Strong Password Policy		RF Shielding			
		Software Update	Null Pointer Checking	File Hashing	File Hash Reputation Analysis

Figure 3.4: MITRE D3FEND matrix

The MITRE ATT&CK Navigator is a dynamic platform that lets the examination of protective layers possible, not only an inert reference tool. This covers assessment of countermeasures and detecting capacity. For every adversary tactic mentioned in the matrix, the utility offers details on mitigating strategies companies could use to lower their risk of exploitation. It also offers understanding of the several detection strategies available to help one properly recognize and handle these approaches. Analyzing protective layers with the MITRE ATT&CK Navigator helps companies change their cybersecurity plans to fit certain vulnerabilities, therefore strengthening their defenses.

Among the most useful applications of the MITRE ATT&CK Navigator is doing a gap analysis. This process contrasts the ATT&CK Matrix's strategies and tactics with an organization's present security posture. This helps companies to find weaknesses and possible protection gaps. One proactive approach to assisting companies give security improvements top priority is security gap analysis. It helps decision-makers distribute funds to enhance their security protocols in areas that most need them. In the end, doing a gap analysis using the MITRE ATT&CK Navigator is a strategic action meant to improve cybersecurity resilience.

More than only graphical depictions of the ATT&CK Matrix, the MITRE ATT&CK Navigator offers tools for better documentation and teamwork. By saving their work inside the program, users guarantee that their analysis and conclusions will then be easily available. Furthermore, the program lets users extract data and export images, therefore enabling the production of thorough reports and the sharing of ideas to stakeholders and colleagues. By means of this documentation and collaborative capabilities, cybersecurity teams may communicate more effectively, thereby ensuring that everyone is in line with the security posture and threat environment of the company.

MITRE D3FEND and the MITRE ATT&CK Navigator are, to conclude, indispensable tools for cybersecurity professionals. D3FEND enables organizations to proactively enhance their defenses, aligning them with MITRE ATT&CK's tactics and techniques of adversaries. Emphasis is placed on the *detect* aspect of defense, network traffic analysis, and establishing baselines to ensure that organizations can quickly identify and respond to potential threats. D3FEND has limitations, but it is essential for proactive defense.

The MITRE ATT&CK Navigator, on the other hand, provides a visual, dynamic representation of the ATT&CK Matrix, enabling organizations to comprehend adversary behaviors and techniques. It facilitates the analysis of defensive layers, supports gap analysis for vulnerability identification, and improves cybersecurity team documentation and collaboration. Together, these instruments provide organizations with the knowledge and capabilities necessary to defend against an ever-changing threat landscape.

Case studies for MITRE D3FEND

Let us examine how businesses proactively strengthen their defenses in order to understand the practical implications of MITRE D3FEND:

- **Case study 1**: A financial institution defending against credential theft.

    o **Background**: A prominent financial institution was concerned about the escalating dangers of credential theft and account compromise. They decided to implement MITRE D3FEND to strengthen their cyber defenses.

    o **Solution**: The organization implemented the MITRE D3FEND recommended techniques for preventing credential theft. This required **multi-factor authentication** (MFA) for user accounts, requiring an additional authentication step even if credentials were compromised. They also deployed strong password policies and routinely conducted user education and awareness training to prevent fraudulent attacks.

  o **Result**: By implementing these D3FEND techniques, the financial institution was able to effectively thwart multiple attempts to capture user credentials. Significantly fewer attempts to gain unauthorized access and accounts were compromised. Not only did the institution's rigid security measures safeguard its consumers, but they also enhanced its reputation for safety.

- **Case study 2**: A healthcare provider employing MITRE D3FEND to prevent ransomware.

  o **Background**: A significant healthcare provider observed an increase in ransomware attacks against healthcare organizations. They turned to MITRE D3FEND to strengthen their defenses against these stealthy threats.

  o **Solution**: The healthcare provider employed D3FEND's recommended ransomware protection techniques. They ensured regular and automated backups of vital patient data, thereby minimizing the potential impact of ransomware attacks. Also, they implemented network segmentation to limit adversary lateral movement and email filtering solutions to block malicious attachments and links frequently used to deliver ransomware payloads.

  o **Result**: Due to their proactive approach guided by D3FEND, the healthcare provider was able to thwart multiple ransomware attacks. Even in instances where ransomware was able to infiltrate their network, the organization was able to quickly restore affected systems from backups, minimizing patient care disruptions.

Cyber Kill Chain

In the ongoing battle against cyber threats, it is crucial for cybersecurity professionals to not only respond to incidents but also to understand how these attacks unfold. This is where the Cyber Kill Chain concept comes into play.

The following figure depicts the Cyber Kill Chain, providing a step-by-step representation of how adversaries progress through an attack, from initial reconnaissance to achieving their objectives. Understanding the Cyber Kill Chain is essential for developing effective cybersecurity defenses. This figure visually outlines the stages where organizations can intervene to disrupt an attack.

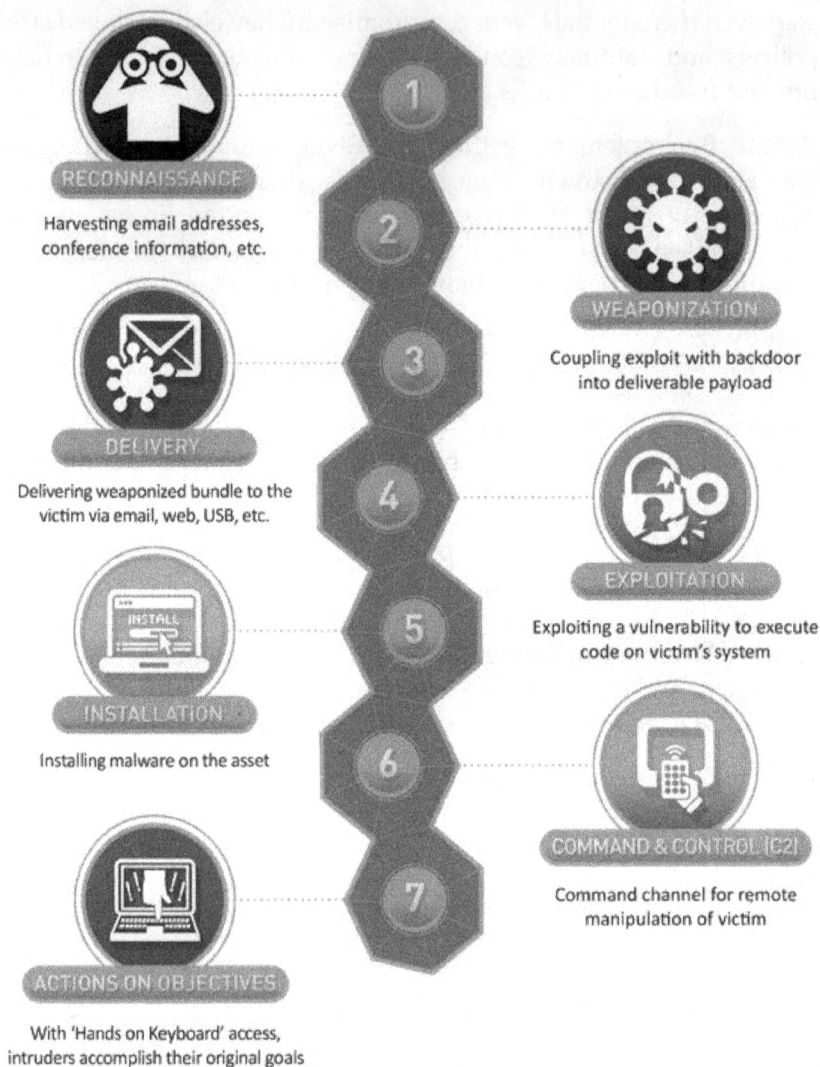

RECONNAISSANCE

Harvesting email addresses,
conference information, etc.

DELIVERY

Delivering weaponized bundle to the
victim via email, web, USB, etc.

INSTALLATION

Installing malware on the asset

ACTIONS ON OBJECTIVES

With 'Hands on Keyboard' access,
intruders accomplish their original goals

WEAPONIZATION

Coupling exploit with backdoor
into deliverable payload

EXPLOITATION

Exploiting a vulnerability to execute
code on victim's system

COMMAND & CONTROL (C2)

Command channel for remote
manipulation of victim

Figure 3.5: Cyber Kill Chain

Let us explore the Cyber Kill Chain in-depth, breaking down its stages, discussing its significance, and providing insights into how organizations can use it to bolster their cybersecurity defenses:

- **Introduction**: Military language inspired the cybersecurity idea known as the **Cyber Kill Chain**, which describes the structured steps involved in a military attack. It provides a methodical approach for grasping and seeing the phases of a cybercrime. Originally presented by defense behemoth *Lockheed Martin*, this idea has evolved into a basic paradigm for incident response and threat analysis. Let us break out the several phases of the Cyber Kill Chain:

o **Stage 1: Reconnaissance**: Reconnaissance is the first step in the Cyber Kill Chain. During this phase, the assailants gather intelligence on the target. This may involve analyzing the target's network for vulnerabilities and identifying possible entry points. To create a profile of their target, attackers frequently use OSINT techniques, such as browsing for publicly accessible information on websites and social media.

To defend against reconnaissance, organizations must monitor for out-of-the-ordinary network surveillance activities and protect sensitive data that could be used by adversaries.

o **Stage 2: Weaponization**: After reconnaissance, the next phase for assailants is weaponization. Here, they transform the gathered information into a weapon. This may entail the creation of malicious payloads, such as malware or fraudulent emails, designed to exploit the vulnerabilities discovered during reconnaissance.

Effective weaponization defenses include robust email filtering to identify and block malicious attachments and **Uniform Resource Locator (URLs)**. Also, it is essential to maintain software and systems patched with the latest security updates.

o **Stage 3: Delivery**: In the phase of delivery, assailants convey their armed payloads to the target. This can occur via a variety of attack vectors, including email attachments, malicious websites, and even USB drives. The objective of attackers is to convince users to execute malicious code, thereby initiating an attack.

Employing email security solutions, web filtering, and educating employees about the perils of opening attachments and clicking on links from unknown sources, organizations can defend against delivery.

o **Stage 4: Exploitation**: Once the delivery is successful, attackers move to the exploitation stage. Here, they take advantage of vulnerabilities in the target's systems or applications. Exploitation often involves gaining unauthorized access, escalating privileges, and establishing a foothold in the target's environment.

To defend against exploitation, organizations must regularly patch and update their systems to fix known vulnerabilities. Employing **intrusion detection systems (IDS)** and **intrusion prevention systems (IPS)** can also help detect and block exploitation attempts.

o **Stage 5: Installation**: During the installation phase, attackers install malicious software or maintain their existence on a compromised system. To maintain control over the target environment, this usually entails constructing backdoors or establishing remote access points.

Organizations require powerful antivirus and endpoint protection solutions to detect and eradicate deployed malware. Also, routine security audits and assessments can help identify unauthorized installations.

o **Stage 6: Command-and-control (C2)**: In the C2 phase, attackers establish channels of communication to sustain control over compromised systems. This typically entails connecting to external servers under the control of the perpetrators so they can send commands and exfiltrate data.

Organizations must monitor network traffic for anomalous patterns or connections to known malicious domains in order to defend against C2 activities. Implementing network segmentation can also restrict the lateral movement of network attackers.

o **Stage 7: Actions on objectives**: The concluding phase of the Cyber Kill Chain consists of objectives-based actions. During this phase, assailants accomplish their final objectives, which may include data abduction, data destruction, or espionage. They may exfiltrate sensitive information, disrupt operations, or accomplish other malevolent goals.

Combining **data loss prevention** (**DLP**) measures, incident response planning, and robust monitoring to detect and respond to anomalous activities is required to defend against actions on objectives.

- **Adaptations and variations of the Cyber Kill Chain**: Cyber Kill Chain is not a static concept; it adapts to the ever-changing threat landscape. The traditional model has been modified and expanded to address contemporary threats. To remain clear of cyber adversaries, it is essential to comprehend these modifications.

- **Mitigating the Cyber Kill Chain**: Just the first step is knowing the Cyber Kill Chain. The final goal is to interrupt the chain in several phases, thereby preventing effective attacks. This calls for a proactive approach to cybersecurity comprising the application of defense-in-depth tactics, the completion of frequent security assessments, and the observation of developing risks.

A logical framework for understanding the stages of a cyberattack is offered by the Cyber Kill Chain. By breaking out every component, companies may create more robust cybersecurity plans and defenses. Though no defense is perfect, Cyber Kill Chain enables cybersecurity experts with a useful tool for proactive threat mitigation and incident response. Knowledge and readiness are absolutely vital to keep one step clear of cyber enemies in the always shifting threat environment of today.

https://www.lockheedmartin.com/en-us/capabilities/cyber/cyber-kill-chain.html

Essential frameworks

In search of a career in cybersecurity, one must first understand cybersecurity frameworks in their whole complexity. These systems act as methodical road maps, guiding digital assets and data security in a society full of always-changing cyber dangers. First of all, they give cybersecurity experts a thorough awareness of the threat environment so they may predict, identify, and react to several attack paths. Second, frameworks help to create thorough security policies, processes, and controls fit for the needs of a company, thereby guaranteeing that security measures follow industry's best standards and legal requirements. They also help to identify and assess system weaknesses in a company, therefore supporting preventative measures. Emphasizing the human aspect of cybersecurity, cybersecurity frameworks help to foster an awareness of security among staff members and adherence. Eventually, by learning these frameworks, cybersecurity experts equip themselves with the knowledge and tools needed to strengthen defenses, reduce risks, and protect sensitive data, enabling themselves to be indispensable stewards of digital ecosystems in a society growingly linked.

The following are some other frameworks:

- **Industrial control system (ICS) cybersecurity framework**: Developed by the U.S. NIST, this framework concentrates on enhancing the cybersecurity of critical infrastructure systems, including those used in industrial and manufacturing contexts.

  https://www.cisa.gov/topics/industrial-control-systems

- **Cloud Security Alliance (CSA) security guidance**: CSA provides guidance on best practices and security controls unique to cloud computing environments, thereby assisting organizations in securing cloud-based assets.

  https://cloudsecurityalliance.org/research/guidance

- **Federal Information Security Modernization Act (FISMA)**: It requires federal agencies to develop, document, and implement comprehensive information security programs to safeguard their information systems.

  https://www.cisa.gov/topics/cyber-threats-and-advisories/federal-information-security-modernization-act

- **Framework for improving critical infrastructure cybersecurity**: Along with the NIST CSF, NIST also provides the Cybersecurity Framework, which is extensively adopted by organizations to enhance cybersecurity practices and manage cybersecurity risk.

  https://www.cisa.gov/resources-tools/resources/framework-improving-critical-infrastructure-cybersecurity

- **Cybersecurity Maturity Model Certification (CMMC)**: This defense industry-specific framework was devised by the *U.S. Department of Defense (DoD)*. It evaluates the cybersecurity maturity of contractors and suppliers, mandating that they meet specific cybersecurity requirements in order to work with the DoD.

  https://www.cisa.gov/resources-tools/resources/cybersecurity-maturity-model-certification-20-program

- **CIS Controls and Critical Security Controls (CSC)**: Developed by the CIS, the CSCs provide a prioritized approach to cybersecurity, concentrating on critical areas where organizations can accomplish the greatest risk reduction.

The **Center for Internet Security (CIS)** provides a set of prioritized best practices known as the CIS Controls. These controls provide detailed recommendations for protecting information systems and data, with an emphasis on implementation.

https://www.cisecurity.org/controls

Other standards and laws

While the frameworks we have explored provide robust foundations for cybersecurity, they often intersect and are sometimes mandated by specific industry standards and legal regulations. This section delves into how standards like PCI DSS, ISO 27001, and GDPR influence and enhance cybersecurity practices, adding another layer of protection and compliance.

PCI DSS

In a world where credit card transactions have become the norm, guaranteeing the security of sensitive payment card data has become of the utmost importance. The **Payment Card Industry Data Security Standard** (**PCI DSS**) plays a vital role in this regard. The PCI DSS is a set of security standards developed by the PCI SSC to safeguard credit card information from cyber threats. Examine the significance and requirements of PCI DSS.

PCI DSS seeks to secure the entire transaction process, from the instant a payment card is swiped or input online to the completion of the payment processing. Its primary objective is to prevent hackers from exploiting cardholder data, including card numbers, PINs, and personal information. By adhering to PCI DSS, organizations can increase consumer confidence, safeguard their brand reputation, and mitigate the risk of incurring monetary losses because of data breaches.

The following are the compliances, requirements, and benefits of PCI DSS:

- **Compliance and requirements**: The PCI DSS establishes a comprehensive framework of requirements that organizations must meet to protect cardholder data. These requirements encompass six important control objectives: constructing and maintaining a secure network, protecting cardholder data, maintaining a vulnerability management program, implementing strong access control measures, regularly monitoring and testing networks, and maintaining an information security policy.

  The standard contains detailed recommendations for data encryption, network segmentation, firewalls, access control systems, and system fortification. Also, it mandates periodic security assessments, such as vulnerability evaluations and penetration tests, in order to promptly identify and resolve potential vulnerabilities.

  All entities that process, hold, or transmit credit card information must comply with PCI DSS. Noncompliance can result in severe penalties, such as monetary fines, loss of consumer confidence, and legal repercussions. Compliance requires ongoing diligence and a dedication to implementing and sustaining comprehensive security measures.

- **Benefits of PCI DSS compliance**: PCI DSS compliance gives businesses many benefits besides just keeping data safe. It helps businesses build strong security, which lowers the chance of data breaches and people getting to private data without permission. When compliance is reached, people are more likely to do business with companies that care about their data safety. Also, following PCI DSS is the same as following other security rules and frameworks, like the GDPR. This makes data safety better in general.

PCI DSS is an important set of rules for keeping payment card information safe in a world where cyber threats are a big problem for both business and customer data security. By following the PCI DSS rules, businesses can create a safe space for handling, keeping, and sending credit card information. Following this standard not only keeps companies from losing money and damaging their reputation, but it also boosts customer trust and the general security of the company.

https://www.pcisecuritystandards.org/

ISO 27001

The **International Organization for Standardization (ISO)** put out a standard called ISO 27001 that is accepted all over the world. It gives a group a plan for setting up an ISMS.

It is the main goal of ISO 27001 to help organizations create, implement, manage, and always make their ISMS better. An IMS is an organized way to handle private company data to keep it safe from many threats, like hackers, data leaks, and other security problems.

In order to get certified, organizations must follow ISO 27001's rules and standards. These standards cover many areas of information security, such as identifying and managing risks, making security policies and procedures, keeping track of assets, controlling access, handling incidents, and planning for business continuity.

By using ISO 27001, businesses can make sure they have a complete and effective information security management system. By doing this, they can fix the problems that come with their information assets and keep private data safe, accessible, and complete.

ISO 27001 can be used by any type of business, no matter how big or small. It is widely used around the world and is used as a standard for managing information protection. Companies can show their clients, customers, and business partners how committed they are to information security by getting certified.

https://www.iso.org/standard/27001

GDPR

In 2018, the **European Union (EU)** put into effect a comprehensive data protection law. GDPR was designed to strengthen and harmonize data protection regulations across EU member states in order to give individuals more control over their personal data.

The main principles of GDPR include:

- **Lawfulness, fairness, and transparency**: Organizations must process personal information lawfully, equitably, and openly.

- **Purpose limitation**: Personal information should only be collected for specified, explicit, and lawful purposes, and should not be processed in a manner inconsistent with those purposes.

- **Data minimization**: Organizations should only collect and process the minimum amount of personal information required for a specific purpose. Relevant and necessary information should determine the scope of data collection.

- **Accuracy**: Personal information should be accurate and kept up to date. Organizations are responsible for taking reasonable measures to ensure its accuracy.

- **Storage limitation**: Personal information should be stored for no longer than is required for the specified purposes.

- **Accountability**: Organizations must be able to demonstrate GDPR compliance and accept responsibility for their data processing activities.

- **Integrity and confidentiality**: Individuals have expanded rights regarding their personal data under GDPR, including the right to access, rectify, eradicate, and restrict the processing of their data. Also, they have the right to data portability and to object to the processing of their data for specific purposes.

GDPR applies not only to organizations within the EU but also to any organization, regardless of location, that processes the personal data of EU inhabitants.

https://gdpr-info.eu/

HIPAA

The HIPAA stands as a foundation in this domain, providing a comprehensive framework for safeguarding **protected health information (PHI)**.

HIPAA is not just about protecting patient privacy; it is about ensuring the integrity and availability of critical health information.

This framework mandates a multi-layered approach to security, encompassing administrative, physical, and technical safeguards. We will discuss this briefly:

- **Administrative safeguards**: These lay the groundwork for a strong security posture. HIPAA requires organizations to do the following:

    o **Implement security management processes**: This includes conducting risk assessments, developing security policies and procedures, and providing workforce training.

o **Designate a security official**: This individual is responsible for overseeing the organization's HIPAA security program.

o **Manage workforce security**: This involves implementing procedures for authorizing access to PHI, terminating access when necessary, and conducting background checks.

o **Establish information access management**: This includes implementing policies for granting access to PHI based on job roles and responsibilities.

o **Implement security awareness and training**: Workforce members must be educated about HIPAA security requirements and best practices.

o **Address security incident procedures**: Organizations must have procedures in place for identifying, responding to, and reporting security incidents.

o **Perform contingency planning**: This includes developing plans for data backup, disaster recovery, and emergency mode operations.

o **Conduct evaluations**: Regular assessments of the HIPAA security program are crucial to ensure its effectiveness.

o **Maintain business associate contracts**: When working with third-party vendors who handle PHI, organizations must ensure these vendors have appropriate security measures in place.

- **Physical safeguards**: These focus on protecting the physical environment where PHI is stored and accessed. HIPAA mandates:

  o **Controlling physical access to facilities**: This includes implementing measures like security guards, locks, and surveillance systems.

  o **Securing workstations and devices**: Protecting devices that access PHI from unauthorized access and theft.

  o **Implementing policies for the use and removal of hardware and electronic media**: This includes procedures for securely disposing of devices and media containing PHI.

- **Technical safeguards**: These address the technological measures necessary to protect **electronic PHI (ePHI)**. The key requirements include:

  o **Access control**: Implementing technical policies and procedures to limit access to ePHI to authorized individuals.

  o **Audit controls**: Implementing mechanisms to record and examine activity related to ePHI.

  o **Integrity**: Ensuring that ePHI is not altered or destroyed in an unauthorized manner.

    o   **Person or entity authentication**: Verifying the identity of users accessing ePHI.

    o   **Transmission security**: Protecting ePHI during electronic transmission, such as through encryption.

HIPAA also highlights the significance of continuous risk management and evaluation. To reduce risks, organizations need to assess their security measures on a regular basis, find any weaknesses, and put the right precautions in place.

Healthcare providers show their dedication to safeguarding patient privacy and preserving the availability, confidentiality, and integrity of sensitive health information by following HIPAA regulations. HIPAA offers a crucial framework for creating a strong security posture and promoting confidence between patients and healthcare providers in a world where cyber threats are ever more complex.

https://www.hhs.gov/hipaa/for-professionals/security/index.html

Conclusion

This chapter explored how cybersecurity frameworks are essential for enabling blue teams to protect against changing cyberthreats. We looked at key frameworks such as NIST, SOC2, and MITRE ATT&CK, emphasizing their methodical approaches to risk management, incident response, and threat identification. You discovered how these frameworks give cybersecurity experts a common language, facilitating easy communication and guaranteeing adherence to industry norms.

The main conclusion is that these frameworks are essential resources for blue team members to use when negotiating the intricacies of the contemporary threat environment. You can proactively improve your company's security posture, handle events efficiently, and eventually protect important digital assets by comprehending and using these frameworks. For any cybersecurity practitioner, understanding these concepts is essential as cyber-attacks continue to increase in complexity and frequency.

After discussing the fundamental concepts that support blue team operations, we now focus on the toolkit available to them. In order to enable defenders to proactively detect, evaluate, and react to cyber threats, the next chapter explores the key tools and methods utilized for threat hunting and blue teaming.

CHAPTER 4

Explore Blue Teaming Strengthening Techniques

The best investment is in the tools of one's own trade.

– Benjamin Franklin

Introduction

While red teams, whose job is to replicate attacks to find weaknesses, get most of the attention, blue teams also play an important but less well-known part. Blue teams work hard to keep their company's data safe and are the defense and guardians of an organization's safety. This chapter looks at the advanced techniques and specialized tools that blue teams use to find, analyze, and react more quickly to possible threats. This is commonly known as **threat hunting**.

Traditional security measures, like firewalls and antivirus software, are like walls that keep out known threats. They work, but they are mostly silent. The vigilant scouts and soldiers who protect the castle and actively look for threats to find and eliminate possible threats before they reach the castle gates are on the blue team. They are equipped with the right tools and methods.

This part is meant to be a must-read for people who work in cybersecurity, make decisions for organizations, and want to improve their security. The more detailed parts of blue teaming and threat management will be discussed in this chapter. The sections that follow will go into more detail about blue teaming methods, the most important parts of threat finding, and the wide range of tools that can be used to do these important jobs. This chapter will take a close look at the main tools that allow proactive cyber defense. These tools range from **endpoint detection and response** (**EDR**) solutions to advanced **security information and event management** (**SIEM**) systems.

We will also talk about the most cutting-edge strategies, like lying and automated reaction playbooks, that raise the level of blue teaming to a whole new level. We hope to give you a full and forward-looking picture by mixing these strategies with real-life examples and future trends, like the part that AI and cloud-native security tools will play.

Put on your seat belts because we are going to talk about the complicated world of danger hunting and blue teams. Clear goal: to give blue teams the skills and tools they need to not only protect their companies from cyber threats but also use those threats to make their defenses stronger.

Structure

In this chapter, we will cover the following topics:

- Blue teaming–Cyber defense and incident response
- Threat intelligence
- File integrity monitoring
- Phishing analysis
- Data loss prevention solutions
- Firewall
- Vulnerability scanning and management
- Identity and access management
- Threat hunting

Objectives

The objective of this chapter is to furnish a complete collection of essential tools for blue team operations and threat-hunting activities. Although the specific requirements and obstacles may vary across organizations, it is important to acknowledge that the following tools have gained significant recognition for their ability to enhance an enterprise's security posture. The primary goal is to provide blue teamers and threat hunters with a comprehensive collection of tools, enabling them to engage in proactive defense measures and swiftly respond to incidents. This will effectively boost the organization's overall cyber resilience.

The primary objective of this chapter is to function as a complete manual for blue team professionals and organizational security teams. It will elaborate on the diverse array of tools and methodologies that form the foundation of contemporary cyber defense and proactive threat detection. Organizations can greatly enhance their security posture and resilience against cyber threats by acquiring a comprehensive understanding of the capabilities, deployment strategies, and best practices associated with these tools.

Blue teaming-Cyber defense and incident response

Intrusion detection system (IDS) and **intrusion prevention systems (IPS)** are indispensable tools in the cybersecurity arsenal. Their role is not limited to merely detecting or preventing intrusions; they serve as the eyes and ears of defensive teams like **Security Operations Center (SOCs)**, **incident response (IR)** teams, and **Computer Security Incident Response Teams (CSIRTs)**, enabling these teams to perform their functions more effectively and efficiently. Given the relentless evolution of cyber threats, the capabilities of IDS and IPS will continue to be a focal point for organizations aiming to strengthen their cybersecurity postures.

Log management and analysis deep dive

Before understanding advanced security platforms, a blue teamer must master the most fundamental element of defensive security: logs. Logs are the digital footprints of every action that occurs on a network, from a user logging in to a firewall blocking a connection. The ability to effectively collect, manage, and analyze these logs is the bedrock skill upon which all threat hunting, incident response, and security monitoring are built. This section provides a deep dive into the raw data that fuels all security operations.

Key log sources for the Defender

An enterprise network generates millions of logs per minute. An effective analyst knows which ones matter most and what to look for in each.

- **Windows Event Logs:** A primary source of information for activity on Windows endpoints. Key logs to monitor include:

  o **Security Log:** Contains crucial audit events. Look for **Event ID 4624** (Successful Logon) to track user access and **Event ID 4625** (Failed Logon) to detect potential brute-force attacks. **Event ID 4688** (Process Creation) can be enabled to see every program that runs on a host.

- **Sysmon:** A free and powerful tool from Microsoft that enhances standard Windows logging, providing deeper visibility into endpoint activity. Key Sysmon events include:

  o **Event ID 1 (Process Creation):** Superior to the standard Windows event, as it includes process hashes and command-line arguments.

- o **Event ID 3 (Network Connection):** Tracks all outbound network connections from a host, which is invaluable for spotting malware beaconing to a C2 server.

- o **Event ID 11 (FileCreate):** Can detect when malware drops or creates malicious files on the system.

- **Firewall Logs:** These logs are the record of what is allowed into or out of your network. Look for high volumes of denied traffic from a single **Internet Protocol** (**IP**) address, which could indicate network scanning. Conversely, allowing traffic to or from a known malicious IP address is a high-priority alert.

- **Proxy Logs:** These logs track the web browsing activity of users. They are essential for identifying users visiting malicious or suspicious websites, spotting unusual user-agent strings that could indicate custom malware, or detecting large file downloads that could be part of data exfiltration.

- **DNS Logs:** One of the most valuable sources for a threat hunter. Since most malware needs to *call home*, it must use DNS. Look for queries to known malicious domains, patterns of **algorithmically generated domains** (**AGDs**) used by botnets, or evidence of DNS tunneling, a technique used to exfiltrate data over the **Domain Name System** (**DNS**) protocol.

Log aggregation and normalization

With logs coming from thousands of different devices in different formats, analyzing them in isolation is impossible. A central log management strategy is crucial and should include the following:

- **Log aggregation:** This is the process of collecting logs from all sources (endpoints, servers, firewalls) and shipping them to a single, centralized location for storage and analysis. A popular open-source platform for this is the **Elasticsearch, Logstash, Kibana** (**ELK**) **Stack**, which can ingest and index massive amounts of log data.

- **Log normalization (Parsing):** Once collected, the logs must be converted into a standardized format. For example, the field for a source IP address might be called src_ ip in a firewall log but SourceAddress in a Windows log. Normalization, or parsing, extracts these key fields and maps them to a common schema (e.g., source.ip). This is a critical step that allows an analyst to write a single query to search for an IP address across every log source simultaneously.

Log Retention Policies

An organization cannot store all logs forever due to high storage costs. A **Log Retention Policy** is a formal guideline that defines how long different types of logs are kept. This policy must balance two competing needs, which are as follows:

- **Security investigations:** Breaches can go undetected for months. To investigate effectively, security teams need access to logs for an extended period (e.g., 90-180 days in *hot*, searchable storage and up to a year or more in *cold*, archived storage).

- **Compliance requirements:** Regulations like PCI DSS and HIPAA mandate minimum log retention periods (e.g., one year for PCI DSS). The security need for logs often exceeds the minimum compliance requirement.

Practical examples of querying and hunting with Logs

This is where theory becomes practice. By writing queries against your centralized log data, you can proactively hunt for threats. While the syntax differs between platforms (like Splunk's SPL or the ELK stack's KQL), the logic is universal.

- **Use case: Hunting for Brute-Force Attacks**

  - **Logic:** Look for a high number of failed login attempts from a single source IP address, followed by a single successful login.

  - **Example query (KQL-like):** `SecurityEvent | where EventID == 4625 | summarize FailedCount = count() by SourceIP, TargetAccount | where FailedCount > 15`

- **Use case: Hunting for C2 Beaconing in Firewall Logs**

  - **Logic:** Look for repetitive, machine-like outbound connections. A compromised host beaconing to a C2 server will often communicate at very regular intervals (e.g., every 5 minutes).

  - **Example query (SPL-like):** `index=firewall action=allowed | bucket _time span=1h | stats count by src_ip, dest_ip | where count > 100`

- **Use case: Hunting for Malicious PowerShell Execution with Sysmon**

  - **Logic:** Search for PowerShell processes that were executed with suspicious command-line arguments, often used to hide malicious activity.

  - **Example query (KQL-like):** `Sysmon | where EventID == 1 and ProcessCommandLine contains "-enc" and ProcessCommandLine contains "-nop" and ProcessCommandLine contains "-exec bypass"`.

Intrusion detection and prevention systems

IDS and IPS are foundational elements of any cybersecurity strategy aimed at identifying and responding to malicious activities and vulnerabilities. While both are designed to monitor network traffic, their functionalities diverge at a crucial point. An IDS identifies and alerts administrators about anomalous or suspicious activities, but does not take any proactive actions to block them. On the other hand, an IPS not only identifies these activities but also takes predetermined actions to prevent or mitigate the detected threats.

Note: In the current threat landscape, perimeter defenses like firewalls are insufficient as standalone measures. According to Verizon's Data Breach Investigations Report, 23% of breaches involved unauthorized access through compromised endpoints or network vectors, accentuating the need for IDS and IPS systems.

How can organizations move beyond simply identifying cyber threats to actively preventing them? The answer lies in understanding and effectively deploying IDS and IPS:

- IDS generates alerts and may integrate with SIEM systems for further investigation.
- IPS takes immediate action based on pre-defined or dynamic security policies to inhibit potential threats.

Here is a simple illustration of IDS and IPS placement on the network. This is just a sample and may vary in each environment.

This figure showcases the interaction between essential security devices, such as firewalls, IDS, and IPS, in a network traffic flow:

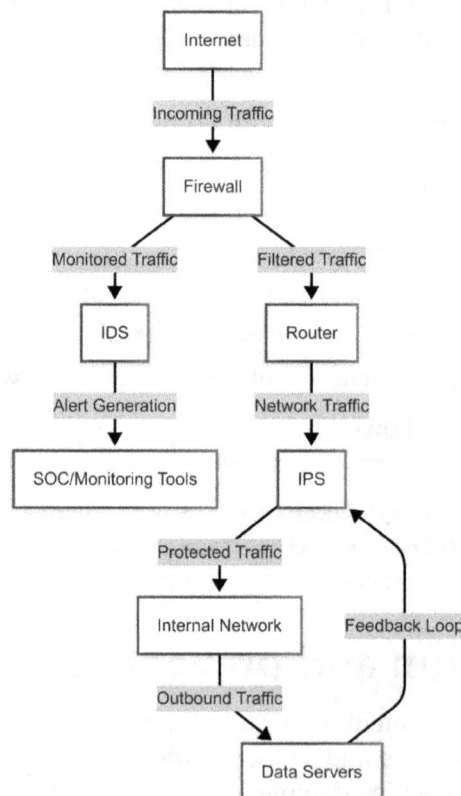

Figure 4.1: IDS and IPS placement on the network

Network-based intrusion detection and prevention systems

Network-based intrusion detection system (**NIDS**) and **network intrusion prevention system** (**NIPS**) are the protectors of network security. NIDS are deployed at a strategic point or points within the network to monitor traffic to and from all devices on the network. Ideally, it performs an analysis of passing traffic on the entire subnet and matches the traffic that is passed on the subnets to the library of known attacks. Once an attack is identified or abnormal behavior is sensed, the alert can be sent to the administrator.

NIDS are placed within the network to monitor and analyze traffic across all devices, seeking signatures or anomalies that indicate malicious activity. An example of this is Snort, an open-source tool that can analyze real-time traffic and log packets on IP networks, providing detailed insights about network intrusions.

On the other hand, NIPS actively responds to detected threats by blocking or redirecting malicious traffic. Modern NIPS evolve with the threat environment, incorporating machine learning and behavior analysis to adapt their detection mechanisms, going beyond signature-based detection to prevent zero-day exploits.

NIPS goes a step further by actively engaging and neutralizing threats. Cisco's Firepower **Next-Generation IPS** (**NGIPS**) is an example of a system that not only detects but also takes automated actions to block threats in real time, thereby preventing potential damage from escalating.

Host-based intrusion detection and prevention systems

While NIDS/NIPS look at the traffic traversing the network, **host-based intrusion detection and prevention systems** (**HIDS/HIPS**) are installed on individual computers or servers to monitor and analyze the internals of the computing system as well as the network packets on its network interfaces. A HIDS can spot if a program is trying to access things it should not, like a Trojan horse trying to sneak in. HIPS is more proactive, not only alerting the teams of potential violations but also taking pre-defined actions to mitigate the threat, often before it executes its payload.

HIDS such as **Open Source HIDS Security** (**OSSEC**) monitor key system files, log files, and configuration databases within a host to detect and report changes that may signal a breach. They provide a layer of defense that is tightly integrated with the host's operating system, enabling deep analysis of the system state.

HIPS, exemplified by McAfee Host Intrusion Prevention, functions by regulating system and application activities on a host, using a policy-based approach to block unauthorized activities, and can often respond to a threat before any actual damage is done.

Web application firewalls

Web application firewalls (**WAFs**) act like a protective barrier between web apps and the internet. Unlike traditional firewalls, WAFs are designed to discern the nuances of HTTP traffic and can prevent attacks that are specific to web applications, such as **cross-site scripting** (**XSS**), SQL injection, and session hijacking. The really advanced WAFs use complex rules and are even starting to use AI to spot weird web traffic that could be a sign of a brand-new kind of attack.

Imperva's Incapsula is an example of a cloud-based WAF that delivers website protection, DDoS mitigation, and load balancing. It uses rule sets such as OWASP Top 10 to protect against vulnerabilities and also offers custom rules for tailored protection.

WAFs can be deployed as either hardware or software appliances, and they can be placed either on premises or in the cloud. Cloud-based WAFs are becoming increasingly popular due to their scalability and ease of deployment.

Some popular WAF vendors include:

- Imperva

- Akamai

- Cloudflare

- AWS WAF

- Azure Application Gateway

When selecting a WAF, it is important to consider the specific needs of the organization, such as the types of web applications being protected, the level of security required, and the budget.

To demonstrate the security measures applied to web traffic, this figure outlines the pathway from the internet through a WAF and load balancer to web servers:

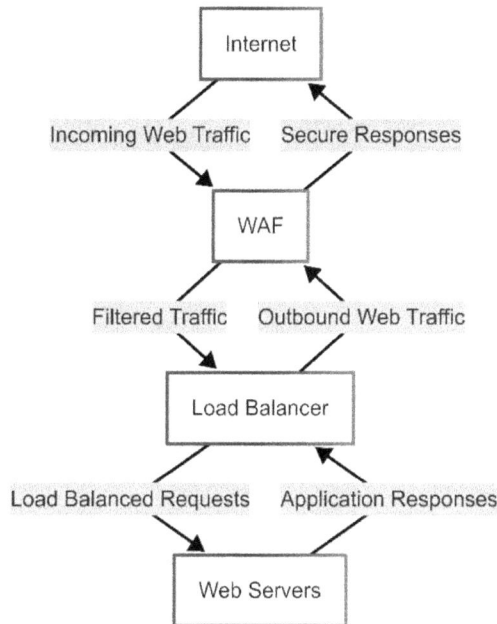

Figure 4.2: *Web traffic flow, WAF to servers*

Endpoint detection and response

EDR tools provide real-time monitoring and response to threats on endpoints. **Extended detection and response** (**XDR**) takes things a step further by looking at the big picture, gathering and connecting data from all sorts of security systems, email, devices, servers, cloud, and the network itself. This enables security teams to detect threats that move laterally across the organization and to streamline response efforts, thereby reducing the attacker dwell time and the potential impact of breaches.

EDR tools, like CrowdStrike Falcon, provide continuous monitoring and response capabilities on endpoints. They combine deep analysis, threat intelligence, and endpoint data to detect subtle threats and provide tools for threat hunting.

XDR solutions such as Palo Alto Networks Cortex XDR extend these capabilities across networks, cloud, and third-party data integrations, enabling cross-layered detection and response. This provides a unified view and can reveal the stealthiest of attacks by correlating disparate data sets.

Some popular EDR vendors include:

- CrowdStrike
- SentinelOne
- Microsoft Defender for Endpoint

- Sophos Intercept X

- VMware Carbon Black

The following figure illustrates the architecture and workflow of an EDR system within an enterprise network. It also depicts the interaction between endpoints, EDR systems, and the SOC and IR teams in a typical enterprise network:

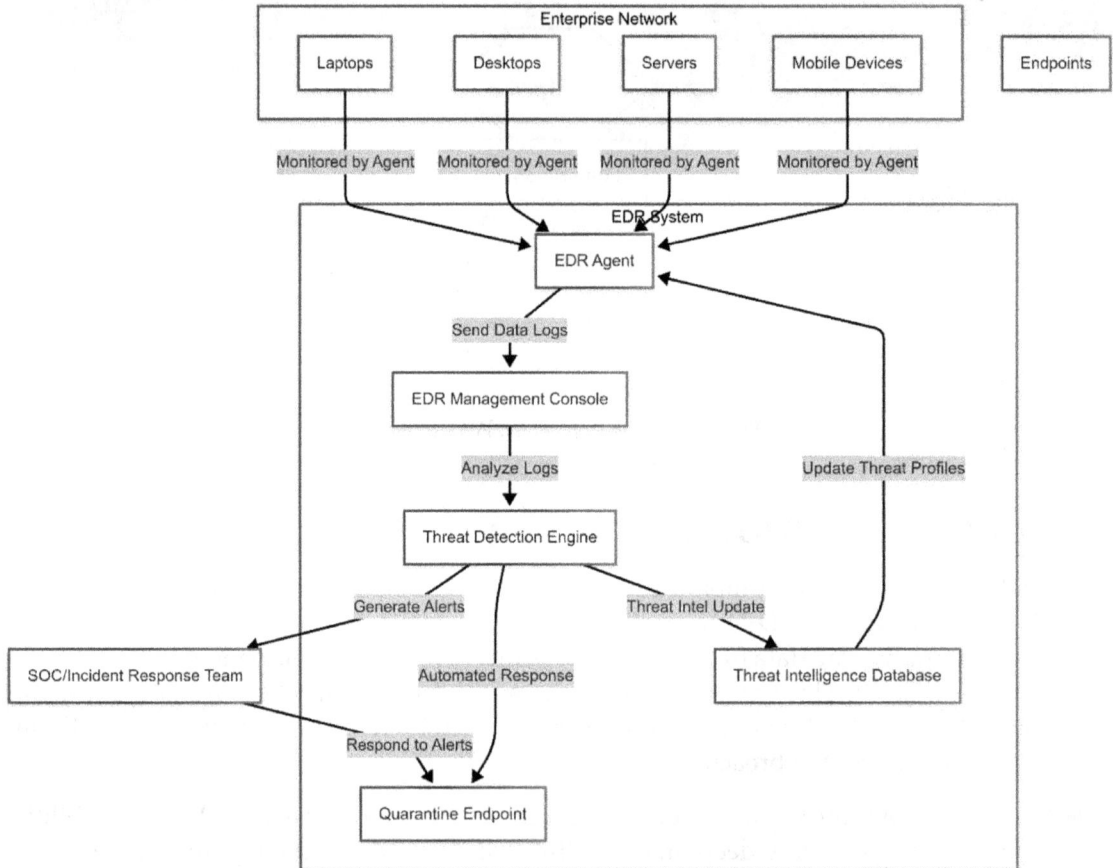

Figure 4.3: *EDR system: endpoints, analysis, alerts, and response*

Security information and event management

SIEM technology provides a 360-degree view of an organization's information security. They collect logs from all over the company, spot anything unusual, and then do something about it, such as alerting, traffic blocking, or triggering automatic responses. Advanced SIEM solutions incorporate **user and entity behavior analytics (UEBA)** and security automation to provide a more comprehensive, proactive approach to threat detection and response.

SIEM systems, such as Splunk or IBM's QRadar, InsightIDR gather logs and security data from all your company's tech, analyze it in real-time to find and rank threats, and make compliance reporting easy. They get smarter over time, using machine learning to spot weird patterns that other systems might miss.

To find potential threats, SIEM systems gather, combine, and sort through tons of data from all kinds of places. Endpoint data, logs, threat intelligence, vulnerability sources, network detection and response data, can all be processed. This ability is super important for really digging into what is happening on your systems and spotting potential threats and attacks.

What sets SIEM apart is how it smoothly uses the latest tech, like AI, machine learning, and analytics. This integration facilitates the generation of high-fidelity alerts and the real-time correlation of diverse data sets. High fidelity, as used in this context, pertains to the care and relevance of the notifications, guaranteeing that cybersecurity experts obtain information that is both significant and implementable.

Nevertheless, cybersecurity analysts frequently encounter obstacles such as fatigue as a result of employing disparate tools and dealing with an excessive quantity of generated alerts. Analysts may be required to manually filter through hundreds, if not thousands, of alerts per day using conventional methods; this is both inefficient and time-consuming. SIEM systems are of great value in this regard, as they optimize the procedure through the filtration of extraneous data and the identification of critical concerns.

Moreover, in order to effectively detect and respond to cybersecurity threats, a proactive and adaptable strategy is required due to their ever-changing nature. SIEM systems are capable of managing this due to their sophisticated analytic functionalities, which empower them to detect patterns and anomalies that may serve as indicators of a security compromise or assault. SIEM systems effectively safeguard against cyber intrusions by perpetually acquiring knowledge and adjusting to emerging threats.

The following figure provides a comprehensive overview of a SIEM system's workflow within an enterprise network, highlighting the collection, analysis, and response process for security events. To illustrate the central role of SIEM in security monitoring, this figure outlines the flow of log data from various sources through analysis and alert generation to incident response:

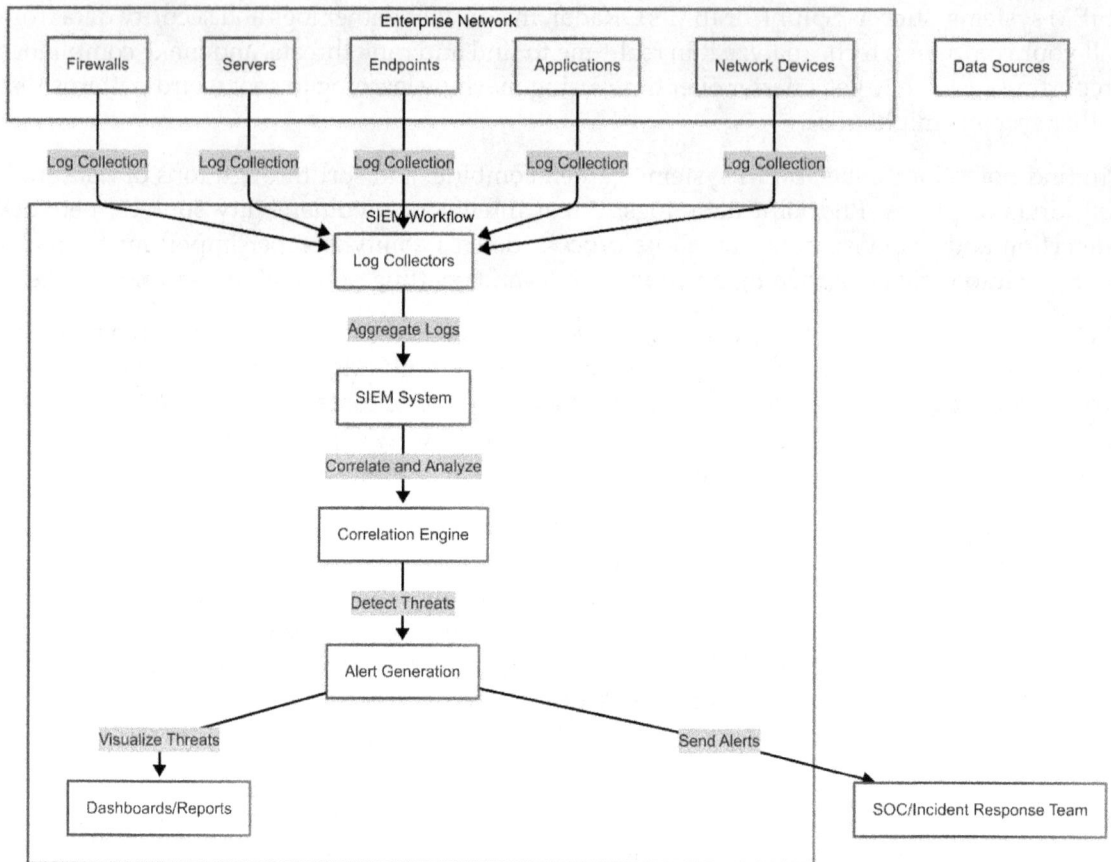

Figure 4.4: SIEM workflow: log collection, analysis, and security response

Components of SIEM

The following are the components of SIEM:

- **Data aggregation**: Collecting data from multiple sources, including network devices, servers, domain controllers, and more.

- **Event correlation**: This involves analyzing and correlating events from different sources to identify patterns that might indicate a security threat.

- **Alerting**: The SIEM system generates notifications about potential security incidents.

- **Dashboards**: These provide visualizations of data to quickly understand what is happening in the network.

- **Compliance reporting**: Many SIEM solutions offer pre-built reports for compliance with various regulatory standards.

Event and log management

SIEM systems collect logs and events from various sources, which are crucial for understanding what is happening in your IT environment. This can include everything from failed login attempts to malware alerts.

Advanced analytics

Modern SIEMs employ advanced analytics, including machine learning and artificial intelligence, to identify anomalous behavior that might indicate a security threat. This predictive capability is vital in detecting **advanced persistent threats** (**APTs**) and insider threats.

IR: SIEM is not just about detection. It also aids in incident response, allowing security teams to quickly address and mitigate threats. This includes providing detailed information about the nature of the threat, its scope, and recommendations for remediation.

Challenges and considerations

The following are the challenges and considerations of SIEM:

- **Complexity**: SIEM systems can be complex to configure and manage.
- **Resource-intensive**: They require significant processing power and storage.
- **Expertise required**: Skilled personnel are needed to interpret SIEM data effectively.
- **Evolving threats**: SIEM systems must continuously evolve to keep up with the changing landscape of cyber threats.

Future of SIEM

SIEM will soon be able to work with other security technologies, such as EDR, **network traffic analysis** (**NTA**), and **security orchestration, automation, and response** (**SOAR**), to make security even better.

In conclusion, SIEM systems are an important part of modern defense systems that cannot be missed. In addition to making threat detection and reaction more effective, they also make the jobs of cybersecurity analysts a lot easier and less stressful. By combining different data sources and using cutting-edge technologies, SIEM systems offer a unified and flexible way for an organization to protect its networks and data. Due to the growing complexity of cyber threats, SIEM has become an important tool for network security and is required for professionals working in cybersecurity.

Security orchestration, automation, and response

The SOAR concept brings together three components: security orchestration, automation, and response. SOAR solutions empower organizations to handle security alerts efficiently, streamlining response processes through orchestration and automation. They enable security teams to focus on more strategic tasks by automating the more routine actions typically performed by analysts, such as gathering threat intelligence or blocking an IP address in a firewall. SOAR tools integrate with a variety of security solutions to provide a platform for managing security operations tasks, processes, and policies.

Each of these tools plays a critical role in the comprehensive strategy necessary for effective blue team operations. They work in concerts, each with specialized functions, but when combined, they provide a formidable defense against cyber threats. Each tool is employed within the context of proactive cyber defense and IR, underscoring the importance of synergy among them to ensure the integrity, confidentiality, and availability of organizational assets.

SOAR platforms, like Fortinet FortiSOAR, Palo Alto CORTEX XSOAR, IBM Resilient, and Splunk SOAR (originally *Splunk Phantom*), help orchestrate the myriad components of a security ecosystem. They automate responses to low-level threats and free up human analysts to concentrate on more complex tasks. For example, upon detecting a phishing attempt, a SOAR platform can automatically isolate the affected endpoint from the network, initiate a scan for threats, and start an investigation into the attack's source.

The following figure provides a visual representation of how SOAR platforms integrate with diverse data sources, analyze threats, and orchestrate automated responses for efficient security management. To demonstrate how SOAR enhances incident response, this figure outlines the process of receiving alerts, triggering playbooks, and automating actions across various security tools:

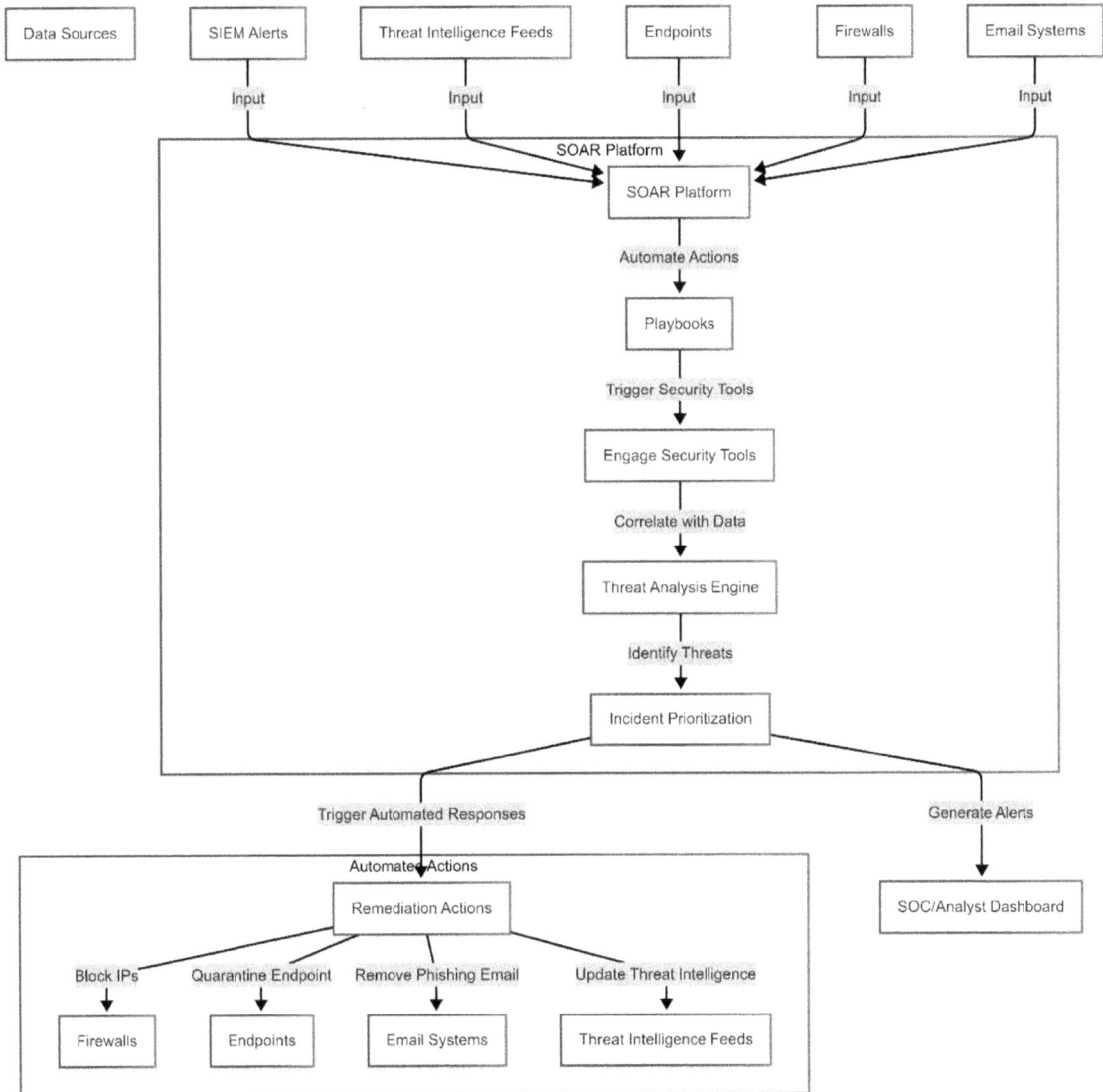

Figure 4.5: SOAR platform: automating security operations and response

Understanding SOAR

SOAR is a technology stack that automates security operations by integrating various security tools, enabling rapid incident response and threat mitigation through predefined playbooks and workflows. It empowers security teams to streamline incident response processes, improve efficiency, and reduce response times by automating tasks such as threat detection, alert triage, and incident remediation.

Orchestration

Orchestration in the context of SOAR refers to the coordinated use of different security tools and systems. A SOAR platform integrates contrasting security products and unifies their capabilities to function as a cohesive unit. This can include everything from IDS to endpoint protection, threat intelligence platforms, and more. By connecting these systems, SOAR enables more comprehensive data sharing and operational efficiency.

Automation

SOAR platforms automate repetitive and low-level tasks that would typically require human intervention. This includes tasks like scanning for vulnerabilities, sorting through false positives in alert systems, or applying patches to software. By handling such tasks, SOAR frees up security analysts to focus on more complex investigations and strategic decision-making. It also enables rapid response to threats, significantly reducing the time from detection to remediation.

Response

The Response in SOAR stands for the actions taken once a threat is identified. SOAR solutions provide tools and workflows that can respond to various security scenarios based on predefined rules and procedures. This can range from simple responses, like blocking an IP address or isolating an infected endpoint from the network, to complex responses, such as coordinating multi-system threat containment strategies or guiding human responders through a step-by-step investigation.

Key components of SOAR

The following are the key components of SOAR:

- **Playbooks**: These are pre-configured sets of rules and processes that the SOAR platform can execute automatically. They are essentially sophisticated **if this, then that** (**IFTTT**) scenarios for incident response. Playbooks can be highly detailed, covering a multitude of potential situations and appropriate responses.

- **Case management**: This feature enables security teams to manage an incident's lifecycle. It allows for logging, tracking, and documenting incidents to ensure a consistent and thorough investigation and remediation process.

- **Dashboard and reporting**: SOAR solutions typically come with a central dashboard that provides an overview of security alerts and incidents. They also have reporting capabilities to help with regulatory compliance and to provide insights into an organization's security posture.

- **Threat intelligence integration**: By integrating threat intelligence feeds, SOAR solutions can aggregate and use the latest information on threats and vulnerabilities to inform response activities and update playbooks.

Threat intelligence

Threat intelligence (**TI**) refers to the methodical gathering and evaluation of data concerning ongoing and potential dangers that pose a risk to an entity's security. TI is not merely the collection of information in the context of blue teaming; rather, it is the transformation of unstructured data into actionable insights that can be used to proactively defend against and mitigate cyber threats.

A crucial blue teaming technique is the operational use of TI. Instead of simply waiting for alerts, this technique involves actively using data about adversaries to anticipate and detect attacks. The primary goal is to shift from a reactive to a proactive defensive posture.

In practice, blue teams leverage threat intelligence by:

- **Integrating indicators of compromise (IOCs):** Actionable IOCs, such as malicious IP addresses, domain names, and file hashes, are fed directly into security tools. For example, a blue teamer will configure the SIEM to generate a high-priority alert if any internal systems communicate with an IP address known to be part of an adversary's command-and-control infrastructure.

- **Guiding threat hunts:** Intelligence on adversary TTPs informs the hunt for threats. If TI reports indicate that an attacker targeting your industry commonly uses PowerShell for lateral movement, the blue team can proactively hunt for unusual PowerShell activity on the network.

- **Prioritizing alerts and vulnerabilities:** Not all alerts or vulnerabilities carry the same risk. TI provides the necessary context to prioritize. An alert involving a TTP used by a group known to target your sector should be investigated before a more generic one. Similarly, a vulnerability known to be actively exploited in the wild will be patched before one that is not.

By integrating threat intelligence into daily operations, a blue team can enhance its detection capabilities, shorten response times, and build a more resilient and predictive defense. A full exploration of the types of threat intelligence and the intelligence lifecycle is covered in *Chapter 9, Deploying and Analysing Threat Vectors.*

The following figure from the CrowdStrike Falcon platform demonstrates its ability to not only identify an IOC but also link it to a specific threat actor, providing valuable context for incident response:

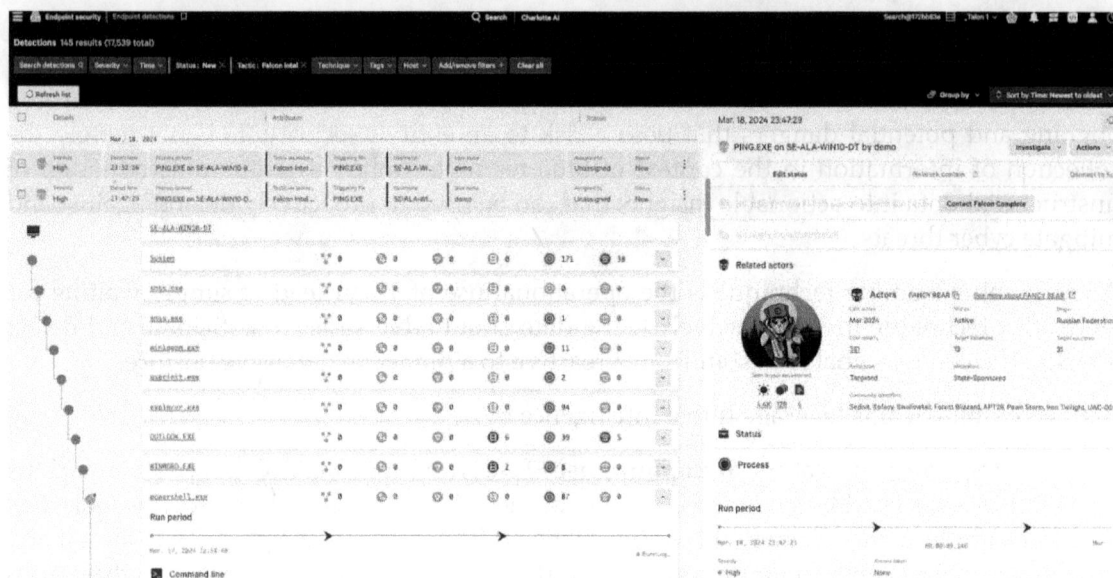

Figure 4.6: CrowdStrike showing details about an IOC and the threat actor

Difficulties and factors to assess

While threat intelligence offers invaluable insights for blue teams, effectively leveraging it presents unique challenges. Organizations must be prepared to address several key factors to ensure their TI initiatives are successful:

- The quantity of data at one's disposal can be too much to handle, and its reliability is questionable at best. Blue teams must acquire the ability to validate and certify TI in order to guarantee its dependability.

- The gap between intelligence reception and implementation can significantly impact the ability of defensive measures, separating an effective intrusion from a successful defense. For blue teams to respond rapidly to TI, processes must be streamlined.

- **Remaining aware of dynamic threats**: Dynamic cyber threats present TI with a formidable challenge in maintaining pace. Adaptation and ongoing education are essential elements of a comprehensive TI strategy.

File integrity monitoring

File integrity monitoring (FIM) is an imperative security procedure that detects and notifies users of any modifications made to IT environment files, directories, or configurations. Understanding and implementing FIM is critical in the domain of blue teaming, which is concerned with safeguarding and defending the information systems of an organization. This is due to the following reasons:

- **Detection of unauthorized changes**: FIM facilitates the detection of unauthorized modifications made to configurations and files, which may serve as an indication of an impending security compromise. This includes modifications introduced by insiders, malware, or unauthorized users.

- **Ensuring compliance**: FIM is required by a number of regulatory frameworks in order to guarantee compliance. Blue teams can ensure that their organization maintains compliance with regulations such as PCI-DSS, HIPAA, and GDPR through the monitoring of file integrity.

- **Baseline security posture**: FIM facilitates the establishment of a system-wide baseline of normal operations. Indicators of prospective security issues may arise from any deviation from this established baseline, thus necessitating additional investigation.

- **Baseline security posture**: **Forensics and incident response**: FIM data can furnish significant insights into the extent and characteristics of a security compromise, thereby facilitating efficient incident response and forensic analysis in the event of a security incident.

- **Forensics and incident response**: **Proactive security measures**: Through the ongoing surveillance and notification of modifications, FIM enables blue teams to proactively patch vulnerabilities prior to their exploitation by malicious actors.

Examples and conceptual screenshots

To illustrate how FIM systems work in practice, let us examine a few examples of their detection capabilities:

- **Example: Detecting malware installation**:
    - **Scenario**: An attacker gains access to a web server and uploads a malicious PHP file (`backdoor.php`) into the web directory (`/var/www/html`) to establish persistent access.

    - **FIM action**: The FIM system is configured to monitor the **/var/www/html** directory for any changes. It continuously checks the files in this directory and compares them against known good baselines (hashes, file sizes, etc.). When the attacker uploads `backdoor.php`, FIM detects this new file and triggers an alert.

    - **Conceptual screenshot**:

```
+-------------------------------------------------+
| FIM Alert - File Change Detected                |
+-------------------------------------------------+
| File Path: /var/www/html/backdoor.php           |
| Change Type: File Added                          |
```

```
| Timestamp: 2024-10-27 10:30:00 UTC          |
| Previous Hash: N/A                          |
| Current Hash: a1b2c3d4... (Hash of backdoor.php) |
| Action Taken: Alert Sent to Security Team   |
+---------------------------------------------+
```

- **Example: Detecting configuration drift**:

  o **Scenario**: A system administrator accidentally modifies a firewall rule while troubleshooting a network issue. This change inadvertently opens a critical port (port 8080) to incoming traffic, potentially exposing the server to attacks.

  o **FIM action**: The FIM system monitors the firewall's configuration file (`/etc/iptables/rules.v4`) for any unauthorized modifications. When the administrator changes the rule, FIM detects the change in the configuration file and generates an alert.

  o **Conceptual screenshot**:

```
+-----------------------------------------------+
| FIM Alert - Configuration Change Detected     |
+-----------------------------------------------+
| File Path: /etc/iptables/rules.v4             |
| Change Type: Rule Modified                    |
| Timestamp: 2024-10-27 11:00:00 UTC            |
| Diff: -A INPUT -p tcp --dport 8080 -j ACCEPT  |
|       +A INPUT -p tcp --dport 8080 -j DROP    | (The change)
| Action Taken: Alert Sent to Security Team     |
+-----------------------------------------------+
```

The **Diff** section shows the specific lines that were changed in the firewall configuration file. In this case:

- `-A INPUT -p tcp --dport 8080 -j ACCEPT` was the original rule, allowing traffic on port 8080.

- `+A INPUT -p tcp --dport 8080 -j DROP` is the modified rule, which now blocks traffic on that port.

FIM highlights this difference to pinpoint the exact configuration change that triggered the alert.

This following figure showcases the SolarWinds **Security Event Manager** (**SEM**) console, specifically highlighting its FIM capabilities for detecting and alerting on file system changes:

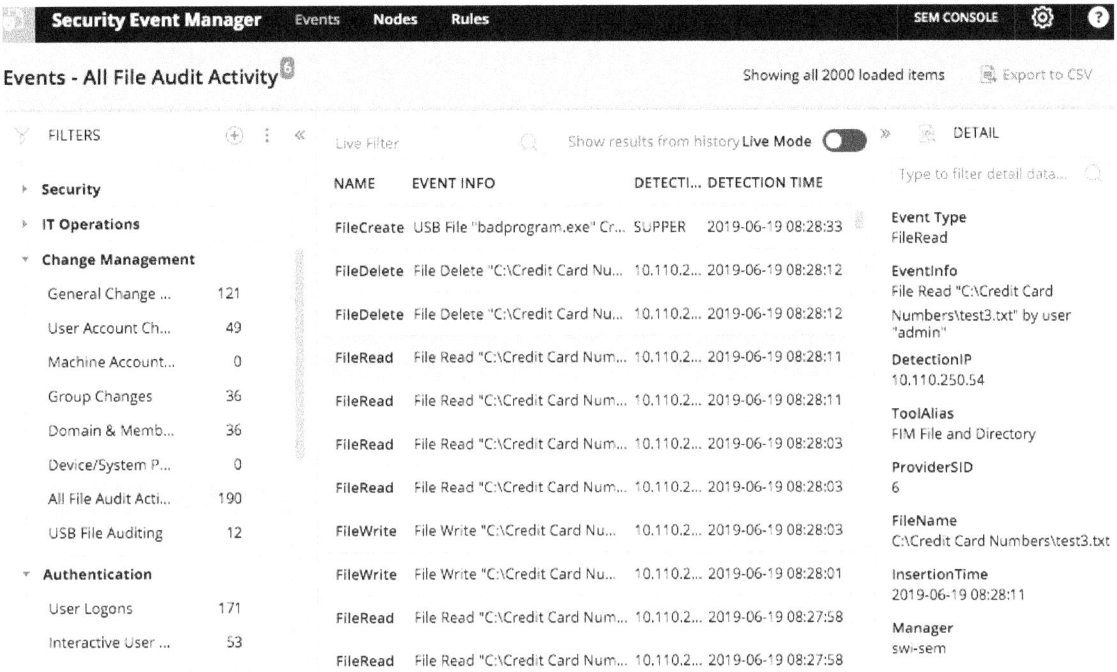

Figure 4.7: SolarWinds Security Event Manager file integrity monitoring tool

Tools used

There are several tools available for FIM, each with its own set of features and strengths. Here are some notable ones used in the industry:

- **Tripwire**: A well-known and widely used FIM tool, Tripwire offers robust file integrity monitoring capabilities. It is particularly known for its comprehensive reporting and alerting system.

- **OSSEC**: This is an open-source tool that provides file integrity monitoring along with log analysis and intrusion detection. It is a good choice for organizations looking for a cost-effective solution.

- **Advanced Intrusion Detection Environment (AIDE)**: Another open-source option, AIDE is suitable for Linux-based systems. It creates a database from the regular expression rules it finds and then helps monitor file integrity against this database.

- **SolarWinds Security Event Manager**: Known for its ease of use and integration with other SolarWinds products, this tool offers FIM as part of a broader suite of security features.

- **Qualys File Integrity Monitoring**: This cloud-based solution is part of the Qualys Cloud Platform, offering scalable and centralized FIM capabilities.

- **ManageEngine File Analysis Suite**: It provides real-time file integrity monitoring and also offers in-depth analysis, which is useful for compliance and security audits.

- **McAfee Integrity Control**: A solution from a well-known cybersecurity company, it provides robust FIM capabilities, especially suitable for organizations already using other McAfee products.

- **AlienVault USM (Unified Security Management)**: This tool not only offers FIM but also integrates other essential security tools, providing a comprehensive security management solution.

Phishing analysis

The cybersecurity landscape has witnessed a marked increase in the complexity and scale of phishing attacks. Phishing analysis, therefore, is a critical skill for any cybersecurity professional. It involves scrutinizing phishing attempts to understand their mechanisms, origins, and purposes. This analysis not only aids in preventing immediate threats but also contributes to broader cybersecurity strategies. This is a vast topic, and writing an entire chapter will not cover everything related to Phishing; however, we shall learn what is required for a Blue teamer for a phishing analysis.

Phishing represents a form of social engineering assault wherein malicious actors assume the guise of a reliable entity with the intention of duping individuals into divulging sensitive data, including login credentials, credit card details, or other personal information. Phishing attacks have the potential to manifest across multiple communication channels, such as electronic mail, telephone conversations, SMS messages, or online social platforms.

Combating phishing threats

Phishing attacks remain a prevalent threat, demanding a multi-faceted approach from blue teams to effectively mitigate their impact. To combat these attacks, organizations must prioritize the following:

- **Comprehending the danger**: Phishing is a fraudulent activity in which assailants assume the identity of reputable organizations in order to obtain sensitive data from their targets. Blue teaming requires the analysis of phishing attempts in order to discern the TTPs of the assailants.

- **Vulnerabilities identification**: Phishing attempt analysis can unveil security posture deficiencies within an organization, including email filtering system weaknesses and employee susceptibility to social engineering.

- **Training and awareness**: The creation of targeted training programs to teach employees about the features of phishing attacks and how to spot them relies heavily on phishing analysis.

- **Strengthening defensive mechanisms**: Blue teams can improve email filtering, establish swift response strategies, and deploy sophisticated security measures by gaining an understanding of the characteristics of phishing attacks.

- **Recovery and incident response**: Phishing research makes it easier to make effective plans for how to handle incidents. Understanding how a phishing attack works is key to stopping it from happening again and lessening its affects.

Phishing analysis

Phishing analysis is a critical aspect of a cybersecurity analyst's role, involving analyzing suspicious emails to determine if they are part of a phishing attack. Here is what to look for:

- **Suspicious sender information**:
  o Email address
  o Display name spoofing

- **Content analysis**:
  o Grammar and spelling
  o Urgent or threatening language
  o Mismatched fonts, logos, or layout inconsistencies are red flags.

- **Link and attachment analysis**:
  o Hover over links
  o Attachments

- **Behavioral indicators**:
  o Unusual requests
  o Unsolicited contact

The following figure displays a phishing email designed to mimic a legitimate communication from PayPal, highlighting the deceptive tactics employed by attackers to steal sensitive information:

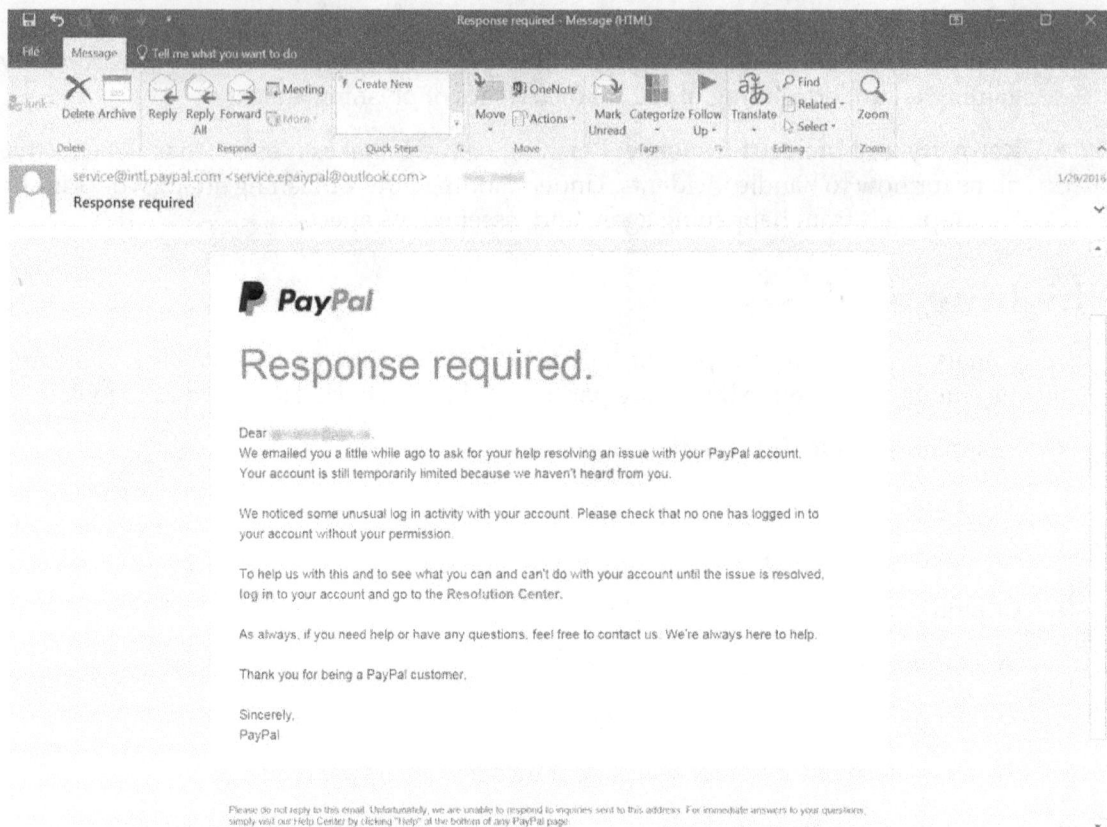

Figure 4.8: Phishing email: PayPal spoofing attempt to harvest credentials

Let us analyze the email in the screenshot for potential phishing indicators:

The following are the key indicators of a phishing/suspicious email:

- **Sender address**:
  - o **Highlighted**: service.epaiypal@outlook.com
  - o **Why it is suspicious**: Legitimate PayPal emails come from addresses ending in @ paypal.com. The use of a public email domain like @outlook.com is a major red flag. Additionally, attackers often use slight misspellings in the sender's name, like epaiypal, to appear legitimate at a glance.

- **Generic greeting**:
  - o **Highlighted**: *Dear Customer* (not shown in *Figure 4.8*)
  - o **Why it is suspicious**: Phishing emails often use generic greetings instead of your name because they are sent out in bulk.

- **Sense of urgency**:

  o **Highlighted**: *Your account is still temporarily limited,* and *Response required.*

  o **Why it is suspicious**: Phishers create a sense of urgency to make you act quickly without thinking. Legitimate companies rarely use such strong language in initial communications.

- **Suspicious link**:

  o **Highlighted**: *Log in to your account and go to the Resolution Center.*

  o **Why it is suspicious**: Hovering over the link (not possible to show in *Figure 4.8*) would likely reveal a non-PayPal URL. Phishers want you to click the link so they can steal your credentials. *Never click links in suspicious emails.* Always navigate directly to the company's website by typing the address in your browser.

- **Grammar and spelling errors**:

  o **Not apparent in this snippet**: While not always present, phishing emails may contain grammatical or spelling errors.

- **Unexpected email**:

  o **Consider**: *Did you initiate any recent activity with PayPal that would warrant this email?* If not, it is likely a phishing attempt.

- **Request for personal information**:

  o **Not directly in this snippet**: While this email does not explicitly ask for information, the linked page (which is the phishing site) would likely ask for your login credentials, credit card details, or other personal information. *Never provide personal information through links in emails.*

- **Disclaimer at the bottom**:

  o **Highlighted**: *Please do not reply to this email.*

  o **Why it is suspicious**: While some legitimate companies may discourage email replies, this can also be a tactic used by phishers to prevent you from questioning the email's authenticity.

In summary, the email in the screenshot exhibits multiple red flags that strongly suggest it is a phishing attempt.

Reading and interpreting email headers

Email headers contain vital information about the journey of an email from sender to recipient, and they can be crucial in phishing analysis. Email headers, while often overlooked, offer valuable forensic evidence in phishing investigations. By examining the headers, blue teams can trace the email's path, identify potential relays or open proxies used to obscure the sender's identity, and gather clues about the attacker's infrastructure. This information can be crucial in identifying the source of the attack and preventing future incidents.

Accessing email headers

To analyze email headers effectively, you first need to know how to access them within your email client. Here is how you can do it in two commonly used platforms:

- **Outlook**: Double-click the email to open it in a new window, then select File | Properties. You will see the headers in the *Internet headers* box.

- **Gmail**: Open the email, click on the three dots in the upper right corner, and select *Show original*.

The following are the key components of email headers:

- **From**: Shows the email address of the sender.

- **To**: Indicates the recipient's email address.

- **Date and time**: When the email was sent.

- **Subject**: The subject line of the email.

- **Received**: A chronological list of all mail servers the email passed through.

- **Return-path**: The email address to which bounce-back messages are sent.

- **Message-ID**: A unique identifier for the email.

- **X-originating-IP**: Shows the IP address from where the email was sent (not always included).

- **Content-type**: Indicates the media type of the email.

The following figure displays the email header section of an email client, revealing key information about the email's origin, route, and authentication:

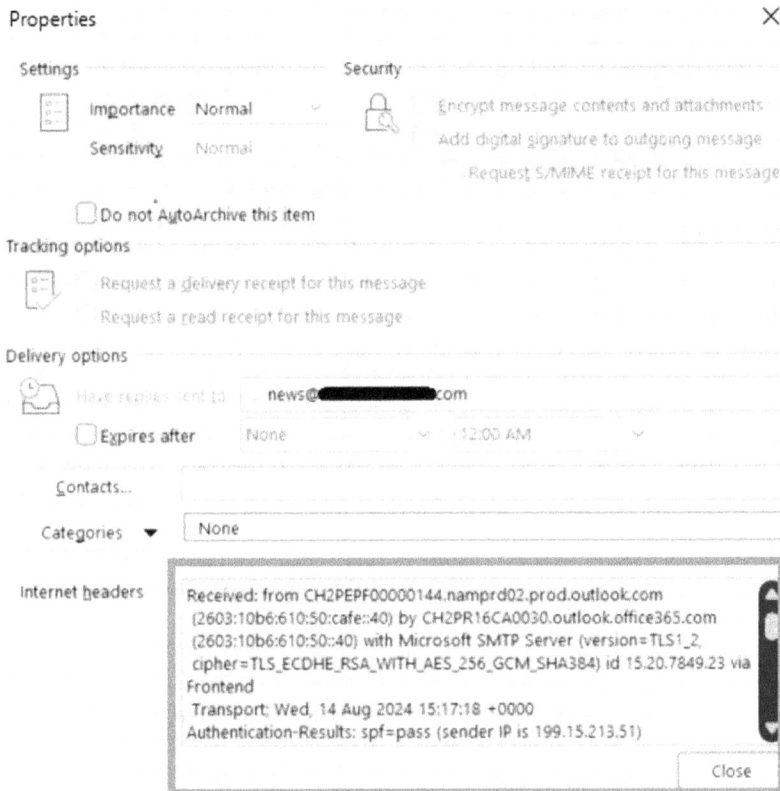

Figure 4.9: Email header analysis

Analyzing the headers

To effectively analyze email headers for signs of phishing, focus on the following key elements:

- **Trace the path**: Use the *Received* lines to trace the email's path. Be cautious if the email appears to originate from a suspicious or unrelated domain.

- **Check for spoofing**: Cross-reference the *From* address with the *Return-Path* and *Received* headers. Discrepancies may indicate spoofing.

- **IP analysis**: Use the IP address in the *X-Originating-IP* (if available) to determine the sender's location, which can be cross-referenced with the supposed location of the sender.

The following are the tools for email header analysis:

- **MXToolbox**: Analyzes and provides a readable output of email headers.

- **MessageHeader Analyzer for Outlook**: An add-on for Microsoft Outlook that simplifies header analysis.

An important aspect of the header is the SPF, DKIM, and DMARK. Let us discuss them.

Sender policy framework

SPF is an email authentication method designed to detect and prevent email spoofing by verifying the sender's IP address. Let us understand it briefly:

- **What it is**: SPF is a robust email authentication mechanism specifically developed to identify and thwart the malicious act of forging sender addresses during the transmission of electronic mail.

- **How it works**: SPF is a crucial mechanism that empowers domain proprietors to precisely define the mail servers that possess the authorization to transmit electronic messages on behalf of their esteemed domain. The implementation of SPF records within the domain's DNS records is the recommended approach to achieving this objective.

- **Verification process**: When an email is received, the receiving mail server checks the SPF record by looking up the domain's DNS. It verifies if the email was sent from a server authorized by that domain's SPF record.

- **Limitations**: SPF only checks the envelope sender address (return-path), not the header from address shown in the email client. Therefore, it can miss certain types of spoofing.

DomainKeys identified mail

DomainKeys identified mail (DKIM) provides a crucial layer of email authentication, helping to verify a message's origin and integrity. Let us understand it briefly:

- **What it is**: DKIM is an email security standard designed to ensure that email content is trustworthy. It uses cryptographic authentication to verify that an email was not tampered with in transit.

- **How it works**: The sending mail server attaches a digital signature to the header of the email message. This signature is created using a private key only known to the sender. The corresponding public key is published in the domain's DNS records.

- **Verification process**: When a recipient server receives an email, it retrieves the DKIM signature from the header and the sender's public key from the DNS. It then verifies the signature to ensure the email has not been altered.

- **Benefits**: DKIM helps to combat email spoofing and phishing by verifying that the content of the email is authentic and unmodified.

Domain-based message authentication, reporting, and conformance

To further enhance email security and combat phishing attempts, it is essential to understand and implement **Domain-based Message Authentication, Reporting, and Conformance (DMARC)**:

- **What it is**: DMARC is an email authentication, policy, and reporting protocol. It is built upon SPF and DKIM and is designed to give email domain owners the ability to protect their domain from unauthorized use.

- **How it works**: DMARC allows domain owners to publish a policy in their DNS record that defines their email authentication practices and how receiving mail servers should handle mail that does not comply (e.g., reject the message, quarantine it, or do nothing).

- **Verification process**: DMARC checks if an email passes SPF or DKIM authentication. If the email fails both checks, DMARC policy dictates what action to take.

- **Reporting**: DMARC also includes a reporting feature where the receiving servers send reports back to the sender about messages that pass and/or fail DMARC evaluation.

Data loss prevention solutions

Nowadays, when things are becoming more and more digital, protecting sensitive info is not just a good idea; it is a must for every business. Adequate **data loss prevention** (**DLP**) is an important part of strong protection measures. It keeps valuable data safe by actively seeking out and stopping any possible unauthorized access, breaches, or data exfiltration attempts. Putting this important safety measure in place is very important because you need to protect private data, like personal, financial, and business data, from anyone who does not have permission to see it. This is to protect privacy and security above all else.

Protection of data has reached levels of importance that have never been seen before. The average cost of a data breach around the world is now a worrisome $3.86 million, and this amount is only going to go up from here. The complexity and size of data grow at an exponential rate as organizations grow, and the range of possible threats increases. As technology changes so quickly, it is important to use strong DLP software that can find, study, and connect data patterns to stop security breaches quickly. Endpoint data, network data, and cloud data are all protected by the suggested solutions. This ensures a complete and all-encompassing security approach.

DLP is a group of tools and methods used to keep important or private data from getting lost, misused, or seen by people who are not supposed to. DLP software and tools keep an eye on, find, and stop private information while it is being used (data in motion), while it is being stored (data at rest), and while it is being sent (data in transit).

Key aspects of DLP

The following are the key aspects of DLP:

- **Identification of sensitive data**: DLP systems are configured to recognize sensitive data. This can include financial information, **personal identifiable information (PII)**, intellectual property, and other confidential data.

- **Monitoring and controlling data transfer**: DLP tools monitor and control the transfer of sensitive data across an organization's network. This includes emails, instant messages, and other forms of data exchange.

- **Data in use protection**: DLP solutions can control what users can do with sensitive data within applications. This includes preventing unauthorized copying, printing, or transferring of sensitive information.

- **Data at rest protection**: DLP tools scan storage systems and databases within an organization to identify and secure sensitive data stored on servers, laptops, and other devices.

- **Data in transit protection**: DLP systems monitor data as it moves across the network to prevent unauthorized data transfers outside the company network.

- **Policy enforcement**: Organizations can set up DLP policies tailored to their specific needs. These policies dictate what is considered sensitive data and the rules for handling it.

- **Incident response and reporting**: DLP tools generate alerts and reports when policy violations occur. This helps in incident response and in understanding the flow of sensitive data within the organization.

Importance of DLP

DLP plays a critical role in safeguarding sensitive information and maintaining the integrity and security of an organization's data. The key benefits of implementing DLP solutions include:

- **Preventing data breaches**: By monitoring and protecting sensitive data, DLP helps prevent data breaches that can lead to financial loss and damage to an organization's reputation.

- **Regulatory compliance**: Many industries are subject to regulations that require the protection of sensitive data. DLP helps organizations comply with regulations such as GDPR, HIPAA, and PCI-DSS.

- **Intellectual property protection**: DLP is crucial for safeguarding intellectual property and trade secrets, which are vital assets for many organizations.

- **Insider threat mitigation**: DLP solutions help in mitigating threats posed by insiders, either through negligence or malicious intent.

Preparation meets prevention

The adage *failing to prepare is preparing to fail* rings especially true in DLP. Preparation encompasses a comprehensive range of activities that form the foundation of the DLP framework, acting as a proactive measure to mitigate the risk of data breaches.

Note: **Actions for security engineers**:

- **Begin with a thorough risk assessment to identify where sensitive data resides, how it moves, and who has access to it. This step will help determine the scope of the DLP program.**

- **Craft DLP policies that align with the organization's data classification framework. Policies should clearly define what constitutes sensitive data and the protocols for handling it.**

- **Build a cross-functional incident response team that includes stakeholders from IT, legal, compliance, and business units. Each member should understand their role in a DLP incident.**

- **Run a pilot DLP program with a limited scope before full deployment. This approach helps in understanding the impact of DLP policies on business operations and fine-tuning them to reduce false positives.**

- **Develop a comprehensive training program to educate users about DLP policies, the importance of data security, and their role in preventing data loss.**

Firewall

In the complicated world of cybersecurity, firewalls are like guardians. They make sure that incoming and outgoing network data follows security rules that have already been set. It is very important for blue teams to learn how to use firewalls because their main job is to protect their company's digital assets. In the context of blue team operations, this chapter gives a thorough look at the strategic implementation, management, and operational challenges of firewalls.

Firewall log analysis and rule tuning

While a well-configured firewall is a foundational security control, the ongoing analysis of its logs and the continuous tuning of its rule-set are critical blue teaming techniques. This proactive approach transforms the firewall from a static gatekeeper into a dynamic source of threat intelligence and a responsive defensive weapon.

A key technique for threat hunting involves the meticulous analysis of firewall logs to find patterns that might indicate a threat that has not triggered a specific alert. This includes searching for:

- **Anomalous traffic patterns:** A high volume of denied connections from a single IP address could indicate a network scan, while traffic on unusual ports might signal tunneling or a rogue service.

- **Suspicious outbound connections:** Monitoring for outbound connections to known malicious domains or geographic regions can be one of the first signs that an internal host has been compromised and is communicating with a C2 server.

Furthermore, blue teams strengthen defenses through **proactive rule tuning**. When new threat intelligence identifies IP addresses or domains associated with an adversary, analysts apply this intelligence by immediately updating firewall rules to block that traffic. This continuous refinement ensures the firewall's defenses evolve in response to the changing threat landscape, making it a much more active component of the organization's security posture.

Vulnerability scanning and management

In cybersecurity, it is very important to stay proactive about detecting and reducing possible threats. In this case, vulnerability scanning and control are very important. The steps include carefully finding, sorting, ranking, and fixing weaknesses in an organization's complex network and systems. When it comes to blue teaming, the goal of strong risk management goes beyond random scanning. In order to always lower risks, it involves creating a strong and forward-looking plan.

Getting to know vulnerability scanning and management: Vulnerability scanning uses automated tools to look for known flaws or gaps in systems, networks, and applications that attackers can use. On the other hand, vulnerability management is a complete method that includes finding these weaknesses, evaluating them, putting them in order of importance, and fixing them.

Leveraging Vulnerability Data For Threat Hunting And Triage

While the comprehensive process of vulnerability management is detailed in *Chapter 10, Implementing Threat and Vulnerability Management on Business Houses*, a key blue team technique involves using the *output* of vulnerability scanners as an active intelligence source. This transforms a routine compliance task into a dynamic tool for threat detection and hunting.

The primary techniques are as follows:

- **Correlating Vulnerability Data with Security Alerts:** Instead of viewing a SIEM alert in isolation, an effective technique is to immediately cross-reference the affected asset with the latest vulnerability scan results. An intrusion alert on a server with a known, unpatched critical vulnerability (e.g., Log4j) is escalated with much higher urgency than an alert on a fully hardened system. This context is crucial for rapid and accurate alert triage.

- **Fueling Hypothesis-Driven Hunts:** Vulnerability data is essential for proactive threat hunting. When a new high-profile vulnerability is disclosed, blue teams should not just wait for a patch. The critical technique is to form a hunting hypothesis, such as *Adversaries are now actively scanning our perimeter for this specific vulnerability.* Analysts can then hunt through firewall and network traffic logs, searching for patterns that match the exploit attempts for that vulnerability, allowing them to identify and block attackers before they succeed.

By treating vulnerability scan results not as a static to-do list for the patching team but as dynamic data to be correlated with real-time events, blue teams can better prioritize threats and proactively hunt for adversaries targeting known weaknesses in their environment.

The following figure showcases the **insightVM** dashboard from Rapid7, a vulnerability management solution that provides a comprehensive view of an organization's security posture across various assets and locations:

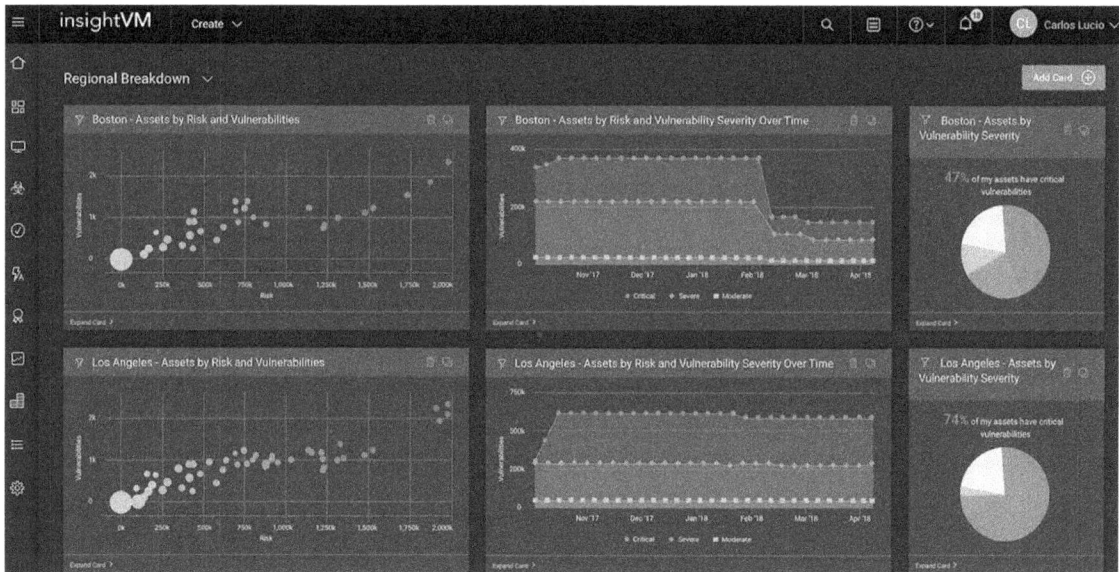

Figure 4.10: InsightVM: Vulnerability assessment, risk analysis, and remediation prioritization

Identity and access management

Identity and access management (IAM) is a key part of a strong blue teaming approach. Its main goal is to restrict user access to company resources, making sure that only authorized people can get private information and processes. Implementing IAM correctly makes security stronger and lowers the risk of breaches and data leaks.

Here is how IAM strengthens blue teaming efforts:

- **Principle of least privilege**: IAM helps enforce the principle of least privilege, granting users only the necessary access to perform their job functions. This minimizes the potential damage from compromised accounts or insider threats.

- **Strong authentication**: Implementing **multi-factor authentication (MFA)** adds an extra layer of security, making it significantly harder for attackers to gain unauthorized access, even if they possess stolen credentials.

- **Access control**: IAM solutions provide granular access control, allowing blue teams to define and manage user permissions based on roles, responsibilities, and specific needs. This ensures that users have appropriate access levels to different resources.

- **Centralized management**: IAM provides a centralized platform for managing user identities, access rights, and authentication policies. This streamlines user onboarding and offboarding processes, simplifies access control management, and improves overall security.

- **Monitoring and auditing**: IAM solutions offer monitoring and auditing capabilities, allowing blue teams to track user activity, identify suspicious behavior, and generate reports for compliance and incident response purposes.

Threat hunting

Threat hunting is an active form of cybersecurity in which skilled security researchers look for and find threats that get past current security measures. Traditional security methods rely on automatic alerts, but threat hunting involves a person using their knowledge along with advanced tools to find threats that are hidden or hard to spot. Here is an example to help you understand.

The following figure illustrates the cyclical process of threat hunting, emphasizing the continuous feedback loop that drives proactive threat detection and response:

Figure 4.11: Threat hunting maturity model cycle

Threat hunting process

Threat hunting is a proactive process aimed at identifying, analyzing, and mitigating security threats that evade automated security tools. The following is a step-by-step outline of the threat hunting process:

1. **Define hypothesis**:

    - **What**: Develop a testable hypothesis about potential attack scenarios based on threat intelligence, observed anomalies, or vulnerabilities.

    - **How**:

        o Leverage threat intelligence feeds (e.g., known IOCs).

        o Use frameworks like MITRE ATT&CK to identify potential adversary tactics and techniques.

    - **Example**: An attacker may have exploited a known vulnerability in a public-facing application to gain initial access.

2. **Collect and prepare data**:

    - **What**: Gather relevant logs and data from various sources across the environment.

    - **How**:

        o Centralize logs using a SIEM system (e.g., Splunk, QRadar).

        o Collect data from endpoints using **endpoint detection and response** (**EDR**) tools (e.g., CrowdStrike Falcon, Microsoft Defender).

        o Capture network traffic using network monitoring tools (e.g., Zeek, Wireshark).

    - **Focus on data sources like**:

        o Endpoint logs (e.g., process execution, file modifications, registry changes).

        o Network traffic logs (e.g., connection logs, DNS queries, HTTP requests).

        o Application logs (e.g., login attempts, database queries).

        o Authentication and access logs.

    - **Goal**: Ensure the data is clean, normalized, and ready for analysis.

3. **Select hunting techniques**:

    - **What**: Choose appropriate methods to detect abnormal or malicious activity.

    - **Techniques**:

-   o   **Behavioral analysis**: Look for deviations from normal user or system behavior (e.g., unusual login times, access to sensitive files).

-   o   **Anomaly detection**: Use statistical models or AI to identify unusual patterns in data (e.g., spikes in network traffic, unexpected user activity).

-   o   **Indicator matching**: Search for known indicators like malicious IPs, file hashes, or domains using threat intelligence platforms (e.g., AlienVault OTX, Recorded Future).

4. **Conduct an investigation**:

   - **What**: Actively search through the data for evidence of malicious activity.

   - **How**:

     - o **Use specialized tools like**:

       - EDR tools for endpoint-level analysis.

       - Network traffic analysis tools to examine network behavior.

       - Threat hunting platforms (e.g., Elastic Security, ThreatHunter.ai) for advanced hunting capabilities.

     - o Apply queries in SIEM tools to narrow down suspicious activities and correlate findings.

   - **Goal**: Validate or invalidate the hypothesis by finding evidence to support or refute it.

Note: **If the investigation does not validate the hypothesis, revisit step 1 (Define hypothesis) or step 2 (Collect and prepare data) to refine the hypothesis or gather additional data. Threat hunting is an iterative process.**

5. **Analyze findings**:

   - **What**: Determine the root cause and scope of the threat if the hypothesis is validated.

   - **How**:

     - o Analyze artifacts (e.g., malicious files, registry changes) in a sandbox environment.

     - o Identify TTPs used by attackers and map them to the MITRE ATT&CK framework.

     - o Correlate findings with threat intelligence sources to identify potential threat actors.

   - **Outcome**: Understand the threat's impact, its entry points, and the extent of the compromise.

6. **Respond and mitigate**:
    - **What**: Neutralize the threat and close vulnerabilities to prevent future attacks.
    - **How**:
        o Quarantine infected endpoints to contain the threat.
        o Block malicious IPs or domains in firewalls.
        o Patch vulnerabilities to eliminate entry points.
        o Update configurations or access policies to strengthen security posture.
    - **Tools**: EDR solutions, firewalls, and incident response playbooks.

7. **Document and share**:
    - **What**: Record the entire hunting process and its results for future reference and knowledge sharing.
    - **How**:
        o Prepare a detailed report including the hypothesis, methods and tools used, findings, outcomes, and mitigation actions.
        o Share insights with the broader security team and relevant stakeholders to enhance organizational security posture and incident response capabilities.

8. **Automate and improve**:
    - **What**: Integrate learnings from the threat hunt into automated detection systems to improve proactive defenses.
    - **How**:
        o Create SIEM alerts based on identified patterns and IOCs.
        o Update playbooks for SOAR to automate incident response actions.
        o Use machine learning models for anomaly detection to proactively identify suspicious activity.
    - **Goal**: Reduce the time required for future hunts and improve overall security posture.

Example of threat hunting

Imagine a financial services company with robust security measures in place. Despite this, a skilled threat hunter, Alice, notices an anomaly: a server in the network is communicating at odd hours with an external IP address that's not part of the usual traffic pattern.

Hypothesis: Alice assumes that the server might be compromised and is possibly part of a C2 attack.

Investigation:

- **Data analysis**: Using SIEM tools, Alice analyzes logs and finds that suspicious communication started two weeks ago.

- **Pattern study**: She studies the pattern of communication and discovers it occurs during off-peak hours, which is unusual for the company's operations.

- **Cross-referencing IOCs**: Alice checks the external IP against threat intelligence databases and finds it has been flagged in recent spear-phishing campaigns.

Discovery: Her investigation reveals that the server is indeed compromised. It is sending out sensitive data to the attacker's IP during times when the detection likelihood is low.

Response and mitigation:

- **Isolation of server**: The compromised server is isolated to prevent further data exfiltration.

- **Root cause analysis**: Further analysis is conducted to understand how the breach occurred.

- **Strengthening security**: The security team updates firewall rules and enhances endpoint security measures.

- **Employee awareness**: Employees are briefed about the latest phishing tactics identified.

Continuous monitoring: Post-incident, continuous monitoring, and additional threat hunting activities are initiated to ensure no other part of the network is compromised.

Conclusion: In this example, threat hunting played a crucial role in identifying and mitigating a sophisticated attack that bypassed standard security measures. The proactive, hypothesis-driven approach of threat hunting allowed the organization to respond effectively to a potential breach, highlighting the importance of this strategy in modern cybersecurity defense.

Concept of threat hunting

Threat hunting is a proactive cybersecurity practice that goes beyond reactive security measures, involving:

- **Proactive approach**: Instead of waiting for alerts from security systems, threat hunters proactively look for IOCs or anomalies that suggest malicious activity.

- **Hypothesis-driven**: Threat hunters often begin with hypotheses based on intelligence reports, recent trends in cyberattacks, or anomalies detected in the system.

- **Use of advanced tools**: They utilize tools like SIEM, EDR, and AI-based analytics for deep investigation.

- **In-depth knowledge**: Requires an in-depth understanding of the organization's normal network behavior to spot deviations that might indicate a threat.

Practical tactics for threat detection and response

Proactive threat detection and response is a critical aspect of modern cybersecurity strategies, especially for organizations looking to stay ahead of emerging threats. Here are some practical tactics that can be employed for effective proactive threat detection and response:

- **Continuous network monitoring**:

    o **Implement real-time monitoring**: Use advanced monitoring tools to continuously observe network traffic for unusual activity or anomalies.

    o **Baseline establishment**: Establish a baseline of normal network behavior to more easily identify deviations that could indicate a threat.

- **Threat intelligence integration**:

    o **Leverage threat feeds**: Subscribe to and integrate real-time threat intelligence feeds to stay informed about new and emerging threats.

    o **Information sharing**: Participate in industry-specific ISACs to share and receive threat intelligence.

- **Advanced security technologies**:

    o **Deploy advanced security solutions**: Utilize NGFWs, IPS, and advanced malware protection to identify and block sophisticated attacks.

    o **Machine learning and AI**: Implement AI and machine learning-based tools for predictive analytics and to identify patterns indicative of cyber threats.

- **Regular vulnerability assessments and penetration testing**:

    o **Conduct regular scans**: Perform regular vulnerability scans to identify and patch vulnerabilities in the network.

    o **Penetration testing**: Regularly conduct penetration testing to simulate cyber attacks and assess the effectiveness of security controls.

- **Behavioral analysis and anomaly detection**:

    o **UEBA**: Implement UEBA tools to detect unusual behavior patterns that may indicate a compromised account or insider threat.

    o **Anomaly detection systems**: Use systems that can detect deviations from normal operations, which might signify a security incident.

- **Incident response planning**:

  o **Develop an incident response plan**: Have a well-defined incident response plan that outlines roles, responsibilities, and procedures for responding to a security incident.

  o **Regular drills and training**: Conduct regular incident response drills and training to ensure preparedness and swift action in case of an actual breach.

- **Security awareness and training**:

  o **Regular employee training**: Conduct regular cybersecurity awareness training for employees to recognize and report phishing attempts and other social engineering attacks.

  o **Simulated attacks**: Use simulated phishing and social engineering attacks to train employees and test their response.

- **EDR**:

  o **Implement EDR solutions**: Use EDR tools for continuous monitoring and response to advanced threats on endpoint devices.

- **Secure configuration and patch management**:

  o **Regular updates and patches**: Ensure all systems and software are kept up-to-date with the latest security patches.

  o **Secure configuration**: Maintain secure configurations of all systems and regularly review configuration settings to ensure they comply with best security practices.

- **Segmentation and zero-trust**:

  o **Network segmentation**: Divide the network into segments to contain breaches and limit lateral movement of attackers.

  o **Implement zero-trust model**: Adopt a zero-trust security model where trust is never assumed, and verification is required from everyone trying to access resources in the network.

Cloud security operations and monitoring

As organizations migrate from traditional on-premises data centers to hybrid and cloud-native environments, the landscape of defensive security fundamentally changes. The ephemeral nature of cloud resources, the use of **Infrastructure as Code (IaC)**, and the unique services offered by **Cloud Service Providers (CSPs)** like **Amazon Web Services (AWS)**, Microsoft Azure, and **Google Cloud Platform (GCP)** require a specialized approach to security operations and monitoring. Blue teamers must adapt their skills to defend this new perimeter.

The shared responsibility model in practice

The foundation of all cloud security is the **shared responsibility model**. This model defines the division of security obligations between the CSP and you, the customer. The CSP is responsible for the *security of the cloud*, protecting the physical data centers, core network infrastructure, and the virtualization layer that powers their services. You, the customer, are always responsible for the *security in the cloud*, securing your own data, applications, and configurations.

How this translates into practice depends on the service model:

- **Infrastructure as a Service (IaaS):** Think of AWS EC2 or Azure VMs. The CSP manages the physical hardware, but *you* are responsible for almost everything else. This includes patching the guest operating system, configuring host-based firewalls, managing network access via security groups, and securing your application and data.

- **Platform as a Service (PaaS):** Think of AWS RDS (a database service) or Azure App Service. The CSP manages the underlying infrastructure and operating system. *You* are responsible for securing the application code you deploy, managing user access and permissions to the platform, and protecting the data you store within it. You do not patch the **Operating System** (**OS**), but you must ensure your application is not vulnerable to **Structured Query Language** (**SQL**) injection.

- **Software as a Service (SaaS):** Think of Microsoft 365 or Salesforce. The CSP manages the entire stack. *Your* responsibility is primarily focused on data and access management. This includes configuring application-level security settings, managing user permissions (who can access what data), and protecting accounts with measures like **multi-factor authentication** (**MFA**).

Cloud-native security tools

Each CSP provides a suite of powerful, integrated security tools that are essential for blue teams to master. While third-party tools are still used, understanding these native services is non-negotiable and includes the following:

- **Network Controls (Security Groups and NACLs):**

  o **Security Groups (SGs):** Act as a stateful firewall for individual instances (like an EC2 or VM). They control inbound and outbound traffic based on port, protocol, and source/destination IP. Because they are stateful, if you allow inbound traffic, the corresponding outbound return traffic is automatically allowed.

  o **Network Access Control Lists (NACLs):** Act as a stateless firewall for an entire subnet. They evaluate rules in order and are stateless, meaning you must define rules for both inbound *and* outbound traffic explicitly.

- **Managed Threat Detection (e.g., AWS GuardDuty):** Services like AWS GuardDuty are a blue team's best friend in the cloud. They are managed threat detection services that continuously monitor cloud logs (like AWS CloudTrail, VPC Flow Logs, and DNS logs) for malicious or unauthorized behavior. GuardDuty uses machine learning and threat intelligence to detect anomalies like cryptocurrency mining activity on your instances, communication with known malicious IPs, or unusual **Application Programming Interface (API)** calls indicative of a compromise.

- **Cloud-Native SIEM (e.g., Azure Sentinel):** Azure Sentinel is a cloud-native **Security information and event management (SIEM)** and **security orchestration, automation, and response (SOAR)** solution. It can ingest and analyze vast amounts of data from Azure services, Microsoft 365, and even on-premises systems and other clouds, providing a unified platform for alert triage and threat hunting.

Cloud logging and monitoring

In the cloud, you can not *walk the floor* of the data center. Visibility comes from logs. Refer to the following list to build an understanding and analyze the right logs, which is the most critical skill for a cloud security analyst:

- **Audit Logs (e.g., AWS CloudTrail):** CloudTrail is the audit log for your entire AWS account. It records nearly every API call made, whether from the console, an SDK, or the command line. It answers the question, *Who did what, where, and when?* If a security group is modified, a new user is created, or an S3 bucket's policy is changed, it is recorded in CloudTrail. This is the primary source for hunting for malicious configuration changes.

- **Service and Performance Logs (e.g., Azure Monitor, Google Cloud Logging):** These services collect performance metrics and logs from various cloud resources. For a blue teamer, they are useful for establishing a baseline of normal activity and detecting anomalies, such as a sudden spike in CPU usage on a VM (which could indicate malware) or a high number of 403 (Forbidden) errors on a web application.

Common cloud attack vectors

While traditional attacks still apply, the cloud introduces unique attack vectors that blue teams must hunt for:

- **IAM Credential Compromise:** An attacker stealing an access key and secret key for an IAM user or role is the cloud equivalent of stealing a password. Attackers can use these credentials to create their own resources, exfiltrate data, or disable security controls.

- **Misconfigured Cloud Storage:** Publicly exposed AWS S3 buckets or Azure Blob Storage containers are a leading cause of major data breaches. While defaults are now more secure, accidental misconfigurations by developers or administrators can expose vast amounts of sensitive data directly to the internet.

- **Server-Side Request Forgery (SSRF) on Cloud Instances:** This is a particularly dangerous cloud attack. An attacker exploits a vulnerability in a web application to force the cloud server to make web requests on their behalf. In the cloud, this can be used to target the **metadata service** (a local API available to all instances). By tricking the server into querying its own metadata service, an attacker can steal the temporary credentials of the IAM role attached to that server, gaining a foothold in your cloud account.

Incident response in the cloud

Incident response procedures must be adapted for the cloud environment, where you do not control the physical hardware.

- **Evidence acquisition**: You can not physically seize a compromised server. Instead, forensic acquisition involves taking **snapshots** of virtual disks (like AWS EBS volumes) to create a forensic image for later analysis. Acquiring a memory dump is also possible on some platforms, but can be more complex. The primary source of evidence is often the detailed logs from services like CloudTrail.

- **Containment**: Instead of unplugging a network cable, containment in the cloud is programmatic and can be much faster. An analyst can immediately contain a compromised instance by modifying its **Security Group** to deny all inbound and outbound traffic except for a specific IP used for investigation. You can also instantly revoke IAM credentials or disable a user account.

- **Interacting with the CSP**: For certain types of incidents, especially those that may involve the underlying infrastructure, you will need to engage with the CSP's support and security teams. It is crucial to understand their support process and know how to report a security incident to them *before* one happens.

Conclusion

This chapter gave a complete rundown of the most important blue teaming technologies and methods. We looked at the main ideas behind cyber defense and incident response. We learned about intrusion detection and prevention systems, web application firewalls, endpoint detection and response, and the power of the combination of SIEM and SOAR.

We also looked at the important part threat intelligence plays in proactive defense tactics, stressing how important it is to collect, analyze, and use threat information to make security stronger. We also talked about file integrity tracking to find changes that were not made by the right person and the methods and tools used in phishing analysis to stop social engineering attacks.

We looked at DLP solutions and the role of firewalls in protecting network perimeters as important ways to keep private information safe. Finally, we talked about vulnerability scans and management as a way to find and fix weak spots, how important IAM is for managing who can access important resources, and how proactive threat hunting can be used to find and stop enemies that are hiding. Organizations can greatly improve their cybersecurity by learning these blue teaming methods. This will help them protect their valuable assets and defend against new threats.

Looking ahead, in the next chapter we will explore the SOC, a centralized hub for coordinating and implementing these blue teaming strategies. We will explore the SOC's structure, functions, and essential role in maintaining a robust security environment.

Join our Discord space

Join our Discord workspace for latest updates, offers, tech happenings around the world, new releases, and sessions with the authors:

https://discord.bpbonline.com

CHAPTER 5

Defensive Strategic Methodology

Introduction

Security is no longer just about reacting after an attack. It is about being proactive. Today, **Security Operations Centers (SOCs)** are proactive. They use advanced technology, skilled people, and improved processes to spot and stop threats before they cause damage. They provide the essential coordination to manage the complex and evolving threat environment.

Note: **A SOC is a core component of an organization's cybersecurity strategy. It provides continuous monitoring for threats, risk analysis, and incident response to protect digital assets in a dynamic threat landscape.**

The modern SOC is very different from its early versions. Previously, SOCs were seen as cost centres. They mainly focused on monitoring security alerts and responding to incidents. Today, SOCs are key assets. They are crucial for managing an organization's overall risk. The SOC's role is always changing. This is due to shifting threats and new technologies coming into play. In the future, SOCs will likely use AI and machine learning more to automate threat detection and response. This will allow analysts to concentrate on more complex investigations.

Structure

In this chapter, we will cover the following topics:

- Introduction to SOC

- SOC operations workflow
- People process technology
- SOC design, architecture, and planning
- Inhouse SOC and MSSP
- Security monitoring and analysis
- SOC incident response procedures
- Key SOC performance indicators and compliance reporting
- SOC compliance, governance, and framework
- SOC best practices
- SOC automation
- Handling security alerts, events, and incidents

Objectives

This chapter aims to give a thorough overview of the defensive approach of SOC, a fundamental part of contemporary cybersecurity protection. You will learn a great deal about the goals, organization, basic operations, and technologies supporting the SOC. Examining the changing function of the SOC, from reactive alarm processing to proactive threat hunting and risk reduction, you will value its strategic relevance in protecting the digital resources of a company. By means of an analysis of real-world examples, difficulties, and best practices, you will be armed with the knowledge to build, deploy, and run a very successful SOC that can adjust to the always-shifting threat environment. This chapter seeks to equip you with the tools you need to create a strong cybersecurity program guaranteeing the availability, integrity, and confidentiality of the vital systems and data of your company.

Introduction to SOC

The SOC watches over the digital strongholds of a company like a guardian. An organization's SOC is like its brain when it comes to cybersecurity. It finds threats, analyzes them, and responds to them in a complete and effective way. As technology gets more complicated and linked, it is impossible to say enough about how important it is to have a SOC that works well.

Defining the SOC

A SOC is a dedicated unit responsible for monitoring, detecting, analyzing, and responding to cybersecurity threats in real-time, mostly 24x7 365 days. It is a command centre where skilled professionals work collaboratively, leveraging advanced technologies to safeguard an organization's critical assets and data.

The SOC is not merely a room filled with blinking screens; it is a dynamic ecosystem of people, processes, and technologies. It is the picture of an organization's commitment to cybersecurity, a proof of its understanding that defence is not a one-time event but an ongoing and evolving process.

Note: **A well-functioning SOC is not just a cost center; it is a strategic investment that can save an organization millions in damages from cyberattacks.**

Evolving role of the SOC

Traditionally, SOCs were primarily reactive, functioning as a digital fire department, rushing in to extinguish flames after a security breach had already occurred. Security analysts spent a significant portion of their time sifting through mountains of alerts, attempting to identify the real threats amidst the noise. This reactive approach left organizations vulnerable to sophisticated attacks that could remain undetected for extended periods, causing significant damage before being discovered.

However, the modern SOC has transformed into a proactive force, adopting a *hunt before you are hunted* mentality. This proactive approach involves leveraging threat intelligence, advanced analytics, and automation to anticipate and neutralize threats before they can cause harm. Threat intelligence provides valuable insights into the **tactics, techniques, and procedures** (**TTPs**) of adversaries, enabling SOC teams to identify potential threats and vulnerabilities before they are exploited. Advanced analytics, powered by machine learning and artificial intelligence, allow SOC analysts to filter through vast amounts of security data more efficiently, identifying hidden patterns and anomalies that may indicate a potential attack. Additionally, automation plays a crucial role in streamlining SOC operations, freeing up security analysts from routine tasks and allowing them to focus on more complex investigations and threat hunting activities.

Today's SOCs go beyond simply monitoring alerts and logs; they actively hunt for threats, analyze patterns of behavior, and identify vulnerabilities before attackers can exploit them. This proactive approach significantly enhances an organization's ability to detect and respond to sophisticated cyber-attacks, reducing the risk of data breaches and operational disruptions.

Value proposition of a SOC

The SOC brings a multitude of benefits to an organization's cybersecurity posture, such as:

- **Enhanced visibility**: The SOC provides a comprehensive view of the organization's security landscape, aggregating and correlating data from various sources to identify potential threats and vulnerabilities. This increased visibility enables security teams to detect and respond to incidents more quickly and effectively.

- **Rapid incident response**: By centralizing security expertise and resources, the SOC enables a swift and coordinated response to security incidents. This can significantly reduce the impact of a breach, minimizing damage to the organization's reputation and bottom line.

- **Proactive threat hunting**: Through proactive threat hunting, the SOC identifies and neutralizes hidden threats that may evade traditional security measures. This reduces the risk of undetected breaches and helps to maintain the integrity of critical systems and data.

- **Improved security posture**: The SOC's continuous monitoring and analysis of security data allows organizations to identify weaknesses and vulnerabilities in their defences. This information can be used to prioritize remediation efforts and strengthen the overall security posture.

- **Compliance and risk management**: The SOC plays a crucial role in ensuring compliance with regulatory requirements and industry standards. It also helps organizations manage risk by identifying and prioritizing threats and vulnerabilities.

Types of SOCs

There are three primary types of SOCs, each with its own advantages and considerations:

- **Internal SOC**: This model involves building and operating a SOC in-house, with a dedicated team of security professionals. Internal SOCs offer greater control and customization, but they can be expensive to build and maintain, requiring significant investment in personnel, technology, and infrastructure.

- **Managed security service provider (MSSP) SOC**: This model involves outsourcing SOC functions to a third-party provider. MSSP SOCs can be a cost-effective option for organizations that lack the resources or expertise to build their own SOC. However, they may offer less flexibility and control than an internal SOC.

- **Hybrid SOC**: This model combines the advantages of both models, leveraging internal staff for certain functions while outsourcing others to an MSSP. Hybrid SOCs can provide a balance of control, expertise, and cost-effectiveness, making them an attractive option for many organizations.

Future of SOCs

The role of the SOC continues to evolve as the threat landscape becomes more complex and sophisticated. Emerging technologies like **artificial intelligence (AI)**, **machine learning (ML)**, and automation are being integrated into SOC operations to enhance threat detection, accelerate incident response, and improve overall efficiency.

Cloud-based SOCs are also gaining popularity, offering scalability, flexibility, and cost-effectiveness. Additionally, collaborative approaches like threat intelligence sharing are becoming increasingly important as organizations recognize the value of sharing information to combat cyber threats collectively.

The SOC is a critical component of a modern cybersecurity strategy. It serves as the central nervous system of an organization's defence, providing the visibility, expertise, and rapid response capabilities needed to protect against ever-evolving cyber threats. By investing in a well-equipped and skilled SOC, organizations can significantly enhance their resilience and safeguard their critical assets.

A comparison of traditional vs. next-gen SOCs

The SOC has changed a lot from its early days. SOCs were initially seen as cost centers. Their main job was to watch for security alerts and handle incidents. But now, SOCs are very important assets. They are essential for managing an organization's risk. SOCs are always changing because of new threats and technologies. Soon, SOCs will probably use AI and machine learning to automate finding and responding to threats, which will let analysts work on more complicated investigations.

The following table provides a comparison of SOCs:

Feature	Traditional SOC	Next-gen SOC
Role	Reactive, focusing on responding to incidents after they occur	Proactive, focusing on threat hunting and prevention
Threat detection	Relies heavily on signature-based detection and manual analysis of alerts	Leverages AI, machine learning, and behavioral analytics to detect anomalies and sophisticated threats
Analysis	Limited correlation of data from disparate sources	Correlates data from various sources to provide a comprehensive view of the security landscape
Automation	Manual processes for alert triage, investigation, and response	Automation of routine tasks to improve efficiency and free up analysts for complex tasks
Technology	Disparate security tools with limited integration	Integrated security platforms with SOAR capabilities for streamlined workflows
Focus	Alert monitoring and incident response	Threat hunting, vulnerability management, and risk reduction
Challenges	Alert fatigue, lack of visibility, and slow response times	Implementation complexity, data integration, and the need for skilled personnel

Table 5.1: Differences in SOCs

SOC operations workflow

The SOC plays a crucial role in safeguarding against the constantly changing cyber threat landscape. This centralized hub of knowledge and technology goes beyond being a reactive alarm system. It is a powerful force that takes proactive measures to identify, analyze, and neutralize threats, ensuring the protection of an organization's digital assets. Let us explore SOC operations, understand its mission, the challenges it encounters, and the strategies it uses to achieve top-notch defense.

A modern SOC operates on a continuous loop of monitoring, detection, analysis, and response. To structure this workflow and understand adversary behavior, SOCs often use established models like the **Cyber Kill Chain** (**CKC**) and the OODA loop.

As detailed in *Chapter 3, Exploring Security Frameworks*, the CKC provides a framework for understanding the stages of a cyberattack. Rather than just waiting for a final security alert, the SOC uses this model to identify an attacker's progress at each stage, from initial reconnaissance to their final actions on objectives. By mapping security alerts to the CKC, analysts can better understand the scope and intent of an attack and deploy countermeasures to disrupt the chain.

For example, the 2020 SolarWinds supply chain attack can be mapped to the CKC: the initial compromise occurred during weaponization (injecting malware into the Orion software), was followed by delivery (via software updates), and led to C2 (through the Sunburst backdoor). Understanding this progression helps SOCs develop defenses targeting each stage, such as enhancing vendor software validation to disrupt the delivery phase.

Importance of the Cyber Kill Chain

The CKC is a valuable framework for understanding the stages of a cyber-attack, from initial reconnaissance to data exfiltration. By understanding the CKC, SOC analysts can identify the TTPs of attackers at each stage and develop strategies to disrupt the attack chain.

Linking CKC to MITRE ATT&CK

While the Cyber Kill Chain provides a high-level view of an attack, frameworks like MITRE ATT&CK offer a more detailed matrix of adversary tactics and techniques. MITRE ATT&CK helps SOC teams understand the specific actions an attacker might take at each stage of the CKC. For example:

- **Reconnaissance**: An attacker might use techniques like *Active Scanning* (T1595) or *Gather Victim Host Information* (T1590) as detailed in MITRE ATT&CK.

- **Weaponization**: This stage might involve techniques like *Spearphishing Attachment* (T1566.001) or *Exploit Public-Facing Application* (T1190).

- **Delivery and exploitation**: Could involve *Phishing* (T1566) or exploiting specific vulnerabilities (e.g., CVE-2021-XXXX).

- **Installation**: Attackers might use techniques like *Persistence* (T1497) to maintain access.

- **Command-and-control**: Might involve establishing a *C2* channel using *Application Layer Protocol* (T1071).

- **Actions on objectives**: Could include techniques like *Data Exfiltration* (T1041) or *Ransomware* (T1486).

By mapping the CKC stages to MITRE ATT&CK techniques, SOC teams can better prepare for and respond to specific attacker behaviors.

Figure 5.1 illustrates the Cyber Kill Chain, detailing the stages of a cyberattack. It aids proactive defense by highlighting intervention points and supports reactive analysis by mapping attack progression.

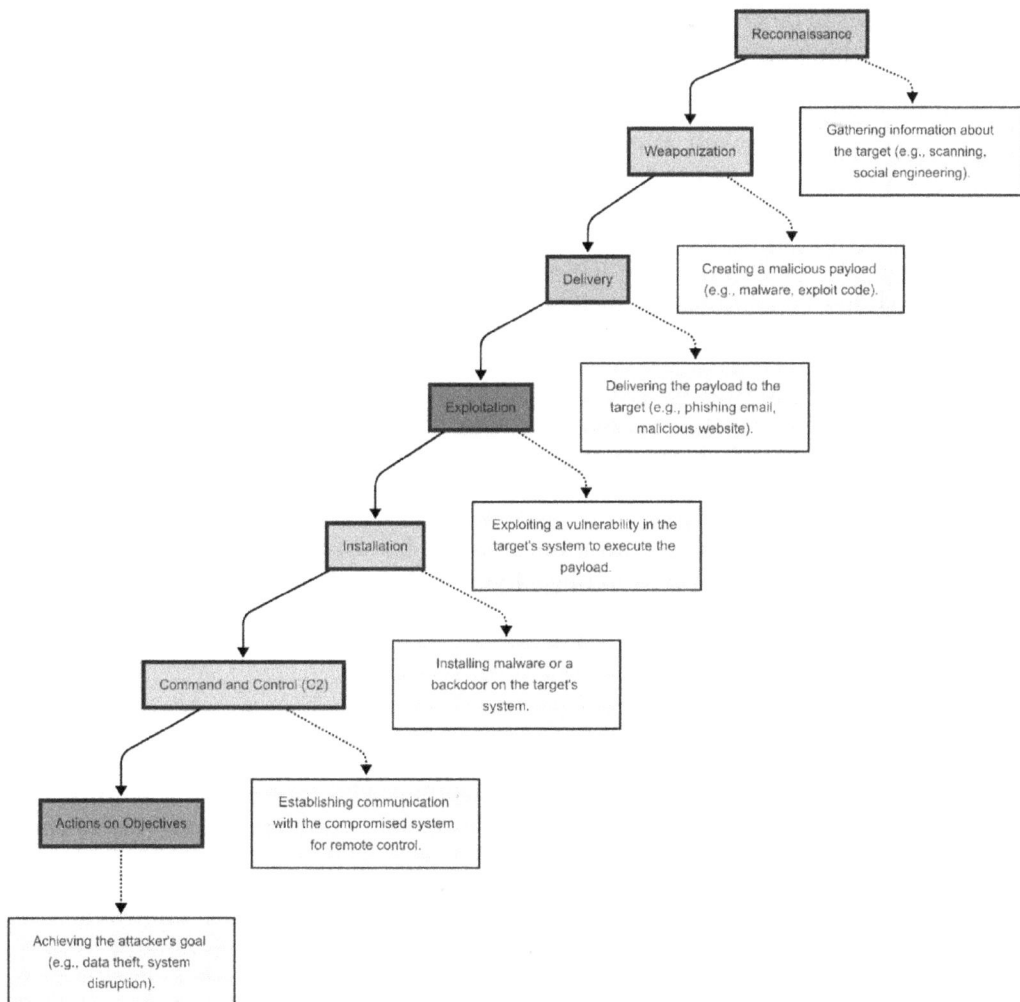

Figure 5.1: *Cyber Kill Chain*

SOC response strategies for each attack stage

For each stage of the Cyber Kill Chain, SOC teams can implement specific response strategies:

- **Reconnaissance**: SOC response: Implement robust logging and monitoring to detect reconnaissance activities like network scanning, use threat intelligence to identify and block known reconnaissance sources, and monitor for social engineering attempts.

- **Weaponization**: SOC response: Use **intrusion prevention systems (IPS)** to detect and block malicious payloads, maintain up-to-date threat intelligence to identify known malware signatures, and implement application whitelisting to prevent the execution of unauthorized code.

- **Delivery**: SOC response: Deploy email security gateways to filter phishing emails, use web proxies to block access to malicious websites, and educate users to recognize and report phishing attempts.

- **Exploitation**: SOC response: Employ vulnerability scanning to identify and patch vulnerabilities, use **web application firewalls (WAFs)** to protect web applications, and implement **intrusion detection systems (IDS)** to detect and block exploitation attempts.

- **Installation**: SOC response: Utilize **endpoint detection and response (EDR)** solutions to detect and block malware installation, implement host-based firewalls to prevent unauthorized access, and monitor suspicious processes or services.

- **Command-and-control**: SOC response: Monitor network traffic for unusual outbound connections, use network firewalls to block communication with known C2 servers, and implement network segmentation to limit the impact of a compromised system.

- **Actions on objectives**: SOC response: Implement **data loss prevention (DLP)** solutions to prevent data exfiltration, monitor for unusual data access patterns, and have incident response plans in place to quickly contain and mitigate the impact of a breach.

OODA loop

The **Observe, Orient, Decide, Act (OODA)** loop is a decision-making framework that is well-suited for the fast-paced and dynamic environment of the SOC. It promotes a continuous cycle of learning and adaptation, enabling the SOC to respond quickly and effectively to changing threats.

The following figure illustrates the OODA loop, which is a model for rapid and effective decision-making in dynamic environments. It emphasizes the iterative flow of information and the critical analysis required before taking action.

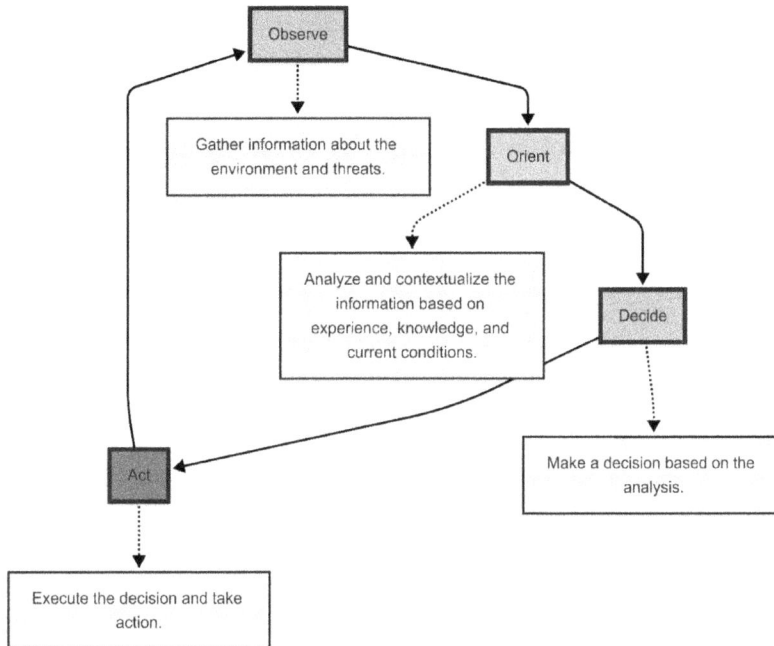

Figure 5.2: OODA loop

This concept, developed by *Colonel John Boyd*, emphasizes a continuous cycle of learning and adaptation, enabling security teams to respond quickly and effectively to changing threats:

- **Observe**: The SOC continuously monitors the environment for signs of malicious activity, utilizing a variety of tools and techniques, such as SIEMs, IDS/IPS, and threat intelligence feeds.

- **Orient**: Analysts analyze the collected data, comparing it to known patterns and threat intelligence to identify potential threats.

- **Decide**: Based on the analysis, the SOC makes a decision on how to respond to the threat, considering factors such as the severity of the threat, the potential impact, and the available resources.

- **Act**: The SOC takes action to mitigate the threat, whether it is blocking a malicious IP address, isolating an infected system, or notifying relevant stakeholders.

By continuously repeating the OODA loop, the SOC can maintain situational awareness, adapt to new threats, and improve its overall effectiveness.

Basic SOC workflow

The typical SOC workflow involves the following steps:

1. **Monitoring**: The SOC continuously monitors network traffic, logs, and security alerts for signs of suspicious activity.

2. **Triage**: When an alert is triggered, analysts assess its severity and potential impact.

3. **Investigation**: If the alert warrants further investigation, analysts gather additional information and analyze it to determine the nature and scope of the threat.

4. **Containment**: If the threat is confirmed, the SOC takes steps to contain it, preventing it from spreading further.

5. **Eradication**: The SOC removes the threat from the environment, such as by quarantining infected systems or removing malicious code.

6. **Recovery**: The SOC restores affected systems and data to a secure and operational state.

7. **Lessons learned**: The SOC conducts a post-incident review to identify lessons learned and improve its incident response capabilities.

The following figure provides a visual representation of the incident response lifecycle, detailing each phase from initial monitoring to post-incident review. It illustrates the core functions of a security operations team during an incident, emphasizing the process from alert to lessons learned.

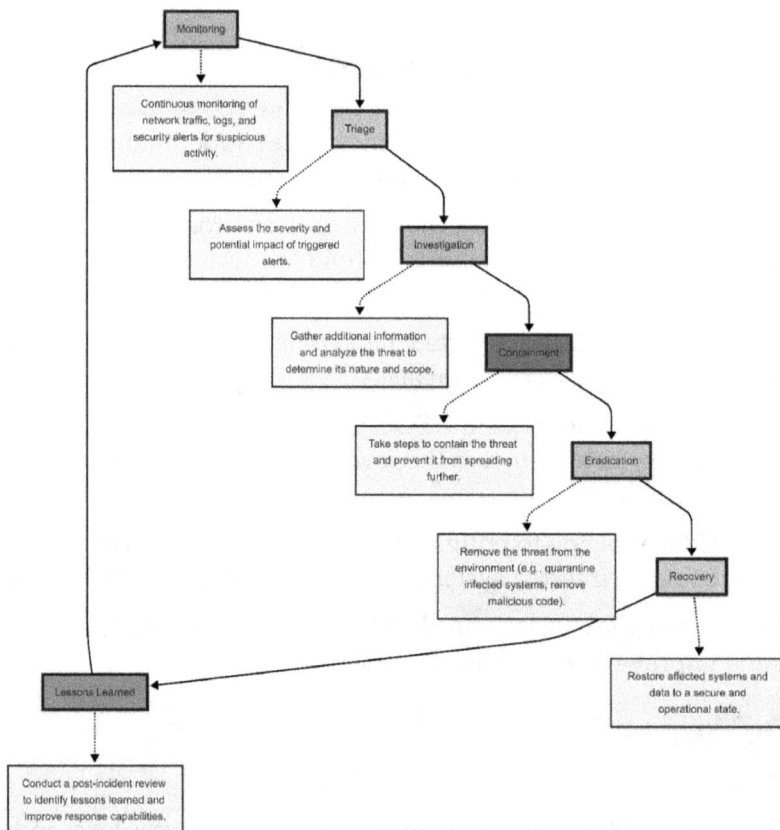

Figure 5.3: Security operations workflow

Core functions

At the heart of any SOC lies a set of core functions that are essential for maintaining a robust security posture. These core functions include the following:

- **Real-time alert monitoring and triage**:
    - Continuously monitoring security alerts from various sources (SIEM, IDS/IPS, etc.).
    - Performing initial triage to assess the severity and potential impact of alerts.
    - Filtering out false positives and escalating legitimate threats for further investigation.

- **Incident reporting**:
    - Receiving and processing incident reports from internal and external sources.
    - Documenting and tracking incident details.
    - Deciding if reported events need more investigation as possible security incidents.

- **Incident analysis and investigation**:
    - Conducting in-depth analysis of suspected incidents to understand their nature, scope, and impact.
    - Gathering evidence and artifacts to support incident analysis.
    - Identifying the root cause of the incident and the threat actors involved.

- **Containment, eradication, and recovery**:
    - Taking immediate action to contain and limit the spread of an incident.
    - Removing malware, malicious code, or unauthorized access.
    - Restoring systems and data to a secure and operational state.

- **Incident management**:
    - Collaborating with internal stakeholders (IT, management, legal) and external parties (law enforcement, CERTs) as needed.
    - Communicating incident details and progress to relevant parties.
    - Coordinating response efforts and ensuring a unified approach to incident resolution.

Specialized functions

Beyond the core functions, many SOCs have specialized teams or individuals focusing on more in-depth security tasks. These specialized functions often require advanced skills and expertise. Some common specialized functions include the following:

- **Forensic artifact analysis:**
  - o Examining digital evidence (hard drives, memory dumps, network captures) to uncover details about an incident.
  - o Analyzing malware, reconstructing timelines, and identifying attacker TTPs.
  - o Providing detailed reports for legal or internal investigations.

- **Malware analysis:**
  - o Analyzing suspicious files to determine if they are malicious.
  - o Reverse engineering malware to understand its functionality and potential impact.
  - o Developing signatures and indicators for detection and prevention.

- **Fly-away incident response:**
  - o Providing on-site incident response services at remote locations when needed.
  - o Deploying specialized tools and expertise to quickly contain and mitigate security incidents.

- **Deception:**
  - o Deploying decoys, honey pots, and misleading information to confuse and detect attackers.

- **Insider threat detection:**
  - o Monitoring user behavior and activity for anomalies that could indicate malicious intent.
  - o Analyzing logs and data to detect insider threats and mitigate risks.

Additional functional areas

Beyond the core and specialized functions, many SOCs have additional functional areas that support the overall security posture of the organization. These areas may not be directly involved in incident response, but they play a crucial role in proactively defending against threats. Some common additional functional areas include:

- **Cyber threat intelligence (CTI):**
  - o **Collection, processing, and fusion:** Gathering threat intelligence from various sources (feeds, reports, open-source intelligence), processing, and integrating it into SOC systems.
  - o **Analysis and production:** Analyzing CTI to identify trends, track adversary behavior, and create reports for decision-makers.
  - o **Sharing and distribution:** Sharing relevant CTI with internal stakeholders and external partners to improve overall security posture.

- **Threat hunting**:
  - o Proactively searching for **indicators of compromise (IOCs)** and hidden threats not detected by existing alerts.
  - o Developing and refining custom analytics and abilities to uncover advanced threats.
- **Sensor and analytics tuning**:
  - o Optimizing detection rules, correlation rules, and response actions in SIEM, EDR, SOAR, and other tools.
  - o Fine-tuning sensors and analytics to reduce false positives and improve threat detection accuracy.
- **Custom analytics and detection creation**:
  - o Developing custom detection rules and analytics based on specific adversary TTPs and the organization's systems.
- **Vulnerability management**:
  - o Identifying, assessing, prioritizing, and remediating vulnerabilities in systems and applications.

    Figure 5.4 illustrates the process flow for vulnerability management, from identification to remediation and reporting.

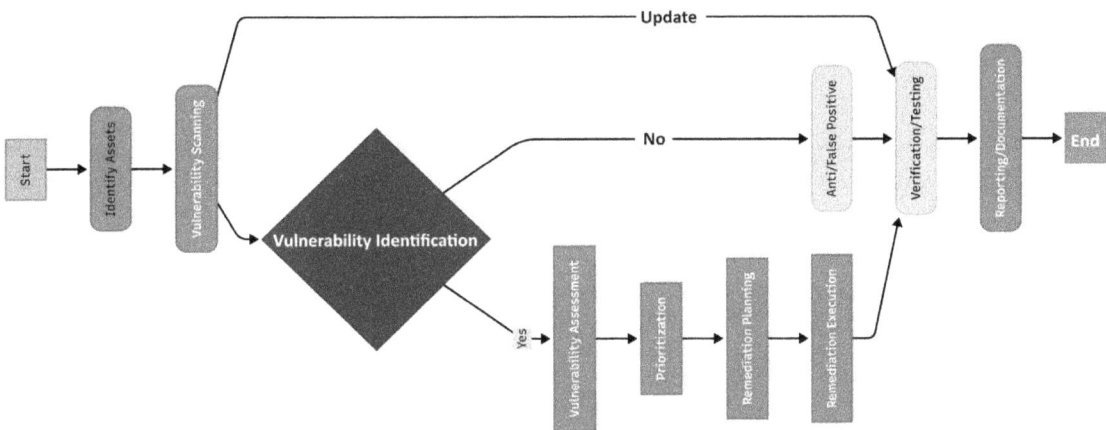

Figure 5.4: Vulnerability management

- **Asset mapping and composite inventory**:
  - o **Discovery and identification**: Identifying all assets within the organization's environment, including hardware, software, data, and network devices.
  - o **Classification and cataloguing**: Categorizing assets based on their function, criticality, and sensitivity.
  - o **Dependency mapping**: Understanding the relationships and interdependencies between assets to assess the potential impact of a compromise.

o **Risk scoring**: Assigning risk scores to assets based on their criticality and vulnerabilities, aiding in prioritization of remediation efforts.

- **Attack simulation and assessments**:

  o **Red teaming**: Simulating real-world attacks to test the effectiveness of security controls.

  o **Penetration testing**: Identifying vulnerabilities by attempting to exploit them.

  o **Adversary emulation**: Mimicking the tactics of specific threat actors to assess resilience.

  o **Purple teaming**: Combining red and blue team efforts for collaborative security improvement.

  o **Breach and attack simulation (BAS)**: Automated testing of security controls against various attack scenarios.

People, Process, Technology

A SOC's effectiveness is not solely determined by advanced technology or cutting-edge tools. It hinges on a delicate interplay of three fundamental pillars, which are People, Process, and Technology. This triad forms the foundation of a strong security operation, ensuring that human expertise, streamlined processes, and innovative technologies work in harmony to detect, analyze, and respond to cyber threats effectively.

Importance of People, Process, Technology framework

The **People, Process, and Technology (PPT)** framework offers a holistic approach to security, recognizing that it is not solely a technical issue but rather a complex problem that demands a multifaceted solution:

- **People**: Skilled professionals are the brain of the SOC. They are the analysts, engineers, and threat hunters who possess the critical thinking, analytical skills, and expertise to interpret complex data, investigate threats, and make crucial decisions. While technology can automate tasks, it is human intuition and experience that ultimately separate false alarms from true incidents and drive a successful defense.

- **Process**: Well-defined processes provide the backbone for consistent and efficient SOC operations. These are the documented workflows that guide the team's actions. Key processes include the overarching **incident response plan (IRP)**, **standard operating procedures (SOPs)** for alert triage and investigation, and automated playbooks that define how the SOC responds to specific types of threats. These procedures ensure that actions are repeatable, predictable, and aligned with the organization's security goals.

- **Technology:** The technology stack acts as a force multiplier, empowering the people and enabling the processes. This includes a range of integrated tools such as **security information and event management (SIEM)** for data aggregation and correlation, **security orchestration, automation, and response (SOAR)** to automate workflows, **endpoint detection and response (EDR)** for endpoint visibility, and **threat intelligence platforms (TIPs)** to provide context on adversaries.

Implementing the PPT framework

A careful and well-thought-out plan that aligns the three parts of the PPT framework is needed to construct a strong SOC. Each part is very important to the success and efficiency of the SOC as a whole, and it is very important that they all work well together. Refer to the following list, which is a roadmap for groups to follow during the implementation process:

- **Assess current capabilities and identify areas for improvement**:

    o **People assessment**: Evaluate the current team's skills and knowledge to identify expertise gaps and training needs.

    o **Process evaluation**: Review existing SOC workflows, such as incident response and threat hunting, to find inefficiencies and opportunities for automation.

    o **Technology audit**: Audit current security tools to ensure they are up-to-date, integrated, and capable of meeting security needs.

- **Develop a comprehensive SOC implementation plan**:

    o **Define objectives**: Clearly define the goals and objectives of the SOC. *What are the key metrics you want to improve (e.g., MTTD, MTTR)? What specific threats and risks do you want to address?*

    o **Resource allocation**: Allocate necessary resources, including budget and staffing, and decide on an in-house, outsourced, or hybrid SOC model

    o **Timeline**: Establish a realistic timeline for the implementation, considering the complexity of the project and the availability of resources.

    o **Incorporate the RACI matrix**: Implement the **Responsibility, Accountability, Consultation, and Informed (RACI)** matrix to clearly define roles and responsibilities within the SOC team and also with the other stakeholders who are involved in building the SOC. This matrix will help avoid confusion and ensure efficient collaboration among team members and teams.

- **Build a high-performing SOC team**:

    o **Recruitment**: Recruit skilled professionals with a mix of technical, analytical, and soft skills.

- o **Training and development**: Invest in continuous training and professional development to keep the team's skills current.

- o **Retention**: Foster a positive and collaborative work environment to retain top talent.

- **Streamline and automate processes**:

  - o **Document processes**: Document all SOC processes using visual aids like flowcharts to ensure clarity and consistency.

  - o **Automate repetitive tasks**: Automate repetitive tasks such as alert triage and log analysis using SOAR platforms.

- **Use technology**:

  - o **Select the right tools**: Select security tools that match your organization's specific needs and risk profile, considering scalability and ease of integration.

  - o **Integrate security solutions**: Integrate security solutions to create a unified view of the security environment for better data correlation and analysis.

  - o **Use threat intelligence**: Incorporate threat intelligence feeds into your SOC tools to improve threat detection and inform incident response.

Challenges and solutions

While SOCs offer significant benefits, they are not without their challenges. Some of the most common challenges include the following:

- **Alert fatigue**: Getting too many security alerts can make you tired and cause you to miss threats. Some solutions are to sort alerts by risk, automate the triage process, and use threat intelligence to get rid of false alarms.

- **Skill shortages**: There are not enough skilled cybersecurity workers to go around. To deal with this problem, businesses can put money into training and development programs, form partnerships with schools, and look into hiring options.

- **Evolving threats**: The threat landscape is always shifting, which makes it hard for SOCs to keep up. Adopting a mindset of continuous improvement means changing tools, methods, and processes all the time to deal with new threats.

Future trends in SOC

The future of SOCs is likely to be shaped by several key trends, which are as follows:

- **AI and ML**: AI and ML are already very important in finding threats, responding to incidents, and automating security, and they will become even more so in the future.

- **Cloud-based SOCs**: The cloud makes SOC processes more scalable, flexible, and cost-effective, and increased adoption is expected.

- **Threat intelligence sharing**: In the fight against cybercrime, it will be even more important for SOCs to work together and share threat intelligence.

- **Focus on resilience**: SOCs will put more effort into making systems more resilient so they can handle and rebound from complex attacks, which will protect business continuity.

SOCs can continue to play very important role in keeping companies safe from online threats as long as they follow these trends and change with the times. Cybersecurity has a bright future ahead of it, and the SOC will be at the heart of new ideas and progress.

SOC design, architecture, and planning

To make a strong SOC, you need to pay close attention to every detail, know what the company needs, and use the latest technologies. This part will talk about the important parts and things to think about when building, architecting, and planning a SOC that can protect against advanced cyber threats. There is not a single SOC that works for everyone, so we will go over all the things you need to know, and then you can use the ones that work best for you.

Designing the SOC

Its goals should be in line with those of the company. To start the design part of a SOC, it is important to know what the organization's goals are, how much risk it is willing to take, and what the rules are. Creating a SOC that not only fits with the company's security plan but also works well with its overall operations is the main goal. Important steps in this phase are:

- **Understanding the SOC's mission and scope**: The design of a SOC begins with a clear understanding of its mission and scope:

  o **Mission**: *What is the SOC's primary purpose? Is it focused on threat detection and response, vulnerability management, compliance monitoring, or a combination of these?*

  o **Scope**: *What are the specific assets, systems, and data that the SOC is responsible for protecting? What are the organization's risk tolerance and security objectives?*

A well-defined mission and scope will guide all subsequent design decisions, ensuring that the SOC's architecture and resources are aligned with the organization's cybersecurity goals.

- **Assessing organizational needs and foundation of SOC design**: A very important step in designing an effective SOC is understanding the unique needs and risk profile of the organization it serves. This involves:

  o **Identifying critical assets**: *What are the organization's crown jewels?* These are the data, tools, and apps that are most important to the business and are also the easiest to hack.

o **Evaluating threat landscape:** *What are the most likely threats facing the organization, and what are the potential attack vectors?*

o **Regulatory compliance:** *What industry-specific or regulatory requirements must the SOC adhere to, and is there any need for your business to adhere to any of these compliance?*

o **Budgetary constraints:** *What financial resources are available for building and operating the SOC?*

Apart from this, the following questions should be asked and answered by the stakeholders:

- *What are our primary cybersecurity goals and objectives?*

  o *Are we primarily focused on threat detection and response, vulnerability management, compliance, or a combination?*

  o *What specific risks are we most concerned about?*

  o *What are our desired outcomes for the SOC (e.g., reduced MTTD/MTTR, improved security posture)?*

- *What is the scope of our SOC?*

  o *Which assets, systems, and data are we going to protect?*

  o *What is our risk tolerance, and what are the potential consequences of a security incident?*

  o *Will the SOC cover on-premises infrastructure, cloud environments, or both?*

  o *Will the SOC be 24x7 365 days?*

- *What resources can we allocate to the SOC?*

  o *What is our budget for building and operating the SOC?*

  o *How many staff members can we dedicate to the SOC?*

  o *What level of expertise do we need in our SOC team (e.g., threat hunters, malware analysts)?*

- *Which SOC model is the best fit for our organization?*

  o *Should we build an internal SOC, outsource to an MSSP (Managed Security Service Provider), or adopt a hybrid model?*

  o *What are the pros and cons of each model in terms of cost, control, and expertise?*

  o *Does our organization have the necessary skills and resources to build and operate an internal SOC?*

- *What are the regulatory and compliance requirements we need to meet?*

  o *Which industry-specific regulations or standards apply to our organization?*

  o *What are the specific security controls and reporting requirements mandated by these regulations?*

o *How will the SOC ensure ongoing compliance with these requirements?*

Answering these questions lays the groundwork for defining the SOC's scope, objectives, and resource requirements.

- **Defining SOC objectives and scope**: Once the organizational needs are understood, the next step is to define clear and measurable objectives for the SOC. SOC objectives should be **Specific, Measurable, Achievable, Relevant, and Time-bound (SMART)**. These objectives should be aligned with the organization's overall security strategy and risk management goals. Examples of SOC objectives could include:

  o **Reduce mean time to detect (MTTD) for phishing attacks by 20% within six months**:

    - **Specific**: Phishing attacks, MTTD metric.

    - **Measurable**: Track average detection time.

    - **Achievable**: Realistic reduction target.

    - **Relevant**: Addresses a common threat.

    - **Time-bound**: Six-month timeframe months.

  o **Reduce mean time to respond (MTTR) for critical incidents**:

    - **Specific**: Focuses on critical incidents and the metric of MTTR.

    - **Measurable**: Tracks the average time to contain and remediate critical incidents.

    - **Achievable**: Sets a realistic reduction target based on current resources and processes.

    - **Relevant**: Aims to minimize the impact of high-severity incidents.

    - **Time-bound**: Specifies a timeframe for achieving the reduction (e.g., by 15% within a year).

Find more examples of SOC objectives on the GitHub page.

Setting the SOC's scope is also very important. This means making a list of the exact systems, apps, and data that the SOC is in charge of protecting and keeping an eye on. The scope should be broad enough to include all important assets but narrow enough to make processes run smoothly, details as follows:

- **SOC architecture and components**: The SOC's architecture is the plan that tells designers and builders how to build and use it. It describes the organization, parts, and connections between the different parts that make up the SOC.

  The key components of a SOC architecture include the following:

- **Data sources:**

  o **Network taps**: Passive devices that copy network traffic for analysis without impacting performance.

  o **Operating systems**: Generate logs about user activity, system events, and security-related incidents.

  o **Applications**: Produce logs that detail application behavior, errors, and potential security issues.

  o **Security elements**: Include firewalls, **intrusion detection/prevention systems (IDS/IPS)**, and other security appliances that generate logs and alerts.

  o **Physical security elements**: Sensors and systems that monitor physical access to facilities and data centers.

  o **Network elements**: Routers, switches, and other networking devices that provide logs on network traffic and configuration changes.

  o **Threat intelligence**: External feeds and sources of information about emerging threats and vulnerabilities.

- **Data collection layer:**

  o It is responsible for gathering raw data from the diverse data sources.

  o It employs various collection methods like syslog, SNMP traps, and API integrations.

  o **Includes:**

    ▪ **Data collection**: The process of aggregating logs and events from all sources.

    ▪ **Event collection**: Gathering security events from various security devices.

    ▪ **Network flow collection**: Collecting network traffic flow data for analysis.

- **Data flow:**

  o Data flows from various sources into the data collection layer.

  o It is processed and enriched in the data processing layer.

  o Processed data is stored and analyzed in the security analytics layer.

  o Alerts are generated and displayed on the dashboard.

  o Analysts investigate alerts, create tickets, and manage incident cases.

  o Reporting provides insights into security trends and the overall security posture.

  o Risk assessments inform decision-making and guide security improvements.

- **Data processing layer**:

  - **Deep packet inspection**: This examines the content of network packets in detail, looking for malicious payloads or suspicious activity.

  - **Rule-based processing**: Applies predefined rules and signatures to identify known threats and anomalies in the collected data.

  - **Sandboxing**: Isolates suspicious files in a safe environment to analyze their behavior and determine if they are malicious.

- **Security analytics**:

  - **Rule-based correlation**: Using correlation rules and data from multiple sources, it finds complicated attack patterns.

  - **Anomaly detection**: Using statistical models and machine learning to find behavior that is not normal or predicted, which could be a sign of a security threat.

- **Storage**:

  - Stores raw and processed data for analysis, historical reference, and forensic investigation.

- **Alert and reporting**:

  - **Alert dashboard**: Provides a visual interface for security analysts to view and prioritize alerts.

  - **Reporting**: Generates reports summarizing security events, incidents, and trends.

- **Ticketing and incident case management**:

  - Keeps track of and handles security issues from the time they are found until they are fixed.

- **Additional components**:

  - **Enrichment**: Enhances collected data with external information like reputation scores, geolocation data, and *WHOIS* records.

  - **Metrics dashboard**: Displays KPIs for evaluating SOC effectiveness.

  - **SOC monitoring**: Continuous monitoring of security events and alerts.

  - **Risk assessment**: Evaluates the overall security risk posture based on collected data and threat intelligence.

- **Technology selection and integration**: The SOC needs to pick the right security tools and solutions. The technology stack should include all the parts that are needed to find threats, analyze them, and respond to them. However, it is just as important that the tools work well together so that knowledge does not get lost.

The following list outlines the key technologies used in SOCs:

o **SIEM**: A central location where security data from different sources can be gathered, analyzed, and linked. SIEMs are very important for finding trends and oddities that could mean there has been a security breach.

o **IDS/IPS**: Monitoring network traffic for signs of malicious activity and blocking threats.

o **EDR**: Providing visibility into endpoint activity and enabling rapid detection and response to threats.

o **TIPs**: Putting together and studying threat data from different sources to help make security decisions

o **SOAR**: Automating security workflows to streamline incident response and free up analysts to focus on more complex tasks.

o **User and entity behaviour analytics (UEBA)**: Using machine learning to detect anomalies in user and entity behaviour that may indicate a security threat.

• **Technology integration strategies**: Successful technology integration is key to building an efficient and effective SOC. Consider the following strategies:

o **Open standards**: Choose technologies that support open standards like **Structured Threat Information eXpression (STIX)** and **Trusted Automated eXchange of Indicator Information (TAXII)**. This helps the exchange of threat intelligence between different tools and platforms.

o **API integration:** Look for solutions that offer strong **application programming interfaces (APIs)** to enable integration with other security tools and systems.

• **The human element**: Technology alone cannot guarantee a successful SOC. The human element is equally important. SOC analysts need to be highly skilled, experienced, and motivated. They must be able to quickly analyze and respond to alerts, collaborate effectively with other teams, and communicate clearly with stakeholders.

The following are the operational considerations:

o **Staffing**: Ensuring adequate staffing levels to handle the volume of alerts and incidents.

o **Training and development**: Providing ongoing training to keep analysts' skills sharp and knowledge current.

o **Processes and procedures**: Establishing well-defined processes and procedures for incident response, threat hunting, and vulnerability management.

o **Metrics and measurement**: Tracking KPIs to measure the SOC's effectiveness and identify areas for improvement.

- **Scalability and adaptability**: The SOC should be designed with scalability and adaptability in mind. The SOC needs to be able to change with the needs of the business and the threats as they appear. This could mean adding new platforms and tools, making the team bigger, or changing how things are done. The SOC has changed a lot over the years to keep up with the constantly shifting world of hacking. We are now in the age of the next-generation SOC, which has more advanced features and is more automated. Modern SOCs use cutting-edge technologies and new strategies to make their defenses against complex cyber dangers more effective and efficient.

- **Continuous improvement and optimization**: A successful SOC must change with the times to deal with new threats, tools, and business needs. To keep the SOC working well in a world where problems are always changing, it needs to keep getting better and better. By using these best practices and adding the key parts we talked about in this section, businesses can create and run a very good SOC that is a key part of their cybersecurity defense. There is more to the SOC than just a room full of screens. It is a strategic asset that can protect the company's most important assets and ensure its long-term success.

Inhouse SOC and MSSP

When deciding on a SOC, organizations can choose between setting up an in-house SOC or outsourcing the services to a **Managed Security Service Provider** (**MSSP**). An in-house SOC offers complete control over security operations, allowing for customization and direct access to security personnel. However, this approach requires significant investment in infrastructure, staffing, and ongoing maintenance.

Conversely, an MSSP provides cost-effective and scalable security services, leveraging specialized expertise and advanced technologies.

MSSPs offer 24/7 monitoring, threat intelligence, and incident response capabilities, freeing up internal resources and reducing the burden on in-house IT teams. However, outsourcing to an MSSP may result in reduced control over security processes and potential reliance on external providers.

In-house SOC vs. MSSP

Choosing whether to build and run an in-house SOC or to hire an MSSP is a strategic decision that can have a big impact on a company's budget, security, and business efficiency. The following list outlines the pros and cons of each type, which can help you make your choice:

- **In-house SOC**: An in-house SOC is built, staffed, and operated entirely within the organization. It offers several key advantages:

    o **Pros**: It offers complete control and customization over security operations, deep integration with existing IT infrastructure, and retention of internal knowledge.

o **Cons**: This approach involves high upfront costs, is resource-intensive, may have limited specialized expertise, and can face challenges in maintaining 24/7 operations.

- **MSSP SOC**: An MSSP SOC provides security services, including threat monitoring, incident response, and vulnerability management, on a subscription basis. The key benefits include:

  o **Pros**: This model provides access to seasoned professionals, scalability to meet changing needs, cost-effectiveness (especially for smaller organizations), and continuous 24/7 monitoring.

  o **Cons**: It may result in less direct control over operations, potential misalignment with an organization's specific security goals, and communication challenges.

Hybrid SOC

A hybrid SOC has parts of both the in-house model and the MSSP model. With this method, companies can use the knowledge and flexibility of an MSSP while still maintaining control over important security tasks.

The following are the key characteristics of a hybrid SOC:

- **Shared responsibility**: The organization and the MSSP are both in charge of security activities. The organization usually makes strategic decisions, decides which incidents are most important, and handles private data. The MSSP, on the other hand, provides specialized knowledge and resources for tasks such as threat monitoring, log analysis, and initial incident response.

- **Flexible and scalable**: With the hybrid approach, businesses can change how much security they have as needed. When demand is high or for special projects, they can use MSSP resources, but they can still keep a core in-house team for ongoing operations.

- **Cost-effective**: By outsourcing certain functions to an MSSP, organizations can reduce their operational costs while still benefiting from advanced security technologies and expertise.

- **Customizable**: The hybrid model is highly customizable, allowing organizations to tailor the SOC to their specific needs and risk profile. They can choose which functions to outsource and which to keep in-house, ensuring that critical security decisions remain under their control.

The following are the use cases for hybrid SOCs:

- **Small and medium-sized enterprises (SMEs)**: SMEs do not always have the monetary resources or the staff to set up and run their own SOC. With a hybrid model, they can use the expertise of an MSSP for important tasks like threat monitoring and incident response, while leaving a smaller team in-house to work on creating and following security policies.

- **Large enterprises with specialized needs**: An MSSP might not be able to fully meet the security needs of a large business because of its complicated IT environment and unique security needs. With a hybrid approach, they can hire an MSSP to do routine tasks like monitoring logs and scanning for security holes. This frees up internal resources to work on more specialized tasks, such as threat hunting or compliance management.

- **Organizations with limited in-house expertise**: A hybrid SOC can bridge the skills gap by providing access to specialized expertise from an MSSP. This allows organizations to quickly ramp up their security capabilities without having to invest in extensive training and recruitment.

Implementing a hybrid SOC

Implementing a hybrid SOC requires careful planning and coordination to ensure seamless integration and avoid potential conflicts or overlaps. A few points to consider are as follows:

- **Clearly define roles and responsibilities**: Establish clear boundaries between the in-house team and the MSSP, outlining their respective roles and responsibilities. This ensures that there is no confusion or duplication of effort.

- **Establish clear communication channels**: Ensure seamless communication and collaboration between the in-house team and the MSSP. This includes regular meetings, shared reporting dashboards, and escalation procedures.

- **Define service level agreements (SLAs)**: Establish clear SLAs with the MSSP, outlining their service commitments, response times, and performance metrics. This ensures that the MSSP is accountable for delivering high-quality services.

- **Conduct regular reviews**: Regularly review the performance of the hybrid SOC, assessing its effectiveness in meeting the organization's security objectives. Adjust the model as needed to ensure continued success.

Choosing the right model

The decision of whether to build an in-house SOC or partner with an MSSP depends on various factors, such as:

- **Organizational size and resources**: Smaller organizations with limited resources may find an MSSP to be a more viable option.

- **Risk tolerance**: Organizations with a high-risk profile may prefer the greater control and customization offered by an in-house SOC.

- **Expertise**: If the organization lacks in-house cybersecurity expertise, partnering with an MSSP can provide access to skilled professionals.

- **Budget**: Consider the costs associated with each model, including upfront investments, ongoing operational expenses, and potential downtime due to security incidents.

The following list outlines some critical questions that are essential to guide an organization's decision between an in-house SOC and an MSSP:

- **Strategic alignment and goals**:
    - *What are our primary cybersecurity goals and objectives?*
        - *Is our focus on threat detection and response, vulnerability management, compliance, or a combination?*
        - *How does the SOC model align with our broader security strategy and risk appetite?*
        - *What specific metrics (MTTD, MTTR, etc.) are we aiming to improve?*

- **Operational capabilities and resources**:
    - *Do we have the necessary in-house expertise to build and operate a SOC?*
        - *Do we have skilled security analysts, incident responders, and threat hunters?*
        - *Can we attract and retain top cybersecurity talent?*
        - *Do we have the internal resources to manage the technology and infrastructure required for a SOC?*
    - *What is our budget for cybersecurity operations?*
        - *Can we afford the upfront investment and ongoing costs of building and maintaining an in-house SOC?*
        - *Are we looking for a more predictable and scalable cost model offered by MSSPs?*
    - *Do we need 24/7 security coverage?*
        - *Are our business operations global, requiring round-the-clock monitoring and response?*
        - *Can we adequately staff an in-house SOC to provide continuous coverage?*

- **Technology and infrastructure**:
    - *What are our existing security tools and infrastructure?*
        - *Do we have a SIEM, IDS/IPS, EDR, and other necessary tools in place?*
        - *Are these tools up-to-date and integrated effectively?*
        - *Do we have the expertise to manage and maintain these tools?*

- o *What is our tolerance for technology risk?*
  - ▪ *Are we comfortable relying on third-party providers for security tools and infrastructure?*
  - ▪ *What level of control do we need over our security environment?*
- o *Compliance and Regulatory Requirements:*
- o *What industry-specific regulations or standards apply to our organization?*
  - ▪ *Do we have specific compliance requirements that an in-house SOC can better address?*
  - ▪ *Can an MSSP demonstrate compliance with our industry regulations?*

- **Additional considerations**:
  - o *How quickly do we need to establish a SOC?*
    - ▪ *Can we afford the time and resources required to build an in-house SOC from scratch?*
    - ▪ *Do we need a faster deployment timeline that an MSSP can offer?*
  - o *What is our incident response maturity level?*
    - ▪ *Do we have established incident response procedures and playbooks?*
    - ▪ *Can an MSSP enhance our incident response capabilities?*
  - o *What are our long-term cybersecurity goals?*
    - ▪ *How will the chosen SOC model support our long-term security strategy?*
    - ▪ *Will the model allow us to adapt to evolving threats and technologies?*

Ultimately, the best choice will depend on the organization's specific needs and circumstances. By carefully weighing the pros and cons of each model, organizations can make an informed decision that aligns with their security goals and budget.

Security monitoring and analysis

Monitoring and analysis are critical components of a company's cybersecurity plan. This process involves continuous collection, correlation, and analysis of security-related data from various sources, transforming raw data into actionable intelligence. Effective security monitoring requires keen observation, analytical skills, and access to current security technology. A SOC's success relies on comprehensive security monitoring and analysis, converting raw data from network traffic, system logs, security events, and user activity into intelligence to proactively counter threats, prevent operational disruptions, data breaches, and reputational damage. Let us look at the most important parts of SOC monitoring and research, which will give cybersecurity experts more in-depth knowledge:

- **Real-time event monitoring**: It means gathering, processing, and studying security events as they happen. There are many sources where these events can come from, such as:

  o **Network devices**: Firewalls, routers, switches, IDS/IPS, and other network security appliances.

  o **Endpoint devices**: Laptops, desktops, servers, mobile devices, and IoT devices.

  o **Applications**: Web applications, databases, cloud services, and other critical software.

  o **Security tools**: SIEM systems, TIPs, vulnerability scanners, and other security solutions.

The key components of real-time events are as follows:

  o **Data collection**: Gathering security events from a wide range of sources in real time.

  o **Data normalization**: Converting raw event data into a standardized format for easier analysis.

  o **Correlation**: Identifying relationships between different events to detect patterns and anomalies.

  o **Alerting**: Generating alerts to notify analysts of potential security incidents.

  o **Investigation and response**: Investigating alerts, determining the root cause of incidents, and taking appropriate action to contain and remediate threats.

By monitoring these events in real-time, SOC analysts can identify anomalies, suspicious patterns, and potential threats before they cause significant damage.

SOC monitoring events and parsing data

SOC depends on a steady flow of data to find and stop possible threats. This data, which comes from many different systems and devices and is usually in the form of logs, provides a deeper understanding of network activity, user behavior, and possible security holes. However, raw log data can be confusing and hard to understand. That is where event tracking and data parsing come in. They turn this huge amount of data into intelligence that SOC analysts can use.

The following figure depicts the critical data flow within a SIEM system, highlighting how raw logs and events are processed to enable effective security monitoring:

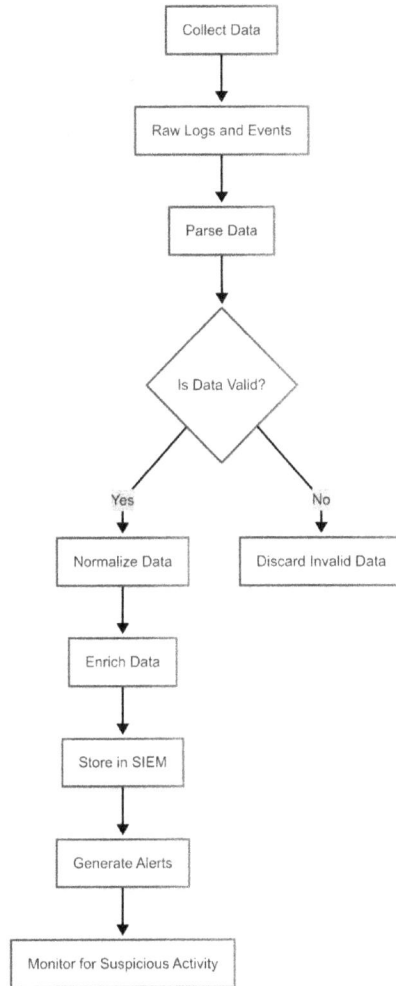

Figure 5.5: Key stages of data processing in a SIEM system

By taking useful information from raw log files and putting it into a structured format that is easy to read and understand, data parsing is the process. In this case, consider the following points:

- **Identifying relevant fields**: Figure out which log data fields are the most important for security research. This could have timestamps, usernames, acts taken, error codes, and source and destination IP addresses.

- **Extracting and transforming data**: Using special parsing tools or scripts to get the important fields out of the raw log data and change them into a standard format. This could mean changing timestamps to a standard style, connecting IP addresses to places on the map, or putting events into groups based on rules that have already been set.

- **Enrichment**: Adding contextual information to the parsed data, such as threat intelligence data, asset information, or user details. This enrichment helps analysts understand the significance of events and prioritize their response.

- **Correlation**: Combining data that has been parsed from different sources to find trends and connections that could point to a security breach is called correlation. To do this, events and logs from different systems may need to be linked to make a record of an attack.

Security event analysis

Security event analysis is both an art and a science. It requires a blend of technical expertise, analytical skills, and an understanding of attacker TTPs. Analysts must quickly assess the relevance and severity of security events, correlate data, and make informed decisions regarding response.

Tools used: SIEM, SOAR, TIPs, **user and entity behavior analytics (UEBA)**, and log analysis tools.

The following table shows various log sources under different categories, which can help a SOC analyst to read and understand alerts:

Category	Log sources
Network security	Firewall logs, IDS logs, IPS logs, web proxy logs, DNS logs, VPN logs, router logs, switch logs, load balancer logs, network traffic logs, wireless access point logs.
Endpoint and user security	Antivirus/Antimalware software logs, EDR logs, operating system logs (Windows event logs), operating system logs (syslog), Active Directory logs, **identity and access management (IAM)** logs, **mobile device management (MDM)** logs, UEBA logs, RADIUS logs, Sysmon Logs, PowerShell logs.
Cloud and application security	Cloud Service Provider logs (AWS CloudTrail), Cloud Service Provider logs (Azure Monitor), Cloud Service Provider logs (Google Cloud logging), application logs, web server logs, database logs, SIEM logs, Office 365 logs, ERP system logs (SAP), CRM system logs (Salesforce), DevOps tools logs (Jenkins), container logs (Docker), Kubernetes logs, blockchain logs.
Operational technology and IoT	**Industrial control systems (ICS)** logs, IoT device logs, physical security logs (badge access), backup and recovery logs, and **point-of-sale (POS)** system logs.
Threat management and compliance	Threat intelligence feeds, vulnerability scanner logs, patch management logs, configuration management logs, deception technology logs (honeypots), SOAR logs, DLP logs.

Table 5.2: Various log sources under different categories

Let us look at some real-time examples of security monitoring and analysis that highlight the diverse tasks and scenarios for security monitoring and analysis encountered within a SOC:

- **Intrusion detection**: If an **intrusion detection system** (**IDS**) sees a sudden rise in traffic from a certain IP address, it will let the user know. This sudden rise in traffic could be a sign of an impending **denial-of-service** (**DoS**) attack, the goal of which is to crush the company's network resources so that approved users cannot access them. The SOC analyst looks into the warning, looks at the traffic trends, and makes sure that the surge was caused by someone who wanted to do harm. After that, the expert takes steps to stop harmful traffic and keep important systems safe. Adding the IP address in question to a *blacklist*, filtering out certain traffic bits, or setting rate-limiting rules on the firewall are some ways to do this. By spotting and stopping the DoS attack early on, the SOC expert makes sure that users can always get to important resources and keeps business operations running smoothly.

- **Phishing email detection**: An email security gateway flags a suspicious email that might be a phishing attempt. The email security gateway sends a warning to the SOC analyst, saying that a suspicious email has been found. The analyst looks for red flags in the email's headers, text, and links. Here, the analyst might look for sender email addresses that look like they were faked to look like real ones (for example, changing one character in a known company email address), scare or urgency language in the email body to get the recipient to click on a malicious link, or language that does not make sense or was translated badly. The analyst may also look at the email's target URLs for anything that seems fishy, like typosquatting (when a real domain name is replaced with one that looks like it), or **Uniform Resource Locator** (**URLs**) that lead to known phishing sites. The SOC analyst says that it is a phishing email that tries to get people to give out private information or click on harmful links that could infect their computers or let hackers into their accounts. The expert then puts the email in a *quarantine*, which keeps it from getting to users' inboxes. The analyst may also take other steps, such as reporting the phishing attempt to a relevant phishing database or letting users know about the particular email campaign to help them spot and avoid future attempts like this.

- **User behavior anomaly**: A UEBA tool can spot strange behavior from an authorized user account. The analyst gets a message telling them that a privileged user account accessed private information outside of regular business hours and from a place they are not familiar with. This is not a good sign because privileged accounts are usually used for administrative tasks and should not be accessing private data outside of business hours or from places that are not supposed to be there. The analyst looks into the activity more by looking at the user's past access logs, finding out what data was read, and looking at the network traffic that was connected to the activity. The analyst may also try to get in touch with the person to make sure the access is real. If the person can't give a good reason for what they were doing, the analyst sees it as a possible breach. The analyst then changes the password for the account that was hacked, takes away access to stop anyone else from getting in without permission, and starts a larger investigation to find out where the hack came from. In this investigation, the investigators may look at logs from the user's endpoint device, try to find signs of compromise (IOCs) that point to malware or remote access tools, and look at network traffic trends to find possible attacker connections. By doing these things, the SOC analyst can lessen the damage the hacked account has done and stop more people from getting into private data without permission.

- **Malware detection**: When a suspicious file is executed, the EDR solution sends out a warning, which makes SOC analysts look into it. Sandboxing lets the analyst put the suspicious file in a controlled setting where they can watch how it acts. When an analyst sees that it does something bad, like encrypting files or trying to talk to known command-and-control services, they know that it is malware. The incident response process then starts, which includes locating the affected endpoint, getting rid of the malware, and checking to see if any other systems have been compromised.

- **Vulnerability scanning**: A SOC needs to keep checking systems and apps all the time to find vulnerabilities before they are used against the company. In real life, a vulnerability scanner might find a major flaw in a well-known computer server. In addition to writing down this fact, the SOC acts right away. Because attackers are likely to use this weakness, the SOC quickly makes patching the most important thing, taking into account how dangerous the risk is. This means that the IT staff needs to work closely with the business to make the necessary changes quickly and keep the digital front door of the company safe.

- **Dark web monitoring**: On the dark web, people often trade stolen data, plans for attacks, and dangerous tools to attack organisations. This makes it a great place for cyber risks to grow. SOCs keep a close eye on marketplaces and discussion boards and carefully watch these less well-known parts of the internet. Say, if they find that an employee's passwords are being sold, that could be a sign of a possible breach. On the other hand, they might hear people talking about a plan to attack their company. Now that the SOC has this information, they can quickly deal with the threat by changing passwords, adding more security, or warning staff about possible social engineering scams.

SOC incident response procedures

While the full methodology of incident response is a discipline, the SOC is the team on the front lines, responsible for executing the process in real-time. The SOC's primary function is to serve as the operational driver for each phase of the incident response lifecycle, as follows:

- **Detection and analysis**: This is the SOC's core, 24/7 function. Analysts use tools like SIEM and EDR to monitor security alerts. They are responsible for the initial triage, validating alerts, filtering out false positives, and determining if a security event constitutes a true incident requiring a full response.

- **Containment, eradication, and recovery**: Once an incident is declared, the SOC team takes immediate action. They leverage SOAR playbooks to automate initial containment steps, such as isolating an infected host from the network. They then use security tools to eradicate the threat, such as removing malware, and support the broader IT team in recovering affected systems from clean backups.

- **Post-incident activity**: Following an incident, SOC analysts are crucial to the *lessons learned* process. They analyze data from the attack to create new detection rules, fine-tune security controls, and provide detailed reports that help improve the organization's overall security posture.

The SOC's hands-on involvement is critical at every step. A full, detailed methodology for the entire incident response lifecycle is covered in *Chapter 6, Incident Response Management*.

Sample alert triage and investigation

At 14:35 UTC, the SOC's SIEM system triggers a high-priority alert. It flags a high volume of TCP SYN packets from the source IP 198.51.100.55 targeting the organization's public-facing web server at 203.0.113.10 on port 443. The alert notes that over 5,000 connection attempts were denied by the firewall in under one minute from this single source. Initial triage

The SOC analyst acknowledges the alert and initiates a preliminary investigation. Reviewing the alert details, the analyst notes the following parameters provided by the SIEM:

- **Source IP**: 198.51.100.55. The analyst queries this address in internal and external threat intelligence feeds. The IP is flagged with a poor reputation, associated with recent scanning activity and botnet **command-and-control (C2)** traffic.

- **Destination and port**: 203.0.113.10 on port 443. This confirms the target is the primary public web server, and the attack is targeting the **Hypertext Transfer Protocol Secure (HTTPS)** service.

- **Traffic profile**: The alert specifically notes a high volume of TCP SYN packets with no corresponding established sessions. This, combined with the volume (5,000+ attempts/minute), is a classic indicator of a TCP SYN flood.

- **Firewall action**: The alert confirms the firewall is denying the connections. This is a positive indicator that perimeter defenses are working as configured, but the volume of traffic itself remains a threat to network and firewall resources.

Based on these initial findings, the analyst forms a working hypothesis: the organization is the target of a DoS attack, specifically a SYN flood, originating from a known malicious IP. The immediate next steps are to check the web server's real-time performance metrics for any signs of degradation and to broaden the query in the SIEM to see if other source IPs are participating in the attack, which would escalate it to a **distributed denial-of-service (DDoS)** event.

Deep dive investigation

Based on the initial assessment, which points to a possible DoS attack, the analyst sends the warning to the IR team for further investigation. To get a better look at the packet grabs, they use tools for **network traffic analysis (NTA)**. The NTA shows a lot of broken TCP connections with spoofed source IP addresses, which supports the idea that there was a SYN flood attack.

Response and mitigation

To effectively contain and mitigate the incident, the analyst takes immediate action, following established incident response procedures. These actions include the following processes:

- **Containment**:
  - o The analyst configures the firewall to rate-limit incoming SYN packets from the suspected IP address.
  - o They also implement temporary rules to block traffic from the entire IP range associated with the botnet.

- **Escalation and communication**:
  - o The analyst escalates the incident to the SOC manager and notifies the IT operations team.
  - o They initiate communication with the company's DDoS mitigation service provider for potential assistance.

- **Eradication**:
  - o The DDoS mitigation service is activated, scrubbing the incoming traffic and filtering out malicious packets.

- **Recovery**:
  - o Once the attack subsides, the analyst gradually relaxes the rate-limiting and blocking rules to restore normal traffic flow.

Post-incident analysis

After the incident is resolved, the SOC/IR conducts a thorough post-incident analysis:

- The analyst examines the attacker's TTPs and updates the organization's threat models accordingly.

- The effectiveness of the existing security controls is evaluated, and recommendations for improvement are made.

- The incident response process is reviewed, and any identified shortcomings are addressed.

This scenario demonstrates the SOC's ability to use real-time monitoring, data analysis, and a combination of tools and expertise to quickly detect, investigate, and mitigate a cyberattack, ensuring the continued availability and security of critical systems.

Key SOC performance indicators and compliance reporting

SOC metrics and reports are essential for demonstrating the effectiveness of security operations and driving improvement. By carefully tracking and reporting on key performance indicators, SOCs can enhance incident management, optimize resource allocation, and communicate the value of their activities to stakeholders. This section provides an in-depth look at the role of metrics and reporting in a SOC.

Measuring and optimizing cybersecurity performance

This process includes coming up with relevant metrics, measuring performance against these metrics, and putting in place plans for ongoing growth. This detailed guide shows you how to check and boost your cybersecurity:

- **Objectives**:
  - Establishing the organization's broader business goals that relate to cybersecurity.
  - These goals could include reducing financial losses due to cyber incidents, protecting sensitive data, maintaining regulatory compliance, and minimizing disruption to operations.
  - By understanding the *why* behind measurement, the SOC can align its efforts with the organization's strategic priorities.
- **Data sources and collection**:
  - SOCs have access to a wealth of data generated by various security tools and systems. This includes security logs collected from different sources, which we learned in the preceding topic, *Security event analysis*.
  - This data contains valuable information about potential threats, vulnerabilities, and the effectiveness of existing security controls.
- **Data synthesis and generating meaning**:
  - This involves analyzing and correlating the collected data to extract meaningful insights.
  - This is where SOC metrics come into play. Metrics are quantifiable measurements that track specific aspects of the SOC's performance and effectiveness.

- o **Examples of SOC metrics include**:
  - ▪ **MTTD**: The average time taken to identify a security incident.
  - ▪ **MTTR**: The average time taken to contain and remediate an incident.
  - ▪ **Number of security incidents**: The total number of incidents detected or reported within a specific period.
  - ▪ **Vulnerability remediation rate**: The percentage of vulnerabilities identified that are successfully addressed.
- **Reporting and presenting metrics**:
  - o Once the data is produced into meaningful metrics, it is crucial to communicate this information effectively to stakeholders.
  - o Reports and dashboards are created to present the metrics clearly and concisely, highlighting trends, areas of improvement, and the overall effectiveness of the SOC.
  - o These reports enable stakeholders to make informed decisions about resource allocation, security investments, and policy changes.
- **Decision-making and action**:
  - o The final phase involves using the insights gained from SOC metrics to drive decision-making and action.
  - o **This can involve**:
    - ▪ Adjusting security controls and processes to improve effectiveness.
    - ▪ Prioritizing vulnerabilities for remediation based on risk.
    - ▪ Allocating resources to areas with the highest security risk.
    - ▪ Identifying areas where additional training or awareness is needed.
    - ▪ Communicating security risks and mitigation strategies to senior management.

The following are the common SOC metrics (relevant to both in-house and MSSP SOCs):

- **MTTD**:
  - o Average time taken to identify a security incident.
  - o Lower MTTD indicates faster threat detection.
- **MTTR**:
  - o Average time taken to contain and mitigate a security incident.

- Lower MTTR indicates faster incident response.

- **Number of security incidents**:

  - Total count of security incidents detected and reported within a given period.

  - Tracks the overall volume and trends in security events.

- **False positive rate**:

  - Percentage of security alerts that turn out to be benign or non-threatening.

  - High false positive rates can lead to alert fatigue and wasted resources.

- **Security alert categorization**:

  - Breakdown of alerts by type (e.g., malware, phishing, intrusion).

  - Helps identify the most prevalent threat types.

- **Vulnerability remediation rate**:

  - Percentage of identified vulnerabilities that are remediated within a defined timeframe.

  - Measures the effectiveness of vulnerability management processes.

- **Compliance metrics**:

  - Percentage of systems or processes compliant with specific regulatory requirements or industry standards.

  - Demonstrates adherence to security regulations.

The following are the metrics more commonly used in in-house SOCs:

- **Staff performance metrics**:

  - Number of alerts triaged per analyst.

  - Number of incidents investigated per analyst.

  - Time spent on each incident.

  - These metrics help assess individual and team performance, identify training needs, and improve staffing levels.

- **Internal process efficiency**:

  - Time taken to complete specific security processes (e.g., patch deployment, configuration changes).

  - Helps identify bottlenecks and inefficiencies in internal workflows.

The following are the metrics more commonly used in MSSP SOCs:

- **Service level agreement (SLA) metrics**:
  o Response times for different types of incidents.
  o Uptime of security tools and services.
  o Customer satisfaction ratings.
  o These metrics are crucial for measuring MSSP performance and ensuring that they meet contractual obligations.

- **Cost per incident**:
  o The average cost incurred by the MSSP to handle a security incident.
  o Helps organizations evaluate the cost-effectiveness of outsourced SOC services.

Reporting

Regular reports are usually made by both in-house and MSSP SOCs that summarize key data and give information about the organization's security. These papers are made for a variety of readers:

- **Executive reports**: Executives should get high-level reports on strategic risks, compliance status, and general security performance.

- **Technical reports**: Detailed reports for IT and security teams, providing in-depth analysis of security events, vulnerabilities, and incident response activities.

- **Compliance reports**: Specifically focused on demonstrating compliance with regulatory requirements and industry standards.

The following are the considerations for SOC managers and leaders:

- **Benchmarking**: Comparing SOC metrics against industry benchmarks can provide valuable context and help identify areas where the organization can improve.

- **Customizable dashboards**: Dashboards that can be tailored to the specific needs of different stakeholders, providing relevant and actionable information at a glance.

- **Automated reporting**: Automating report generation can save time and resources while ensuring the timely delivery of information.

SOC metrics benefit the organization in the following ways:

- **Improved security posture**: By identifying weaknesses and areas for improvement, SOC metrics help organizations strengthen their defenses and reduce the risk of successful cyberattacks.

- **Improved resource allocation**: Metrics enable informed decision-making about where to allocate resources, ensuring that investments are focused on the most critical areas.

- **Demonstrable ROI**: By tracking the effectiveness of security measures, metrics can demonstrate the **return on investment** (**ROI**) in cybersecurity initiatives.

- **Enhanced communication**: Metrics help IT, security, and business stakeholders work together by giving them a common language to talk about cybersecurity risks and success.

- **Regulatory compliance**: Many regulations require that businesses should track and report on how well they keep their data safe. Metrics for SOC can help show that these standards are being met.

SOC compliance, governance, and framework

SOCs are not just technical teams; they also play a vital role in safeguarding trust. This trust is built on adherence to industry regulations, data protection laws, and internal policies. SOC compliance ensures alignment with these standards, protecting sensitive information and mitigating legal and reputational risks. Building on the cybersecurity compliance, control, and framework concepts covered in earlier chapters, this section will address aspects specific to SOCs.

Compliance in SOC

The following are the key compliance factors:

- **Data protection and privacy**: Regulations like the **General Data Protection Regulation** (**GDPR**) and **California Consumer Privacy Act** (**CCPA**) set stringent standards for collecting, processing, and storing personal data. SOCs must ensure that their practices align with these laws, encompassing areas like data minimization, consent, and data subject rights.

- **Industry-specific regulations**: Many sectors, such as healthcare (**Health Insurance Portability and Accountability Act** (**HIPAA**)), finance [**Gramm-Leach-Bliley Act** (**GLBA**), also known as the **Financial Services Modernization Act of 1999**, **Sarbanes-Oxley Act** (**SOX**), and critical infrastructure [**North American Electric Reliability Corporation Critical Infrastructure Protection** (**NERC CIP**)], have specific cybersecurity requirements. SOCs operating in these sectors must adhere to the specific security controls and reporting obligations mandated by these regulations.

- **Contractual obligations**: A lot of businesses have agreements with clients or business partners that require them to take certain security steps. It is up to the SOC to make sure that these formal duties are carried out.

Governance in SOC

Governance sets the strategy direction for the working of SOC. It includes the rules, procedures, and ways of making decisions that make sure the organization's cybersecurity actions are in line with its overall goals and objectives.

The following are the key governance factors:

- **Leadership and oversight**: A good framework for governance starts with clear direction and oversight from the board of directors and senior management. Making sure that cybersecurity is a top concern for the company and giving the SOC enough resources is done this way.

- **Risk management**: For finding, evaluating, and lowering hacking risks, you need a clear risk management process. The SOC is very important to this process because it gives risk ratings, incident reports, and suggestions for how to make things better.

- **Policies and procedures**: The SOC's actions are governed by clear policies and procedures that make sure everyone is held accountable. Some of the things that these should cover are responding to incidents, managing vulnerabilities, managing changes, and controlling access.

- **Roles and responsibilities**: Roles and responsibilities must be clearly stated within the SOC team in order for operations to run smoothly and efficiently. This includes giving analysts, incident responders, and other team members clear jobs to do

- **Communication and reporting**: The SOC should set up good ways for other stakeholders, like IT, legal, and senior management, to talk to each other. Reporting on the SOC's performance, security, and new threats on a regular basis helps keep everyone up to date and allows decisions to be made quickly.

Frameworks in SOC

Cybersecurity frameworks provide a structured approach to managing cybersecurity risks and improving a SOC team for any organization's security posture. They offer a set of guidelines, best practices, and standards that can be adopted and adapted to meet the specific needs of the SOC.

The following are the key cybersecurity frameworks:

- **NIST Cybersecurity Framework (CSF)**: A widely adopted framework that provides a common language for understanding and managing cybersecurity risk.

- **ISO 27001/27002**: A family of international standards for **information security management systems (ISMS)**.

- **CIS Controls**: A prioritized set of security controls designed to protect organizations against the most common cyber-attacks.

The following are the benefits of using a framework:

- **Structured approach**: Provides a structured approach to cybersecurity, ensuring that all aspects of security are considered.

- **Best practices**: Incorporates industry-proven best practices and lessons learned from past incidents.

- **Compliance**: Aligns with many regulatory requirements, simplifying compliance efforts.

- **Continuous improvement**: Promotes a continuous improvement cycle, ensuring that security practices evolve with the changing threat landscape.

SOCs can manage cyber risks, protect important assets, and build trust with stakeholders by putting in place a strong governance framework, following relevant compliance requirements, and using industry-recognized frameworks.

SOC best practices

While building a SOC is a significant undertaking, ensuring its ongoing success requires adherence to a set of best practices. These practices, distilled from industry experience and real-world lessons, empower SOC teams to proactively detect, respond to, and mitigate cyber threats, ultimately fortifying an organization's cybersecurity posture.

To establish and maintain a successful SOC, it is essential to follow a set of best practices that have been proven effective in real-world scenarios. The following are the best practices that encompass various aspects of SOC operations, and the following are the points to consider:

- **Define clear objectives and metrics**:

    o **Mission-driven**: Start by articulating a clear and concise mission statement for the SOC, outlining its purpose and goals. This mission should be aligned with the organization's overall security strategy and business objectives.

    o **Measurable goals**: Establish **Specific, Measurable, Achievable, Relevant, and Time-bound (SMART)** goals for the SOC. These goals should focus on KPIs such as MTTD, MTTR, and the number of successful attacks prevented.

    o **Regular review**: Continuously review and refine the SOC's objectives and metrics to ensure they remain relevant and aligned with the organization's evolving needs and the changing threat landscape.

- **Use threat intelligence**:

    o **Integrate threat feeds**: Incorporate threat intelligence feeds from reputable sources into your SIEM and other security tools. This provides valuable insights into the latest threats, vulnerabilities, and attacker TTPs.

- Contextualize alerts: By adding relevant information to security alerts with threat intelligence, analysts can quickly figure out how bad a threat is and how it might affect the system.

- Prioritize investigations: Use threat intelligence to prioritize investigations and focus resources on the most critical threats.

- **Automate and orchestrate security operations**:

  - Identify automation opportunities: Analyze your SOC workflows and identify repetitive, time-consuming tasks that can be automated. This could include alert triage, incident enrichment, and vulnerability scanning.

  - Implement SOAR: Deploy a SOAR platform to automate and streamline security operations. SOAR solutions can integrate with various security tools, allowing for automated incident response, threat hunting, and vulnerability management.

  - Continuously refine automation: Regularly review and improve your automation workflows to ensure they are efficient and effective.

- **Conduct regular testing and exercises**:

  - Penetration testing: Simulate real-world attacks to identify vulnerabilities in your systems and defenses.

  - Red team exercises: Emulate adversary tactics to test the SOC's detection and response capabilities.

  - Tabletop exercises: Simulate incident scenarios to practice and refine incident response procedures.

- **Embrace continuous improvement**:

  - Post-incident reviews: Conduct a thorough post-incident review to identify lessons learned and areas for improvement.

  - Regularly assess SOC performance: Track key metrics like MTTD and MTTR to evaluate the SOC's effectiveness and identify areas for optimization.

  - Adapt to evolving threats: Stay informed about emerging threats and vulnerabilities and adjust your security controls and processes accordingly.

- **Communication and collaboration**:

  - Maintain open communication channels: Ensure clear and timely communication between the SOC team, other departments, and senior management.

  - Share threat intelligence: Share threat intelligence with other organizations and participate in information-sharing communities.

- Build relationships with law enforcement: Establish relationships with law enforcement agencies to facilitate collaboration in the event of a major security incident.

- **People**:

  - Skilled and experienced personnel: How well the SOC works depends on how knowledgeable and dedicated its staff is. Security analysts, threat hunters, incident responders, engineers, and managers are all important parts of a well-rounded team because they each bring different skills and information to the table.

  - Continuous training and development: Cybersecurity is always changing, and people who work in SOCs need to stay on top of it. To keep your skills at a high level, you need to get training on the newest threats, vulnerabilities, and tools on a regular basis.

  - Mentoring and collaboration: Building a mindset of mentoring and teamwork within the SOC team helps people share their knowledge and learn new skills. Senior experts can help less experienced team members, and working together across departments can help people solve problems and make decisions more quickly.

  - Clear roles and responsibilities: Set clear roles and responsibilities for each team member so that everyone knows what they need to do to help the goal succeed. This clarity cuts down on confusion and boosts efficiency during incident reaction.

  - Promote a positive work environment: A positive work environment fosters teamwork, creativity, and innovation. Recognize and reward individual contributions, encourage work-life balance, and provide opportunities for career growth to attract and retain top talent.

- **Processes**:

  - Standardized workflows: Set up clear steps for all SOC tasks, like sorting alerts, responding to incidents, managing vulnerabilities, and looking for threats. Standardized processes make sure that everything is the same, works quickly, and can be done again and again. This lets the SOC run like a well-oiled machine.

  - Incident response playbooks: It make thorough plans for how to handle different kinds of security incidents. These playbooks show step-by-step ways to find, analyze, contain, eradicate, and recover, making sure that the reaction is quick and well-coordinated.

  - Change management: Implements a rigorous change management process to ensure that changes to systems and configurations are properly assessed and authorized before implementation. This helps prevent unintended security vulnerabilities from being introduced into the environment.

- o **Documentation**: Maintain comprehensive documentation of all SOC processes, procedures, and configurations. This documentation serves as a valuable reference for training, auditing, and troubleshooting.

- **Procedures**:

  - o **Standard Operating Procedures (SOPs)**: SOPs are detailed instructions for performing specific tasks within the SOC. They provide clear guidance for activities like log analysis, alert triage, and incident investigation, ensuring that tasks are performed consistently and accurately.

  - o **Runbooks**: Runbooks are more comprehensive than SOPs, providing step-by-step instructions for complex processes like incident response or disaster recovery. They often include checklists, decision trees, and escalation procedures to guide analysts through challenging situations.

  - o **Playbook execution**: During an incident, the SOC team follows the relevant playbook to ensure a coordinated and effective response. This involves identifying the type of incident, gathering necessary information, escalating to the appropriate stakeholders, and taking actions to contain and remediate the threat.

- **Ensure compliance and audit readiness**:

  - o **Compliance monitoring**: Continuously monitor and ensure compliance with relevant regulations and standards [e.g., GDPR, HIPAA, **Payment Card Industry Data Security Standard (PCI DSS)**].

  - o **Audit preparation**: Maintain detailed documentation and evidence to support internal and external audits.

- **Invest in strong access and identity management**:

  - o **Least privilege principle**: Implement the principle of least privilege to restrict access to sensitive systems and data.

  - o **Multi-factor authentication**: Enforce **multi-factor authentication (MFA)** for critical systems and privileged accounts.

- **Use metrics for performance measurement and improvement**:

  - o **Key metrics**: Track KPIs such as MTTD, MTTR, false positive rate, and incident volume.

  - o **Continuous improvement**: Use metrics to identify areas for improvement and implement changes to enhance SOC performance.

- **Adopt a security-first culture**:

  - o **Awareness programs**: Run security awareness programs to educate employees about their role in maintaining security.

- o **Encourage reporting**: Foster a culture where employees are encouraged to report suspicious activities without fear of repercussions.

- **Scalability and flexibility**:

  - o **Scalable solutions**: Implement solutions that can scale with the organization's growth and evolving threat landscape.

  - o **Flexible procedures**: Ensure SOC procedures are flexible enough to adapt to new technologies and changing business needs.

SOC automation

SOCs are dealing with a problem that has never been seen before: a huge amount of security alerts and data. Cyber threats are coming at us so fast and in such large numbers that manual analysis and reaction just cannot keep up. This is where SOC automation is essential, as it changes the way security teams work by automating boring chores, streamlining workflows, and making threat detection and response faster, more accurate, and more effective.

Need for SOC automation

Since we have already discussed the importance of automation for cybersecurity, let us observe how important it is for the SOC. SOC today get a lot of security reports from firewalls, intrusion detection systems, endpoint protection solutions, and threat intelligence feeds, among other places. Even the best security analysts can get overwhelmed by this alert storm, which can cause alert fatigue, slow reaction times, and missed threats.

Also, cyberattacks are getting smarter, which means they need more in-depth research and investigations, which puts even more pressure on SOC resources. Tasks like triaging alerts, adding more information to incidents, and gathering proof by hand take a lot of time and can go wrong.

These problems can be solved by SOC automation, which uses technology to make security processes more efficient and faster. By automating tasks that are done over and over again and take a lot of time, analysts are free to work on more important tasks like looking for threats and investigating incidents.

The following are the key benefits of SOC automation:

- **Increased efficiency and productivity**: Automation eliminates manual tasks, allowing analysts to focus on high-value activities like threat hunting and investigation. This leads to faster response times, improved productivity, and a more efficient use of resources.

- **Reduced MTTD and MTTR**: Automated workflows can quickly triage and prioritize alerts, reducing the time it takes to detect and respond to security incidents. This is critical in today's fast-paced threat landscape, where every second counts.

- **Improved accuracy and consistency**: Automated processes are less prone to human error than manual tasks, ensuring consistent and reliable results. Automation can also help to enforce standardized procedures, improving the overall quality and accuracy of security operations.

- **Scalability**: Automation enables SOCs to scale their operations without the need for proportional increases in staff. This is especially important for organizations with limited resources or those experiencing rapid growth.

- **Cost reduction**: By automating repetitive tasks, SOCs can reduce their operational costs and free up budget for other security initiatives.

The following are the key areas for SOC automation:

- **Alert triage and enrichment**: Automation can help filter out false positives, enrich alerts with contextual information from threat intelligence feeds, and prioritize alerts based on severity and risk.

- **Incident response**: Automated workflows can guide analysts through the incident response process, from initial triage to containment, eradication, and recovery. This ensures a consistent and efficient response to security incidents.

- **Threat hunting**: Automation can assist in threat hunting by automating data collection, analysis, and reporting. This allows analysts to focus on identifying patterns and anomalies that may indicate advanced threats.

- **Vulnerability management**: Automated tools can scan for vulnerabilities, prioritize them based on risk, and even apply patches automatically, reducing the time and effort required for remediation.

- **Reporting and compliance**: Automation can generate reports on SOC performance, compliance status, and other key metrics, streamlining communication with stakeholders and ensuring that the SOC meets regulatory requirements.

Implementing SOC automation

While implementing automation in a SOC environment can seem daunting, a strategic approach focusing on starting with small, manageable steps, selecting appropriate tools, and developing well-defined processes can pave the way for a smooth and successful automation journey.

A successful automation journey is built on a solid foundation. Consider these key steps and pillars for your implementation strategy:

1. **Start small and iterate**: Do not try to automate everything at once. Begin with low-hanging fruit, such as automating repetitive tasks that are prone to human error. As you gain experience and confidence, you can gradually expand your automation efforts.

2. **Choose the right tools**: Select automation tools that are compatible with your existing security infrastructure and can be easily integrated with your other security solutions. Consider factors like scalability, ease of use, and customization options.

3. **Develop well-defined processes**: Before automating any process, ensure that you have a clear understanding of the steps involved and the desired outcomes. Document your processes in detail to ensure consistency and accuracy.

4. **Monitor and measure**: Continuously monitor the performance of your automated workflows and measure their effectiveness. Adjust your processes and automation rules as needed to ensure that they are meeting your objectives.

Some practical examples

To bridge the gap between theoretical knowledge and real-world application, this section delves into practical examples of SOC operations. The following are some practical examples with code samples, demonstrating how security professionals can utilize various tools and techniques to enhance threat detection and response. More examples can be found on the GitHub page.

Log parsing examples

Log parsing is crucial for transforming raw log data into a structured format that security analysts can easily understand and analyze.

Example: Firewall log

- **Raw log entry**:

```
Oct 24 10:00:00 firewall1 IN=eth0 OUT=eth1 SRC=192.168.1.20 DST=10.0.0.5
PROTO=TCP SPT=5000 DPT=80 SYN
```

- **Parsed output**:

```
{
  "timestamp": "Oct 24 10:00:00",
  "source_interface": "eth0",
  "destination_interface": "eth1",
  "source_ip": "192.168.1.20",
  "destination_ip": "10.0.0.5",
  "protocol": "TCP",
  "source_port": "5000",
  "destination_port": "80",
  "tcp_flags": "SYN"
}
```

A parsing tool reads this string and extracts the key-value pairs. It identifies *SRC=192.168.1.20* as the source IP address, *DST=10.0.0.5* as the destination IP, and *DPT=80* as the destination port, indicating a web traffic request. Other important fields, like the *PROTO (TCP)* and *TCP_ Flags (SYN)* are also extracted and categorized. This structured data is then sent to the SIEM for analysis.

This same principle applies to all data sources, whether it is a web server log, where the parser extracts the HTTP method and status code, or a Windows Event Log, where it identifies the Event ID and username. Effective parsing is the foundation of all security monitoring and analysis, and it is typically handled by log shippers or built-in SIEM ingestion capabilities.

Note: Significance of Event ID 4624 (Successful Logon)

The 4624 event ID in Windows logs is essential for monitoring and analyzing account activity, particularly for security purposes:

- **Indicates legitimate user logins or service authentications.**

- **Useful for identifying potential unauthorized access or lateral movement within a network.**

- **If an unusual IP address is present, it could indicate an external threat or compromised credentials.**

- **Provides a record of logon activities for auditing purposes, such as monitoring privileged account access.**

Tools and techniques for log parsing: SOC analysts use various tools and techniques for log parsing, including the following:

- **Regular expressions**: Defining patterns to match and extract specific data from log files.

- **Log parsing tools**: Using specialized software like **Fluentd**, **Logstash**, or **Syslog-ng** to automate the parsing process.

- **SIEM systems**: SIEM systems often have built-in parsing capabilities to process log data.

SIEM query writing and rule creation examples

A core skill for any SOC analyst is writing queries to search through vast amounts of log data and create custom detection rules. While the specific syntax varies between platforms like **Splunk**, **Azure Sentinel**, or the **ELK Stack**, the underlying logic is the same, which is to identify patterns that match known malicious behavior.

Let us look at a common example, creating a rule to detect a potential brute-force login attack. An analyst would write a query to find a high number of failed login attempts from a single source. Using a syntax similar to Splunk's **Search Processing Language** (**SPL**), the query logic would be:

1. **Search and filter**: First, search through authentication logs for all events that represent a failed login.

    eventtype=authentication_failure status=failure

2. **Aggregate and count**: Next, count the number of these failures for each unique source IP address over a short time frame (e.g., five minutes).

    | timechart span=5m count by src_ip

3. **Set a threshold**: Finally, filter those results to only show the IP addresses that cross a specific threshold (e.g., more than 10 failed attempts).

    | where count > 10

Once this query is validated, it can be saved as a real-time detection rule. If an IP address ever meets these conditions, the SIEM will automatically generate a high-priority alert for the SOC team to investigate immediately. This same logical approach, which is filtering, aggregating, and setting thresholds, is used to build custom rules for detecting other threats, such as malware activity or data exfiltration patterns.

More examples can be found on the GitHub page.

SOAR playbook automation using Python API scripts

SOAR platforms use automation to streamline incident response, threat hunting, and vulnerability management. Python is commonly used to write scripts that integrate different security tools via their APIs. Some examples are as follows:

Example 1: Automating alert enrichment: This script demonstrates how to automatically enrich security alerts with threat intelligence data using a Python script to integrate with a TIP API.

*   **Python script**:

```
import requests
import json


def enrich_alert_with_threat_intel(alert_data):
    """
    Enriches a security alert with threat intelligence data.
    """
    ip_address = alert_data.get("ip_address")
```

```
    # Threat intelligence API endpoint
    tip_api_url = f"https://api.threatintelligenceprovider.com/ip/{ip_
address}"

try:
    response = requests.get(tip_api_url)
    threat_data = response.json()

    # Extract relevant threat information
    reputation = threat_data.get("reputation")
    malware_families = threat_data.get("malware_families")

    # Add threat intelligence data to the alert
    alert_data["threat_reputation"] = reputation
    alert_data["malware_families"] = malware_families

    print(f"Alert enriched with threat intelligence: {alert_data}")

except requests.exceptions.RequestException as e:
    print(f"Error querying threat intelligence: {e}")

return alert_data

# Example alert data
alert_data = {"ip_address": "192.168.1.10"}
enriched_alert = enrich_alert_with_threat_intel(alert_data)
```

- **Explanation**:
  - The script takes **alert_data** as input, which contains information about the security alert, such as the IP address involved.
  - It uses the **requests** library to make a GET request to a threat intelligence API endpoint to retrieve information about the IP address.
  - The script parses the JSON response from the API and extracts relevant threat information, such as the IP address's reputation and associated malware families.
  - This threat intelligence data is added to the **alert_data** dictionary, enriching the alert with valuable context.
  - The enriched alert data is then printed to the console.

    o   Error handling is included to manage potential issues with the API request.

Example 2: Automating incident response: This script demonstrates how to automate incident response actions, such as isolating an infected host, using a Python script to integrate with an EDR API.

- **Python script**:

```python
import requests
import json

def isolate_host(host_id):
    """
    Isolates an infected host using the EDR API.
    """
    edr_api_url = f"https://api.edrprovider.com/hosts/{host_id}/isolate"
    headers = {
        "Authorization": "Bearer YOUR_API_KEY",
        "Content-Type": "application/json"
    }

    try:
        response = requests.post(edr_api_url, headers=headers)
        response.raise_for_status()  # Raise an exception for bad status codes

        if response.status_code == 200:
            print(f"Host {host_id} successfully isolated.")
        else:
            print(f"Failed to isolate host {host_id}.")

    except requests.exceptions.RequestException as e:
        print(f"Error isolating host: {e}")

# Example usage
host_id = "example-host-123"
isolate_host(host_id)
```

- **Explanation**:

    o   The script defines a function **isolate_host** that takes **host_id** as input, which is the unique identifier of the host to be isolated.

o   It constructs the EDR API endpoint URL for isolating the specified host.

o   The script sets the necessary headers, including the authorization token for accessing the EDR API and the content type.

o   It uses the **requests** library to make a POST request to the EDR API endpoint to initiate the host isolation.

o   The script checks the response status code. If the host is successfully isolated (status code 200), it prints a success message. Otherwise, it prints a failure message.

o   Error handling is included to manage potential exceptions during the API request.

These examples illustrate how Python scripts can be used to automate security operations by integrating with different security tools via their APIs. SOAR platforms leverage these types of scripts to create playbooks that orchestrate complex workflows and automate security tasks. More samples and examples can be found on the GitHub page.

Future of SOC automation

SOC automation has a bright future ahead of it. As AI and machine learning keep getting better, we can expect to see even more advanced automation features that will make SOC processes even more efficient and effective.

By using automation, SOCs can stay ahead of the curve and handle the growing amount of security data and risks more efficiently. This will let them focus on more important tasks, like looking for threats and making their company's security better on purpose.

Handling security alerts, events, and incidents

A SOC is constantly bombarded with a barrage of security alerts, events, and potential incidents. Each signal, whether a minor anomaly or a full-blown attack, requires careful attention and a well-defined response strategy.

Understanding alerts, events, and incidents

Understanding the differences between alerts, events, and incidents is critical in cybersecurity. These terms, while seemingly interchangeable, represent distinct stages in the lifecycle of a potential security breach:

- **Security alerts**: A notification generated by a security tool or system indicating a potential security issue. Alerts can range from benign informational messages to critical warnings of active attacks.

- **Security events**: An observable occurrence within a system or network. Not all events are security-related, but those that deviate from normal behavior or match known threat patterns are flagged as potential security concerns.

- **Security incidents**: A confirmed security event that compromises the confidentiality, integrity, or availability of an organization's assets. Incidents typically require a coordinated response to contain, eradicate, and recover from the breach.

The following are the best practices for handling security alerts, events, and incidents:

- **Establish clear procedures**: Develop comprehensive and well-documented incident response procedures that outline the steps to be taken for each type of incident. These procedures should be regularly reviewed and updated to reflect the latest threats and best practices.

- **Prioritize alerts**: Not all alerts are created equal. Prioritize alerts based on their severity, potential impact, and relevance to the organization's critical assets.

- **Use threat intelligence:** Use threat intelligence to contextualize alerts and identify known threats and vulnerabilities. This helps to focus investigations and prioritize response actions.

- **Automate repetitive tasks**: Automate routine tasks like alert triage and incident enrichment to free up analysts' time for more complex investigations.

- **Collaborate effectively**: Incident response is a team effort. Ensure clear communication and collaboration between SOC analysts, incident responders, IT teams, and other stakeholders.

- **Document everything**: Thoroughly document all aspects of the incident response process, including the timeline of events, actions taken, and lessons learned. This documentation is essential for forensic analysis, compliance reporting, and continuous improvement.

- **Continuous improvement**: Regularly review and refine your incident response procedures based on lessons learned from past incidents. Conduct tabletop exercises and simulations to test your incident response plans and identify areas for improvement.

In the preceding sections, we thoroughly understood the ways to handle these security signals, from the first detection to the final resolution. We emphasized how important the SOC is to keeping an organization's cyber resilience. Here is a more in-depth look at the different types of security reports, events, and incidents that the SOC team usually deals with, along with the evidence and data that need to be gathered for an investigation and the next steps that need to be taken in each case. In terms of protection, these are some common situations:

- **Phishing alert**:
    - **Description**: An email security gateway (e.g., Microsoft Defender) flags a potentially malicious email containing a suspicious link or attachment.
    - **Artifacts/Information**:
        - **Alert metadata**: Source IP address, destination IP address, timestamp, severity level, alert type/category, event description.

- **Email headers**: Analyze for spoofed addresses or unusual routing patterns.
- **Link analysis**: Determine the destination of the link and its reputation.
- **Attachment scanning**: Scan attachments for malware or other malicious content.
- **Threat intelligence**: Correlate with known phishing campaigns and IOCs.

o **Actions**:

- **Verification**: Analyze email headers and contents to verify the phishing attempt.
- **Notification**: Inform the targeted user(s) and provide guidance on recognizing phishing emails.
- **Containment**: Block the malicious **Uniform Resource Locator** (**URLs**) or email addresses on email gateways and proxy servers. Quarantine the email.
- **Investigation**: Check for any signs of successful phishing attacks, such as unauthorized access to accounts.
- **Awareness training**: Conduct user awareness training to prevent future phishing incidents.
- **Reporting**: Document the incident and update threat intelligence feeds with new IOCs.

- **Malware alert**:

  o **Description**: EDR or antivirus software detects a potentially malicious file execution.

  o **Artifacts/Information**:

    - **Alert metadata**: File Hash, Timestamp, Severity level, Alert type/category, Event description.
    - **Network traffic logs**: **Packet captures** (**PCAP**), NetFlow data, firewall logs, IDS/IPS logs.
    - **System logs**: Operating system logs, endpoint security logs.
    - **Endpoint data**: File system artifacts (file hashes, file metadata), memory dumps, running processes.
    - **Threat intelligence feeds**: IOCs such as file hashes, domain names.
    - **User and access data**: User activity logs

- **File hash**: Check against threat intelligence databases for known malware.

- **Process information**: Identify the process associated with the file execution.

- **Network connections**: Monitor for any unusual outbound traffic.

- **Memory dumps**: Capture memory snapshots to analyze for malicious activity.

o **Actions**:

- **Initial analysis**: Verify the alert by analyzing system and network logs to confirm the presence of malware.

- **Containment**: Isolate the infected system from the network to prevent further spread.

- **Eradication**: Remove the malware using antivirus or EDR tools.

- **Recovery**: Restore the system from clean backups and re-image if necessary.

- **Post-incident analysis**: Conduct a root cause analysis to determine how the malware entered the system and identify any security gaps.

- **Reporting**: Document the incident, findings, and remediation steps in an incident report.

- **Intrusion alert**:

o **Description**: An IDS or IPS detects a possible network intrusion attempt.

o **Artifacts/Information**:

- **Alert metadata**: Source IP address, destination IP address, timestamp, severity level, alert type/category, event description.

- **Network traffic logs (PCAP)**: Analyze network traffic for suspicious activity.

- **Firewall logs**: Review firewall logs for blocked or allowed traffic.

- **IDS/IPS alerts**: Examine alert details for attack signatures and patterns.

- **Threat intelligence**: Correlate with known attack techniques and IOCs.

o **Actions**:

- **Verification**: Analyze IDS/IPS logs and other network traffic logs to verify the intrusion attempt.

- **Containment**: Isolate the affected systems or network segments to prevent further intrusion. Block malicious traffic.

- **Investigation**: Identify the method and extent of the intrusion by examining system and network logs. Investigate the source of the attack and any potential impact.

- **Eradication**: Remove any malicious software or unauthorized access points found during the investigation.

- **Recovery**: Restore systems to a known good state and patch vulnerabilities.

  o **Post-incident analysis**: Conduct a detailed analysis to identify security gaps and improve defenses. Harden security controls and update IDS/IPS signatures.

- **Reporting**: Document the incident, the investigation process, and the remediation steps taken.

- **Account compromise alert**:

  o **Description**: Unusual login activity or unauthorized access attempts on a user account.

  o **Artifacts/Information**:

    - **Alert metadata**: Source IP address, destination IP address, timestamp, severity level, alert type/category, event description.

    - **System logs**: Authentication logs, Active Directory logs, Operating system logs, Application logs, File system artifacts, Network connections, Running processes.

    - **Authentication logs**: Review login failures, successful logins from unusual locations, or multiple failed attempts.

    - **User activity logs**: Look for unauthorized actions or unusual behavior.

    - **Endpoint data**: Analyze for suspicious processes or files on the user's device.

    - **Threat intelligence feeds**: Known attacker TTPs

  o **Actions**:

    - **Verification**: Confirm the account compromise by analyzing authentication logs and user activity.

    - **Containment**: Disable the compromised account or reset its credentials.

    - **Investigation**: Determine how the account was compromised (e.g., phishing, brute force, credential stuffing).

    - **Eradication**: Remove any malware or unauthorized access mechanisms associated with the compromise.

- **Recovery**: Reinstate the account with enhanced security measures such as MFA.

- **Awareness training**: Educate the affected user(s) on recognizing phishing and securing accounts.

- **Reporting**: Document the incident, including the method of compromise and steps taken to secure the account.

- **DLP alert**:

  o **Description**: A DLP solution detects a policy violation, such as the attempted transfer of sensitive data outside the organization.

  o **Artifacts/Information**:

    - **Data in motion**: Analyze the content and destination of the data transfer.

    - **User involved**: Identify the user responsible for the data transfer.

    - **Data classification**: Determine the sensitivity of the data.

  o **Actions**:

    - **Verification**: Confirm the DLP alert by analyzing logs and identifying attempts to move sensitive data outside the organization.

    - **Containment**: Block the data transfer and isolate the affected systems if necessary.

    - **Investigation**: Identify the source, method, and intent of the data loss attempt. Investigate the reason for the transfer and any potential policy violations.

    - **Eradication**: Remove any software or mechanisms used for data exfiltration.

    - **Recovery**: Restore any affected systems and reinforce DLP policies.

    - **Post-incident analysis**: Review the incident to identify any gaps in DLP controls and enhance monitoring. Remediate any vulnerabilities that may have allowed the transfer.

    - **Reporting**: Document the incident, including the type of data involved and the remediation steps taken.

- **Anomaly detection alert**:

  o **Description**: A UEBA tool flags unusual behavior that deviates from established baselines.

  o **Artifacts/Information**:

- **User activity logs**: Review the user's recent activity for anomalies.

- **Endpoint data**: Analyze for any suspicious processes or files.

- **Network traffic logs**: Examine network connections for unusual destinations or protocols.

  o **Actions**:

- **Verification**: Confirm the anomaly by cross-referencing logs and understanding the baseline behavior.

- **Containment**: If the anomaly indicates a threat, isolate the affected systems or users.

- **Investigation**: Determine the cause of the anomaly and assess if it indicates a security incident.

- **Eradication**: If malicious activity is confirmed, remove the threat actor's access and any related malware.

- **Recovery**: Restore affected systems to normal operation and validate their integrity.

- **Monitoring**: Increase monitoring on systems showing anomalies to detect any further suspicious behavior.

- **Reporting**: Document the incident, including the nature of the anomaly, the investigation process, and actions taken.

- **Ransomware attacks**:

  o **Description**: EDR or antivirus software detects file encryption activity or ransom notes on endpoints.

  o **Artifacts/Information**:

- **File system changes**: Examine file modifications and newly created files (e.g., encrypted files, ransom notes).

- **Network traffic**: Look for communication with known ransomware C2 servers.

- **Endpoint data**: File system artifacts, memory dumps, running processes.

- **Backup status**: Verify the availability and integrity of backups for recovery.

- **Threat intelligence feeds**: IOCs such as ransomware signatures and file hashes.

  o **Actions**:

- **Verification**: Confirm the ransomware attack by identifying encrypted files and ransom notes.

- **Containment**: Isolate infected systems to prevent the spread of ransomware.

- **Eradication**: Remove ransomware using decryption tools if available or format and restore from clean backups.

- **Recovery**: Restore affected systems and files from backups.

- **Post-incident analysis**: Conduct a root cause analysis to determine how the ransomware entered the system and address vulnerabilities.

- **Awareness training**: Educate users on recognizing and preventing ransomware.

- **Reporting**: Document the incident, remediation steps, and lessons learned in an incident report.

Handling security alerts, events, and incidents is a complex and demanding task, but it is also a critical one. By implementing a structured incident response process, leveraging the right tools and technologies, and investing in the training and development of SOC analysts, organizations can significantly improve their ability to detect, respond to, and mitigate cyber threats. The SOC serves as a vital hub for cybersecurity operations, protecting critical assets and ensuring business continuity in the face of an ever-evolving threat landscape.

Conclusion

Throughout this chapter, we have thoroughly examined the intricate aspects of SOCs, including their fundamental functions, architectural considerations, and the crucial trio of people, process, and technology. We have witnessed the transformation of SOCs from being reactive alert centers to becoming proactive cybersecurity powerhouses. They now use advanced technologies and methodologies to swiftly and accurately detect, analyze, and respond to threats.

We have thoroughly analyzed the various models of SOC implementation, including in-house, MSSP, and hybrid options. Each model has its own unique strengths and considerations to take into account. We have covered the essential aspects of SOC operations, including establishing clear objectives and promoting teamwork, utilizing threat intelligence, and embracing automation. We have emphasized the crucial role of incident response and the significance of constantly adjusting to the constantly evolving threat landscape.

Understanding the importance of a SOC goes beyond the mere utilization of tools and technologies. It is a crucial investment that has the potential to greatly strengthen an organization's cybersecurity defenses. With a deep understanding of the principles and practices outlined in this chapter, you have the knowledge and skills to create, construct, and manage a SOC that will successfully safeguard your organization's vital assets and data.

Always keep in mind that achieving cybersecurity excellence is an ongoing process. As technology advances, new threats will inevitably arise, and it is crucial for the SOC to adapt and stay ahead. With a proactive, adaptable, and collaborative approach, your SOC can become a powerful force in combating cybercrime and protecting your organization's future in the digital age

In the next chapter, we will look into the critical components of **incident response (IR)**, exploring its fundamental concepts, stages, and its importance within the larger threat management environment. It will cover the creation of a strong IR plan, outlining procedures for detection, containment, eradication, and recovery. We will also discuss the composition of an effective IR team and the collaborative efforts required to minimize the impact of security incidents.

Join our Discord space

Join our Discord workspace for latest updates, offers, tech happenings around the world, new releases, and sessions with the authors:

https://discord.bpbonline.com

CHAPTER 6
Incident Response Management

Introduction

In cybersecurity, change is the only constant. Companies must deal with a growing number of complex dangers. Being able to quickly and effectively handle events is not only a strategic advantage in this ever-changing world, but it is also a must considering the business perspective. This chapter is a complete guide for cybersecurity experts, people who react to cyberattacks, and everyone else who wants to break into cyberspace. This chapter carefully balances academic background with useful tips for figuring out how to handle complicated incident response situations. Strategic integration of threat intelligence is at the heart of this complete guide that offers a forward-looking method that will change incident response from a reactive necessity to a proactive defense mechanism.

This chapter gets down to the specifics of finding incidents, containing them, getting rid of them, and recovering from them. Real-life examples and useful insights provided in this chapter will give readers methods that they can use to deal with problems quickly and effectively.

Structure

This chapter will include the following topics:

- Introduction to incident response

- Incident response team

- Incident response planning: preparation and procedures

- Incident response detection and analysis

- Containment

- Eradication

Objectives

In the field of cybersecurity, professionals are always on guard. Despite all the work that has been put into keeping intrusions out, even the strongest security methods can be broken. Right now, incident reaction is a tool that cannot be done without. Security incident management is a well-planned way to find, stop, get rid of, and recover from security breaches; to ensure that they cause minimal or no damage to our important data and systems. Well-thought internal risk management plans that are regularly carried out are not just nice to have, but they are also essential for effective danger management and being able to do this makes it easier to switch from a protective to an active stance, which restores balance and mitigates the risk of harm.

In this chapter, an all-encompassing plan for building and running a strong IR program is laid out. In the first step in our study of IR, we will look at its basic ideas and stages, along with its importance and place in the larger threat management environment. Next, we will discuss the most important parts of building a good internal relations team, including laying out roles and responsibilities, and making sure there are good lines of contact. This chapter is mostly about making an all-encompassing IR strategy, which includes planning, methods, and ways of communicating. Towards the end of this chapter, we will provide the information and tools that you would need to handle every part of the incident response cycle, like finding the problem, analyzing it, containing it, getting rid of it, and recovering from it.

Introduction to incident response

In the face of a security breach, a well-coordinated response is important. While *Chapter 1, Introduction to Blue Teaming,* introduced the concept of **incident response** (**IR**), this chapter provides the operational blueprint for execution. A successful response is not improvised; it is the result of a dedicated team operating with a clear, pre-defined plan. We will begin by detailing the essential roles and responsibilities that form a capable incident response team and then proceed to the critical process of building and maintaining a comprehensive **incident response plan** (**IRP**)

This figure illustrates the life cycle of an incident, explaining the incident response management:

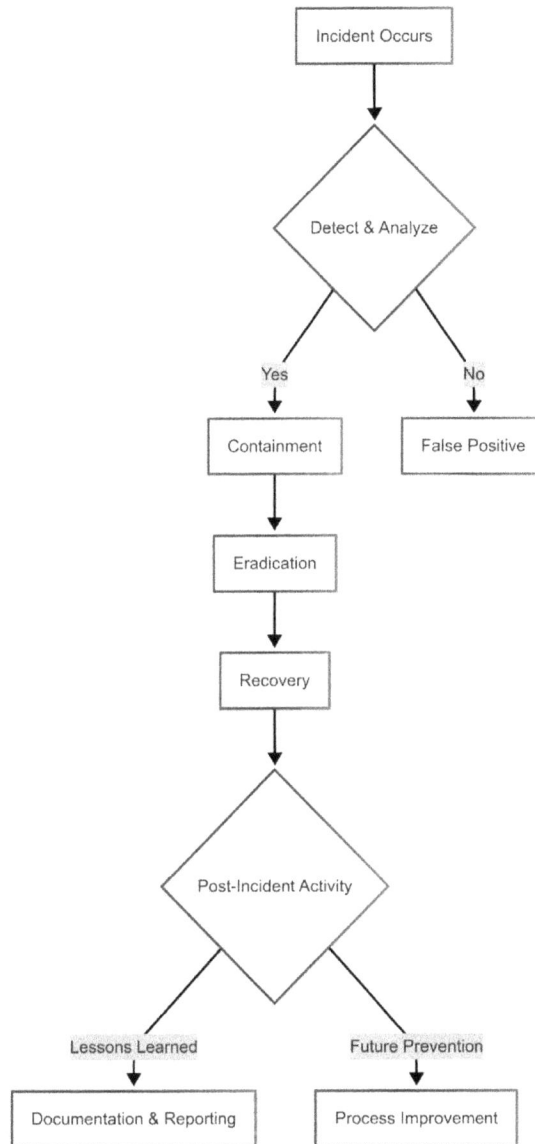

Figure 6.1: Incident response management

Incident response team

Building a high-performing incident response team requires skill, synergy, and trust. Building a diverse team requires careful selection of individuals skilled in both technical expertise and strong communication, analysis, and critical thinking. It is paramount to build a culture of trust and cooperation, to keep them running smoothly when things get busy. Remember, the IR team is also called the **Computer Security Incident Response Team** (**CSIRT**).

Spending money to build up, teach, and improve your IR team is not a cost, but an investment to strengthen your company. You can use this powerful tool to protect yourself from constantly changing cyber threats. A skilled team with clear communication and sharp analysis will shield your company from any digital storm.

This is just the beginning; there is still a lot to learn about incident response teams. In the upcoming sections, we will describe each role in detail, along with the specific skills and tools needed to fight cyber threats.

Note: **Please keep in mind that these jobs may have different names or descriptions in different organizations.**

Now, let us look at what they do and how they do it.

Scope of work

The IR or CSIRT team is assigned a wide range of activities, all of which are designed to reduce the severity and consequences of security incidents, listed as follows:

- **Detection and analysis of incidents**: The IR team continuously monitors networks, log data, and threat intelligence reports to detect any anomalies that could indicate malicious activity. You can consider them as cyber-sentinels that are constantly on the lookout for even the tiniest indication of an impending attack.

- **Containment and isolation**: After identifying a potential threat, the team promptly initiates measures to prevent additional harm by isolating compromised systems and networks. One can envision them constructing firewalls to encircle compromised areas, thereby preventing the fire from spreading to the entire digital landscape.

- **Eradication and remediation**: The next step is to figure out the cause of the event and stop it. This could mean cleaning up the system, fixing bugs, and getting rid of malware. As cyber-exterminators, their job is to carefully examine and get rid of digital pests.

- **Recovery and restoration**: After the danger has been neutralized, it might be necessary to get back data, fix systems, and get things back to normal without stopping. Think of them as the digital doctors who fix broken systems and heal wounds.

- **Post-incident analysis and adaptation**: IR team thoroughly examines the incident, detects the exploited vulnerabilities, and revises its protocols and defenses to enhance readiness against forthcoming threats. They assume the role of digital battlefield historians, guaranteeing that the organization gains insights from previous conflicts and improves its defensive measures.

Roles

The IR team comprises the following roles:

- **Incident commander**: The incident commander leads the CSIRT team's response to a security incident. They are responsible for making decisions about how to contain the incident, eradicate the threat, and recover from the incident.

- **Security analyst**: Security analysts are responsible for investigating security incidents and identifying the root cause of the problem. Additionally, they might be responsible for developing and implementing security controls to prevent future incidents.

- **Network engineer**: Network engineers are responsible for troubleshooting and repairing network problems. They may also be responsible for implementing security controls on the network.

- **Forensics investigator**: Forensics investigators are responsible for collecting and analyzing evidence from security incidents. Additionally, they might be responsible for providing information about their findings.

- **Threat intelligence analyst**: Threat intelligence analysts are responsible for collecting and analyzing information about cyber threats. They may also be responsible for developing and implementing threat detection and prevention strategies.

- **Vulnerability researcher**: Vulnerability researchers are responsible for identifying and reporting vulnerabilities in software and systems.

- **Malware analyst**: Malware analysts are responsible for analyzing malware samples to understand how they work and how to detect and prevent them.

- **Threat hunter**: Threat hunters employ their analytical ability and innovative thinking to systematically examine networks and data to detect vulnerabilities and potential attacks before their escalation, thereby improving the incident prevention capabilities of the team as a whole.

Establishing incident response preparation and procedures

A primary challenge in incident management is the operational chaos that impedes an effective response to a cybersecurity event. An **incident response plan** (**IRP**) directly addresses this challenge by functioning as an authoritative guide. It equips the team with the necessary instructions and framework to facilitate timely, coordinated, and effective decision-making throughout the incident lifecycle.

Complete preparedness

IRP is a comprehensive roadmap to navigate the complexities of an incident. It needs to address every aspect, right from detection and containment to recovery and post-incident analysis. Key areas to cover include, are roles and responsibilities, communication protocols, customer notifications, cyber insurance involvement, and many more, which we will learn as we proceed further in this chapter. Let us start by creating the plan for IR in the following subsection.

Creating incident response plan

Building a robust IRP requires a structured approach. The following is a roadmap, which provides a step-by-step guide to get you started:

1. **Risk assessment**: Identify your organization's critical assets and potential threats to understand your vulnerability landscape.

2. **Define response stages**: Outline the phases of incident response, from detection and containment to eradication and recovery.

3. **Develop procedures**: For each stage, create detailed procedures, including specific actions, tools, and decision-making frameworks.

4. **Identify resources**: The management should allocate the necessary personnel, tools, and budget to support your IR plan.

5. **Testing and refinement**: Regularly test your plan through tabletop exercises and simulations to ensure its effectiveness and identify areas for improvement.

Your IR plan is a living document; it should evolve with your organization and be updated as the threat landscape changes. You need to test your plan regularly with the aid of tabletop exercises and simulations, which will help you identify weaknesses and ensure everyone knows their role.

Role of tabletop exercises

In real life, fire drills teach us how to get out of a building quickly and quietly, in case of an emergency. Similarly, in the digital world, tabletop drills simulate cyber incidents so that we can test our IRPs and prepare our team for when things go wrong. These drills are not just discussions about theory; they are full-immersion simulations that put your team in the middle of a cyber crisis. This lets them practice their skills, find holes in the plan, and learn how to work together effectively when things get tough.

Importance of tabletop exercises

How would your organization respond to a sophisticated ransomware attack that cripples critical systems and threatens sensitive data? Tabletop exercises provide a safe environment to explore this scenario and prepare for the unexpected. In the previous subsection, we understood the roles that tabletop exercise plays. Now, let us understand the importance of tabletop exercises:

- **Testing the plan**: IRP might look great on paper; however, whether it will work in the real world is always a concern. Tabletop activities point out the weaknesses, vulnerabilities, and gray areas, which can help you improve the steps and ensure you make sure everyone on your team understands them.

- **Training the team**: These activities give your IR team very useful real-world experience. They practice using their skills in a simulated setting, which helps them get better at leadership, speaking, and making decisions in a safe setting.

- **Identifying gaps**: Simulations highlight the improvement areas, thus pointing out where you need to improve your resources, tools, or knowledge. During these exercises and simulations, you might identify that there are not enough ways to communicate, or some team members lack a few skills, or they do not have enough access to the technology required.

- **Building confidence**: Getting through a simulated event successfully boosts team spirit and confidence. They learn how to trust themselves and work well with others, which helps them to understand how to act in a real situation.

- **Improving collaboration**: Tabletop exercises help groups like IT, security, legal, and other departments to work together more easily and break down barriers between them.

In the following subsection, let us learn how to conduct effective tabletop exercises.

Conducting effective tabletop exercises

Understanding the importance of tabletop exercises is the first step. Now, let us explore the key elements of designing and conducting these exercises for maximum impact:

- **Choose a realistic scenario**: Pick a scenario that fits the risk profile and possible threats of your company. Make it just hard enough to test your skills, but avoid making it unnecessarily difficult.

- **Gather the right participants**: Include important people on your IR team, people with a stake in the matter from other areas, and even outside experts to get more points of view.

- **Lead the exercise**: Choose someone to lead the talk, insert simulated events, and add unexpected turns to keep everyone interested.

- **Encourage open communication**: Create a safe place where everyone can talk about their worries, ask questions, and allow them to question what they think they know. Here, criticizing people is not the point; the point is to learn and get better.

- **Document and analyze**: Write down your learnings, find places for improvement, and update your IRP based on your learnings.

In the next subsection, let us explore other options to improve our IRP.

Beyond the tabletop

Tabletop exercises are just one element of an IR program. You can combine them with other training opportunities, vulnerability assessments, and plan regular reviews to build a robust and well-tested response ecosystem.

The effectiveness of any incident response plan is determined by the team's ability to implement it. Tabletop exercises are the primary method for ensuring this operational readiness. They convert procedural documentation into practical skills, equipping the team to respond to security incidents with confidence and precision. This results in a more capable response team, a more resilient business, and better-protected digital assets.

Beyond periodic testing, the long-term effectiveness of an incident response plan hinges on two critical, ongoing efforts:

- **Continuous review and updates**: As mentioned earlier, the types of online threats are always changing, and so should your IRP. Review and change your plan often to keep up with new threats, tools, and organizational changes. Remember, a static plan is a vulnerable plan.

- **Integration with other security measures**: IRP is not alone; other security measures, such as vulnerability management, threat intelligence, and security awareness training, should work with it without any problems. This all-around method improves your security and makes sure that everyone works together when the digital alarm goes off.

Incident escalation and response procedures

An effective incident response requires a well-defined escalation process to ensure timely and appropriate action. This process involves categorizing incidents based on severity and impact and escalating them to the appropriate teams or individuals.

This structured approach to incident escalation comprises several integral parts that ensure a coordinated response:

- **Escalation levels**: Organizations commonly define escalation levels to structure their incident response efforts. These levels typically represent increasing levels of severity and impact.

  o **Tier 1**: Initial triage and assessment of security alerts.

  o **Tier 2**: In-depth analysis, containment, and eradication of incidents.

- o **Tier 3**: Handling of critical incidents with significant business impact, requiring coordination with multiple teams and potentially executive management.

- **Escalation matrix**: The following table is an example of some sample incident types with severity and escalation level. This may differ from organization to organization.

Incident type	Severity	Escalation level
Phishing	Low	Tier 1
Malware	Medium	Tier 2
Ransomware	High	Tier 3
Data breach	High	Tier 3
DDoS attack	Medium	Tier 2
Insider threat	Medium	Tier 2
Zero-day exploit	Critical	Tier 3

Table 6.1: Sample incident types with severity and escalation level

- **Service level agreements (SLAs)**: SLAs define the expected response times for different escalation levels. SLAs help to ensure that incidents are addressed in a timely manner and that stakeholders have clear expectations regarding response times.

- o **Tier 1**: Acknowledge within 15 minutes, begin triage within 30 minutes.

- o **Tier 2**: Begin analysis within 1 hour, initiate containment within 2 hours.

- o **Tier 3**: Immediate acknowledgement, continuous communication.

- **Automated playbooks**: SOAR platforms can automate escalation and initial response actions, improving efficiency and reducing response times.

  Example: A SOAR playbook can automatically escalate a high-severity alert (e.g., multiple failed login attempts followed by a successful login from an unknown location) to *Tier 3* and notify the on-call incident commander.

  The playbook can also automatically isolate the affected host and block the attacker's IP address.

  Automated playbooks can significantly speed up the initial response to incidents, allowing security analysts to focus on more complex tasks.

It is essential to spend time and money on crafting and improving your IRP, and it is a critical must. A clear plan and set of clear steps to follow transforms your team into smart players from weak pawns on the cyber battlefield. Remember that planning and getting ready are your most powerful tools against threats that are sure to come your way.

There is a lot to learn about IR planning, and this is just the beginning. We will go into more detail about each step of the IR process, give you useful tips on how to make and test your IRP, and look at how to combine it with other security measures to get full safety. Building your digital shield together, one brick at a time, will make you powerful in a world that is always changing.

Incident response detection and analysis

Finding and analyzing security events quickly is one of the most important parts of any IR program that works. This important step lays the groundwork for quick containment, eradication, and recovery. We will talk about the art and science of IR detection and analysis in this section. This section will give you all the information, along with the best practices you need, to find threats that are hiding in plain sight. Let us begin with detection.

Detection

In IR, the first line of defense is to set up strong monitoring systems that can pick out possible incidents in the constant stream of system events. This requires a layered approach that combines tools like **security information and event management (SIEM)** systems, **network traffic analysis (NTA)** solutions, **endpoint detection and response (EDR)** agents, threat intelligence feeds, etc.

Once a possible incident is found, it is important to do a full study to find out what it is, how big it is, and what effects it might have. Log analysis, forensic analysis, threat hunting, and integrating threat intelligence are some of the things that are part of this more in-depth study.

Let us understand this using some real-time examples.

Scenario one phishing attack

Detection: An employee gets an email that seems to come from a reliable source and tells them to click on a link to change their account information. However, when you look more closely, the email has small signs that it is a phishing email, like an odd sender email address or writing mistakes in the message. The letter is marked as suspicious by an email security gateway, which sends an alert to the company's security team and is shown in *Figure 6.2*:

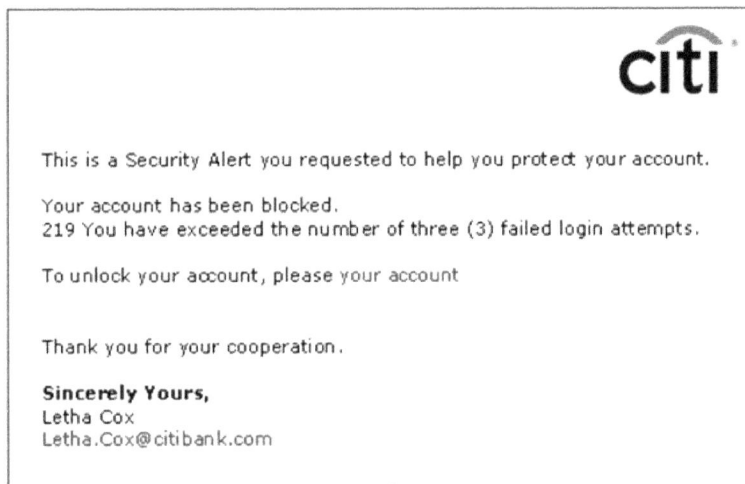

Figure 6.2: Phishing email

Analysis: As soon as the security team gets the warning, they start an analysis to find out how big and bad the phishing attack is. They look at the email header and text with a forensic eye, looking at metadata and possible malicious payloads. They also check to see if any workers have been scammed by the phishing attempt by keeping an eye on network traffic and endpoint activity for signs of stolen credentials or attempts to log in without permission.

Scenario two malware infection

Detection: An endpoint security solution detects anomalous behavior on a company computer, which could mean that malware is installed. The **endpoint detection and response/extended detection and response (EDR/XDR)** solution sends out a warning when it detects suspicious activity, like downloading files without permission or trying to change system files. Users also report slow system performance and pop-up messages that do not make sense, which makes it even more likely that malware is present.

In a **Security Operations Center (SOC)**, these endpoint alerts are often correlated with other security events using a SIEM system. For example, a SIEM rule might be in place to detect suspicious patterns indicative of **command-and-control (C2)** activity after a potential infection.

SIEM rule example

SIEM rule: Detect multiple failed login attempts followed by a successful login from a different IP.

The following is an example of rule **suspicious_login_activity**:

```
{
  events:
    e1 = from login_failure
    e2 = from login_success
  condition:
    e1.user == e2.user and
    e1.src_ip != e2.src_ip and
    e1.time within 5 minutes
    count(e1) >= 5
}
```

Analysis: The incident response team, or the SOC analyst handling the alert quickly starts a study to figure out what kind of malware was installed and how widespread it is. To facilitate this, analysts may employ YARA rules to identify specific malware families based on known patterns. For instance, a YARA rule to detect WannaCry ransomware might look like this:

- **YARA rule**: Detect WannaCry ransomware:

```
rule WannaCry
{
  meta:
    description = "Detects WannaCry ransomware"
    author = "SOC Analyst"
  strings:
    $mz = { 4D 5A }                      // Magic number (MZ header)
    $sig1 = { 0F 0B 6B 0A 15 15 4F 1A 28 09 17 09 } // Specific byte sequence
    $sig2 = "WannaCryptor"        // Ransomware string
  condition:
    $mz at 0 and                  // MZ header at the beginning of the file
    ($sig1 or $sig2)              // Either signature must be present
}
```

To prevent further spread, the affected computer is isolated from the network. The team then conducts a detailed analysis of system logs, registry entries, and network activity. This analysis aims to identify the specific malware, its propagation mechanisms, and any **indicators of compromise (IOCs)** that can be used for eradication and future prevention.

Remember that detection and analysis are repetitive processes. As you encounter new threats, refine your understanding of your IT environment, continuously adapt your detection mechanisms and analysis procedures to maintain the upper hand against adversaries.

Containment

Imagine you are the first person to arrive at the scene of an accident. Your immediate action would not be to attempt surgery on the wounded. Instead, the first action would be to fix the situation and try to stop any further damage. Similarly, when it comes to hacking, containment is also used in IR. During this crucial stage, you must promptly stop the attack from spreading. This will limit the damage and buy time for further research and recovery. Let us look at the strategies and things to think about for successful containment in a world where threats are always changing.

Real-world examples

The following list outlines a few real-world examples:

- **Ransomware outbreak**: A user's device gets infected with ransomware through a fake email, which locks up important files. To contain an infection, you need to put the affected device in a special area, stop it from talking to the C2 server, and stop it from moving laterally within the network.

- **Data breach**: Malicious actors exploit a web application vulnerability to steal customer data. Containment focuses on isolating the compromised server, patching the vulnerability, and revoking any stolen credentials to prevent further data exfiltration.

- **Denial-of-service (DoS) attack**: Hackers flood a website with traffic, making it unavailable. Containment strategies might involve filtering malicious traffic, scaling up resources, and collaborating with internet service providers to mitigate the attack.

Practical suggestions for IR responders

As we discussed, a few real-world examples and how to contain them, here are a few suggestions that will help you while you are trying to contain the attacks:

- **Know your environment**: To find and stop suspicious behavior rapidly, you need to know your network's structure, its most important assets, and its security controls inside and out. Do vulnerability surveys and penetration tests on a regular basis to look for possible weak spots.

- **Predefined action plans**: Write down containment methods for all kinds of incidents, like ransomware, data breaches, and DoS attacks. Make sure your IR team knows how to implement these methods thoroughly so that they can act swiftly and together in case of an attack.

- **Segmentation and access control**: Use network segmentation to make it harder for attackers to get into your surroundings. Enforce strong access control policies based on the principle of least privilege to minimize the effects of passwords being stolen.

- **Isolation and quarantine**: Ensure that you have quick ways to separate systems or user accounts that have been hacked. You might want sandbox files or processes that you think are suspicious, so you can look at them without causing more damage.

- **Kill switches**: For critical systems, consider implementing *kill switches* that can be activated remotely to halt operations, thus preventing widespread damage in extreme cases.

- **Threat intelligence**: Use threat intelligence feeds and analysis tools to stay up to date on new threats and make sure your containment tactics are up to date as well.

Containment strategies

A few containment strategies are as follows:

- **Rapid isolation**: Once a security incident is found, it is paramount to move rapidly and decisively. Start quickly isolating systems that are affected to stop threats from moving laterally within the network. For instance, if a computer is found to be infected, it should be disconnected from the network right away to stop any further infection.

- **Network segmentation**: Network segmentation is a proactive way to reduce the damage from an incident. By splitting the network into sections, each with its entry controls, it becomes much harder for people to move from one section to another. This containment approach was very important in stopping the *WannaCry ransomware attack* in 2017 (**https://en.wikipedia.org/wiki/WannaCry_ransomware_attack**). Segmented networks stopped the malware from spreading to many computers.

- **Endpoint quarantine**: In cases where the incident involves endpoints, consider applying endpoint quarantine measures. This involves isolating affected devices from the network while allowing incident responders to conduct thorough analysis and remediation. Endpoint quarantine was notably effective in curtailing the impact of the *NotPetya malware*, which spread laterally across networks.

- **Application whitelisting**: Using application whitelisting can help keep problems with illegal executables under control. When you only let approved programs run, the attack area gets a lot smaller. For example, whitelisting could stop harmful encryption tools from being used during a ransomware attack.

- **Cloud service deactivation**: As companies use cloud services more, incident responders need to be aware of possible threats in cloud settings. If your cloud services have been hacked, you might want to temporarily turn them off to stop more data from being stolen or illegal access.

- **User account lockdown**: Threat actors often use user accounts that have been hacked as entry points. During an incident, lock down accounts that have been hacked right away to stop people from getting in without permission. A real-time account lockdown can be a key way to stop possible data leaks or other illegal activities.

- **Deploying automated threat response tools**: To speed up and improve the effectiveness of control efforts, think about using automated threat response tools. These tools can automatically carry out actions that have already been planned, like stopping malicious IP addresses or isolating devices that have been hacked. Adding these kinds of tools to the incident reaction process can cut containment time by a significant amount.

- **Communication**: During the containment phase, keep open lines of communication with all parties. Make it clear what is being done to lessen the effects of the event. Work with the right teams, like IT, legal, and communications, to ensure that the response is well-coordinated and efficient. The Equifax data breach shows how important it is to communicate openly and work together during the control phase.

- **Post-containment analysis**: Once the incident has been contained, a careful analysis should be done to find the root cause, the weaknesses that were used, and the lessons that were learned. In addition to eradication and recovery, use this analysis to strengthen defenses, update policies, and improve incident reaction procedures to make the system more resilient in the future.

The following is a simplified network figure illustrating network segmentation and how it contains the spread of an incident:

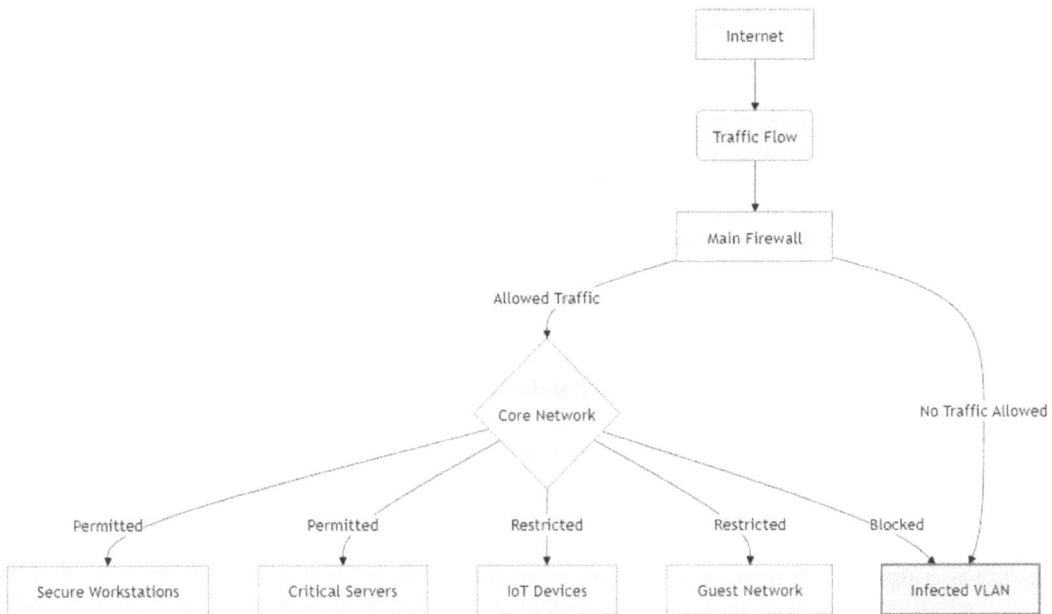

Figure 6.3: *Network segmentation*

Note: **Containment is a race against time. The attacker cannot do much damage if you move quickly. Invest in automation tools and well-trained processes to make your reaction faster and lessen the damage from security incidents.**

To sum up, incident containment needs a planned and multifaceted method. By incorporating these real-time examples and practical suggestions into the incident response playbook, organizations can effectively minimize the impact of security incidents and fortify their cybersecurity posture. Now, let us look at the following scenarios and their containment.

Scenario one phishing attack

Containment: When the incident response team confirms that there has been a phishing attack, they swiftly put containment in place, which is meant to keep organizational assets from being stolen again. The affected employee's computer is cut off from the network so that it cannot communicate with the attacker's infrastructure. They also use email filtering rules to stop similar phishing emails from getting into the inboxes of other workers. This lowers the risk of more breaches. The security awareness team also holds targeted training sessions to teach workers how to spot and report phishing attempts. This makes the company more resistant to future attacks of this kind.

Scenario two malware infection

Containment: When malware infiltrates an organization's network, swift containment is crucial to prevent further damage and lateral movement. The incident response team, often operating within a SOC, initiates containment procedures to isolate affected systems and limit the malware's spread.

A primary containment action involves disconnecting the infected computer from the network. This prevents the malware from communicating with C2 servers or spreading to other network devices. Network segmentation is also employed to restrict the infected workstation's communication with critical systems or network zones. This limits the blast radius of the infection and protects sensitive assets.

To automate and expedite these containment actions, SOAR platforms are often utilized. A simplified SOAR playbook for automated containment might resemble the following:

SOAR playbook example: Isolate the infected host and notify

Playbook: Malware containment

Description: Automatically isolates a host upon malware detection and notifies the security team.

Refer to the following steps:

1. **Get alert details (host IP, malware alert ID, severity)**
   * Action: `Get_Alert_Details(alert_id)`
2. **Isolate host from the network**
   * Action: `EDR.isolate_host(host_ip)`
3. **Block host IP on firewall (if applicable)**
   * Action: `Firewall.block_ip(host_ip)`

```
4. Create incident ticket
   * Action: Create_Ticket(title="Malware Infection",
     severity=severity, host=host_ip)
5. Notify security team via chat
   * Action: Chat.send_message(channel="SOC Alerts",
     message="Malware detected   and host isolated: " + host_ip)
6. Run vulnerability scan on other hosts in the same subnet
    * Action: Vulnerability_Scanner.scan_subnet(host_ip)
```

This playbook demonstrates how a SOAR platform can automate key containment steps, reducing response time and analyst workload.

Concurrently, the endpoint security solution distributes updated malware signatures and heuristic detection rules to all endpoints. This proactive measure enhances the organization's overall threat detection capabilities and reduces the likelihood of reinfection from similar malware variants.

Eradication

When it comes to IR, containment buys time; however, removal is the only way to win. At this point, you need to get rid of the attacker completely from your systems, so they cannot come back to do more damage. It is like getting rid of the root of a weed instead of just cutting off its leaves. Let us talk about effective ways to get rid of threats and useful advice for IR professionals dealing with today's complex threats.

Real-world examples

The eradication phase of incident response focuses on completely removing the root cause of the security incident. This is crucial to prevent reinfection and ensure the system returns to a secure state. Let us explore some real-world scenarios to illustrate how eradication works in practice:

- **Ransomware eradication**: The IR team works on getting rid of the ransomware itself after isolating the infected device and stopping data encryption. In the worst cases, this could mean deleting files by hand, using specialized anti-malware software, or even reimaging the whole system. Also, the attack would need to reset any passwords that were stolen or used without permission.

- **Data breach eradication**: Once the compromised server has been contained, the focus changes to getting rid of the attacker's tools and access points. This means finding backdoors, harmful scripts, and user accounts that are not supposed to be there and removing them from the system.

Conclusion

This chapter provided a comprehensive blueprint for building and executing a robust IR program. We moved from theory to practice, establishing that effective IR is not an improvised reaction, but a well-structured discipline built on preparation and process. We began by defining the essential roles and responsibilities that form a capable Incident Response Team (CSIRT) and underscored the critical importance of a detailed, tested IRP as the foundation for any successful operation.

We then journeyed through the complete incident lifecycle, starting with the proactive phases of detection and analysis, where raw alerts are transformed into actionable intelligence. We detailed the crucial immediate actions of containment to limit an attack's spread, followed by the methodical processes of eradication to remove the threat's root cause, and recovery to restore systems to a secure, operational state. Finally, we emphasized that the work is not over once the incident is resolved; the post-incident activity, including forensic analysis (DFIR) and a thorough *lessons learned* review, is what transforms a single event into an opportunity for strengthening an organization's long-term resilience.

Now that we have mastered the framework for responding to security events, the next chapter will delve into the specific threats that IR teams face daily, exploring the anatomy of different attack types, from malware to advanced persistent threats.

Join our Discord space

Join our Discord workspace for latest updates, offers, tech happenings around the world, new releases, and sessions with the authors:

https://discord.bpbonline.com

CHAPTER 7

Effective Threat Management for Enterprises

Introduction

This chapter will be focused on understanding the kinds of risks faced by businesses daily. We examine the goals and strategies of threat actors, investigate how digital transformation is making the attack area bigger, and how to get the information we need to build a strong defense. The goal is not only to understand the risks, but also to give you, the reader, the information you need to protect your company's digital assets.

There are many different types of threats, right from sophisticated nation-state actors, all the way up to hidden malware operations. By the end of this chapter, you will know how to spot the signs, understand the tactics, and put these strategies into action, to protect yourself from these constant risks. Together, we will find our way through the dangerous digital world and be ready to protect our company from those who are out to harm it.

Before we start this journey to understand the risks businesses face, we need to be clear that these enemies are not like other enemies. Despite being very smart and determined, we cannot find them until they have done the damage. This chapter will talk about the hidden threats that modern businesses face, such as the cloak-and-dagger tactics used by nation-state players and cybercriminal gangs, as well as the sneaky threats that can come from inside an organization. Not only will we investigate the *what*, but also the *why* and *how* of these dangers. We equip ourselves with all the information and tools we need to protect and strengthen our digital worlds.

Structure

This chapter will include the following topics:

- Types of malwares
- Social engineering
- Phishing attacks
- Ransomware
- Denial-of-service and distributed denial-of-service
- Advanced persistent threats
- Insider threat
- Insider threat intelligence
- Physical security

Objectives

This chapter provides a comprehensive view of modern cyber threats. The aim is to equip the readers with the skills required to spot, evaluate, and successfully deal with the possible threats by breaking down the anatomy of cyber threats, the threat landscape, and the constantly changing **tactics, techniques, and procedures** (**TTPs**). This chapter will help blue teamers develop a proactive, threat-hunting attitude with the aid of real-life examples and information about how adversaries work, thus improving their cybersecurity and thereby protecting important assets. Towards the end, readers will learn how to confidently and safely manage the ever-changing threat landscape.

In this chapter, we will understand how to spot and differentiate between different types of malware, study how they act, learn the tricks and methods used in phishing scams, and how to protect yourself from them. We will also learn more about the insider danger, which is often overlooked but has a big effect.

Threat actors have a plethora of tools at their expense, right from complex malware to smart social engineering schemes. Through case studies and real-life examples, we will see how dangerous cyber threats can be and how they can affect businesses of all kinds. This chapter establishes key threat-hunting tactics, emphasizing proactive threat detection. Understanding adversaries helps companies strengthen defenses and stay ahead in cybersecurity.

Types of malwares

Malware, or malicious software, encompasses a diverse range of threats designed to compromise digital systems. Viruses, for instance, require a host file to propagate, embedding themselves within legitimate software and spreading as infected files are shared. Worms, in contrast, are self-replicating and can spread autonomously across networks, exploiting vulnerabilities without user interaction. Trojans masquerade as legitimate software, tricking users into installing them, while spyware covertly monitors user activity, stealing sensitive data. Ransomware encrypts files and demands payment for decryption, and rootkits conceal the presence of other malware, allowing them to operate undetected. Adware, though often less harmful, inundates users with unwanted advertisements. Understanding these distinct malware types is crucial for implementing effective cybersecurity defenses. Let us understand malwares and look at their types:

This figure illustrates the classification of malware into two main categories: Non-replicating and self-replicating malware:

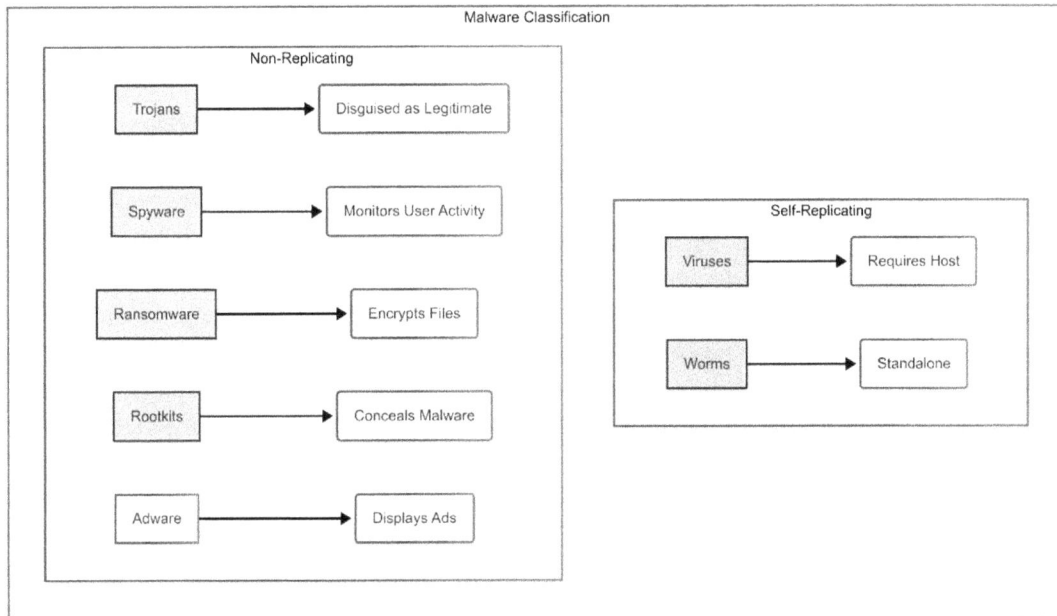

Figure 7.1: Malware classification: non-replicating and self-replicating

Each category contains specific types of malwares along with a brief description of their functionality:

- **Viruses [Example: The Melissa Virus (1999)]:** One of the best-known and longest-lasting types of software is the virus. Viruses are malicious code that inserts itself into executable files or documents. When the infected file is executed, the virus code also runs, potentially replicating and spreading to other files or systems. The following figure depicts the Melissa virus, which showed up in 1999, is one of the first cases of a computer virus. It was sent through infected email files as a macro in a Microsoft Word document. When Melissa was opened, it sent infected documents to the first 50 email names in the victim's Microsoft Outlook address book. This caused a problem with email around the globe.

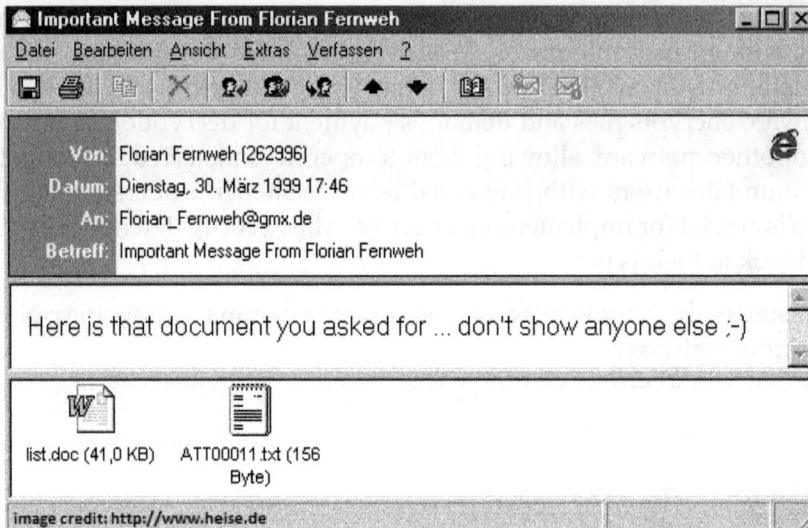

Figure 7.2: This image is a screenshot of an email showing how the Melissa virus spread in 1999

- **Worms [Example: The Conficker Worm (2008)]:** Worms are self-replicating malware that can propagate across networks without requiring a host file. They exploit vulnerabilities in operating systems or applications to spread automatically. In 2008, the Conficker worm became famous for taking advantage of flaws in Microsoft Windows. It quickly spread to millions of computers around the world, creating a huge botnet. Conficker was a major threat because it used complex methods to spread and was resistant to cleanup tools. This shows how powerful worm-based attacks can be. The same can be observed in the following figure:

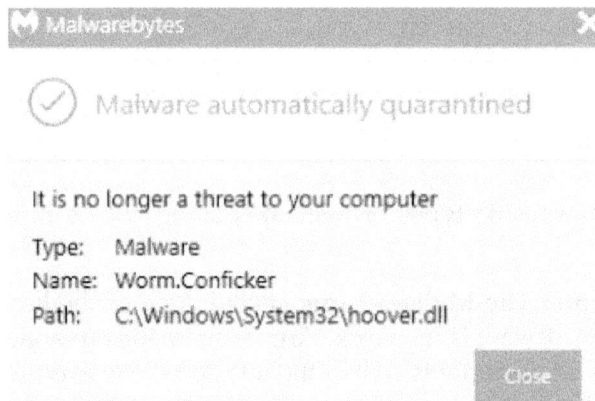

Figure 7.3: Worm Conficker being removed by Malwarebytes. Image take from Malwarebytes labs blog

Reference: https://www.malwarebytes.com/blog/detections/worm-conficker

- **Trojans (Example: Zeus (Zbot) Trojan):** Trojans are malicious programs disguised as legitimate software. Unlike viruses, they do not self-replicate. They rely on users to execute them, after which they can perform various malicious actions, such as stealing data or creating backdoors. The name comes from the mythical Greek horse made of wood. Once they are turned on, they can do many bad things, like steal private information or let people in who are not supposed to be there. This is shown very well by the Zeus Trojan, which is also called **Zbot**. It went after online banking systems and stole user information and financial information. It was a key part of financial fraud plans all over the world.

- **Ransomware [Example: WannaCry Ransomware (2017)]**: Ransomware is a type of malware that encrypts a victim's files or entire systems, rendering them inaccessible. Attackers then demand a ransom payment in exchange for a decryption key. Attackers want you to pay a ransom to get the access key. The 2017 WannaCry virus attack was a major problem for computers around the world. It infected hundreds of thousands of computers, including ones that were used for healthcare and key infrastructure. This caused governments and organizations to respond with emergency plans.

Refer to *Figures 7.4 and 7.5* for ransomware figures.

- **Spyware [Example: FinFisher (FinSpy) Spyware]**: Spyware is malware that covertly monitors and collects user information without their consent. This can include browsing history, keystrokes, login credentials, and other sensitive data. FinFisher, which is sometimes called FinSpy, is a well-known case. It is commercial spyware that is sold to law enforcement and government organizations. FinFisher gets into devices and gathers information, like emails, live feeds, and keystrokes. Putting it into use has caused a lot of privacy and moral issues.

- **Adware (Example: Superfish Adware)**: Adware, while not always malicious, inundates users with unwanted advertisements. In some cases, adware can become invasive, slowing down system performance and tracking users' online behavior. Superfish is an infamous example; it came pre-installed on some Lenovo laptops and injected third-party ads into web browsers, compromising user privacy.

- **Keyloggers (Example: DarkTequila Keylogger)**: Keyloggers are a type of malware that captures and records every keystroke entered on an infected device. Attackers use this to steal sensitive information like passwords, credit card numbers, and personal messages. One example is DarkTequila, which was aimed at people in Latin America. It kept track of keystrokes to get private data like passwords and banking information. Secret agents and people who steal identities often use keyloggers like DarkTequila.

- **Rootkits [Example: Stuxnet Worm (2010)]**: Rootkits are a type of malware designed to conceal their presence and the presence of other malicious software on an infected system. They operate at a low level, often modifying core system files or processes to evade detection. When Stuxnet was founded in 2010, it was a very important example. It was meant to get into industrial systems and mess up Iran's nuclear program. Since Stuxnet was so complicated and could stay hidden for a long time, it started a new era in cyber-espionage.

- **Botnets (Example: Mariposa Botnet)**: Botnets are networks of compromised computers (bots) controlled remotely by an attacker (botmaster). Botnets are used to conduct various malicious activities, including DDoS attacks, spam distribution, and malware spreading. When it was found in 2008, the Mariposa botnet attacked millions of computers around the world. This lets hackers steal private data, commit identity theft, and spread malware. It showed how big and bad botnet-driven attacks can be.

- **Fileless Malware (Example: Poweliks Malware)**: Fileless malware operates in a computer's memory, **random-access memory** (**RAM**), and other non-file-based objects, rather than relying on executable files on the hard drive. This makes it harder to detect by traditional antivirus software. One example is Poweliks, which used rogue PowerShell scripts to run payloads without leaving behind normal file remnants. Since it did not have any files, it was hard for regular protection software to find.

- **Mobile Malware [Example: Android.Fakebank (BankBot) Malware]**: Malware that targets smartphones and tablets takes advantage of flaws in mobile systems and phones. One example is Fakebank, which is also called BankBot. It looked like a real banking app and got people to give it their login information. Malware like BankBot shows how important it is to protect pocket-sized electronics.

- **Cryptojacking Malware (Example: Coinhive Cryptojacking)**: Cryptojacking malware hijacks a victim's computing resources to mine cryptocurrencies, such as Bitcoin or Monero, without their consent. Coinhive, a notorious cryptojacking script, was embedded in websites and executed by visitors' browsers, consuming CPU power. Websites employing Coinhive often did so without informing users, sparking ethical debates.

There are many malwares and the list is long. However, the following table, *Table 7.1*, summarizes the top ten malwares of their time:

Name	Description	Key factors	Impact	Expected loss (Million dollars)
WannaCry	Ransomware that exploits Windows vulnerabilities	Rapid propagation, encryption	Global disruption, critical infrastructure	Hundreds of millions
NotPetya	Wiper disguised as ransomware	Rapid spreading, data destruction	Data loss, operational downtime	Over $10 billion
Conficker	Self-propagating worm	Network-based propagation, persistence	Botnet control, potential for widespread attacks	Over $9 billion
Mydoom	Worm and backdoor	Email propagation, DDoS capability	Email disruption, DDoS attacks	Over $3 billion

Name	Description	Key factors	Impact	Expected loss (Million dollars)
SQL Slammer	Worm targeting SQL Server vulnerabilities	Rapid propagation, network impact	Internet slowdown, critical systems affected	Over $1 billion
Zeus (Zbot) Trojan	Banking Trojan	Credential theft, widespread	Financial fraud, data breaches	Hundreds of millions
Sasser	Worm targeting Windows vulnerabilities	Rapid propagation, memory usage	System instability, network congestion	Over $500 million
Code Red	Worm exploiting IIS vulnerabilities	Self-propagation, web defacement	Website defacement, network disruption	Over $2 billion
Blaster (MSBlast)	Worm targeting Windows vulnerabilities	Rapid propagation, DDoS attacks	Network congestion, system instability	Over $320 million
Slingshot	Sophisticated malware	Stealthy, data exfiltration	Espionage, data theft	Unknown

Table 7.1: Top ten malwares

These diverse types of malwares serve as a testament to the relentless creativity of cybercriminals. They have been employed in a wide array of cyberattacks, from data breaches and financial fraud to espionage and infrastructure disruption. Understanding these malware types is crucial for cybersecurity professionals tasked with defending against the ever-present threat of digital adversaries.

Tip: **A career in malware analysis is a highly specialized and rewarding path within the field of cybersecurity. Malware analysts play a crucial role in identifying, dissecting, and mitigating malicious software threats.**

Malware analysis

From a threat intelligence perspective, malware analysis can be defined as *decoding the enemy's playbook for enhanced threat intelligence*. It is like meticulously dissecting the weapons used by attackers to understand their motives and strategies. Through the process of deciphering the mechanisms of malevolent software, blue teams acquire indispensable knowledge that directly enhances their threat intelligence endeavors. In this discourse, we shall examine the ways in which malware analysis enhances the resilience and adaptability of a defense system:

- **Understanding malware behavior**: Analyzing malware code and its runtime actions reveals how the malware compromises systems, communicates with command-and-control servers, exfiltrates data, or evades traditional detection. For example, analyzing a ransomware sample might reveal its encryption techniques and network propagation mechanisms.

- **Identifying IOCs**: Malware leaves behind a trail of tell-tale signs. Malware analysis uncovers file hashes, unique registry entries, network traffic patterns, and other IOCs. Sharing these IOCs across your security systems enhances proactive detection.

- **Attribution and TTP analysis**: Malware analysis can help link attacks to known threat actors based on code similarities, infrastructure, or unique tools. Understanding a threat actor's preferred TTPs helps defend against similar future attacks.

- **Improving detection and prevention**: New malware signatures and behavioral patterns extracted through analysis strengthen your firewalls, endpoint protection, and intrusion detection systems. Analysis of zero-day attacks refines your ability to spot previously unknown threats.

- **Incident response**: When a breach occurs, malware analysis is vital for determining the root cause, the scope of the compromise, and the precise malware variant used. This empowers faster containment and targeted remediation.

Example scenario: Imagine malware analysis uncovers a new ransomware variant that encrypts files using a novel algorithm and spreads laterally via a specific SMB vulnerability. These insights would drive the following threat intelligence actions:

- **IOC distribution**: File hashes, network communication patterns, and other IOCs are shared within the organization and externally to help others detect the ransomware.

- **Signature creation**: Security vendors are provided with malware sample to develop updated antivirus signatures, enhancing protection for a wider audience.

- **Patch prioritization**: The SMB vulnerability is flagged for immediate patching across the organization.

- **Threat hunting playbook**: Incident responders develop a checklist based on the ransomware's lateral movement techniques to identify further signs of compromise within the network.

Malware analysis is not just about malware itself; it is about the insights gathered to prevent, detect, and respond to the constantly evolving threat landscape. By treating malware as an intelligence source, blue teams build a more informed and resilient defense posture. In the next section, let us look at insider threat intelligence.

Social engineering

Social engineering is a sophisticated and cunning tactic employed by malicious actors within the cyber realm to exploit the vulnerabilities inherent in the human factor of cybersecurity. Social engineering attacks, rather than employing direct technological targeting or exploiting vulnerabilities, are designed to deceive individuals into revealing sensitive information, executing specific actions, or making decisions that ultimately favor the attacker. These cyber-attacks leverage sophisticated techniques such as psychological manipulation, trust establishment, and exploitation of human psychology to accomplish nefarious objectives.

Types of social engineering attacks

Social engineering attacks exploit human psychology to manipulate individuals into disclosing confidential information or performing actions that compromise security. Here are the common types of social engineering attacks:

Phishing

Clearly, phishing is the most common way that social engineering techniques are used. Phishing is a malevolent tactic in which false emails, messages, or websites with an outward look of legitimacy are specifically meant to entwine naive recipients into revealing sensitive information, including but not limited to login credentials, credit card details, or personal data.

Using a phishing method, a threat actor creates an email that looks somewhat like a well-known financial institution, claiming to have compromised the account of the target. The email has a link to an artificial login page meant to illegally gain the target's credentials, including username and password. Often used as a tool for financial fraud and personal identity theft, phishing attacks help to enable these crimes.

Pretexting

Threat actors use a complex method called pretexting to create a scenario or pretext and hence take advantage of human weaknesses. The main goal is to control people into unintentionally revealing private information or engaging in behavior that can undermine security. Often assuming the appearance of a respectable person, such as a client, supplier, or co-worker, the opponent often hides behind this front.

Pretending to be a real IT assistance expert from the company, a malicious actor contacts an employee via phone. The assailant lies to the staff by claiming to have a network-related issue, therefore influencing their computer system permission of remote access. Once privileged access has been acquired, the hostile actor can either exfiltrate extremely private data or run the deployment of harmful software. Malicious actors often use pretexting attacks; a tactic used for illegal access and data theft, to get in.

Baiting

Malicious actors use baiting attacks, a deceitful strategy, to seduce gullible victims with enticing offers, including the enticement of a free software download or a highly sought-after reward. The intended person is driven to participate in an activity that later causes sensitive data to be compromised or dangerous software to be introduced.

Using compromised USB devices placed on company premises, a malevolent actor labels them as either *Employee Bonuses* or *Confidential Payroll Data*. Inadvertent computer infection is the result of curious workers unintentionally acquiring and connecting these disks, therefore bringing dangerous malware into their systems. Baiting assaults deftly use human curiosity to help malware spread subtly.

Tailgating

Under the sinister practice known as tailgating, also known as piggybacking, threat actors surreptitiously follow an authorized person into a highly guarded zone or facility under the cover of an employee, guest, or service professional.

Disguised as a delivery worker, a prospective threat actor posts himself at the door of an office building, deliberately waiting for the arrival of an authorized employee with a valid access badge. Later, the assailant enters illegally, claiming to have left their identity badge behind by accident. After successful penetration, hostile actors could try to gain illegal access to very sensitive areas. Attacks using tailgating leverage weaknesses in physical security systems, which we will cover in the upcoming section.

Quid pro quo

Quid pro quo attacks, also referred to as reciprocal exchanges, involve sensitive information or illegal access being returned for a valuable service or advantage. Adversaries use enticing strategies by providing incentives for cooperation.

Using social engineering techniques, a malevolent actor calls naive staff members pretending to be a reputable technical support agent. The dishonest person cleverly lures the targets by suggesting complementary antivirus software. The employee is asked to permit remote access to their computer system so they may acquire the allegedly *complimentary* software. The found access point has natural weaknesses that could be used by threat actors for illegal data exfiltration or malicious software deployment. Quid pro quo attacks deftly use the natural human drive toward obtaining either highly sought-after or gratis services.

Social engineering attacks leverage the intricate nuances of human psychology, trust dynamics, and emotional vulnerabilities, thereby rendering them highly efficacious. These malicious activities are commonly observed in diverse scenarios, encompassing cyber espionage, identity theft, financial fraud, and corporate espionage. Mitigating social engineering attacks necessitates the implementation of a comprehensive approach encompassing employee education, security awareness initiatives, and technical countermeasures to effectively detect and neutralize these deceptive maneuvers.

Phishing attacks

We all know what phishing attacks are, but before we talk about them, let us look at some shocking facts and see what a blue teamer must deal with; for him, every day is a hacking attack. This is one of the most common cyber threats to businesses and comes very high on the list. We will talk about some basic and important parts of the different types of phishing, including how to stop them and how to defend yourself. In later chapters, which will be more technical and interesting, we will look at some real-life cases of these kinds of attacks and how a blue team member handles them for companies. Here are a few facts pertaining to phishing attacks:

- 2022 was a record year for phishing, with the APWG logging more than 4.7 million attacks. Since the beginning of 2019, the number of phishing attacks has grown by more than 150% per year.

- **Business email compromise** (**BEC**) attacks continued to menace enterprises. The average BEC attack attempted to steal USD 132,559.

- The COVID-19 pandemic created fertile ground for phishing attacks. Cybercriminals exploited the crisis with pandemic-themed phishing emails, resulting in a surge of COVID-19-related phishing scams. In the early months of the pandemic, phishing attempts related to COVID-19 saw a significant spike.

- According to the 2021 *Data Breach Investigations Report* by Verizon, 36% of data breaches involved phishing, with a significant portion being spear phishing attacks.

- Certain industries are more heavily targeted than others. The financial sector, healthcare, and technology companies are often prime targets due to the valuable data they hold.

- Email continues to be the primary vector for phishing attacks. According to the *State of Email Security 2021* report by Mimecast, 61% of organizations reported an increase in phishing attacks via email.

- Phishing attacks increasingly rely on sophisticated social engineering tactics. Cybercriminals craft convincing emails, often impersonating trusted entities, to deceive recipients.

- One of the primary objectives of phishing attacks is credential theft. Cybercriminals seek to steal usernames and passwords, which can be used for various malicious purposes, including account takeover.

- Phishing emails are frequently used to deliver malware payloads. These can include ransomware, spyware, and keyloggers.

- With the increasing use of mobile devices, phishing attacks targeting smartphones and tablets have become more common. Mobile phishing, or smishing, often involves text messages and mobile apps.

- Cybercriminals are increasingly turning to **phishing-as-a-service (PaaS)** platforms on the dark web. These services provide phishing tools and resources, making it easier for even less technically skilled individuals to launch attacks.

Phishing attacks have been a common cyber threat for decades. They affect individuals, businesses, and groups. They are a type of social engineering attack that tries to trick and control people into doing things that usually lead to theft of data, loss of money, or unauthorized entry to private systems. Looking at the trends of attacks, we can say that fake attacks have changed a lot over the years, getting smarter and harder to spot.

More than 90% of successful attacks against businesses originate from phishing.

– Knowbe4

Principal attributes of phishing attacks

In this subsection, we will deeply understand the principal attributes of phishing attacks:

- **Deceptive communication**: Phishing attacks usually start with a fake message or email, like a smishing text message, a vishing phone call, or a social media message. These texts look like they came from a trustworthy source, like a business, the government, or a co-worker.

- **Social engineering**: Phishing relies heavily on psychological manipulation. Attackers send messages that make people feel things like fear, urgency, curiosity, or joy to get them to act right away, like clicking on a link or downloading an attachment.

- **Urgency and emotion**: Phishers often use a sense of urgency or an emotional pitch, to get people to make decisions that they do not want to. Phishers might say that right away, something needs to be done, like updating account information or verifying a payment, to get the target to act without thinking about it too much.

- **Imitating trusted entities**: Phishing emails and messages often look like they come from legitimate businesses by using logos, email themes, and language that looks a lot like those used by real businesses. People who receive these messages have a hard time telling the difference between real and fake messages.

- **Malicious links and attachments**: Phishing emails often have harmful links that take people to fake websites that are meant to steal their login information or spread malware. They might also have harmful files that infect the victim's device when they are opened.

Now that we have understood the principal attributes of phishing attacks, in the next subsection, let us understand the motive behind phishing attacks.

Common objectives of phishing attacks

Here are a few reasons and objectives for phishing attacks:

- **Credential theft**: One of the major uses of phishing attempts is to steal people's credentials. These attacks get private login information, like usernames and passwords, without permission. Attackers might be able to use the stolen credentials to get into company systems, hacked email accounts, or cloud-based services without permission.

- **Financial fraud**: In cybersecurity, financial fraud causes great worry. Phishing attacks, which are especially meant to target financial departments or people with access to corporate funds, are one of the common strategies used by hostile actors. These strikes seek to fool and control naive victims into revealing private financial data or making illegal purchases. Organizations and people must be alert and use strong security policies to reduce the hazards related to such illegal behavior. Cyber attackers use social engineering to subtly control staff members, therefore enabling them to carry out illegal cash transfers or expose private financial information.

- **Data breach**: Targeting valuable company assets, such as customer data, intellectual property, and confidential business information, is a common way for scammers to get into computers without permission. If threat actors can get into an organization's network, they can steal important data with malicious intentions or from the network to make money.

- **Malware delivery**: Phishing emails often have harmful files or links that are designed to make it easier for malware to get onto the system of the person being scammed. There are many different types of this malware, such as ransomware, spyware, and keyloggers. It is very dangerous to the targeted organization's security because it can change into these different types.

- **BEC**: A bad idea we come across in the field of cybersecurity is called **BEC**. This type of attack is carried out by smart phishers who carefully plan how to pretend to be respected executives or other high-level employees of the target company. Attackers use this sneaky method to trick workers who are not paying attention, forcing them to approve fraudulent wire transfers or accidentally giving out highly sensitive and private information.

- **Network access**: Some bad actors use hacking to get into an organization's network or systems without permission from that organization. Once threat actors get inside a network, they can move from one part of it to another, possibly getting more powerful until they control important parts of the system.

- **Intellectual property theft**: Identity theft is another big problem. Phishing attacks are one way that hackers perform this crime. These attackers are especially trying to get employees' personal information so that they can steal identities. People and businesses need to stay alert and put in place strong security measures to lower their chances of falling victim to these kinds of bad activities. If someone gets this information without permission, it could be used in a variety of malicious ways, like setting up fake accounts without permission and making it easier to do harmful actions later. People can launch targeted strikes on businesses that have valuable intellectual property, like trade secrets, product designs, or secret algorithms. Phishing is often the first step in getting unauthorized entry or data breaches.

- **System compromise**: In certain instances, the primary goal entails compromising the target's system or device, leveraging it as a springboard for subsequent assaults, such as **distributed denial of service (DDoS)** attacks or engagement in botnet activities.

- **Propagation**: Phishing attacks have the potential to propagate through the internal network of an organization, thereby penetrating numerous devices and jeopardizing the overall security of the infrastructure.

- **Ransomware deployment**: There are phishing campaigns that are specifically meant to deliver ransomware, which is used to encrypt important files and systems. Attackers use coercion by demanding money in return for a decryption key, which stops businesses from running normally until the payment is made.

- **Espionage and nation-state attacks**: Sophisticated phishing attacks, which are often carried out by threat actors funded by states, are designed to get inside companies to steal private information or carry out secret operations for political or economic reasons.

- **Distributed attacks**: It is possible for phishing attempts to spread malware or other types of malicious payloads to a lot of people. These attacks might use systems that have been hacked to plan coordinated strikes on different companies.

- **Fraudulent transactions**: Cybercriminals who take advantage of staff accounts can carry out unauthorized transactions, such as purchases, money transfers, or changes to payment information that are not supposed to be made.

Comprehending the prevalent objectives of phishing attacks, it is imperative for blue teams to formulate resilient cybersecurity strategies, encompassing comprehensive employee training, stringent email filtering mechanisms, and well-defined incident response plans. Taking these steps is very important for finding, stopping, and lowering the risks that come with hacking.

Types of phishing attacks

Now, let us understand phishing attacks and look at its types with examples:

- **Email phishing**: Email phishing is the most common type of phishing. It involves cybercriminals sending fake emails to a large group of people who do not know what is going on. The majority of the time, these electronic messages have harmful links or files.

Example: Criminals use a trick where they send fake emails that look like they are from a well-known package service company. In these fake letters, it says that an earlier attempt to deliver failed because the address given was wrong. The email has a link that is supposed to let you track your package. However, you must be very careful because this link takes you to a fake login page that is meant to steal the target's login information. It is common for identity thieves and attackers who are spreading malicious software to use this type of attack route.

- **Spear phishing**: As a very specific type of phishing, spear phishing is when attackers try to get financial information from certain people or companies. People who pose a threat are very good at making their words fit the target perfectly, which makes the attack very convincing.

  Example: A threat actor carefully gathers information about a company during reconnaissance and successfully finds a high-value executive target. The criminal cleverly uses a method called *spear phishing*, in which they send an executive a custom email while pretending to be a familiar and trustworthy co-worker. Their true goal is to trick people into giving them access to private financial records that are meant to be kept secret. This type of attack is often used for business espionage or to commit financial fraud.

- **Whaling**: Also called **CEO/CFO spear phishing**, is a sophisticated type of targeted cyberattack that goes after top leaders in a company. There are people who want to take advantage of these people to make money or get unauthorized access to important company data.

  Example: Attacker pretends to be a well-known executive and sends an email to the finance department, telling them about a time-sensitive business opportunity that requires them to send a large amount of money to an overseas account right away. Cybercriminals often use complex and dangerous methods called *whaling attacks*, which are also called *CEO fraud* or *BEC*, to commit financial fraud.

- **BEC**: In BEC attacks, hackers pretend to be company leaders or trusted vendors. Their workers are tricked into sending fake money or giving out private information. Cybercriminals use complex methods to take advantage of workers who do not know what is going on, forcing them to do illegal things like sending money to fake accounts or giving out highly sensitive and private information.

  Example: An attacker gets into a vendor's email account and writes an email that is sent to the accounting department of the company being targeted. This email lies when it asks for a change to be made to the payment information for an upcoming bill. After that, the illegal movement of funds takes place, sending the money to the accounts that are under the attackers' control. Conspirators of financial fraud often use BEC hacks to do their dirty work.

- **Vishing**: A type of cyberattack that is carried out over the phone is called vishing, which is also known as voice hacking. A lot of cyber criminals are very good at pretending to be real businesses or people in order to get private information or force people to do bad things.

  Example: A malicious actor initiates a social engineering attack by calling and pretending to be from a financial institution. They want to trick an employee into thinking that their account has been hacked because of strange activity. The attacker is able to use social engineering to trick the innocent employee into giving up their account number and PIN under the guise of verification, making it easier for financial theft to happen. The term *vishing*, which is short for *voice phishing*, is often used by cyber criminals to steal identities and do illegal financial transactions.

- **Smishing**: Smishing refers to SMS phishing, a type of cyberattack that uses text messages to trick people into clicking on dangerous links or giving out private information. A lot of the time, these messages make it sound like time is running out.

  Example: The person being targeted receives a fake text message that seems to come from a legitimate business in the shopping sector. The content of that letter tells the recipient false information that they have been chosen to receive a gift card. If the person wants to win the prize, they should finish the verification on the given link. People should be careful not to click on any sketchy links or give out personal information. Smishing, which comes from the words *text message* and *phishing*, is a sneaky way that threat actors often steal people's identities and spread harmful software, or malware.

- **Clone phishing**: Clone phishing is a trick that malicious individuals use to trick people. They carefully make copies of real emails that people have already received without paying attention. Many times, cloned emails have harmful links or files that are a major security risk.

  Example: If someone is trying to do harm, they can successfully copy and send a recent security alert email from an organization's IT staff to everyone who works there. As a warning, the email says that security may have been compromised and includes a link to start the process of changing passwords. Unfortunately, when workers click on the link by accident, they give the attackers their login information. Malicious people often use clone hacking to get around security measures and spread harmful software.

- **Evil twin phishing**: It is also known as rogue **Wireless Fidelity (Wi-Fi)** access point phishing, which encompasses the deceptive practice of fabricating a counterfeit wireless network that imitates a genuine network. When individuals inadvertently establish a connection with this nefarious network, their online data transmission becomes susceptible to interception and unauthorized manipulation.

  Example: Malicious actors have set up an evil twin Wi-Fi access point close to a coffee shop in the area. It is possible for people who are not paying attention to connect to the fake coffee shop network by accident, thinking it is the real one. It is possible for the attacker to steal the login information or add harmful content to the targeted people's computer traffic.

- **Pop-up phishing**: Pop-up windows used in phishing attacks are a common type of cyber danger. These fake pop-up windows are meant to trick users who are not paying attention into giving out private information or doing bad things. Attackers use phishing to trick people into giving them their personal or financial information by making fake pop-up windows on websites that look like real login or security alerts. These sneaky pop-up windows use a variety of tricks to get people to reveal private and sensitive information.

  Example: While browsing a website that seems to be real, a person is interrupted by an annoying pop-up message saying that their computer has been hacked and forcing them to call a certain number right away to get technical help. The attackers on the other end of the communication line can trick the user into giving up private or sensitive financial or personal information or install malicious software on their system without their knowledge.

- **Watering hole phishing**: Watering hole phishing is a complex form of cyberattack that targets specific groups of people by taking advantage of flaws in websites that those targeted groups of people often visit. Code injection is a method used by cybercriminals to sneakily add harmful code to trustworthy websites. This makes it easier for malware to infect users who are not paying attention.

  Example: Cybercriminals are good at figuring out a well-known industry site that employees from a certain company, whom the cybercriminals are targeting, regularly visit. Malicious code has been added to the forum, making it vulnerable. When workers go to the forum, they get and install harmful software on their computers without meaning to. This puts them at risk of data breaches or system compromise.

- **Angler phishing**: As the name suggests, angler phishing is a more advanced form of phishing that uses a mix of social engineering and misleading techniques to get people to do what the attacker wants. These acts usually involve giving out private information or downloading harmful files without meaning to. False LinkedIn profiles made by malicious actors, that look like they are recruiters from a well-known company, is one way that these attackers try to trick people.

  Example: Using a fake LinkedIn profile, malicious players pretend to be recruiters connected to a reputable company. Cyber attackers aggressively engage in conversations with possible targets and start connection requests. In due time, the offenders start the incredibly convincing electronic correspondence, claiming to be a valid job offer, accompanied by a hyperlink leading to a job application form that has been subtly infiltrated with harmful software.

- **Website spoofing**: It is a malicious technique that involves the creation of fraudulent websites designed to closely mimic authentic ones. Perpetrators employ deceptive tactics to mislead unsuspecting individuals into perceiving a website as trustworthy, thereby luring them into divulging confidential data.

Example: Malicious actors employ the tactic of fabricating a counterfeit online banking portal, meticulously mimicking the visual aesthetics and interface of a legitimate financial institution's website. The targeted individuals are being subjected to phishing emails containing hyperlinks that redirect them to a fraudulent website. On this deceptive platform, they are deceitfully prompted to disclose their sensitive account credentials. The threat actors leverage these compromised credentials to perpetrate illicit activities related to financial fraud.

- **Pharming attacks**: These involve the manipulation of **Domain Name System** (**DNS**) settings or the utilization of malware to surreptitiously redirect unsuspecting users to malevolent websites. The targeted individuals are deceived into perceiving that they are accessing authentic websites.

    Example: Malicious actors have effectively compromised the DNS settings of a router, therefore directing all network traffic toward fake banking websites. User login attempts allow the evil actors to effectively get and document their authentication credentials. Often used by hackers as a malevolent tool, pharming is a means of financial fraud and identity theft.

Using voice cloning technology, threat actors construct convincing audio messages in the field of advanced phishing assaults, therefore improving the deception carried out against gullible victims via voice-based channels. Malicious actors use voice cloning techniques to copy the vocal traits of a well-known CEO in a company, therefore misleading staff members in the finance department during phone contacts. The aforementioned misleading move is planned specifically to persuade the intended entity to approve a large electronic fund transfer. Given the very convincing character of the copied speech patterns, the use of voice cloning technology poses a great challenge for individuals in discriminating between honest activities.

The aforementioned instances provide useful illustrations of the wide spectrum and sophisticated features of phishing campaigns, a preferred strategy used by hostile organizations in cyberspace. Designed with the intention of accomplishing several hostile objectives, including but not limited to illegal financial gains, compromising data integrity, and identity theft, these cyberattacks are finely engineered. These elements draw attention to the clever and dishonest methods used by hostile players in cyberspace to take advantage of vulnerabilities and control companies and people. Prioritizing increased knowledge, thorough education, and the implementation of resilient security measures will help to sufficiently handle the hazards these attacks bring.

Ransomware

Malicious malware known as ransomware encrypts victim files, thus making them inaccessible, and then the attackers demand a ransom payment for the decryption key. Early ransomware was fairly simple, depending on simple encryption and crude payment systems. However, over time, ransomware has developed into a sophisticated and extremely profitable business among the attackers who are using advanced tactics like double extortion, whereby data is not only encrypted but also stolen and threatened to be leaked. Now-a-days ransomware-as-a-service is also available, which lets even low-skilled attackers easily launch ransomware attacks. This development has rendered ransomware a major hazard, to both people and businesses equally, requiring strong security policies and aggressive defense systems.

Types of ransomwares

Various types of ransomwares exist in the cyber threat landscape, each exhibiting distinct characteristics and techniques. It is crucial to understand these types to enhance your knowledge of potential cyber threats. Here are some examples of ransomware:

CryptoLocker

CryptoLocker is a notorious strain of ransomware that has gained significant recognition in the cyber security landscape. The propagation of this particular threat vector commonly occurs via the utilization of malicious email attachments or hyperlinks, subsequently resulting in the encryption of an extensive array of files residing on the compromised individual's computing device.

In the year 2013, a notorious botnet known as *Gameover ZeuS* successfully propagated the malicious ransomware known as **CryptoLocker**, causing widespread infection across a multitude of computer systems on a global scale. The targeted individuals were subjected to a stringent deadline within which they were required to remit the demanded ransom, failing which they would be confronted with irrevocable deprivation of their data, as shown in *Figure 7.4*:

Figure 7.4: Screenshot of the system encrypted by CryptoLocker

WannaCry

Also known as **WannaCrypt**, it is a destructive ransomware variant that exploits a critical Windows vulnerability to propagate swiftly within interconnected networks. This particular malicious software employs encryption algorithms to render files inaccessible and then extorts victims by demanding a monetary payment in exchange for their release.

In 2017, this well-known virus spread to more than 150 countries and caused harm to respected organizations like the **National Health Service (NHS)** in the UK. This caused a lot of chaos and trouble all over the world. *Figure 7.5* shows a screenshot of a system attacked by WannaCry:

Figure 7.5: Screenshot of the system encrypted by WannaCry

Ryuk

Ryuk is a highly advanced strain of ransomware that is frequently linked to meticulously planned and executed cyber assaults targeting prominent enterprises. The delivery mechanism commonly employed is spear-phishing emails.

In the year 2019, a notorious cyber threat known as Ryuk strategically focused its attacks on a multitude of entities, encompassing municipal bodies, healthcare institutions, and media outlets. The threat actor had shown a financially motivated behavior by forcing a large ransom amount.

Sodinokibi

Sodinokibi, also known as **REvil**, was known as a dreadful **ransomware-as-a-service (RaaS)** entity. This entity has gained its reputation for its expertise in exploiting weaknesses, particularly within software systems and the **Remote Desktop Protocol (RDP)**.

A highly published cyberattack was directed towards Kaseya, a prominent software enterprise, resulting in significant impacts for numerous managed service providers and their clientele. The malicious actors have asked for a substantial monetary sum in exchange for decryption keys.

Maze

Maze ransomware is another type of harmful software that has become well-known for using two types of blackmail. Attackers use a complex strategy that includes not only encrypting files but also stealing highly sensitive data and threatening to make it public if the ransom is not paid.

Targeted attacks by Maze have been seen happening against companies in the manufacturing, healthcare, and banking industries. Attacks using ransomware have become even more complicated since they now include data theft and bribery.

The following table shows a few ransomware attacks:

Ransomware group	Targeting industry	Tactics used	Noteworthy impact
REvil (Sodinokibi)	Various, including healthcare, legal	Data encryption, data theft, and double extortion	Executed a massive supply chain attack via Kaseya software, affecting numerous managed service providers and their clients globally.
DarkSide	Various, including energy, logistics	Data encryption, double extortion	Forced a multi-day shutdown of the Colonial Pipeline, a critical U.S. fuel supplier, leading to widespread fuel shortages on the East Coast.
Conti	Healthcare, government, critical infrastructure	Data encryption, double extortion	Caused severe disruption to Ireland's national health system (HSE), forcing the shutdown of IT systems and the cancellation of patient appointments.
Ryuk	Healthcare, government, finance	Data encryption, manual intervention	Targeted large enterprises, including **Universal Health Services (UHS)**, causing significant disruption to hospital operations and patient care across the U.S

Ransomware group	Targeting industry	Tactics used	Noteworthy impact
Maze	Various, including healthcare, finance	Data encryption, data theft, and double extortion	Pioneered the 'double extortion' tactic of stealing sensitive data before encryption and threatening public release to pressure victims like Cognizant.
DoppelPaymer	Manufacturing, healthcare, education	Data encryption, double extortion	Known for targeting critical sectors, including healthcare facilities, during the COVID-19 pandemic, and exfiltrating data for additional leverage.
LockBit	Various, including manufacturing, finance	Data encryption, double extortion	Operates as one of the most prolific RaaS groups, known for its speed and high-profile attacks on organizations like Accenture.
NetWalker	Healthcare, education, government	Data encryption, data theft, and double extortion	Specifically targeted the healthcare and education sectors, including the **University of California, San Francisco (UCSF)**, disrupting operations and research.
Ragnar Locker	Manufacturing, financial services	Data encryption, double extortion	Known for targeting large corporate networks and exfiltrating sensitive data before encryption, as seen in the attack on energy giant EDP Renewables.
Babuk	Various, including manufacturing, healthcare	Data encryption, double extortion	Gained notoriety for its attack on the Washington D.C. Police Department, where it stole and subsequently leaked sensitive internal data.

Table 7.2: Top ransomware attacks

Ransomware is a real threat that businesses must deal with, and it changes with time. It can put their finances, operations, and image at risk. Implementing comprehensive cybersecurity measures must be the top priority for all organizations to successfully deal with this threat. These steps should include strong backup plans, thorough training for employees, careful management of vulnerabilities, and careful planning for handling incidents.

The next few years are likely to be very interesting for ransomware. Malicious actors will keep changing and adapting their software, and things will get harder for both businesses and individuals. The constantly changing nature of ransomware surely brings many challenges and chances to cybersecurity. Organizations must always be alert, giving cybersecurity priority and developing all-encompassing IRPs to effectively minimize the consequences of ransomware events. Cyber attackers are honing their tactics; hence, cybersecurity defenders must be proactive in updating their techniques to keep ahead in the never-ending struggle against ransomware attacks.

Denial-of-service and distributed denial-of-service

A DoS attack involves a single attacker overwhelming a target system with traffic or requests, making it unavailable to legitimate users. In contrast, a DDoS attack uses multiple compromised computers (a botnet) to launch an attack, significantly amplifying its scale and impact. Let us look at a DoS attack first.

Denial-of-service attack

A DoS attack is an attempt by a malicious actor to disrupt the services or resources of a single computer, server, or network. The attacker does this by overwhelming the target with a high volume of traffic or by exploiting vulnerabilities to exhaust system resources. Now, in the next sub-section, let us understand what a DDoS attack is.

Distributed denial-of-service attack

DDoS attacks are a constant and changing threat to businesses. The goal of these attacks is to stop their online services from working by sending too much traffic to them at once. These attacks come in different forms and use different weaknesses in the application and network core layers.

DoS and DDoS attacks on businesses cause traffic overload, service interruptions, loss of money and reputation, and problems with operations. The following figure shows a representation of both attacks:

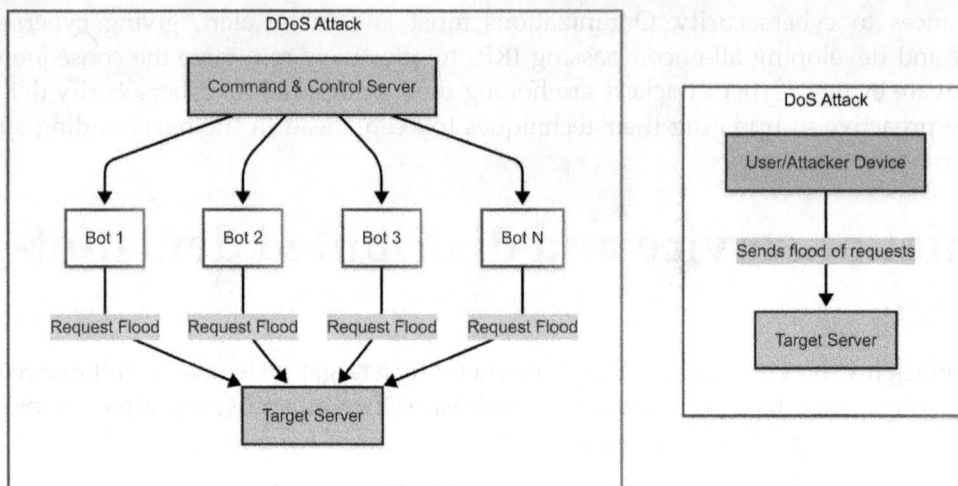

Figure 7.6: DoS and DDoS explanation

DoS and DDoS attack types

Let us look at some of the top DoS and DDoS attack types, along with a few real-time examples:

- **TCP/IP exhaustion attack**: TCP/IP exhaustion attacks, such as **synchronize (SYN)** floods, exploit the TCP handshake process. The attacker sends a high volume of SYN requests to the target server but does not complete the handshake, leaving the server waiting for acknowledgments and exhausting its connection resources.

   Example: A huge TCP/IP exhaustion attack happened on the *Dyn DNS service* in 2016. This stopped people from accessing popular websites like Twitter, Netflix, and Reddit. The attackers used a botnet of **Internet of Things (IoT)** devices to launch the attack, showing how devastating these kinds of strikes can be.

- **User datagram protocol (UDP) reflection attack**: UDP reflection attacks leverage the fact that many servers respond to UDP requests with larger packets. The attacker sends UDP requests to these servers with the victim's IP address as the source. The servers then send the large responses to the victim, overwhelming their network.

   Example: In 2018, *GitHub* was hit by a major UDP reflection attack. The attackers used Memcached servers to make their strike stronger. With a peak bandwidth of 1.35 Tbps, the strike showed how destructive UDP reflection attacks can be.

- **SYN flood attack**: A SYN flood attack sends a huge number of TCP SYN requests to a target server, making it unable to finish the three-way handshake process and make connections.

   Example: The 2016 Dyn DNS attack used a huge network of hacked IoT devices as a botnet and had SYN flood parts. The different attack methods worked together to cause a lot of trouble.

- **DNS amplification attack**: DNS amplification attacks leverage open DNS resolvers to send a large number of DNS queries with forged source IPs to the target. The resolvers respond with amplified DNS responses, flooding the victim with data.

  Example: In 2013, *Spamhaus*, an anti-spam organization, suffered a DNS amplification attack that reached 300 Gbps, making it one of the largest such attacks at the time. The attackers used misconfigured DNS servers to amplify their assault.

- **HTTP flood attack**: HTTP flood attacks bombard a web server with a high volume of HTTP requests. These requests can be simple GET requests or more complex requests designed to consume server resources, ultimately leading to service unavailability.

  Example: *Cloudflare* said in 2020 that it had stopped a huge HTTP flood attack that was sending 800 million requests per minute. The goal of the attack was to overload the infrastructure of the website being attacked so that users could not get to it.

- **ICMP flood attack**: ICMP flood attacks, which are also called Ping floods, send a lot of ICMP echo request (Ping) packets to the target network, using up a lot of data and resources.

  Example: An ICMP flood attack on *GitHub* in 2018 reached a peak speed of 1.3 Tbps, making it one of the biggest DDoS strikes at the time. DDoS security services helped GitHub lessen the damage of the attack.

- **Slowloris attack**: Attacks called **Slowloris**, target web servers by starting many HTTP connections and sending HTTP headers very slowly. This uses up server resources and makes website replies take a long time.

  Example: Over the years, Slowloris has been used in several strikes on websites. Even though it does not get as much attention as some other attacks, this one is still a threat, and attackers often use it to stay hidden.

- **Network time protocol (NTP) amplification attack**: NTP amplification attacks use NTP servers that are weak to send more DDoS data to the target.

  Example: In 2015, the *BBC* was hit by a 300 Gbps NTP amplification attack that was very strong. Attackers went after the BBC's online services, which were temporarily interrupted.

- **Ping flood attack**: Ping flood attacks send a lot of ICMP echo requests (Ping) packets to the victim's network, which fills up the bandwidth and slows things down.

  Example: Ping flood attacks have been used in the past, though they have not been used as much in recent years. They have been used to damage networks and flood individual users' internet connections.

Understanding these top ten DoS and DDoS attacks and seeing examples of them in real time makes it very clear how important it is to use strong DDoS mitigation strategies to protect businesses from these annoying threats. These include traffic monitoring, rate limiting, and using **content delivery networks (CDNs)**.

Figure 7.7 represents the largest recorded Layer 7 DDoS attack, peaking at 46 million **requests per second** (**RPS**). The graph illustrates how the attack rapidly escalated, reaching its peak within seconds, before being mitigated and eventually neutralized by Google's cloud-based security systems:

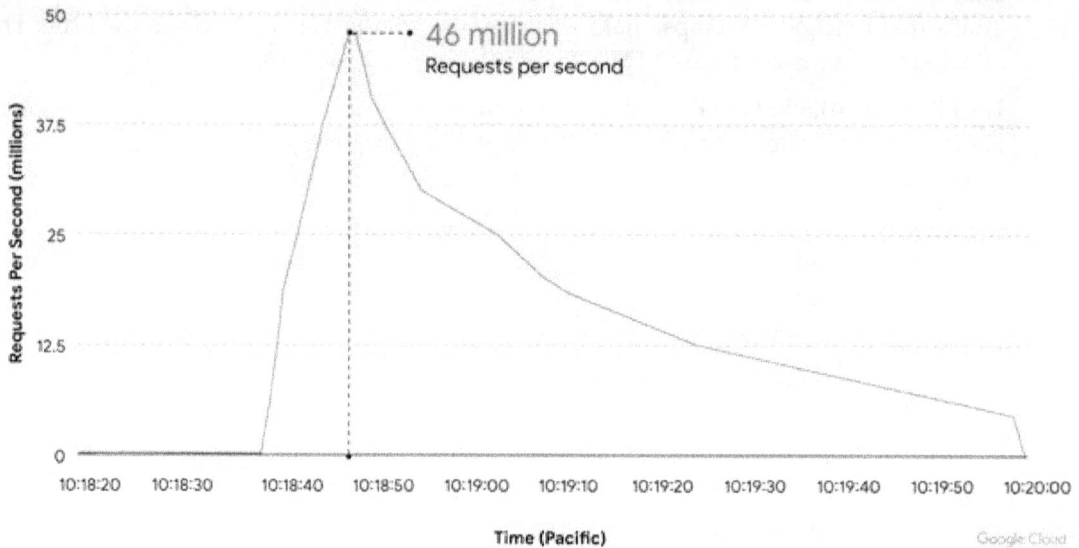

Figure 7.7: *DDoS attack graph peaking at 46M requests per second*

Source: *https://cloud.google.com/blog/products/identity-security/*
how-google-cloud-blocked-largest-layer-7-ddos attack-at-46-million-rps

Advanced persistent threat

An **advanced persistent threat (APT)** is a carefully planned and sustained cyberattack that poses a significant risk to many different entities, especially companies. Unlike opportunistic attacks, APTs show a great degree of complexity and are painstakingly well-planned and executed by skilled threat actors, usually with the help of highly organized criminal syndicates or national entities. The attackers breach the network of a targeted entity using a wide range of **tactics, methods, and procedures** (**TTPs**), then persist secretly for extended lengths of time, sometimes spanning years, and achieve different, strategic goals.

Usually starting their activities by carefully performing thorough reconnaissance operations, APTs exercise seeks to provide insightful knowledge about the intended company, its staff, and its technology base. Usually, the main entrance vectors are well-crafted spear-phishing emails, meant to capture selected people. Once illegal access is obtained, hostile actors can use covert techniques to move horizontally throughout the network, increasing their privileges and guaranteeing their ongoing presence. To hide from traditional security systems, cyber attackers can use customized malicious software and take advantage of zero-day exploits, i.e., undiscovered flaws.

APTs have several main goals, including espionage, illegal data collecting, and possible disturbance of important infrastructure, targeting valuable assets including intellectual property, proprietary data, and confidential government information. Malicious actors deliberately seek to illegally remove them from their proper owners. Cyber enemies might also engage in cyber-espionage activities meant to provide political, financial, or military advantage.

Organizations that want to properly reduce the risks of APTs must adopt a proactive cybersecurity posture. Moreover, companies must aggressively create a strong IRP if they are to quickly spot and stop APT strikes.

Organizations must embrace a proactive attitude and admit their vulnerability to APTs in the contemporary digital scene marked by high risks, understanding the complex nature of these approaching hazards, and allocating funds towards implementing strong and all-encompassing cybersecurity measures that will help people and businesses to strengthen their capacity to resist and minimize the possible damage caused by these quite advanced attacks.

Attributes of an advanced persistent threat attack

A key characteristic of APTs is their focus on long-term persistence within the target's network. Attackers establish multiple backdoors and maintain a low profile to ensure continued access, even if some of their entry points are discovered and blocked. In this way, they hope to get what they want without being caught by security measures. APT strikes specifically aimed at certain people, businesses, or industries are accurate. The other side spends a lot of money and time on extensive reconnaissance operations to learn useful information about the people they are after. APTs use sophisticated methods to stay hidden, such as custom malware, encryption, anti-forensics techniques, and being stealthy. APT groups often make custom malware that is designed to take advantage of the target environment, which makes it hard to find using the standard security measures.

Stages of an advanced persistent threat

In this subsection, we will understand various stages of APT:

- **Reconnaissance**: In the reconnaissance phase, threat actors gather information about the target group to collect intelligence about it. As part of this, you should learn about its employees, processes, weaknesses, and possible entry points. For example, open-source intelligence gathering, social engineering (using psychological tricks on people to get what you want), or carefully checking systems for flaws and holes are all possible parts of the process at hand.

- **Primary compromise**: Adversaries use many methods, like spear-phishing emails, malicious files, or taking advantage of weaknesses, to get into a specific network for the first time. Their main goal is to get a strategic base in the system once they have successfully compromised it.

- **Persistence**: Establishing persistence is an important part of APT tactics. Threat actors use a variety of methods to make sure they stay in systems that have been compromised. This could mean setting up hidden entry points, putting complex malware in place, or changing system settings to avoid being caught.

- **Lateral movement**: Lateral movement involves attackers navigating within the compromised network to gain access to valuable assets. They use techniques like pass-the-hash, privilege escalation, and exploiting internal vulnerabilities to move from one system to another. They do this by strategically moving around within the network environment; their goal is to take control of important resources.

- **Data exfiltration**: APT attacks are mostly about data exfiltration because they want to get private and valuable information, like personal data and intellectual property, without permission. The thieves are very good at finding, stealing, and often encrypting the data that they take, which may be stored on computers they control.

- **Covering tracks**: APT groups use a variety of techniques to hide their activities and make it harder for incident rescuers to figure out what they were doing. As part of these steps, logs are deleted, timestamps are changed, and anti-forensic methods are used. Through these actions, APT groups hope to make it very hard for people who are looking into their malicious activities.

- **Maintaining access**: Threat players carefully watch the compromised system, change their plans based on the company's defenses, and change their methods as needed to avoid being caught. Even after exfiltrating data, attackers may maintain access to the network for future use. They may leave backdoors or hidden entry points to regain access when needed, continuing to exploit the system over time.

- **Command-and-control (C&C)**: APT attackers establish C&C channels to communicate with and control compromised systems within the target network. These channels may use various techniques to blend in with legitimate traffic and evade detection, such as using encrypted protocols or hiding within legitimate network services.

Gaining a comprehensive comprehension of an APT attack is of utmost importance for organizations to formulate and implement robust cybersecurity strategies. To effectively counter the risks posed by APTs, it is imperative to adopt a proactive stance encompassing ongoing surveillance, the exchange of threat intelligence, and meticulous incident response preparation. The following table summarizes a few APT groups, their characteristics, and other details:

APT group	Characteristics	Major incidents	Associated malware
APT29 (Cozy Bear)	Believed to be Russian state sponsored	Accused of hacking the Democratic National Committee in 2016	Hammertoss, MiniDuke
	Known for sophisticated spear phishing campaigns	Impersonated U.S. State Department email system	
	Targets government entities, defense, think tanks	Suspected involvement in SolarWinds supply chain attack	
APT28 (Fancy Bear)	Linked to Russian military intelligence (GRU)	Accused of hacking the Democratic National Committee in 2016	Sofacy/Sednit, XAgent, Xtunnel,
	Notorious for cyber espionage and disinformation	Infiltration of the World AntiDoping Agency	
	Targets governments, military, critical infrastructure	Attempted interference in elections in multiple countries	
APT34 (OilRig)	Believed to be Iranian state sponsored	Targeted the U.S. and Middle Eastern organizations	Helminth, HyperShell, PoisonFrog
	Known for spear phishing and social engineering	Data theft from U.S. universities	
	Focuses on espionage and stealing sensitive data	Cyberattacks against Saudi Arabian infrastructure	
APT35 (Charming Kitten)	Linked to Iranian government	Targeted U.S. government officials and dissidents	BONDUPDATER, QUADAGENT, INFY, Catfish, Sniff, Jason
	Utilizes spear phishing and social engineering	Impersonated journalists and academics	
	Focuses on cyber espionage and surveillance	Attempts to collect intelligence on political opponents	

APT group	Characteristics	Major incidents	Associated malware
Lazarus Group	Associated with North Korean government	Infamous for the Sony Pictures hack in 2014	WannaCry, Destover, Lazarus,
	Engages in cyber espionage, financial theft	Attacked banks, cryptocurrency exchanges	
	Targets financial institutions, cryptocurrency	Attempted theft of funds from the Bangladesh Bank	

Table 7.3: APT attacks, their characteristics and impact

Gaining an in-depth understanding of an APT attack is of utmost importance for organizations to formulate and implement robust cybersecurity strategies. To effectively counter the risks posed by APTs, it is imperative to adopt a proactive stance encompassing ongoing surveillance, the exchange of threat intelligence, and meticulous incident response preparation. In our future chapters, we shall learn how a blue teamer can be on top of these attacks to safeguard organizations.

Insider threat

Insider risks are a big problem, and they happen when people inside a company, like workers or contractors, abuse their access to hurt the company's data or security. These threats can be made on purpose, with foul intentions, or by accident, due to carelessness or human error. To keep private information safe, you need to understand and deal with both types.

Threats from inside can look like many things. Insiders can be people who are out to do harm and do bad things on purpose, like stealing data or sabotaging, or insiders can be people who are careless and often cause security problems by falling for fake scams or setting up systems incorrectly. Third parties, like contractors and vendors, can be dangerous if they abuse the information, they are allowed access to.

Insider threats are caused by several different things. People may steal and sell data or participate in insider trading to make money. Employees who are angry about being fired or having problems at work may try to get back at their employers. Due to politics or beliefs, espionage can lead to the release of private information. Accidental data release and carelessness can also do a lot of damage.

It is very important to know the signs of insider danger, which can include strange patterns of data access, failed login attempts over and over, illegal device use, changes in behavior like withdrawal or discontent, and data theft for no good reason.

In real life, an angry worker at the big UK bank, *Tesco Bank* used his access to other employees' computers to steal £2.28 million from customer accounts in 2016. He took advantage of flaws in the bank's systems to move money to his own accounts. This event shows how bad insider threats can be and how important strong security means and keeping an eye on employees are.

Insider threat intelligence

In the field of cybersecurity, insider threats present an exceptional and enduring obstacle. Perpetrators of sabotage, contractors, or authorized personnel may inadvertently or deliberately cause substantial damage through the use of their authorized privileges to compromise systems, steal confidential information, or disrupt operations. Insider threat intelligence is a specialized field of study that aims to proactively detect, assess, and alleviate the dangers presented by individuals who have already breached the perimeter of your organization.

Insiders turning into threats

It is not always a clear-cut case of someone being a bad actor. Insider threats can happen for a bunch of reasons, like money troubles, feeling disgruntled at work, maybe being pressured by someone outside the company, or plain old carelessness. Understanding why people turn on their own organization is key to figuring out who might pose a risk.

Insider threat damage

The damage insiders can do is wide-ranging. They might steal sensitive data, swipe company secrets, mess with systems on purpose, bring in malware from outside, some even open the door wider for other attackers.

Key pillars of insider threat intelligence

Effective insider threat intelligence relies on several key pillars to detect and respond to potential threats before they cause harm, which are mentioned as follows:

- **Data-driven detection:**
    - o **Log analysis**: Scrutinizing SIEM logs, file access logs, network traffic, and authentication patterns for anomalies.
    - o **User behavior analytics (UBA)**: Machine learning and statistical models establish behavioral baselines for individuals and entities, flagging deviations that might indicate risk.
    - o **Risk-based prioritization**: Assigning risk scores to users, behaviors, and assets allows teams to focus resources on the most critical potential threats. Context is key; an employee accessing sensitive financial data outside normal working patterns warrants higher concern.

- **Mitigation strategies:**

  o **Principle of least privilege**: Granting users only the minimum necessary access rights reduces the potential impact of compromised accounts.

  o **Privileged access management (PAM)**: Enforcing stricter controls, monitoring, and auditing privileged accounts.

  o **Data loss prevention (DLP)**: Tools to detect and block unauthorized exfiltration of sensitive information.

  o **Exit procedures**: Swift revocation of access and disabling credentials of departing employees is crucial.

Challenges and best practices

In this subsection, we will look at a few challenges and best practices pertaining to insider threats:

- **Balancing privacy**: Monitoring must be proportionate to risk and adhere to privacy regulations and company policies.

- **False positives**: Behavioral analysis can sometimes generate alerts on benign anomalies. Tuning models is essential to reduce noise.

- **Human element**: Educate employees about insider threats, how to spot suspicious behaviors, and establish clear reporting channels.

It is not just technology that insider threat intelligence is about; to lower the risk of insiders doing harm, it is important to create a strong security culture, encourage open communication, and stick to clear policies. By using threat intelligence principles in your company, you make it much less likely that someone will do something bad or careless from inside.

Physical security

While cybersecurity focuses on protecting digital assets, these efforts can be undermined if an attacker can simply gain physical access to equipment. **Physical security** is the practice of safeguarding personnel, hardware, and tangible assets from real-world threats like theft, vandalism, or unauthorized entry. It is a foundational layer of a comprehensive security strategy because it protects the very infrastructure that hosts an organization's critical data and systems.

An effective physical security program is essential for mitigating a range of threats. It prevents unauthorized individuals from accessing sensitive areas like data centers and server rooms, thereby protecting against data breaches and the physical theft or destruction of critical equipment. Furthermore, strong physical controls are a key component in mitigating **insider threats**, as they limit the ability of even authorized personnel to access areas or systems outside of their specific job functions.

To build a robust physical security posture, organizations should implement a layered defense that includes:

- **Access control:** Employing measures such as keycards, biometric scanners, and secure locks to ensure only authorized individuals can enter sensitive facilities.

- **Surveillance:** Using CCTV cameras and monitoring systems to deter intruders and provide evidence for investigations. Intrusion detection systems, including alarms and sensors, provide early warnings of unauthorized entry.

- **Visitor management:** Implementing strict sign-in protocols and issuing temporary access badges to control and monitor all non-employees within a facility.

- **Integrating physical and cybersecurity:** In a modern enterprise, physical and digital security are not separate. They should be seamlessly integrated to provide unified protection. For example:

  o **CCTV footage** can be analyzed with AI-powered software to detect suspicious behavior, and these alerts can be correlated with digital security logs in a SIEM.

  o **Badge access systems** should be tied to user accounts, so that disabling a user's network access also revokes their physical entry privileges.

  o **Network access control (NAC)** solutions can be used to enforce security policies at the point of connection, preventing a device from joining the network unless it meets predefined security criteria, effectively creating a digital checkpoint that complements a physical one.

By treating physical security as an integral part of the overall cybersecurity strategy, organizations can close critical gaps that attackers are eager to exploit. After all, the most sophisticated firewall is useless if an intruder can walk in and unplug the server.

Remember, the most sophisticated cyber-attack can be rendered ineffective if the attacker can simply walk in the front door.

Conclusion

This chapter has provided a comprehensive overview of the main and disruptive cybersecurity risks that companies come across on the modern digital terrain. The listed risks, which include sophisticated kinds of malicious software and APTs, showcase the complex nature and ongoing existence of cyberattacks in the modern digital scene.

We looked closely at DDoS assaults, which can seriously disable web systems, and it underlined especially the great need to use strong mitigating techniques to stop such harmful behaviors. Being a destructive program capable of paralyzing companies and demanding outrageous ransoms, ransomware clearly shows the financial motivations motivating attackers. Strategic cybersecurity strategy now depends much on the understanding and preemptive readiness for ransomware attacks. Moreover, it is important to recognize the serious character of APTs, which represent the deliberate and relentless strategies used by state-sponsored or highly organized enemies. As such, companies must start strengthening their protection systems from a proactive standpoint.

Towards the end, we saw how important it is to realize that social engineering strategies work as a continual reminder of the inherent vulnerability presented by the human element, which remains among the most vulnerable features of the field of security.

The knowledge acquired in this chapter helps to build a strong cybersecurity posture and strengthen the digital assets of companies in a world of ever-greater connectivity. This chapter covers all the theoretical parts of cyber threats. In the next chapters, we shall learn about these topics more by technically diving deep into the practical aspects of these topics and understand what a blue teamer is expected to do in a real cyber threat scenario.

Join our Discord space

Join our Discord workspace for latest updates, offers, tech happenings around the world, new releases, and sessions with the authors:

https://discord.bpbonline.com

CHAPTER 8
Threat Hunting Exploration

Introduction

In the modern cybersecurity landscape, a reactive posture is no longer sufficient. Organizations must transition from simply responding to alerts to actively seeking out threats that evade traditional defenses. This chapter provides a comprehensive guide to proactive threat hunting, equipping security professionals with the knowledge and techniques to uncover hidden adversaries and fortify their defenses. We must therefore reframe defense in a different way. We cannot simply wait for the alarms to sound and wait for attacks passively. We must become proactive and unrelenting hunters ourselves. You can learn how to become a cyber danger hunter from this chapter. It will teach you how to actively find dangers in your network, including those adept at hiding. After finishing this chapter, you will be able to identify threats, before those assailants have a chance to cause any significant harm, you will be able to expel them and safeguard your company.

Structure

This chapter will include the following topics:

- Importance of threat hunting
- Deception technology
- Threat hunting techniques

- Planning, preparation, and process

- Experience, efficiency, and expertise

- Proactive threat hunting and advanced threats

Objectives

This chapter aims to transform your defensive cybersecurity approach. You will develop the proactive mindset of a threat hunter, embracing hypothesis-driven investigations to uncover even the most well-hidden threats. You will gain a clear understanding of why traditional security tools often fall short and why threat hunting has become essential for protecting enterprise environments. This chapter will teach you how to leverage threat intelligence to anticipate attacker behaviors and optimize your hunts. Additionally, you will master practical tools and techniques for network analysis, log review, and malware investigation. Finally, hands-on exercises will solidify your knowledge and give you direct experience applying your threat-hunting skills to realistic scenarios.

Importance of threat hunting

Consider a situation where in your home is being broken into, reconnaissance is the time before they enter, boom is the actual act of breaking in, and post-boom is the time it takes to find and recover. This implies that there are dangers in your systems that go unnoticed until they do harm. The goal of threat hunting is to proactively identify these dangers before they cause chaos.

Hunting for threats constitutes a proactive cybersecurity strategy. It is the distinction between waiting passively for an attack to occur and actively scanning your network for concealed threats. Imagine oneself in the role of an experienced investigator, scrupulously scrutinizing each indication and irregularity, to reveal the truth before the time runs out.

The consequences are unquestionably high in the digital world of today. A successful cyberattack has the potential to cause substantial financial harm, undermine consumer confidence, and impair a business. Our adversaries are relentless and perpetually inventive in their strategies. The frequency of data intrusions is increasing, ransomware attacks are becoming more sophisticated, and the threat posed by nation-state actors is expanding. Exclusively depending on conventional security measures is tantamount to blindly wishing for the best.

The problem: Traditional security focuses on reactive responses after threats are detected. However, the time between an attack and its discovery can be significant, leading to extensive data loss and financial damage. The average time to identify a threat is 200 days, and containment takes another 70 days, totaling a staggering 270 days of vulnerability. (**Source**: **https://www.threatintelligence.com/blog/soc-data-security#:~:text=Data%20Breach%20 Lifecycle%3A,and%20contain%2C%20averaging%20292%20days**)

The solution: Threat hunting

Threat hunting focuses on two primary types of clues:

- **Indicators of compromise (IOCs)**: These are the static artifacts or *evidence* left behind after an attack, such as a malicious file's hash, a known-bad IP address, or a specific registry key created by malware. IOCs confirm a compromise has occurred.

- **Indicators of attack (IOAs)**: These focus on an adversary's actions and intentions, regardless of the specific malware or exploit used. An IOA might be a process attempting to scrape credentials from memory or an unusual PowerShell command being used for lateral movement. IOAs help detect an attack in progress."

Advantages of threat hunting

Now, let us look at the advantages of threat hunting:

- **Lower risk**: Identify and eliminate dangers before they have a chance to do harm.

- **Quicker reaction**: Reduce the amount of time that passes between an attack and containment.

- **Reduced expenses**: Prevent the monetary consequences of outages and data breaches.

- **Better security posture**: Learn more about your security weaknesses.

Recall that threat hunting can help you go from a reactive to a proactive cybersecurity posture, thereby lessening the effect of possible assaults and safeguarding your important data. Additionally, to improve your abilities, think about taking part in threat-hunting activities and communities.

Continually assess and revise your threat-hunting approach, considering your unique requirements and security environment. You may secure your vital systems and create a strong defense against online attacks by combining these precautions with the advice given here.

Effective strategies for threat hunting

Conventional security measures such as antivirus software and firewalls have proven to be inadequate. Sophisticated adversaries consistently modify their strategies, utilizing intricate methods to penetrate security perimeters and acquire vital systems and data. Cyber threat hunting is an advantageous proactive strategy that enables security teams to detect concealed hazards that may be present within the network.

The scenario: Imagine a company that uses popular accounting software. Their security team learns (through threat intelligence sources, entity-driven hunting), that a new vulnerability in this software is being actively exploited by hackers to steal financial data.

Now, with the help of the aforementioned scenario, let us understand the various effective strategies for threat hunting.

Structured hunting by targeting TTPs

Structured hunts are methodical and targeted, by leveraging IoAs, and **tactics, techniques, and procedures** (**TTPs**) associated with known threat actors. Think of it as hunting a specific animal; you know its tracks, its behavior, and the signs it leaves behind.

By aligning hunts with the MITRE ATT&CK framework, which catalogs adversary TTPs, hunters can identify potential threats even before they cause damage. This framework offers a comprehensive knowledge base, encompassing both pre-attack (PRE-ATT&CK) and enterprise-specific techniques. Structured hunts leverage this knowledge to identify the *paw prints* of specific threat actors within your network.

Action in the scenario: The team starts with a structured hunt. They use the MITRE ATT&CK framework to identify the TTPs, commonly used by attackers exploiting this vulnerability. They know these attackers often try to escalate privileges and move laterally within the network after gaining access. So, they focus their search on unusual activities related to user permissions and network connections.

Unstructured hunting and following the clues

Unstructured hunts, on the other hand, are more exploratory. They are often triggered by a single IOC, such as a suspicious file hash or a malicious IP address. This single clue acts as a thread, and the hunter's job is to unravel the entire tapestry of malicious activity. They may need to analyze historical data, searching for pre- and post-detection patterns associated with the initial IOC. Think of it as following a trail of breadcrumbs left behind by an unknown animal; you do not know what you are looking for, but you keep following the clues.

The depth and breadth of an unstructured hunt depend on data retention policies and the availability of historical security incidents. The more data available, the further the hunter can trace the attacker's footsteps.

Action in the scenario: During the structured hunt, they discover a suspicious login attempt from an unknown **Internet Protocol** (**IP**) address (IOC), on a server running the vulnerable accounting software. This triggers an unstructured hunt. They investigate the server logs and find evidence that the attacker downloaded a malicious file. They analyze the file and discover it is a custom backdoor, allowing the attacker persistent access.

Situational and entity-driven hunting

The final approach combines internal intelligence with external threat data. Situational threat hunting leverages information gleaned from internal risk assessments and vulnerability analyses specific to your organization's IT environment. Think of it as understanding the unique vulnerabilities of your landscape. Entity-driven hunting, on the other hand, draws insights from crowd-sourced attack data. By analyzing reports from other organizations, hunters can identify the latest TTPs used by current cyber threats. They can then tailor their investigations to search for these specific behaviors within your network. Imagine learning from other animal trackers about the latest hunting techniques used by specific predators.

Action in the scenario: Now, they combine their knowledge of the attacker's TTPs with their understanding of their own network (situational awareness). They know their financial data is stored on a separate, highly secure server. They focus their efforts on analyzing logs and network traffic related to that server, looking for any signs of the attacker attempting to access it. They also prioritize patching vulnerability on all systems running the accounting software.

Understanding the adversary mindset

Effective cyber threat hunting requires a shift in perspective. It is about thinking like an attacker and understanding their motivations, TTPs. Threat actors can range from financially motivated cybercriminals deploying ransomware to nation-state actors conducting espionage. Each has distinct goals and utilizes specific tools and techniques. Threat intelligence plays a crucial role here. By leveraging threat intelligence feeds, security teams can gain insights into current attack trends, adversary TTPs, and IOCs, indicating that a system might be compromised.

Toolkit and the human element

There is no one tool that can ensure that threat hunting will work. It is a mix of techniques and tools that are used in a planned way. The most important thing a threat hunter has is their information and experience. To be successful, you need to be meticulous, have a deep knowledge of how attackers act, and have the ability to think critically. As we dive deeper into this chapter, we will learn more about the tools used to look for threats.

Even though tools are very important for threat hunting, people are still very important. To make sense of data, find oddities, and put the pieces of the puzzle together, security researchers need to be good at analysis. They can do thorough investigations and successfully deal with threats found because they have experience with malware analysis, digital forensics, and incident response frameworks. A threat hunter must also be creative and ready to think outside the box to excel at their job.

Collaborating via cyber threat intelligence sharing platforms

Cyber threat intelligence sharing platforms facilitate collaboration among organizations, enabling the exchange of threat intelligence, IOCs, and best practices. By participating in threat intelligence-sharing communities, organizations can enhance their threat detection capabilities and strengthen their overall cybersecurity posture. A few examples of cyber threat intelligence sharing platforms include **Information Sharing and Analysis Centers (ISACs)**, Government-led initiatives like the **Cybersecurity and Infrastructure Security Agency (CISA)** in the US, Open-source platforms like **Malware Information Sharing Platform (MISP)**, etc.

The timely sharing of information about new threats, weaknesses, and attack trends is made easier by these platforms. This lets businesses protect themselves against known threats. These platforms give a fuller picture of the threat landscape by collecting threat data from various sources.

Sharing the best ways to handle incidents and the lessons learned can help other businesses make their own processes better. Working together during active events can help containment and cleanup go more quickly, which can lessen the damage from attacks. This collaborative space makes it easier for people to share private data and works to protect everyone from cyber dangers.

Deception technology

While threat hunting involves actively searching for adversaries, deception technology is a proactive strategy that flips the script: it creates attractive, decoy targets to lure attackers into revealing themselves. Instead of you finding them, you make them come to you. By setting up these digital traps, any interaction becomes a high-fidelity alert, providing an early and unambiguous warning of malicious activity on your network.

Honeypots, honeytokens, and honeynets, the concepts of deception

Deception technology is built on several core components designed to mimic legitimate assets:

- **Honeypots**: A honeypot is a computer system or service designed to be an attractive target for attackers. Its value lies in the fact that no legitimate user should ever interact with it. Honeypots range in complexity:

    o Low-interaction honeypots emulate common services (like SSH or a web server) and can capture initial connection attempts and basic commands. They are relatively safe and easy to deploy.

    o High-interaction honeypots are fully functional systems (e.g., a real Windows or Linux OS) that allow an attacker to interact with them deeply. While more complex to manage, they provide invaluable intelligence on an attacker's **tools, techniques, and procedures (TTPs)**.

- **Honeytokens:** These are digital bait or canary tokens seeded within your environment. They are designed to be stolen or used by an attacker. Like a honeypot, they should never be accessed by a legitimate process. Examples include:

    o A fake AWS API key placed in a configuration file or code repository.

    o A fake database connection string embedded in an application's code.

    o A Word document named `Executive Salaries.docx` that contains a token that *calls home* to an external server the moment it is opened.

- **Honeynets:** This is a more advanced concept, consisting of a network of multiple, interconnected honeypots. A honeynet is designed to simulate a larger, more realistic corporate network, allowing defenders to observe how attackers perform lateral movement and interact with multiple systems after the initial compromise.

Practical deployment

You can start implementing deception technology with simple, high-impact deployments which are as follows:

- **Simple honeypot setup:** An easy starting point is to deploy a low-interaction SSH honeypot like Cowrie. You could place this decoy system in your network (perhaps in a DMZ or a user segment) and configure it to forward all of its logs to your SIEM. Any attempt to log into this non-production system is an immediate red flag and warrants investigation.

- **Honeytoken creation:** Creating a honeytoken can be highly effective. For example, you can generate a new, fake AWS API key within your AWS account but assign it no permissions. Place this key in a developer's configuration file on a server or within a private code repository. Then, create a high-priority alert in your SIEM or cloud monitoring tool to trigger the moment that specific key is ever used in an API call.

Monitoring and alerting the high-fidelity signal

The primary advantage of deception technology is the quality of its alerts. Unlike alerts from an IDS or antivirus, which can often be false positives triggered by benign activity, an alert from a deception asset is almost always a sign of a real threat, details as follows.

- **Zero false positives (in theory)**: Since these assets have no production value, no legitimate user or process should ever interact with them. Therefore, any interaction is a high-fidelity alert that indicates an unauthorized presence on your network.

- **Monitoring and alerting**: All logs from honeypots should be ingested by your SIEM. Alerts for any access attempt on a honeypot or any use of a honeytoken should be configured at the highest priority, triggering an immediate incident response or threat hunt.

Use cases for deception technology

Beyond just detection, deception serves several strategic purposes for a blue team:

- **Early and accurate warning of a breach**: An attacker interacting with a decoy is often one of the very first actions they take after gaining initial access. This provides a very early warning, long before they can reach their true objective.

- **Gathering high-context threat intelligence**: Observing an attacker in a high-interaction honeypot provides invaluable, real-time intelligence. You can see the specific commands they run, the tools they download, and the vulnerabilities they try to exploit. This is intelligence about an adversary actively targeting *your* environment.

- **Slowing down adversaries**: Attackers waste valuable time and resources attempting to exploit decoy systems, which gives your blue team more time to detect their presence on the real network and mount an effective response.

Threat hunting techniques

Threat actors never stop, hence we cannot either. Patching systems and teaching people to be careful is important; however, these days, we need to be more proactive. We need to think like hunters, anticipating the moves our adversaries might make, as mentioned earlier.

The best hunters know their prey. In the cyber world, that means understanding what is normal for your network. Think of it like knowing the usual sounds and rhythms of your own home. Once you know what normal looks like, you can start to spot those weird things that might be a sign of trouble.

Understanding the adversary

Effective threat hunting hinges on a deep understanding of your network's normal state, i.e., its baseline behavior. This baseline serves as the standard for identifying anomalies, i.e., potential indicators of malicious activity. Here is a two-pronged approach to establish this crucial foundation:

1. **Active and passive asset management**:

    *   Maintain a comprehensive inventory of all devices and systems on your network. This includes both IT and **operational technology (OT)** assets.

    *   Utilize vulnerability scanners to identify potential weaknesses associated with these assets.

    *   Regularly review and update your asset inventory to ensure its accuracy.

2. **System and network monitoring**:

    *   Implement system-level monitoring to track processes, network communications, and SSL/TLS encryption activity.

    *   Leverage **security information and event management (SIEM)** solutions to collect and analyze logs from various security tools like firewalls, **intrusion detection systems (IDS)**, and endpoints.

    *   Correlate system-level data with firewall alerts to gain a holistic view of potential threats.

Threat hunting methodologies and frameworks

Cyber threat hunting is not a random search; it is a structured process guided by methodologies and frameworks. Here are a few common approaches:

*   **Hypothesis-driven hunting**: This approach leverages threat intelligence and identified vulnerabilities to formulate specific hypotheses about potential threats. Hunters then

utilize various tools and techniques to investigate those hypotheses. For example, if intelligence suggests a rise in phishing attacks targeting your organization's executives, hunters might focus on email logs and user behavior to identify suspicious email activity.

- **Indicator-based hunting**: This method involves searching for known IOCs associated with specific malware or attack campaigns. While effective for identifying known threats, it can miss novel attack methods (zero-day exploits) employed by advanced adversaries.

- **Structured vs. unstructured hunting**:

  o **Structured hunting**: A methodical approach where you follow predefined procedures and checklists, and it is often used for routine checks or compliance audits.

  o **Unstructured hunting**: A more exploratory approach where you follow your intuition and investigate anomalies or suspicious events, and is more suitable for uncovering new or unknown threats.

- **Entity-driven hunting**: This approach focuses on understanding the TTPs of specific threat actors or groups.

  o **Example**: If you know a particular APT group is known for using spear-phishing attacks, you can proactively hunt for signs of such attacks targeting your organization.

Core techniques for proactive threat hunting

Once you have established a strong understanding of your network baseline, you can employ the following techniques to actively hunt for threats:

- **Monitoring for auto-starts and suspicious processes**:

  o Pay close attention to auto-start locations within the operating system's registry and startup folders.

  o Monitor for unexpected applications or services automatically starting at system boot.

  o Utilize tools to query the environment for fileless malware and anomalous process behavior.

  o Deviations from the established baseline could indicate potential compromise.

- **Network traffic analysis (NTA)**:

  o Analyze network connections for signs of beaconing behavior, malicious communication between compromised systems, and a **command-and-control** (**C2**) server.

    o   Monitor DNS data for abnormal activity. Adversaries may attempt to resolve unusual domains for malicious purposes, such as phishing campaigns or malware distribution.

- **Identifying discrepancies in system behavior:**

    o   Look for inconsistencies in software usage across similar systems. For instance, a sudden surge in unexpected software execution on a particular machine could be a sign of compromise.

    o   Investigate deviations from the established security configurations or baseline settings.

    o   Significant discrepancies might indicate tampering by an adversary.

- **Focusing on specific segments:**

    o   Instead of casting a wide net, prioritize threat hunting efforts on specific network segments or user groups.

    o   Consider factors like high-risk users (privileged accounts, remote access users), critical assets (data servers, financial systems), or network segments housing sensitive data when selecting targets for your hunt.

    o   This targeted approach allows for a more in-depth investigation and faster identification of potential threats.

- **Leveraging threat hunting tools:**

    o   Beyond traditional security tools, several specialized threat hunting tools can significantly enhance your capabilities:

        ■   **ELK Stack**: This open-source platform excels at log analysis. It allows you to parse security events from various sources, identify patterns indicative of malicious activity, and create custom dashboards for threat hunting visualization.

        ■   **OSQuery**: This lightweight tool facilitates system baselining and enables you to write custom queries to hunt for specific indicators within your Windows environment. You can leverage OSQuery to query the registry, file system, running processes, and more, allowing for in-depth investigations.

        ■   **PowerShell**: For Windows environments, PowerShell scripting empowers you to automate tasks, query system data (like OSQuery), and generate reports to streamline your threat hunting process.

- **Outbound data transmission analysis:**

    o   Do not focus only on inbound traffic; analyze outbound data transmissions to identify potential exfiltration attempts of sensitive information.

- o   Look for unusual file types like encrypted archives or large volumes of data leaving the network unexpectedly.

- o   Correlate outbound data anomalies with user activity and access controls to determine legitimacy.

- o   For instance, a large data exfiltration attempt originating from a user account without proper access privileges would warrant further investigation.

- **DLL analysis**:

  - o   Investigate the presence of **dynamic link libraries** (**DLLs**) within the system, especially if the corresponding files are missing.

  - o   Adversaries may inject malicious DLLs into legitimate processes to gain persistence or escalate privileges within the system.

  - o   Utilize security tools that can identify suspicious DLL loading patterns and alert you for further investigation.

- **Using honeypots/honeynets**:

  - o   **Strategic placement**: Do not just scatter canaries randomly. Place them in locations attackers are likely to target, such as user folders, shared drives, or privileged access points.

  - o   **Monitoring and alerting**: Implement automated monitoring to detect unauthorized access or modification of canary tokens. Configure alerts to notify your security team for immediate investigation.

  - o   **Rotation and updates**: Regularly rotate your canary tokens to prevent attackers from becoming familiar with them. Update the content and location of your tokens to maintain their effectiveness as decoys.

- **Identifying unusual network activities**:

  - o   Look for unexpected file types on the network, such as **Hangul Word Processor** (**HWP**) files (a Korean word processing format) or top-secret **Portable Document Formats** (**PDFs**) appearing in unauthorized locations.

  - o   Investigate lateral movement attempts within the network. Adversaries may pivot between compromised systems to achieve their objectives, such as accessing sensitive data or deploying ransomware across your network.

  - o   Analyze network traffic for signs of tunneling or encryption used to mask malicious communication.

  - o   Tunneling protocols can be used to encapsulate malicious traffic within legitimate protocols, making it appear innocuous to traditional security controls.

- **Threat intelligence integration**:

  o   Threat intelligence feeds, provide valuable insights into the latest adversary TTPs.

  o   Integrate threat intelligence feeds with your SIEM or other security tools to enrich your security data and prioritize threat hunting activities based on real-world threats.

  o   Utilize the MITRE ATT&CK framework to map identified IOCs or behaviors to specific adversary groups and their known TTPs. This allows you to tailor your investigation and implement targeted mitigation strategies.

- **Hunting in small groups**:

  o   Consider forming small hunting teams with diverse skill sets, including network security analysts, incident responders, and threat intelligence analysts.

  o   Brainstorming and sharing knowledge within these teams can lead to a more comprehensive understanding of potential threats and faster identification of root causes.

In the next section, let us understand the process of planning to be prepared.

Planning, preparation, and process

Threat hunting is not a haphazard venture. It requires meticulous planning, thorough preparation, and a well-defined process to yield successful results. Here is a roadmap to guide you through each stage:

Stage 1: Planning

The first stage is planning, which is like setting the stage for the hunt. You can start this stage with the following steps:

1. **Define your objectives**:

   - *What are you hoping to achieve with your threat hunt?*

   - *Are you looking for specific threats, identifying general security weaknesses, or validating existing security controls?*

   - Clearly defined objectives will guide your hunt strategy and resource allocation.

2. **Scope and prioritization**:

   - You cannot hunt everything at once. Consider factors like critical assets, high-risk users, or network segments with sensitive data when prioritizing your targets.

   - Start with a well-defined scope that aligns with your objectives and gradually expand your hunting efforts as you gain experience.

3. **Threat intelligence integration**:

   • Leverage threat intelligence feeds to gain insight into the latest adversary TTPs.

   • This knowledge will aid your hunt planning by allowing you to tailor your approach to specific threats relevant to your industry or organization size.

4. **Hunting methodology**:

   • Select appropriate threat-hunting techniques based on your objectives, available resources, and target environment.

   • Refer to the previous topic, *Threat hunting techniques*, for a detailed explanation of various techniques like anomaly detection, network traffic analysis, and process monitoring.

5. **Hunt team assembly**:

   • Consider forming a dedicated threat hunting team with diverse skillsets.

   • Include network security analysts, incident responders, and threat intelligence analysts to leverage their expertise and foster a collaborative hunting environment.

Stage 2: Preparation

The second stage is preparation, it can be thought of as sharpening your hunting tools. You can proceed with this stage by following steps:

1. **Environment baseline establishment**:

   • Before you can hunt for anomalies, you need to understand your network's normal behavior.

   • Establish a baseline by collecting and analyzing system configuration data, process execution patterns, and network traffic flows.

   • Utilize tools like OSQuery or system monitoring solutions to gain comprehensive insights.

2. **Security tool tuning**:

   • Fine-tune your security tools (SIEM, EDR, NTA) to focus on threat hunting activities.

   • Configure alerts to identify suspicious activity based on the chosen hunting techniques and established baselines.

3. **Threat hunting playbook development**:

   • Develop a playbook that outlines the steps involved in your threat hunt, including data collection methods, analysis procedures, escalation protocols, and reporting templates.

- A well-defined playbook ensures consistency and streamlines the hunting process for your team.

4. **Hunting rules creation**:

- Depending on your chosen techniques, you may need to create custom rules or queries for threat hunting.

- For instance, you might develop queries to identify unauthorized application executions, unusual network connections, or suspicious file modifications.

5. **Test and refine**:

- Before launching a full-scale hunt, test your tools, rules, and playbooks in a non-production environment.

- This allows you to identify and address any potential issues before hunting on live systems.

Stage 3: Process

After planning and preparation, the final stage is the process. This refers to the stage where the hunt began, and the hunt is on. You can follow these steps in this stage:

1. **Data collection and analysis**:

- Utilize your chosen threat hunting techniques to collect data from various sources like logs, network traffic, endpoint data, and system configuration.

- Leverage SIEM, EDR, and NTA tools to aggregate and analyze this data for potential IOCs or suspicious activity.

2. **Hypothesis generation and prioritization**:

- Based on your analysis, formulate hypotheses about potential threats.

- Consider factors like the severity of the potential impact, the likelihood of the threat, and the available evidence when prioritizing your investigation.

3. **Investigation and validation**:

- Conduct a deeper investigation of the prioritized threats.

- This may involve forensic analysis, endpoint investigation tools, and threat intelligence research to validate or disprove your hypothesis.

4. **Containment and remediation**:

- If a threat is confirmed, take immediate action to contain the incident and remediate the compromised systems.

- This may involve isolating infected systems, removing malware, patching vulnerabilities, and implementing additional security controls.

5. **Reporting and lessons learned**:

- Document your findings, including the identified threats, investigation steps, and remediation actions taken.

- Conduct a post-hunt analysis to identify any shortcomings in your approach and refine your hunting methodology for future endeavors.

Experience, efficiency, and expertise

Threat hunting is a complex and dynamic field. While the tools and techniques discussed previously are crucial, success hinges on three key pillars, which are experience, efficiency, and expertise. Mastering these aspects will transform you from a novice hunter into a seasoned guardian of your organization's digital domain.

Experience for the hunt

Experience is the cornerstone of effective threat hunting. It allows you to:

- **Develop intuition**: As you conduct hunts and encounter various IOCs or suspicious activity, you will develop a sense of what normal looks like within your network. This intuition becomes invaluable in identifying subtle anomalies that might slip past automated tools.

- **Refine your approach**: Through experience, you will learn which techniques are most effective in your specific environment and against the threats you face. You will also develop the ability to adapt your hunt strategy based on the latest threat intelligence and adversary TTPs.

- **Identify false positives**: Threat hunting often involves sifting through large volumes of data. Experience helps you distinguish between genuine threats and false positives triggered by benign activity or misconfigurations.

Gaining practical experience in threat hunting

You can enhance your skills in threat hunting with the following ways:

- **Participate in threat hunting simulations**: Many security vendors offer threat hunting exercises that simulate real-world scenarios. These exercises provide a safe environment to hone your threat hunting skills and learn from experienced professionals.

- **Join online threat hunting communities**: Engaging with online communities allows you to learn from other threat hunters, share best practices, and stay updated on the latest threat hunting trends.

- **Conduct scenario-based threat hunting**: Develop scenarios based on real-world cyberattacks or industry trends. Simulate adversary behavior within your environment and practice hunting for evidence that aligns with the scenario.

Streamlining the hunt with efficiency

Efficiency is vital in threat hunting. You need to optimize your process to maximize your coverage and minimize wasted time. Here is how:

- **Automation**: Leverage automation tools to streamline repetitive tasks like data collection, log analysis, and rule-based anomaly detection. This frees you to focus on higher-level analysis and investigation.

- **Threat intelligence integration**: Utilize threat intelligence feeds to prioritize your hunting efforts. By focusing on threats relevant to your industry or organization size, you can avoid wasting time chasing irrelevant leads.

- **Collaboration**: Form a threat hunting team with diverse skillsets. Collaboration fosters knowledge sharing, reduces investigation time, and allows team members to leverage each other's expertise.

Expertise in threat hunting

Expertise is the foundation for effective threat hunting. It encompasses knowledge in various areas:

- **Adversary TTPs**: Familiarize yourself with the MITRE ATT&CK framework. This comprehensive knowledge base categorizes adversary TTPs, allowing you to tailor your hunts to specific attack methods.

- **Network security concepts**: Possess a strong understanding of network security fundamentals, including protocols, firewalls, intrusion detection systems, and endpoint security solutions.

- **Threat hunting techniques**: Master various threat hunting techniques such as anomaly detection, network traffic analysis, and process monitoring to apply these techniques effectively in your chosen hunting methodology.

- **Digital forensics and incident response**: Understanding digital forensics allows you to collect and preserve evidence in case of a confirmed threat. Incident response knowledge ensures you can effectively contain and remediate threats once identified.

Developing your threat hunting expertise

You can develop your expertise in threat hunting in the following ways:

- **Attend threat hunting workshops and trainings**: Many security vendors and training providers offer workshops and courses specifically designed to enhance threat hunting skills.

- **Read security blogs and publications**: Stay updated on the latest threat hunting trends and adversary tactics by following reputable security blogs and publications.

- **Pursue industry certifications**: Consider industry certifications like **Global Cyber Threat Intelligence Professional** (**GIAC GCTI**) or **SysAdmin, Audit, Network, and Security** (**SANS**) threat hunting to validate your expertise and demonstrate your commitment to continuous learning.

Tools and technology

No single tool can guarantee successful threat hunting. It is a combination of techniques and technologies deployed strategically. Here are some key elements of a cyber threat hunter's toolkit:

- **Endpoint detection and response (EDR)**: It provides visibility into endpoint activity, allowing hunters to detect suspicious behaviors like unauthorized file access or lateral movement within the network.

- **Network traffic analysis (NTA)**: It analyzes network traffic for anomalies that might indicate malicious activity, such as unusual communication patterns or data exfiltration attempts.

- **Behavioral analytics**: It discovers deviations from normal user behavior, helping identify potential insider threats or compromised accounts.

- **SIEM**: It aggregates security logs from various sources, allowing hunters to correlate events and identify potential attack patterns.

- **Sysmon**: This free tool from Microsoft is a game-changer for Windows endpoint visibility. Sysmon logs detailed system activity, including process creation, file creation, network connections, and more. This granular data empowers threat hunters to reconstruct the footsteps of malicious actors within the endpoint environment.

- **User and entity behavior analytics (UEBA)**: UEBA solutions focus on user activity and identify deviations from typical behavior patterns. A sudden surge in login attempts from an unknown location or a user accessing unauthorized files can trigger alerts, prompting further investigation.

- **Threat hunting tools**: Specialized tools can automate specific tasks like IOC hunting, log analysis, and anomaly detection, freeing up analysts' time for in-depth investigations.

- **Sandbox analysis**: It provides a safe environment to execute suspicious files or URLs to observe their behavior and identify malware.

- **MITRE ATT&CK framework**: This comprehensive knowledge base serves as a roadmap for threat hunters. It categorizes adversary TTPs, allowing you to tailor your investigations to specific techniques used by malicious actors.

- **Scripting languages**: Proficiency in scripting languages like Python or PowerShell can significantly empower your threat hunting endeavors. You can automate repetitive tasks, create custom queries to analyze logs, and develop bespoke hunting scripts to identify specific threats within your environment.

Proactive threat hunting and advanced threats

In today's dynamic cybersecurity landscape, traditional reactive security measures are no longer enough. Advanced threats, deployed by sophisticated adversaries, can bypass static defenses and wreak havoc on your organization. This is where proactive threat hunting comes in, a powerful approach to identify and neutralize these threats before they cause significant damage.

Note: **ESG's 2022 cybersecurity trends report found that 61% of organizations surveyed leverage threat hunting as part of their security strategy. This statistic indicates a growing recognition of the value proactive threat hunting brings to cybersecurity.**

Advanced threats

Advanced threats are malicious campaigns meticulously crafted by skilled attackers. These threats often exhibit the following characteristics:

- **Targeted attacks**: Adversaries meticulously research their targets, exploiting specific vulnerabilities within their systems or leveraging social engineering tactics to gain initial access.

- **Custom malware**: APTs often develop custom malware that evades traditional signature-based detection methods.

- **Living off the Land (LoLbins)**: Attackers may exploit legitimate system tools and binaries (LoLbins) to perform malicious activities, making them difficult to distinguish from normal operations.

- **Lateral movement**: Once inside the network, attackers move laterally across systems to achieve their objectives, such as stealing data or deploying ransomware.

- **Persistence**: Advanced threats can establish persistence mechanisms within the network, ensuring continued access even after a reboot or security update.

Necessity of proactive threat hunting

Traditional security solutions like firewalls and antivirus are essential, however they have limitations due to which advanced threats can bypass these controls, highlighting the need for a proactive approach:

- **Early detection**: Threat hunting allows you to identify threats before they cause significant damage. By uncovering IOCs early on, you can prevent attackers from achieving their objectives.

- **Improved security posture**: The continuous process of threat hunting helps you identify vulnerabilities and weaknesses within your security posture and by addressing these vulnerabilities, you make it more difficult for attackers to gain a foothold in your network.

- **Enhanced threat intelligence**: Threat hunting activities contribute to your overall threat intelligence and by analyzing the TTPs observed during hunts, you can gain valuable insights into the evolving threat landscape and adapt your defenses accordingly.

Benefits of proactive threat hunting

By implementing proactive threat hunting, you gain several advantages:

- **Reduced dwell time**: Early detection of threats minimizes the time attackers must operate within your network, limiting the potential damage they can inflict.

- **Improved incident response**: Threat hunting activities prepare your security team to respond more effectively to security incidents.

- **Enhanced security culture**: A proactive approach to security fosters a culture of vigilance within your organization.

Conclusion

In today's dynamic threat landscape, organizations cannot afford to be passive. This chapter has equipped you with the knowledge and strategies to become a proactive threat hunter. We explored the fundamental why behind threat hunting; to uncover hidden threats before they wreak havoc. We delved into the how of threat hunting, outlining a structured approach encompassing planning, preparation, and a well-defined process.

We discovered various threat hunting techniques, from anomaly detection to network traffic analysis, empowering you to identify suspicious activity. We emphasized the importance of experience, efficiency, and expertise; the pillars that elevate a threat hunter's effectiveness.

Tools, techniques, and technology were explored, highlighting how the right combination empowers your hunting endeavors. We discussed strategies for making threat hunting successful, including fostering a continuous learning mindset and refining your approach based on experience. Finally, we addressed proactive threat hunting and its crucial role in countering advanced threats.

By embracing the concepts presented in this chapter, you can transform your organization's security posture from reactive to proactive. Remember, threat hunting is a continuous journey; stay curious, stay vigilant, and keep hunting.

In the next chapter, we shall look into the critical role of threat intelligence in supporting cybersecurity defenses. We will explore the various types of cyber threat intelligence, from open-source and indicators of compromise to in-depth malware analysis and the often-overlooked area of insider threats. Additionally, we will examine the strategic importance of dark web intelligence, dissect the threat intelligence cycle, and review the essential tools used in this vital field.

Join our Discord space

Join our Discord workspace for latest updates, offers, tech happenings around the world, new releases, and sessions with the authors:

https://discord.bpbonline.com

CHAPTER 9

Deploying and Analyzing Threat Vectors

Introduction

Imagine a network where threats lurk in the shadows, their motives and capabilities obscured. This is the challenge cybersecurity professionals face daily. Traditional perimeter defenses are no longer enough. **Cyber Threat Intelligence** (**CTI**) illuminates the battlefield, providing insights into attacker **tactics, techniques, and procedures** (**TTPs**), enabling proactive defense and informed decision-making.

You get the information and resources in this chapter to become a proactive hunter rather than a passive defender. We will explore CTI, a thorough method of collecting, evaluating, and sharing vital information regarding cyber threats. You will learn here how CTI enables you to reveal the opponent, enabling you to foresee their future action in addition to identifying any dangers.

Prepare to investigate the several CTI categories, each catering to a certain requirement. We will break down tactical intelligence to provide practical insights to stop impending assaults and strategic intelligence to give a broad picture of the threat environment. By learning to extract insightful information from publicly available data, you will become an expert in **open-source intelligence** (**OSINT**).

Without knowing **indicators of compromise** (**IOCs**), the digital fingerprints left by malevolent actors, no CTI conversation is complete. We will provide you with the ability to recognize and evaluate IOCs, so you can spot breaches before they become serious problems.

This chapter will serve as your all-inclusive manual for implementing and evaluating threat vector analysis. We will look at sophisticated ways to map the attack surfaces, find weaknesses, and determine the most likely entry points. Knowing the playbook of your opponent can help you to tactically distribute resources and rank your defenses.

We will also get into the fundamental resources that enable CTI specialists. Learn about anything from sophisticated threat intelligence feeds to open-source platforms to create a strong CTI toolset that is customized for your company.

By the time this chapter ends, you will know how to use threat intelligence to find the opponent. Using CTI to light the battlefield and obtain a critical advantage in the continuous fight against cyber threats, you will change from a blind defender to a proactive threat hunter.

Structure

This chapter will include the following topics:

- Importance of threat intelligence and its benefit
- Cyber threat intelligence types
- Open-source intelligence
- Indicators of compromise
- Malware analysis
- Insider threat intelligence
- Dark web intelligence
- Threat intelligence cycle
- Tools

Objectives

This chapter gives you the tools you need to use **cyber threat intelligence** (**CTI**), to become a proactive threat hunters. We will look at several kinds of CTI, from strategic summaries to doable strategies, and we will learn how to get useful information from freely available sources. To spot intrusions early, you will need to become an expert at recognizing IOCs. After that we turn our attention to deploying and evaluating threat vectors, so you can map attack surfaces, identify weaknesses, and predict enemy strategies. Towards the end of this chapter, you will know how to use CTI and have an advantage over cybercriminals.

Importance of threat intelligence and its benefit

In the high-stakes area of cybersecurity, to operate blindly, acting without clear visibility, intelligence, or a strategic approach, is a recipe for failure. Organizations are exposed and vulnerable to an ever-changing threat landscape due to the traditional security techniques that concentrate only on perimeter defenses. Here is where CTI shines, enabling you to see through the fog of battle and secure a certain edge over opponents.

Imagine if you could foresee possible breaches, give your defenses priority, and successfully eliminate threats before they do serious harm, rather than having to react quickly after one. CTI's foundation is this proactive strategy. By gathering and analyzing intelligence about threat actors, their TTPs, CTI allows you to:

- **Make informed decisions**: Move beyond reactive security based on guesswork. CTI provides actionable insights into the evolving threat landscape, empowering you to allocate resources strategically and make informed decisions about security investments.

- **Optimize security spending**: Focus your defenses on the threats that matter most. CTI helps you identify the most likely attack vectors and vulnerabilities, allowing you to prioritize security controls and optimize security spending for maximum impact.

- **Reduce dwell time**: The longer an attacker operates undetected within your network, the greater the potential damage is. CTI empowers you to detect intrusions early, minimizing dwell time and thus mitigating potential losses.

- **Improve incident response**: When a breach occurs, every second counts. CTI provides valuable context about the attacker's goals and TTPs, enabling a faster and more targeted incident response, minimizing the impact of the attack.

- **Enhance situational awareness**: Gain a comprehensive understanding of the ever-changing threat landscape. CTI keeps you informed about emerging threats, allowing you to proactively adjust your defenses to stay ahead of the curve.

There are more benefits to CTI than just reducing the fear of an imminent threat. CTI helps employees make smart decisions and spot odd behavior by creating an organization-wide mindset that is aware of threats. Additionally, effective CTI may improve an organization's overall cybersecurity, which could lead to lower insurance costs and a public show of commitment to strong security procedures. CTI that works well is a must in today's threat world. With CTI, an organization can successfully change its stance from a passive target to a proactive defender. This protects important assets and gives the organization a big competitive edge in this digital age.

This is just the beginning of our journey into the world of CTI. The sections that follow will go into more detail about the different types of CTI, look at advanced methods for implementing and evaluating threat vectors, and give you the knowledge and tools you need to use CTI successfully.

Cyber threat intelligence types

The domain of CTI is extensive and provides direct capabilities to blue teams in order to fortify their defenses. Every category of intelligence provides distinct advantages, bolstering various facets of preemptive measures, identification, and reaction. This manual will provide an analysis of the four main categories of threat intelligence and demonstrate how blue teams can utilize them strategically to advance their operations.

Strategic intelligence

Strategic intelligence provides high-level insights into the overall threat landscape. It focuses on long-term trends, risks, and potential impacts on an organization's business strategy. It is designed for executives, boards, and other high-level decision-makers, offering a broad view of cyber threats and their implications. Let us take a look at them:

- **Focus**: Strategic intelligence provides a panoramic view of an organization's threat environment. It concerns itself with high-level trends, geopolitical influences, industry-specific vulnerabilities, and the risk of the potential impact of business decisions.

- **Audience**: This non-technical intelligence serves executives, boards, and stakeholders. It usually takes the form of reports and assessments.

- **Blue team applications**:
  o Aligning defensive priorities with the organization's risk appetite.
  o Informing resource allocation and budget decisions regarding security measures.
  o Long-term strategic planning considering emergent threat trends.

Operational threat intelligence

Operational intelligence talks about the specifics of ongoing or imminent cyberattacks. It provides detailed information about the nature, timing, and intent of attacks, aiding in incident response and mitigation. Let us take a look at its features:

- **Focus**: Operational intelligence delves into the motivations, infrastructure, and targeting patterns of specific threat actors or groups. It answers the *who*, *why*, and potentially the *when* of cyber-attacks.

- **Audience**: Security analysts, vulnerability management, and incident response teams.

- **Blue team applications**:
  o Enhancing threat modeling and scenario analysis.
  o Anticipating likely attack vectors based on known adversary preferences.

o   Proactively monitoring dark web chatter for hints of impending targeting.

Technical threat intelligence

Technical intelligence focuses on the specific technical details of cyber threats, it involves analyzing IOCs to detect and prevent attacks. This type of intelligence is often used to automate security tools and processes. Its features are as follows:

- **Focus**: Technical intelligence is a hyper-focused, forensic lens applied to past attacks. It involves dissecting malware code, network anomalies, and artifacts left behind by intrusions.

- **Audience**: Malware analysts, reverse engineers, and security researchers.

- **Blue team applications**:

    o   Developing advanced detection rules to catch similar attacks proactively.

    o   Identifying subtle behavioral indicators for sophisticated threat hunting.

    o   Retrospectively improving defenses by understanding how an intrusion unfolded.

Tactical threat intelligence

Tactical intelligence focuses on the **tactics, techniques, and procedures** (**TTPs**) used by threat actors. It provides specific details on how attacks are carried out, enabling security teams to understand and defend against current threats. Let us take a look at its features:

- **Focus**: Tactical intelligence concerns the actionable technical details of threats. It encompasses IOCs, vulnerability data, and adversary TTPs.

- **Audience**: SOC analysts, incident responders, and threat hunters.

- **Blue team applications**:

    o   Configuring firewalls, IDS/IPS, and endpoint protection based on the latest IOCs.

    o   Proactive threat hunting guided by known attack patterns and behaviors.

    o   Swift incident response aided by analysis of associated malware or exploits.

Integrating intelligence for maximum impact

True strength in blue teaming comes from the combined power of these intelligence types. Strategic views inform tactical prioritization. Tactical IOCs can be enriched by operational context about threat actors, and technical analysis of past incidents further refines future detection. By actively integrating intelligence, blue teams gain a more profound and actionable understanding of their unique threat landscape.

Open-source intelligence

OSINT encompasses a wide range of publicly available information, such as print materials, electronic media, online resources, and commercial databases. It involves data that can be accessed without any unauthorized means or hacking. Utilizing OSINT tools is essential for gathering and analyzing this information to strengthen security measures, identify threats, and improve decision-making processes. These tools are helpful for collecting data from public sources about websites, servers, devices, geolocation, and other relevant details. Recognizing role of OSINT in reducing the attack surface is essential for identifying risks, vulnerabilities, and suspicious connections in an organization's digital environment. Efficient utilization of OSINT tools is crucial for security teams to enhance their cybersecurity position and remain up-to-date on potential risks and weaknesses.

Enhancing blue team strategies with OSINT

Let us understand the role of OSINT in the blue team's defense:

- **Low barrier to entry**: OSINT leverages readily accessible, often free resources. This reduces the cost and complexity of information gathering for resource-constrained security teams.

- **Rich information landscape**: The vastness of the internet, social media, public records, and other open sources offers a treasure trove of potential insights on adversaries, vulnerabilities, and emerging threats.

- **Proactive defense**: OSINT facilitates early detection of threats. Monitoring leaked credentials, stolen data on dark web marketplaces, or chatter about exploits against an organization's software stack can lead to timely mitigation.

- **Incident contextualization**: OSINT enriches incident response investigations. Identifying the origins of a malware sample or the broader infrastructure used by threat actors can speed up containment.

Key applications of OSINT for threat mitigation

Here are key applications of OSINT for threat mitigation:

- **Phishing and social engineering**: OSINT reveals patterns in phishing domains, social media impersonation, or leaked employee emails; improving spam filtering and user education initiatives.

  o Identifying domain registration patterns associated with phishing campaigns (e.g., names subtly misspelling your brand, or using recently expired, legitimate-sounding domains).

    o   Proactively searching for impersonation accounts on social media platforms that mimic executives or use your organization's branding.

    o   Cross-referencing leaked email lists with your employee directory to check for compromised credentials that could be abused in targeted attacks.

- **Malware and ransomware**: OSINT uncovers malware **command-and-control** (**C2**) infrastructure, distribution methods, and early discussion of ransomware strains. This helps block malicious domains and update signature-based detection.

    o   Tracking discussions on malware forums or dark web marketplaces where early versions of ransomware or exploit kits are sold, potentially revealing attack patterns before they become widespread.

    o   Decoding naming conventions used by malware families, aiding in tracking their evolution and potentially identifying infrastructure.

    o   Discovering **domain generation algorithms** (**DGAs**) used by malware to contact C2 servers, allowing for predictive blocking.

- **APTs**: Monitoring for indicators associated with known APTs, including unusual domains, IP addresses, or references to a specific organization in attacker forums, can provide early warnings.

    o   Actively searching for mentions of your organization's name or specific technologies used in conjunction with keywords associated with reconnaissance and intrusion activity.

    o   Analyzing any publicly exposed code or documents from your organization for sensitive metadata that could be used for targeting.

- **Vulnerability mapping**: Tracking disclosures of vulnerabilities in software your company uses, via resources like CVE databases and vendor advisories, supports proactive patching.

Operationalizing OSINT for threat intelligence

Operationalizing OSINT means systematically collecting, analyzing, and applying OSINT data in real-world security workflows. We can turn OSINT into a practical, actionable tool for improving cybersecurity defenses and threat detection. Let us look at how we can do that:

- **Intelligence requirements**: Clearly define what information is required; some questions might include:

    o   *Are our employees' credentials exposed?*

    o   *Are there new vulnerabilities impacting our systems?*

Focus on your OSINT efforts accordingly. Emphasize the iterative nature of this process. Intelligence requirements evolve as your understanding of the threat landscape deepens, and vulnerabilities shift within your organization.

- **Data gathering**: Explore these OSINT sources:

  o **Social media**: Monitor platforms for mentions of your organization, threat discussions, or disgruntled employee posts.

  o **Dark web/Deep web**: Carefully access forums, marketplaces, and chats where data leaks or exploits are traded (consider specialized tools).

  o **Search engines**: Use advanced search operators for precise queries.

  o **Code repositories**: Find exposed API keys or inadvertent information leaks.

- **Domain registrars**: Observe newly registered, suspicious domains mimicking your organization.

- **Analysis and integration**: Analyze collected data, correlating it with internal logs and existing threat intelligence feeds. This reveals context and significance.

- **Action**: Use intelligence to update firewall rules, improve user awareness training, accelerate vulnerability patching, and refine detection mechanisms.

Developing an OSINT-driven program

Now, let us look at how to develop an OSINT-driven program:

- **Tools and automation**: Consider OSINT aggregation platforms and tools tailored to specific use cases (e.g., domain monitoring, dark web intelligence). Automation enhances efficiency.

  o **Maltego**: It is a powerful tool for link analysis and visualization of relationships between domains, IPs, and people.

  o **Spiderfoot**: A Versatile OSINT automation tool that is capable of gathering data from numerous sources.

  o **MISP**: Open-source threat intelligence platform for sharing and analyzing OSINT-derived indicators.

- **Skills development**: Train blue teams in OSINT collection techniques, search operations, and analytical approaches.

- **Ethical and legal considerations**: Ensure your OSINT practices comply with data privacy regulations and do not involve ethically questionable scraping tactics.

- **Collaboration**: Share threat findings with relevant teams, establishing a culture of intelligence-driven security throughout the organization.

OSINT challenges and best practices

In this subsection, we will look at a few challenges and best practices pertaining to OSINT:

- **Information overload**: Implement filtering and prioritization mechanisms to combat noise.

- **Verification and contextualization**: Verify the results, especially in high-risk situations that change quickly and where false information is common. Understanding the context in which information is presented is essential for accurate analysis.

- **Operational security (OPSEC)**: Take precautions to mask your own digital footprint when using OSINT for investigations to avoid alerting adversaries.

- **Clearly defined objectives**: Start with specific questions or goals to guide your OSINT collection efforts.

- **Source selection**: Choose reliable and reputable sources that align with your information needs.

- **Data verification**: Cross-check information from multiple sources to ensure accuracy and avoid misinformation.

The OSINT framework

Justin Nordine's OSINT framework is an extraordinarily beneficial resource for blue teams. The website is exceptionally well structured in its organization of free tools and resources, which serve to optimize the procedure of collecting open-source intelligence. Consider it as an exhaustive compilation of websites that specialize in various fields, such as domain lookups, public records searches, searching people, and more. Blue teams are assisted by the OSINT framework in the areas of threat intelligence, identification of vulnerabilities, and incident response. Its emphasis on easily accessible tools and intuitive navigation establishes it as a fundamental component of the cybersecurity toolkit.

Note: **Readers are requested to visit the OSINT framework website (https://osintframework. com/) and scroll through all the options.**

Indicators of compromise

IOCs are pieces of information that point to a security breach or event in a system or network. They are like traces that attackers leave behind, showing what TTPs were used by the attackers. Their principal responsibility is to aid in the detection, analysis, and prevention of future cyberattacks.

Importance of indicators of compromise for blue teams

Having a solid grasp on IOCs is crucial for preventing cyber-attacks and protecting against potential threats. IOCs are crucial indicators of a breach or threat, usually discovered during incident response procedures. Being able to detect these warning signs early on allows for a faster response and thereby minimizes any potential damage.

Various types of indicators of compromise

Let us take a closer look at the key categories of IOCs that you should keep in mind:

- **Network IOCs**: Identifying network IOCs can help uncover potential intrusions on your network. These may include suspicious IP addresses, domains, or unusual network traffic patterns.
    - o Suspicious IP addresses that are communicating with known command-and-control servers.
    - o Domain names that are associated with malware or phishing campaigns.
    - o URLs that host malware or phishing pages.
    - o Network traffic patterns that suggest malicious activity, such as beaconing or large data transfers.
    - o Suspicious DNS queries, such as queries for known malicious domains or newly registered domains.
- **Host-based IOCs**: Identifying signs of compromise within individual systems includes unauthorized logins, changes to system files or registry keys, or the presence of unknown processes.
    - o File names that are associated with malware or other malicious software.
    - o File hashes that match known malware samples.
    - o Registry keys that have been modified by malware to establish persistence.
    - o Process names that are associated with malware or other malicious software.
    - o System configurations that have been changed by malware or other malicious software.
- **File-based IOCs**: Identifying file-based IOCs is crucial in detecting potential malware on your systems. Keep an eye out for file hashes, names, or any unusual locations that may indicate the presence of malicious software.
    - o File names that are associated with malware or other malicious software.
    - o File hashes that match known malware samples.

o   Registry keys that have been modified by malware to establish persistence.

o   Process names that are associated with malware or other malicious software.

o   System configurations that have been changed by malware or other malicious software.

o   The location of a file on a system, which can be suspicious if it is in a sensitive directory or created by an unknown process.

o   The extension of a file can sometimes indicate its type and potential risk (e.g., `.exe`, `.dll`, `.scr`).

o   An unusually large or small file size can be an indicator of malicious activity.

o   Metadata embedded within files can reveal suspicious details, such as creation or modification dates, author names, or hidden content.

o   Files can contain malicious code or macros that are executed when the file is opened or processed.

o   High entropy can indicate encrypted or compressed malware.

o   Specific patterns or strings within files that can be used to identify known malware or suspicious content.

- **Behavioral IOCs**: Identifying behavioral IOCs is crucial in detecting potential threats. Any anomalies in user behavior, application activity, or system performance might be indicative of malicious intent.

o   Unusual user activity, such as a user accessing sensitive files that they do not normally need to access.

o   System behaviour that deviates from the norm, such as a sudden increase in CPU usage or network traffic.

o   Data access patterns that suggest malicious activity, such as a user downloading large amounts of data or accessing data that they are not authorized to access.

Note: **In 2023, the exploitation of a vulnerability in MOVEit Transfer software led to a widespread data breach affecting hundreds of organizations. A key IOC was the presence of a web shell file named human2.aspx with a specific hash value. This file was used by attackers to maintain persistence and steal sensitive data.**

Utilizing indicators of compromise for defense

IOCs are not merely forensic artifacts; they are actionable intelligence that directly empowers your blue team to improve defenses. Here is how to strategically leverage IOCs' action items for your operations:

- **Integrating IOCs into security tools:**
  - o Configure your SIEM solution to ingest IOC feeds and trigger alerts based on matches in log data. Correlate IOCs with other events to gain a broader context.
  - o Update firewall rules and **intrusion detection/prevention systems (IDS/IPS)** signatures with the latest IOCs to block malicious traffic at the network perimeter.
  - o Enrich your EDR software with IOCs to identify malware variants, suspicious files, and unusual process behaviors on your workstations and servers.

- **Augmenting threat intelligence:**
  - o When you discover IOCs during an incident investigation, analyze them to understand the attacker's TTPs. This knowledge will help you tailor defenses specifically for your environment.
  - o Contribute IOCs to trusted threat intelligence platforms or industry-specific ISACs. In return, you will benefit from the collective intelligence of the security community.

- **Proactive threat hunting:**
  - o Comb through historical logs using known IOCs to uncover previously undetected attacks or security gaps.
  - o Develop threat hypotheses based on intelligence reports or your organization's risk profile and search for corresponding IOCs to catch attackers in the early stages.

- **Optimizing incident response:**
  - o Utilize IOCs (e.g., malicious IPs, hashes, domains) to swiftly identify and isolate infected systems. This prevents lateral movement and further compromise within your network.
  - o Trace the attacker's actions across your network based on related IOCs, correlate related IOCs to reconstruct the attacker's activities, and understand the full extent of the breach.
  - o Use IOCs to precisely target cleanup efforts. Remove malicious files, terminate malicious processes, and eradicate any persistence mechanisms established by the attacker.

Key considerations

Here are a few key considerations:

- **IOC prioritization**: Focus on IOCs with high confidence levels and relevance to your organization's threat environment to avoid alert fatigue.

- **Automation**: Automate the ingestion and deployment of IOCs across your security tools wherever possible to enhance efficiency and reduce response times.

- **Context**: Combine IOC analysis with other threat intelligence sources for a holistic understanding of the threat and to improve decision-making.

By effectively utilizing IOCs, you transform your defense from reactive to proactive, staying ahead of evolving cyber threats.

Malware analysis

A key intelligence function is malware analysis, the process of reverse-engineering malicious software to extract **indicators of compromise (IOCs)** and understand attacker techniques, as was detailed in *Chapter 7, Effective Threat Management for Enterprises*.

Insider threat intelligence

While a significant portion of threat intelligence focuses on external adversaries, a mature security program must also address risks from within. **Insider threat intelligence** is the specialized discipline of gathering, analyzing, and acting upon data to identify and mitigate threats posed by employees, contractors, or partners with legitimate access.

This practice moves beyond traditional security by leveraging **user and entity behavior analytics (UEBA)** to establish baseline behaviors and detect significant deviations, such as an employee suddenly accessing unusual amounts of data or logging in at odd hours. The goal is not only to find malicious insiders but also to identify unintentional threats, like those caused by negligence or compromised credentials. A comprehensive breakdown of insider threat profiles and the specific defensive strategies to counter them is detailed in *Chapter 7, Effective Threat Management for Enterprises*.

Dark web intelligence

The dark web is a part of the deep web that is intentionally hidden and requires specific software like **The Onion Router (TOR)** or **Invisible Internet Project (I2P)** to access. The dark web is often thought of as a bad place; however, blue teams can also find a lot of useful information there. Professionals in cybersecurity can learn how to better spot risks, anticipate new attacks, and protect their companies from harm by going into these depths. Dark web intelligence involves collecting and analyzing data from the dark web to identify and mitigate potential cyber threats. It provides valuable insights into the activities of cybercriminals.

Understanding the dark web intelligence

While the dark web hosts legitimate content, it is also a hub for cybercriminal activity, making it a valuable source of threat intelligence for cybersecurity experts, law enforcement, and businesses. Here is key intelligence that can be gathered from the dark web:

- **Leaked data**: Dark web marketplaces and forums are rife with stolen data, including compromised credentials, financial information, and intellectual property. Monitoring for the appearance of your organization's data can provide early warning of a breach.

- **Exploit kits and zero-days**: Cybercriminals sell or trade zero-day vulnerabilities and exploit kits on the dark web. Identifying these gives you a head start in patching critical vulnerabilities before widespread exploitation occurs.

- **Threat actor discussions**: Monitoring dark web forums provides glimpses into the tools, techniques, and plans of hacking groups and threat actors. Understanding their chatter aids in predicting their potential targets or modus operandi.

- **Early-stage malware**: Dark web markets often serve as a testing ground for new malware strains before they hit mainstream networks. Analyzing these samples can help develop signatures and protections for your security infrastructure.

- **Hacker-for-hire services**: The availability of hacker-for-hire services on the dark web highlights trends in cybercrime and may signal the potential for targeted attacks towards specific industries or organizations.

Harnessing dark web intelligence

Now, let us see how to harness the dark web intelligence:

- **Specialized tools and access**: Navigating the dark web safely and effectively often requires specific tools and access controls. Options include threat intelligence platforms with dark web monitoring capabilities, or, for larger organizations, dedicated in-house analysts.

- **Risk analysis**: Due to its volatile nature, dark web intelligence needs careful contextualization. Assess the reliability of sources and the likelihood of threats directly impacting your organization.

- **Operationalizing intelligence:**

  o **IOC updates**: New malware hashes, malicious domains, or IP addresses gleaned from the dark web should be swiftly integrated into firewalls, IDS/IPS, and endpoint protection tools.

  o **Vulnerability management**: Prioritize patching software flaws or misconfigurations discussed in dark web forums and marketplaces.

  o **Proactive threat hunting**: Use dark web intelligence about threat actor tactics or tools to inform proactive hunt activities on your own networks.

Important considerations

Here are a few things to be mindful about while working with dark web intelligence:

- Be mindful of laws in your jurisdiction and source data ethically.

- Avoid engaging in activities that could put your organization at legal risk.

- Analysts should use dedicated, isolated systems and anonymization techniques to protect themselves while exploring the dark web.

- Dark web information can be intentionally misleading; hence, corroborate findings with reliable external sources whenever possible.

- Share anonymized dark web findings with trusted partners, threat intelligence sharing platforms, or law enforcement (in cases of severe criminal activity). This collective pooling of intelligence benefits the broader security community.

Dark web intelligence, when approached cautiously and with expertise, provides a unique window into the evolving threat landscape. By shining a light into these hidden corners of the internet, blue teams can uncover valuable insights that allow them to better predict, prepare for, and mitigate the risks posed by cyber adversaries.

Threat intelligence cycle

The threat intelligence cycle is a structured, iterative process that turns raw data into information that can be used by blue teams to make smart security decisions. In contrast to a linear model, the cycle focuses on constant improvement so that it can react to a threat landscape that is always changing. Let us break down each step:

1. **Planning and direction**:

   - **Understanding your needs**: Before gathering intelligence, blue teams must define clear objectives by answering questions like; *What are your organization's most critical assets? What specific threats are you most concerned about (ransomware groups, APTs targeting your industry, etc.)?*

   - **Intelligence requirements**: This step involves articulating specific questions you want the threat intelligence process to answer. Tailoring questions leads to more focused data collection and analysis.

2. **Collection**:

   - **Data sources**: Tap into a diverse array of sources:

     o **Internal logs and data**: SIEMs, endpoint logs, network traffic, vulnerability scan reports.

     o **OSINT**: Reputable security blogs, vendor reports, dark web monitoring (with caution), social media chatter.

o **Threat intelligence feeds**: Subscribe to commercial feeds providing curated, relevant threat data.

o **Information sharing communities**: Participate in ISACs or community forums for sector-specific insights.

3. **Processing**:

- **Normalization and filtering**: Convert raw data into standardized formats for efficient analysis. Remove irrelevant or low-quality data to reduce noise.

- **Context enrichment**: Correlate threat data with your own asset inventory, vulnerability data, and knowledge of existing security controls. This context determines the true relevance of threats to your environment.

4. **Analysis**:

- **Identifying patterns**: Analyze the processed data to uncover trends, relationships, and potential attacker TTPs.

- **IOC extraction**: Identify specific IOCs like malware hashes, malicious domains, or suspicious IP addresses.

- **Attribution (where possible)**: Attempt to link threat activity to known threat actors or groups based on tools, infrastructure, and attack patterns.

- **Impact assessment**: Evaluate the potential damage a threat could inflict if successfully exploited against your organization's specific assets.

5. **Dissemination**:

- **Target the audience**: Tailor the format and technical depth of reports for different stakeholders (technical teams vs. executives).

- **Actionable recommendations**: Do not just present threats; provide clear, prioritized actions to mitigate them (patching, security control configuration, awareness campaigns).

- **Integration**: Feed IOCs directly into your security tools (firewalls, IDS/IPS, SIEMs) for automated blocking and alerting.

6. **Feedback**:

- **Evaluate effectiveness**: Gather feedback from stakeholders and operational teams on the usefulness of the intelligence provided. Try to answer the question, *did it lead to successful threat detection or mitigation?*

- **Iterative improvement**: Use the feedback loop to continually refine your intelligence requirements, collection sources, and analysis methods.

Benefits of the cycle for blue teams

The effectiveness of the blue team is enhanced, and the cycle ensures that the blue team stays proactive and adaptive against evolving threats by:

- **Proactive defense**: The cycle shifts your posture from reactive to proactive, allowing you to anticipate attacks and implement countermeasures before they strike.

- **Prioritized decision-making**: Intelligence helps prioritize the threats that pose the most significant risk, optimizing resource allocation.

- **Enhanced detection**: Integrating fresh IOCs into your security tools bolsters your ability to spot malicious activity early.

- **Informed incident response**: During an incident, threat intelligence aids in understanding the attacker's methods, scoping the breach, and containing the issue quickly.

The threat intelligence cycle is not a one-time activity but an ongoing engine that powers your defensive operations. By systematically gathering, analyzing, applying, and refining your understanding of the adversaries you face, blue teams gain a decisive edge in protecting their organizations from an ever-evolving array of cyber threats.

Tools

To gather the right intel information and act upon it, you should have the right tool in place. Specialized tools and platforms are essential for managing the vast amounts of threat data, automating tasks, streamlining analysis, and ultimately translating intelligence into concrete defensive actions. We have read about tools like SIEM, EDR, vulnerability management systems, network security tools, etc., which could be the primary tools to gather threat intel for any organization, in our previous chapters. Let us explore the other key categories of tools and how they enhance a blue team's effectiveness:

1. **Threat intelligence platforms (TIPs)**:

   - TIPs serve as the core hub for threat intelligence, aggregating data from internal and external sources (OSINT feeds, commercial feeds, ISAC intelligence).

   - **Capabilities**:

     o **Deduplication and normalization**: Ensure consistent formatting for efficient analysis.

     o **Correlation and enrichment**: Link IOCs with internal assets, vulnerability scans, and contextual data to reveal the most relevant threats.

     o **Search and visualization**: Enable analysts to query data, uncover trends, and pivot quickly during investigations.

- **Collaboration**: Allow secure intelligence sharing with partners.

- **Examples**: Maltego, EclecticIQ, ThreatConnect, Talos intelligence

2. **IOC management tools**:

   - **Operationalizing IOCs**: These tools specialize in storing, organizing, and tracking the lifecycle of IOCs (like hashes, domains, IP addresses).

   - **Prioritization and deployment**: They allow teams to prioritize IOCs based on relevance and confidence level, enabling automated push of high-confidence IOCs to firewalls, IDS/IPS, and EDR tools.

   - **Examples**: MISP (open source), ThreatConnect, Anomali ThreatStream

3. **OSINT gathering and analysis tools**:

   - **Eyes and ears on the open web**: Specialized tools streamline open-source intelligence collection and analysis from sources like:

     o **Domain and DNS tools**: Domaintools, SecurityTrails

     o **Dark web monitoring (with caution)**: Surface web search engines tailored for the dark web; dedicated services for those with clearance and specific needs.

     o **Social media monitoring**: Tools to track mentions and sentiment relevant to the organization, potential leaks, or threat chatter.

   - **Examples**: Spiderfoot, Hunchly, Shodan, Maltego (for open-source data)

4. **Threat data marketplaces and feeds**:

   - **Curated, actionable intelligence**: Commercial vendors offer various feeds tailored to specific industries, threat types, or regions.

   - **Quality and relevance matter**: Evaluate the quality of the feed, and its alignment with your organization's threat model.

   - **Examples**: Recorded Future, FireEye iSIGHT, Flashpoint, CrowdStrike Falcon

5. **Workflow and collaboration tools**:

   - **Streamlining the process**: These tools optimize the threat intelligence lifecycle.

     o **Incident ticketing and integration**: Automate the creation of tickets based on threat alerts, ensuring timely action.

     o **Reporting and visualization**: Facilitate customized analytics and dashboards for various stakeholders.

   - **Examples**: Jira, TheHive/Cortex (case management and orchestration)

Investing in the right threat intelligence tools and platforms is not optional; it is fundamental to proactive cyber defense. By equipping your blue team with tools that transform threat data into timely, actionable insights, you enable efficient threat detection, mitigation, and an overall more resilient security posture.

Conclusion

In this chapter, we have really dug into the power of threat intelligence. We have seen how it is the key to getting ahead of the attackers instead of just reacting to attacks. We explored different kinds of intelligence, how to uncover those sneaky clues from open sources, and the importance of those IOCs for spotting attackers on our networks. The threat intelligence cycle gave us a roadmap to make sense of it all and the amazing tools out there. They make this whole threat intel process way easier. The bottom line is, by making threat intelligence central to our defense, and always getting better at it, we can seriously strengthen our security and stay a few steps ahead of the threats out there.

The next chapter dives into the practical application of threat management, covering crucial elements like establishing strong cybersecurity policies and procedures, implementing effective security controls, adopting a robust security management framework, and integrating **governance, risk, and compliance (GRC)** activities. These components work together to create a comprehensive security posture, enabling organizations to proactively address threats, mitigate risks, and ensure compliance with industry standards and regulations. By mastering these concepts, organizations can effectively navigate the complexities of the ever-evolving threat landscape and safeguard their critical assets.

Join our Discord space

Join our Discord workspace for latest updates, offers, tech happenings around the world, new releases, and sessions with the authors:

https://discord.bpbonline.com

CHAPTER 10
Threat and Vulnerability Management

Introduction

Now that the world is so connected, cyber threats are not a matter of *if* but *when* for businesses of all sizes. One breach can put private information at risk, stop work, and hurt the image and reputation of any organization. As organizations face an increasingly sophisticated and persistent threat landscape, the ability to swiftly detect, contain, and mitigate security incidents is vital. That is why threat management is not just a technical matter; it is also important for business. This chapter will show you the most important steps you need to take to make a strong threat control program. You can expect us to talk about a lot of things, from strong policies and real security controls to ongoing monitoring, risk assessments, and confusing rules about data privacy. However, it is not just about checking off boxes; we will talk about creating a culture that cares about security through training, education, and a framework that fits your business goals. Think of this chapter as your blueprint to not only survive cyber threats but thrive in the face of them.

Structure

This chapter will include the following topics:

- Implementing cybersecurity controls with the CIS Framework
- Cyber security audit

- Cyber security and data privacy regulations
- Security management framework
- Governance and compliance
- Training and awareness programs for cybersecurity
- Risk management
- Cyber threat management best practices
- Cyber threat management challenges

Objectives

By the end of this chapter, you will gain understanding of the most important parts of threat management and the best ways to do them. As a part of our goals, we want to give you the tools required to set up strong physical and cyber defenses, make and follow clear policies, proactively assess risks, find your way around the legal landscape, and pick the right security controls. In addition, you will learn how to perform security audits, make your employees more security-aware, and set up a governance framework that fits the needs of your company. The main goal of this chapter is to give you the knowledge and tools you need to protect your organization's most important assets from cyber threats and manage these threats.

Implementing cybersecurity controls with the CIS framework

While frameworks like NIST and ISO 27001 provide the high-level structure for a security program, the **Center for Internet Security** (**CIS**) Critical Security Controls offer a prioritized, practical, and actionable set of safeguards for defending against the most common cyberattacks. CIS Controls are an excellent guide for implementing specific technical and organizational measures. They are grouped into three categories based on priority.

- **Basic CIS Controls (CIS Controls 1-6)**: These six controls are considered essential *cyber hygiene* and should be the starting point for any organization. They provide the foundational layer of defense.

    o **Control 1 and 2**: Inventory and Control of Enterprise and Software Assets.

    o **Control 3**: Data Protection.

    o **Control 4 and 5**: Secure Configuration of Enterprise Assets and Software.

    o **Control 6**: Account Management.

- **Foundational CIS Controls (CIS Controls 7-16)**: These controls build upon the basic set and are crucial for managing a more mature security environment. They address a broader range of attack vectors and system vulnerabilities.

- o **Control 7**: Continuous Vulnerability Management.

- o **Control 8**: Audit Log Management.

- o **Control 9**: Email and Web Browser Protections.

- o **Control 10**: Malware Defenses.

- o **Control 11**: Data Recovery.

- o **Control 12-16**: Address Network Infrastructure Management, Network Monitoring, Security Awareness Training, Service Provider Management, and Application Software Security.

- **Organizational CIS Controls (CIS Controls 17-18)**: These controls are focused on the people and processes required to sustain a robust cybersecurity program.

  - o **Control 17**: Incident Response Management.

  - o **Control 18**: Penetration Testing.

By adopting CIS Controls, an organization can implement a defense-in-depth strategy that is both effective and resource-efficient, focusing first on the controls that provide the greatest risk reduction.

Cyber security audit

Security audit is not just about finding faults in your system and processes; it is about the holistic evaluation and continuous improvement of your organization's cybersecurity posture.

Auditing in cyber security

Organizations must prioritize the implementation of robust security measures to protect their critical assets. However, merely deploying security controls is not sufficient; continuous monitoring and auditing are essential to ensure their effectiveness and identify potential vulnerabilities. This article delves into the crucial aspects of auditing pertaining to cyber security, providing insights and best practices for organizations seeking to strengthen their defenses.

Understanding the need for auditing

Regular audits give you a thorough picture of your security posture, highlighting areas for improvement and enabling proactive mitigation strategies. Cybersecurity threats are always changing, with attackers using ever-more-sophisticated tactics to exploit vulnerabilities and gain unauthorized access to sensitive information. Organizations are constantly under siege, facing a barrage of cyberattacks ranging from ransomware and **Advanced Persistent Threat** (**APTs**) to phishing scams and malware attacks. Static security measures are simply inadequate in this dynamic environment.

Key components of auditing

Effective auditing encompasses a range of activities, including:

- **Planning and preparation**:

  - **Scope definition**: Clearly define the scope of the audit, identifying the systems, applications, data, and processes that will be included in the assessment. This ensures that the audit is focused and aligned with the organization's specific needs and priorities.

  - **Audit objectives**: Establish clear and measurable audit objectives. These objectives should be based on the organization's risk profile, compliance requirements, and overall security goals.

  - **Audit methodology**: Select an appropriate audit methodology, such as a risk-based approach or a compliance-based approach. This methodology will guide the audit process and determine the types of tests and assessments that will be performed.

  - **Resource allocation**: Allocate the necessary resources, including personnel, time, and tools, to ensure a thorough and efficient audit.

- **Data gathering and analysis**:

  - **Document review**: Review relevant documentation, such as policies, procedures, standards, and risk assessments, to gain an understanding of the organization's security framework.

  - **Interviews**: Conduct interviews with key personnel, including IT staff, security managers, and business stakeholders, to gather information about security practices and controls.

  - **Technical testing**: Perform technical assessments, such as vulnerability scans, penetration testing, and configuration reviews, to identify weaknesses in systems and applications.

  - **Log analysis**: Analyze security logs to detect anomalies, unauthorized access attempts, and other signs of malicious activity.

  - **Data analysis**: Review data handling practices to ensure compliance with privacy regulations and data protection policies.

- **Findings and recommendations**:

  - **Document findings**: Document all audit findings, including the severity of each issue, its potential impact, and recommended remediation steps.

  - **Prioritize findings**: Prioritize findings based on risk, with critical issues addressed first.

o **Develop recommendations**: Provide actionable recommendations for addressing each finding. These recommendations should be **specific, measurable, achievable, relevant, and time-bound** (**SMART**).

- **Reporting**:

  o **Executive summary**: Provide a concise summary of the audit findings, highlighting key risks and recommendations for improvement.

  o **Detailed report**: Present a comprehensive report detailing the audit methodology, scope, findings, and recommendations. Include supporting evidence and technical details as necessary.

  o **Communication**: Clearly communicate audit findings and recommendations to relevant stakeholders, including management, IT staff, and security personnel. Ensure that the report is understandable and actionable.

- **Follow-up and remediation**:

  o **Track remediation efforts**: Track the implementation of recommended remediation measures.

  o **Verify effectiveness**: Verify that the implemented controls are effective in mitigating the identified risks.

  o **Continuous monitoring**: Continuously monitor the organization's security posture to detect and address new risks as they emerge.

Best practices for effective auditing

Here are the best practices for effective auditing:

- **Define clear objectives and scope**:

  o **Strategic alignment**: Ensure the audit objectives align with the organization's overall cybersecurity strategy and risk management goals. Define the specific areas to be assessed, whether it is a comprehensive audit of the entire IT infrastructure or a focused review of a particular system or process.

  o **Stakeholder input**: Involve key stakeholders in defining the audit scope and objectives. This ensures that the audit addresses their concerns and provides actionable insights that can be used to improve security.

- **Assemble a qualified audit team**:

  o **Expertise**: The audit team should possess a diverse range of skills and expertise, including knowledge of cybersecurity frameworks, technical controls, risk assessment, and compliance requirements.

- o **Independence**: The audit team should be independent and objective, free from any conflicts of interest that could compromise the integrity of the audit.

- o **Certification**: Consider auditors with relevant certifications, such as **Certified Information Systems Auditor (CISA)** or **Certified Ethical Hacker (CEH)**, to ensure a high level of professionalism and competence.

- **Employ a risk-based approach**:

  - o **Focus on high-risk areas**: Prioritize audit activities based on the organization's risk profile. This means focusing on the areas that pose the greatest risk to the organization's assets and data.

  - o **Risk assessment integration**: Integrate the audit findings with the organization's risk assessment process. This allows for a more holistic understanding of the organization's risk posture and enables informed decision-making about risk mitigation strategies.

- **Utilize a variety of audit techniques**:

  - o **Documentation review**: Thoroughly review policies, procedures, standards, and risk assessments to understand the organization's security framework and identify any gaps or inconsistencies.

  - o **Interviews**: Conduct interviews with key personnel to gather information about security practices, controls, and awareness.

  - o **Technical testing**: Utilize a combination of technical testing methods, such as vulnerability scanning, penetration testing, and configuration reviews, to identify weaknesses in systems and applications.

  - o **Log analysis**: Analyze security logs to detect anomalies, unauthorized access attempts, and other signs of malicious activity.

  - o **Data sampling**: Use data sampling techniques to assess the effectiveness of data security controls and identify potential data leaks.

Benefits of auditing

Implementing a robust auditing program offers several benefits, including:

- **Enhanced security posture**: By identifying and addressing vulnerabilities, you can significantly improve your organization's overall security posture and reduce the risk of cyberattacks.

- **Improved incident response:** Continuous monitoring enables faster detection and response to security incidents, minimizing the potential damage and downtime.

- **Compliance adherence**: Regular audits ensure compliance with relevant industry regulations and standards, mitigating legal and financial risks.

- **Informed decision-making**: Audit findings provide valuable insights into your security posture, enabling informed decision-making regarding security investments and resource allocation.

Security frameworks

Several security frameworks and best practices can guide your auditing program, including:

- **NIST cybersecurity framework**: The NIST cybersecurity framework provides a voluntary framework for managing cybersecurity risk. It consists of five core functions: *Identify*, *Protect*, *Detect*, *Respond*, and *Recover*.

- **ISO 27001**: ISO 27001 is an international standard for information security management. It provides a set of requirements for establishing, implementing, maintaining, and continually improving an **information security management system (ISMS)**.

- **CIS Controls**: The CIS Controls are a set of 18 cybersecurity controls that are essential for protecting critical systems and data. They are divided into three domains: *Basic*, *Foundational*, and *Organizational*.

- **COBIT 5**: COBIT 5 is a framework for IT governance and management. It provides a set of principles, processes, and practices that can be used to govern and manage IT effectively.

Authorization processes and governance

Auditing authorization processes and governance is essential for ensuring that users have the appropriate access to systems and data. This involves:

- **Checking access control policies**: Defining who has access to what systems and data.

- **Validating granted access**: Validating granted access to users based on their job roles and responsibilities.

- **Reviewing access**: Periodically review and update access permissions.

Enterprise identity and information access management

Enterprise identity and **information access management (IAM)** is a set of processes and technologies that are used to manage user identities and access to systems and data, and it plays a vital role in security audits. This involves:

- **Identity governance**: Assess the policies and procedures for managing user identities, including provisioning, de-provisioning, and lifecycle management. Verify that user identities are properly authenticated and authorized.

- **Access controls**: Evaluate the effectiveness of access controls, such as **role-based access control (RBAC)**, **attribute-based access control (ABAC)**, and least privilege principles. Ensure that access rights are regularly reviewed and updated based on changing roles and responsibilities.

- **Authentication and authorization**: Assess the strength of authentication mechanisms, such as passwords, **multi-factor authentication** (**MFA**), and biometrics. Verify that authorization processes are in place to ensure that users can only access the resources they are entitled to.

- **Privilege management**: Review privileged access management practices, ensuring that privileged accounts are tightly controlled and monitored. Implement measures like password vaulting and session recording to mitigate the risks associated with privileged access.

- **Password management**: Assess password policies and practices, including password complexity requirements, password expiration, and account lockout policies. Encourage the use of strong, unique passwords and consider implementing passwordless authentication methods wherever appropriate.

- **Single sign-on (SSO)**: If SSO is implemented, assess its security and effectiveness. Verify that SSO is configured securely, and it does not introduce new vulnerabilities.

Cyber and legal regulatory requirements

Organizations must comply with a variety of cyber and legal regulatory requirements, including:

- **Scoping and planning**: At the outset of an audit, identify the specific regulations and standards that apply to the organization. This will determine the scope of the audit and the specific controls that need to be assessed.

- **Control mapping**: Map the organization's security controls to the relevant regulatory requirements. This helps ensure that all necessary controls are in place and operating effectively.

- **Evidence collection**: Gather evidence to demonstrate compliance with regulatory requirements. This can include documentation of policies and procedures, security logs, vulnerability scan reports, and incident response documentation.

- **Gap analysis**: Identify any gaps between the organization's current practices and the regulatory requirements. Develop remediation plans to address these gaps and bring the organization into compliance.

- **Reporting**: Include a section in the audit report that specifically addresses regulatory compliance. Detail the organization's compliance status with each applicable regulation and provide recommendations for addressing any non-compliance issues.

Auditing is an essential component of any effective cybersecurity strategy. By proactively identifying and addressing vulnerabilities, organizations can strengthen their defenses and stay ahead of evolving threats. By implementing the best practices outlined in this article, you can establish a robust auditing program that enhances your security posture and protects your organization's critical assets.

Cyber security and data privacy regulations

Data is the lifeblood of organizations and individuals alike. It drives decision-making, fuels innovation, and underpins nearly every aspect of modern life. However, the immense value of data also makes it a prime target for malicious actors. As cyber threats evolve and become more sophisticated, the need to safeguard sensitive information has never been more critical. This is where data privacy regulations come into play.

Role of data privacy regulations

Data privacy regulations are legal frameworks designed to protect the personal information of individuals. They establish rules and guidelines for how organizations collect, store, process, and share data. These regulations aim to ensure that sensitive data remains confidential, is used only for legitimate purposes, and is protected from unauthorized access, disclosure, or misuse.

While the specific provisions of data privacy regulations vary from region to region, their overarching goals remain consistent, which are as follows:

- **Protection of individual rights**: Data privacy regulations empower individuals by granting them control over their personal information. They often provide rights such as access to data, rectification of errors, and the ability to erase data in certain circumstances.

- **Accountability for organizations**: Regulations hold organizations accountable for their data practices. They establish clear requirements for data protection measures, incident reporting, and data breach notifications.

- **Promotion of trust**: By establishing a legal framework for data protection, regulations foster trust between organizations and individuals. This trust is essential for the functioning of the digital economy.

Key data privacy regulations

The global landscape of data privacy regulations is constantly evolving. Some of the most influential regulations include:

- **General Data Protection Regulation (GDPR)**: The GDPR is a comprehensive data protection law that applies to all organizations operating within the **European Union (EU)** or processing the personal data of EU residents. It sets strict standards for data protection and imposes hefty fines for non-compliance.

- **California Consumer Privacy Act (CCPA)**: The CCPA is a landmark data privacy law in the United States that grants residents of California specific rights regarding their personal information. It requires businesses to disclose the categories of personal information they collect, the purposes for which it is used, and the categories of third parties with whom it is shared.

- **Personal Information Protection and Electronic Documents Act (PIPEDA)**: PIPEDA is the federal privacy law for private-sector organizations in Canada. It sets ground rules for how businesses must handle personal information in the course of commercial activities.

Implications for cybersecurity professionals

Data privacy regulations have profound implications for cybersecurity professionals. They must ensure that their organization's security practices align with these regulations. This involves:

- **Understanding regulatory requirements**: Cybersecurity professionals must stay up to date with the latest data privacy regulations that apply to their organization. This involves understanding the specific provisions of the regulations, their scope, and their enforcement mechanisms.

- **Implementing technical and organizational measures**: Cybersecurity professionals must implement technical and organizational measures to protect personal data. This includes data encryption, access controls, regular security assessments, and incident response procedures.

- **Conducting privacy impact assessments (PIAs)**: PIAs are systematic evaluations of the potential privacy risks associated with new projects or initiatives. Cybersecurity professionals play a key role in conducting PIAs and recommending measures to mitigate privacy risks.

Implementing data privacy regulations in an organization

Implementing data privacy regulations is not merely a legal checkbox; it is a fundamental component of a robust cybersecurity strategy and a cornerstone of building and maintaining customer trust. Here is a breakdown of the essential steps organizations should take:

1. **Comprehensive data inventory**:
   - **Identification**: Begin by thoroughly cataloging all personal data your organization collects, stores, or processes. This includes customer information, employee records, vendor details, and any other data that could identify an individual.

- **Classification**: Categorize the data based on its sensitivity and the level of protection it requires. Highly sensitive data, like financial information or health records, will necessitate stricter safeguards than less sensitive data like email addresses.

2. **Gap analysis and risk assessment**:

   - **Regulatory mapping**: Map the data inventory against the specific requirements of applicable data privacy regulations. This helps identify areas where your current practices may fall short of compliance.

   - **Privacy impact assessment (PIA)**: For new projects or initiatives, conduct PIAs to evaluate potential privacy risks. This helps proactively identify and address privacy concerns before they become issues.

   - **Risk assessment**: Identify and assess the risks associated with the collection, storage, and processing of personal data. This includes the likelihood of data breaches, unauthorized access, and other threats.

3. **Develop a data privacy program**:

   - **Policies and procedures**: Establish comprehensive data privacy policies and procedures that align with relevant regulations. These should cover data collection, storage, retention, access controls, data subject rights, and incident response.

   - **Data protection officer (DPO)**: Appoint a DPO or designate a team responsible for overseeing data privacy compliance. This individual or team should have the authority and resources to ensure compliance and act as a point of contact for data subjects.

   - **Employee training**: Provide regular training to employees on data privacy regulations, company policies, and best practices for handling personal data. This is crucial for fostering a culture of privacy awareness within the organization.

4. **Implement technical and organizational controls**:

   - **Technical controls**: Implement robust security measures like encryption, access controls, firewalls, intrusion detection systems, and data loss prevention tools. Regularly update and patch software to protect against vulnerabilities.

   - **Organizational controls**: Establish clear roles and responsibilities for data handling, implement data access policies, and conduct regular security audits and reviews. Develop incident response plans to address data breaches promptly and effectively.

5. **Vendor management**:

   - **Due diligence**: Conduct due diligence on third-party vendors who handle personal data on behalf of your organization. Ensure they have adequate data protection measures in place and comply with relevant regulations.

- **Contractual agreements**: Establish data processing agreements with vendors that clearly define the responsibilities of vendors for protecting personal data.

6. **Monitoring and review**:

   - **Ongoing monitoring**: Continuously monitor data processing activities to ensure compliance with privacy regulations. Conduct regular audits and reviews to identify and address any gaps or weaknesses.

   - **Incident response**: Develop and test incident response plans to handle data breaches or other privacy incidents swiftly and effectively.

7. **Communication and transparency**:

   - **Privacy notices**: Provide clear and concise privacy notices to individuals, explaining how their data is collected, used, and shared. Ensure that these notices are easily accessible and understandable.

   - **Transparency**: Be transparent about your data practices. Respond promptly and effectively to data subject requests for access, rectification, or erasure of their personal data.

Security management framework

In the ever-changing world of cybersecurity, where new threats arise and weaknesses are exposed, organizations must adopt a systematic approach to mitigate risk and safeguard their valuable assets. Security management frameworks are crucial in establishing a solid foundation for maintaining a robust security posture.

Understanding security management framework

A security management framework is a set of policies, procedures, guidelines, and best practices that help organizations systematically identify, assess, and mitigate cybersecurity risks. These frameworks offer a structured approach to information security, providing a roadmap for organizations to follow to protect their sensitive data and systems. Firstly, we need to understand the importance of a security management framework.

Importance of security management frameworks

A comprehensive approach to cybersecurity is provided by security frameworks, which cover organizational, operational, and legal facets in addition to technical controls. This all-encompassing method guarantees that every aspect of security is considered and incorporated into a coherent plan. Additionally, frameworks help firms prioritize and identify risks, allocate resources efficiently, and implement the appropriate controls for risk mitigation. The most important locations will be the focus of security efforts, thanks to this risk-based strategy.

Furthermore, a lot of security frameworks are in line with legal and industry standards, which makes it simpler for businesses to prove compliance and stay out of trouble. Finally, frameworks support an ongoing development cycle where businesses regularly assess their security posture, identify areas for improvement, and implement necessary changes. This guarantees that security precautions continue to work even when threats change. Now, in the next subsection, let us look at various frameworks available and their characteristics.

Types of security management frameworks

There are several widely recognized security management frameworks, each with its own strengths and focus areas. Some of the most prominent frameworks include:

- **ISO/IEC 27001**: This international standard provides requirements for establishing, implementing, maintaining, and continually improving an **information security management system** (**ISMS**). It covers a wide range of security controls and is widely adopted across the globe.

- **NIST Cybersecurity Framework (CSF)**: Developed by the **National Institute of Standards and Technology** (**NIST**), the CSF is a flexible framework that helps organizations identify, assess, and manage cybersecurity risk. It provides a common language for understanding and managing cybersecurity risk and is widely used in the United States.

- **CIS Controls**: These controls, developed by the **Center for Internet Security** (**CIS**), offer a prioritized set of actions for cybersecurity defense. They are designed to be practical and effective for organizations of all sizes.

- **COBIT**: Developed by ISACA, COBIT is a framework for IT governance and management. It provides a comprehensive set of best practices for managing IT risk and ensuring that IT investments align with business goals.

Choosing the right framework

The best security management framework for your organization will depend on several factors, including:

- **Industry**: Different industries have varying levels of cybersecurity risks and may be subject to specific regulatory requirements. For instance, healthcare organizations may need to consider frameworks that address patient privacy regulations like HIPAA, while financial institutions may need to focus on frameworks that comply with data security standards like PCI DSS.

- **Size and complexity**: Larger organizations with complex **Information Technology** (**IT**) environments may benefit from a more comprehensive framework like ISO/IEC 27001, while smaller organizations may find a more lightweight framework like CIS Controls to be more manageable.

- **Maturity level**: Organizations with a mature security program may already have many controls in place and may benefit from a framework that helps them refine their existing practices. On the other hand, organizations with a less mature security program may need a framework that provides more guidance on building a security program from the ground up.

- **Resources**: Implementing any security framework requires resources, including personnel, budget, and time. Organizations should choose a framework that aligns with their available resources to ensure successful implementation.

By implementing a robust security management framework, organizations can establish a solid foundation for cybersecurity to mitigate risks and ensure the ongoing resilience of their digital assets.

Implementing security management framework

Implementing a security management framework is a multi-step process that requires careful planning and execution. Here is a general outline of the key steps involved:

1. **Scoping**: Determine the scope of the framework implementation by identifying the systems, processes, and data that will be covered.

2. **Gap analysis**: Assess your organization's current security posture against the requirements of the chosen framework to identify gaps and areas for improvement.

3. **Risk assessment**: Conduct a comprehensive risk assessment to identify and prioritize the most significant risks to your organization.

4. **Implementation plan**: Develop a detailed plan for implementing the necessary security controls and processes.

5. **Implementation**: Execute the implementation plan, deploying the required controls and processes.

6. **Monitoring and review**: Continuously monitor the effectiveness of the security controls and processes. Conduct regular reviews and audits to ensure ongoing compliance with the framework.

In the next section, we will look at effective governance and compliance, that are essential pillars of managing cybersecurity.

Governance and compliance

In the ever-changing world of cybersecurity, where new threats arise and weaknesses can appear out of nowhere, having strong governance and compliance measures is crucial for building a strong defense against cyberattacks. Although frequently used synonymously, these ideas have separate functions in safeguarding the security and reliability of a company's digital resources. Let us understand this distinction in the following subsection.

Governance

Organizations' cybersecurity efforts are greatly influenced by governance, which defines the long-term security vision and goals, the precise responsibilities and duties of key personnel, and the alignment of security measures with the organization's overarching goals and purposes.

Establishing a cybersecurity strategy, which entails determining the organization's risk tolerance, identifying vital assets, and laying out a plan to safeguard those assets from cyber threats, is one of the most important components of governance.

Furthermore, cybersecurity governance creates distinct lines of authority and accountability, with the board of directors and senior executives actively participating in the supervision and encouragement of security activities. Additionally, governance guarantees that cybersecurity programs receive sufficient financial and human resources, guaranteeing that security measures are correctly enforced and consistently upheld. Finally, governance includes creating thorough cybersecurity policies, guidelines, and standards that direct the company's security operations.

Compliance

Making sure a company complies with laws, rules, industry standards, and internal data security and protection policies is the main goal of compliance in cybersecurity. It entails putting in place the controls and safeguards required to bring organizational procedures into compliance with these specifications. Regulatory compliance, which mandates that businesses should abide by particular laws and rules controlling cybersecurity, privacy, and data protection, such as the HIPAA or GDPR, is one of the most important components of compliance.

For businesses processing credit card data, it also entails following industry requirements like the PCI DSS. Organization-specific internal regulations must also be adhered to, guaranteeing that their own protocols are in place to preserve cybersecurity. Additionally, to ensure that security controls are operating efficiently, compliance frequently necessitates routine audits and evaluations, and reporting systems are put in place to notify stakeholders of the organization's compliance status, guaranteeing accountability and transparency.

Interplay between governance and compliance

Governance and compliance are complementary elements of a comprehensive cybersecurity program. Governance provides a strategic direction, while compliance ensures that the tactical implementation aligns with established requirements.

A strong governance framework is essential for establishing a culture of security within the organization, while robust compliance measures ensure that the organization operates within the boundaries of legal and regulatory frameworks.

Best practices for effective governance and compliance

Here are a few recommended strategies, principles, and procedures organizations should follow to ensure they operate within legal, ethical, and regulatory frameworks:

- **Establish a cybersecurity steering committee**: This committee, which is composed of senior executives and representatives from key departments, should provide oversight and guidance for the organization's cybersecurity program.

- **Conduct regular risk assessments**: Regularly assess the organization's risk profile, considering evolving threats, vulnerabilities, and changes to the business environment.

- **Develop comprehensive cybersecurity policies**: These policies should cover all aspects of cybersecurity, from data protection and access controls to incident response and disaster recovery.

- **Implement robust security controls**: Deploy technical and organizational security controls to mitigate identified risks. This may include firewalls, intrusion detection systems, encryption, access controls, and employee training.

- **Monitor and review**: Continuously monitor the effectiveness of security controls and processes. Conduct regular audits and reviews to ensure ongoing compliance with regulatory requirements and internal policies.

- **Incident response and reporting**: Establish a robust incident response plan to address security incidents promptly and effectively. Ensure that incidents are reported to relevant authorities and stakeholders as required by law or policy.

By effectively implementing governance and compliance practices, organizations can build a strong foundation for cybersecurity, mitigate risks, protect their assets, and maintain the trust of their customers and stakeholders.

Training and awareness programs for cybersecurity

Organizations frequently make significant investments in state-of-the-art technology to strengthen their defenses. Nevertheless, even the most advanced security infrastructure can be rendered ineffective by a single mistake from an unaware employee. It is essential to have strong training and awareness programs as a crucial part of a comprehensive cybersecurity strategy. Let us first look and understand how humans play a significant role in strengthening security.

Understanding the human factor

Humans are complex and multifaceted. They bring a wealth of creativity, adaptability, and problem-solving skills to the table, making them invaluable assets in any organization. However, these same human characteristics can also introduce vulnerabilities in the cybersecurity landscape. Here is a deeper dive into why humans can be both the strongest asset and the weakest link in cybersecurity:

- **Strengths**: Humans possess the critical thinking skills to analyze information, identify suspicious activity, and make informed decisions. They can adapt to changing situations, improvise solutions, and collaborate effectively to address security challenges. Additionally, human vigilance is crucial for detecting social engineering tactics that may bypass automated security controls.

- **Weaknesses**: Humans are susceptible to cognitive biases and social engineering techniques. Phishing emails can exploit our natural tendency to trust authority figures or urgency. Fear of punishment or the desire to be helpful can lead employees to inadvertently click on malicious links or disclose sensitive information. Additionally, human error, such as weak password hygiene or accidental data leaks, can create security vulnerabilities.

By acknowledging these strengths and weaknesses, organizations can develop training programs, addressing the human element of cybersecurity effectively. Training should not only equip employees with knowledge of security threats but also empower them to make informed decisions and mitigate risks based on their unique skills and experiences.

Importance of training and awareness programs

Employees who receive cybersecurity training are better equipped to make educated judgments and refrain from dangerous behavior, which greatly lowers the possibility of successful assaults.

Frequent training helps staff members understand the value of cybersecurity and fosters a sense of shared accountability, fostering a culture where security is a team effort. Furthermore, well-designed programs guarantee adherence to industrial and regulatory frameworks that require cybersecurity training, preventing any legal and financial consequences.

Additionally, training can give staff members the information and abilities they need to identify security events and report them right away, allowing for a rapid and efficient reaction that can greatly lessen the damage in case of a breach.

Key elements of effective training programs

Cybersecurity training programs should be tailored to the specific needs and roles of different employee groups within the organization. Executives need to understand the strategic cybersecurity landscape, current threats, and the potential impact of breaches, while technical staff require in-depth knowledge of specific security tools and procedures relevant to their daily tasks.

Non-technical staff can benefit from training tailored to their roles, such as HR personnel being aware of social engineering tactics and customer service representatives being trained on identifying and handling suspicious inquiries. Engaging delivery methods, such as interactive modules and simulations, should be used instead of dry presentations. Regular reinforcement through refresher training and phishing simulations is crucial for keeping security top of mind. Finally, training effectiveness should be tracked through assessments, surveys, and metrics to allow for continuous improvement and optimization of the program.

Essential topics for cybersecurity training

According to IBM's *Cost of a data breach report 2023*, the average cost of a data breach in 2023 was a staggering $4.45 million. This figure includes the direct costs of investigating and remediating the breach, as well as the indirect costs of lost business, reputational damage, and legal fees. The report also found that breaches caused by human error were among the most expensive to resolve, further emphasizing the need for comprehensive cybersecurity training to minimize the risk of human-induced security incidents. Let us look at a few topics of training:

- **Phishing attacks:**

    o **Understanding the threat**: Educate employees on the various types of phishing attacks, including spear phishing, whaling, and **SMS phishing** (**smishing**).

    o **Recognizing red flags**: Teach employees to identify common indicators of phishing emails, such as suspicious links, urgent requests, and requests for sensitive information.

    o **Reporting suspicious activity**: Establish a clear reporting mechanism for suspected phishing attempts and encourage employees to report suspicious activity promptly.

- **Passwords and authentication:**

    o **Strong password hygiene**: Emphasize the importance of creating strong, unique passwords for each account and using password managers to securely store credentials.

    o **Multi-factor authentication (MFA)**: Encourage the use of MFA wherever possible, to add an extra layer of security beyond passwords.

    o **Password policies**: Implement and enforce robust password policies that require regular password changes and prohibit password reuse.

- **Working remotely:**

  o **Secure network connections**: Encourage employees to use secure Wi-Fi networks at home and avoid using public Wi-Fi for sensitive work.

  o **Virtual private networks (VPNs)**: Provide and require the use of VPNs for accessing company resources remotely.

  o **Home office security**: Offer guidance on securing home offices, including securing routers, using strong passwords, and updating software regularly.

- **Social engineering attacks on employees:**

  o **Understanding the tactics**: Educate employees on common social engineering techniques, such as phishing, pretexting, and baiting.

  o **Recognizing red flags**: Help employees identify warning signs of social engineering attempts, such as unsolicited requests for information or unusual urgency.

- **Removable media:**

  o **Understanding the risks**: Explain the risks associated with using removable media, such as USB drives, external hard drives, and CDs, which can easily introduce malware or facilitate data theft.

  o **Safe handling practices**: Provide guidelines for the secure use of removable media, including scanning for malware, encryption, and proper disposal procedures.

- **Physical security:**

  o **Securing workspaces**: Teach employees to lock their workstations when unattended, keep sensitive documents stored securely, and be mindful of shoulder surfing (unauthorized viewing of sensitive information).

  o **Tailgating awareness**: Educate employees on the risks of tailgating and encourage them to challenge unauthorized individuals attempting to enter secure areas.

  o **Visitor management**: Implement visitor policies and procedures to track and monitor visitors within the workplace.

- **Mobile device security:**

  o **Device hardening**: Explain the importance of enabling strong passwords or biometric authentication, encrypting data, and installing security software on mobile devices.

  o **Public Wi-Fi risks**: Warn employees about the dangers of connecting to public Wi-Fi networks and encourage the use of VPNs for secure connections.

- o **Mobile device management (MDM)**: Implement MDM solutions to enforce security policies on company-issued devices and enable remote wiping in case of loss or theft.

- **Public Wi-Fi:**

  - o **Avoiding sensitive activities**: Warn employees against accessing sensitive company data or conducting financial transactions over public Wi-Fi networks.

  - o **Using VPNs**: Recommend using VPNs to encrypt traffic when using public Wi-Fi.

- **Cloud security:**

  - o **Data protection in the cloud**: Explain how data is stored and protected in cloud environments and emphasize the importance of strong passwords and MFA for cloud accounts.

  - o **Shared responsibility model**: Educate employees about the shared responsibility model in cloud security, clarifying their role in protecting data stored in the cloud.

- **Social media use:**

  - o **Privacy settings**: Encourage employees to review and adjust privacy settings on social media platforms to limit the visibility of personal information.

  - o **Over-sharing risks**: Explain the risks of sharing sensitive information or company details on social media and emphasize the importance of maintaining a professional online presence.

- **Internet and email use:**

  - o **Safe browsing habits**: Teach employees to be cautious when clicking on links or opening attachments in emails, and to avoid downloading software from untrusted sources.

  - o **Email security**: Explain the importance of using strong passwords for email accounts and enabling two-factor authentication.

- **Security at home:**

  - o **Personal device security**: Extend security awareness training to personal devices, encouraging strong passwords, regular updates, and antivirus software.

  - o **Smart home security**: Discuss the potential risks associated with internet-connected devices and provide guidance on securing smart home devices and networks.

Beyond training, building a security-aware culture

While training is a crucial foundation, fostering a security-aware culture goes beyond formal programs. Encourage employees to report security concerns, share security tips and news, and participate in security-related activities like lunch-and-learns or workshops. Recognize and reward employees who demonstrate exemplary security practices.

In the ongoing battle against cyber threats, organizations cannot afford to overlook the human element. By investing in comprehensive training and awareness programs, they can empower their employees to become active participants in cybersecurity, creating a resilient defense against the ever-evolving landscape of cyber-attacks. In the next section we will dive deeper and understand risk management.

Risk management

Since new threats and vulnerabilities continue to emerge each day, effective risk management is the linchpin of a successful threat and vulnerability management program. By quantifying and prioritizing risks, blue teams can make informed decisions about where to focus their resources, ensuring the most critical vulnerabilities are addressed promptly.

Intersection of risk and vulnerability

At its core, risk management in this context involves a calculated balance of risk and vulnerability:

- **Understanding vulnerabilities**: A vulnerability assessment unveils the weaknesses in your systems and software. These are potential entry points for attackers.

- **Assessing the threat landscape**: Threat intelligence provides insights into the TTPs of adversaries, shedding light on which vulnerabilities are most likely to be exploited.

- **Quantifying the risk**: By combining knowledge of vulnerabilities with the threat landscape, you can assess the likelihood and potential impact of each vulnerability being exploited. This is the essence of risk assessment.

Risk-driven vulnerability prioritization

Rather than simply patching vulnerabilities in the order they are discovered, a risk-based approach prioritizes remediation efforts based on the severity of the associated risk. For instance:

- **Critical risk**: A vulnerability that, if exploited, could lead to a complete system compromise, significant data loss, or financial damage would be assigned a critical risk level and require immediate attention.

- **High risk**: A vulnerability with a high likelihood of exploitation and significant impact would also warrant swift action.

- **Medium/Low risk**: Vulnerabilities with lower likelihood or impact may be addressed on a scheduled basis, allowing resources to be focused on the most pressing threats.

- **Practical risk management in action**: Consider a scenario where your vulnerability scan identifies a critical vulnerability in a widely used web server software. Threat intelligence indicates that a sophisticated threat actor group is actively exploiting this vulnerability in the wild. In this case, a risk-based approach would prioritize patching this vulnerability immediately, even if other vulnerabilities have been identified earlier.

Risk identification by understanding the attacker's mindset

The first step in effective risk management is comprehensive risk identification. This involves not only cataloguing vulnerabilities but also understanding the motivations and tactics of potential threat actors.

Two primary attacker mindsets are crucial to consider:

1. **Explorative**: These attackers are probing for weaknesses, often indiscriminately scanning for vulnerabilities they can later exploit or sell.

2. **Exploitative**: These attackers have a specific target or objective in mind and are actively seeking vulnerabilities they can use to achieve their goals.

Understanding these mindsets helps security teams anticipate potential attack vectors and prioritize their defenses accordingly. Additionally, tools like the **Cyber Kill Chain** (**CKC**) framework can aid in risk identification by mapping out the stages of a cyber-attack, from initial reconnaissance to data exfiltration. By analyzing potential attack paths within the CKC, security teams can proactively identify and mitigate risks at each stage.

Risk quantification by measuring the threat landscape

Once risks are identified, it is essential to quantify them to understand their potential impact. This involves assessing both the likelihood and the potential consequences of a successful attack, detail as follows.

- **Likelihood**: This refers to the probability that a specific threat will exploit a given vulnerability. Factors to consider include the prevalence of the threat, the skill level of potential attackers, and the presence of existing security controls.

- **Impact**: This encompasses the potential damage that could result from a successful attack, including financial loss, operational disruption, reputational harm, and legal liabilities.

A useful tool for visualizing risk quantification is a risk matrix, as depicted as follows:

LIKELIHOOD	IMPACT →				
	1	2	3	4	5
1	LOW **1**	LOW **2**	LOW **3**	MEDIUM **4**	MEDIUM **5**
2	LOW **2**	MEDIUM **4**	MEDIUM **6**	HIGH **8**	HIGH **10**
3	LOW **3**	MEDIUM **6**	HIGH **9**	HIGH **12**	EXTREME **15**
4	MEDIUM **4**	HIGH **8**	HIGH **12**	HIGH **16**	EXTREME **20**
5	MEDIUM **5**	HIGH **10**	EXTREME **15**	EXTREME **20**	EXTREME **25**

Figure 10.1: Risk matrix

The risk matrix allows you to plot identified threats based on their frequency and potential impact, providing a clear visual representation of which risks demand immediate attention.

Risk treatment strategies

Once risks are prioritized, you can implement various strategies to mitigate them:

- **Mitigation**: Implement security patches, strengthen access controls, or deploy additional security measures to reduce the likelihood or impact of a vulnerability being exploited.

- **Avoidance**: If a risk is too high and cannot be adequately mitigated, consider eliminating the vulnerable system or process altogether.

- **Transfer**: Cyber insurance can transfer some of the financial risk associated with a cyber-attack.

- **Acceptance**: In some cases, the cost of mitigating a risk may outweigh the potential impact. In such situations, organizations may choose to accept the risk, documenting their decision and implementing monitoring to track any changes.

Continuous risk monitoring and review

The cybersecurity landscape is dynamic, with new threats and vulnerabilities emerging constantly. Therefore, risk management must also be an ongoing process. Regularly reassess risks, update your vulnerability assessments, and adjust your risk treatment strategies as needed, to ensure your defenses remain effective.

By integrating risk management into your threat and vulnerability management program, you can make informed, data-driven decisions that prioritize the most critical risks, optimize resource allocation, and ultimately strengthen your organization's overall security posture.

Risk management is not merely a theoretical concept but a practical necessity for blue teams in the fast-paced world of cybersecurity. By embracing a risk-based approach to threat and vulnerability management, organizations can make strategic decisions, prioritize resources, and ultimately strengthen their overall security posture. In the next section, we will talk about the best practices.

Cyber threat management best practices

Cyber threats are a constant and evolving menace, targeting organizations of all sizes and sectors. Effective CTM is not just a technological challenge; it is a strategic imperative that requires a holistic approach encompassing people, processes, and technology. Let us delve into a comprehensive set of best practices designed to build a resilient defense against the ever-changing threat landscape.

Strategic alignment and risk-based prioritization

Cybersecurity should not operate in isolation, but instead, CTM efforts should be aligned with the organization's broader business objectives.

This means understanding the critical assets, processes, and data that drive the business and tailoring the security strategy to protect them. A thorough risk assessment forms the foundation of CTM, where potential threats are identified, assessed based on likelihood and potential impact, and prioritized accordingly. This risk-based approach allows for the efficient allocation of resources and focuses on the most critical risks.

Proactive defense and continuous vigilance

Making threat hunting a fundamental habit can help you move from a reactive to a proactive security approach, which will improve your security posture. Even when there is not an active attack, threat hunting entails actively looking for signs of network intrusion. This calls for knowledgeable analysts who are familiar with the strategies, methods, and processes used by attackers.

Since no single security control is infallible, it is imperative to implement a multi-layered defense plan, commonly referred to as defense in depth. Numerous technologies, such as firewalls, intrusion detection and prevention systems, endpoint detection and response, and security information and event management solutions, should be included in this plan. Furthermore, being ahead of the curve by utilizing threat intelligence from reliable sources gives you important knowledge about the most recent threats, weaknesses, and attacker strategies, enabling you to proactively fortify your defenses. Let us understand this from the **People, Process, and Technology** terms.

People as the first line of defense

Many organizations have started building a robust security posture that starts with their employees, considering them as the first line of defense.

- **Security awareness training**: The human factor remains a critical vulnerability. Invest in comprehensive security awareness training to educate employees about common threats like phishing, social engineering, and malware. Teach them how to recognize and report suspicious activities.

- **Create a culture of security**: Encourage employees to be vigilant and take ownership of security. Adopting a culture where security is everyone's responsibility, and not just that of IT department or any other single department.

Process of streamlining security operations

Standardizing the procedures ensures consistency and efficiency in all security-related activities. Some of them are listed as follows:

- **Incident response planning**: Develop and regularly test a robust IRP. This ensures that you have a well-defined process for detecting, containing, and eradicating threats, as well as recovering from incidents.

- **Change management**: Implement a rigorous change management process to ensure that changes to systems and configurations are properly assessed and authorized. This helps prevent unintended vulnerabilities from being introduced into the environment.

- **Vulnerability management**: Establish a structured vulnerability management program to identify, prioritize, and remediate vulnerabilities promptly. This involves regular scanning, patching, and configuration management.

Technology for leveraging advanced tools

Maximizing the security capabilities involves harnessing the power of automation and intelligent systems. Let us take a look at them:

- **Embrace automation**: Automate repetitive security tasks like vulnerability scanning, patch management, and log analysis. This frees up valuable time for security analysts to focus on more complex investigations and threat hunting.

- **Explore artificial intelligence (AI) and machine learning (ML)**: AI and ML can be leveraged to enhance threat detection, automate incident response, and identify patterns that human analysts might miss.

- **Continuous monitoring and logging**: Monitor your systems and networks 24/7, collecting and analyzing logs to detect anomalies and suspicious activity. This provides early warning of potential threats, enabling swift action.

Cyber threat management is an ongoing challenge, requiring a holistic approach, and by embracing these best practices, organizations can build a resilient defense that protects their critical assets, safeguards their data, and minimizes the risk of disruption from cyber-attacks.

Cyber threat management challenges

While CTM is essential for safeguarding organizational assets, it is not without its challenges. These obstacles can hinder the effectiveness of even the most well-intentioned security programs. Let us delve into some of the most pressing challenges faced by organizations in their CTM efforts:

- **Evolving threat landscape**: Cyber threats are constantly evolving, with attackers employing new techniques and technologies to evade detection and exploit vulnerabilities. This dynamic nature of threats makes it difficult for organizations to keep pace and adapt their defenses accordingly.

- **APTs**: APTs are sophisticated, well-funded, and highly motivated attackers who often target specific organizations or industries. They are patient and persistent, often lurking in networks for extended periods to steal sensitive data or cause disruption. Detecting and mitigating APTs requires advanced threat hunting capabilities and a deep understanding of their TTPs.

- **Zero-day attacks**: Zero-day attacks exploit vulnerabilities that are unknown to software vendors and security researchers. These attacks are particularly dangerous because there are no patches or fixes available, leaving organizations vulnerable until a solution is developed.

- **Shortage of skilled cybersecurity professionals**: The cybersecurity industry faces a significant shortage of qualified professionals. This skills gap makes it difficult for organizations to find and retain the talent needed to effectively manage cyber threats.

- **Complexity of IT environments**: Modern IT environments are increasingly complex, with a proliferation of devices, applications, and cloud services. This complexity makes it difficult to secure all endpoints and maintain visibility across the entire network.

- **Limited resources**: Many organizations, especially smaller ones, have limited resources to dedicate to cybersecurity. This can make it difficult to implement comprehensive CTM programs, including investing in advanced security technologies and hiring skilled personnel.

- **Compliance and regulatory requirements**: The ever-changing landscape of cybersecurity regulations can be overwhelming for organizations. Ensuring compliance with various standards like GDPR, HIPAA, and PCI DSS can be a significant challenge, requiring ongoing monitoring and adaptation of security practices.

- **Balancing security and usability**: Implementing strict security controls can sometimes hinder productivity and usability for employees. Striking the right balance between security and usability is a constant challenge, requiring careful consideration of the trade-offs involved.

- **Insider threats**: Not all threats come from external attackers. Malicious insiders, whether disgruntled employees or unwitting victims of social engineering attacks, can pose a significant risk to an organization's security.

- **Lack of visibility and control over third-party risk**: Many organizations rely on third-party vendors and partners for various services. These third parties can introduce security risks if they do not have adequate security practices in place. Maintaining visibility and control over third-party risk is a growing concern for organizations.

- **Data breaches and incident response**: Despite best efforts, data breaches can still occur. Having a robust incident response plan in place is crucial to minimizing the impact of a breach. This involves quickly identifying and containing the breach, notifying affected parties, and implementing measures to prevent future occurrences.

- **Emerging technologies**: As new technologies like artificial intelligence, machine learning, and the internet of things become more prevalent, they also introduce new security risks. Organizations must stay abreast of these emerging technologies and adapt their security strategies to address the unique challenges they pose.

By acknowledging and proactively addressing these challenges, organizations can enhance their cyber threat management capabilities and build a more resilient security posture.

Conclusion

We have examined the diverse aspects of this field throughout this chapter, highlighting its significance in protecting organizational resources and information.

We explored the core ideas of cyber threat management and realized that it is a proactive effort that foresees, detects, and eliminates dangers before they have a chance to do serious harm, rather than just a reactive reaction to attacks.

A key component of efficient threat management was emphasized as being the development of unambiguous cybersecurity policies and procedures. By offering a framework for decision-making, these policies make sure that everyone involved is aware of their obligations and roles in protecting the organization's cybersecurity posture.

We examined best practices for managing cyber threats, stressing the value of a proactive, risk-based strategy. Key tactics for remaining ahead of the curve and successfully reducing risks were emphasized, including threat hunting, vulnerability management, incident response planning, and the use of cutting-edge security solutions.

In summary, managing cyber threats is a continual process that calls for constant attention to detail, flexibility, and creativity. Businesses can create a robust cybersecurity ecosystem that protects their vital assets, data, and long-term success in an increasingly digital world by adopting a comprehensive strategy that takes into account people, processes, and technology.

Remember that the best defense is a multi-layered one that incorporates a variety of technological, operational, and human-centric approaches as you set out to improve your organization's cybersecurity posture.

The future and extent of threat management and blue teaming will be covered in the next chapter. We will examine what can be automated, new and developing tools and technologies, CTI's future, and future-ready skills.

Join our Discord space

Join our Discord workspace for latest updates, offers, tech happenings around the world, new releases, and sessions with the authors:

https://discord.bpbonline.com

CHAPTER 11

Future of Blue Team and Threat Management

Introduction

The blue team plays a crucial role in cybersecurity as digital footprints expand and threats grow more complex. Cyber adversaries are improving their tactics and weaponry; therefore the defenders must too. This chapter will investigate the future of blue teaming and threat management. It shows defenders' resilience, adaptation, and creativity in cybersecurity. We shall also look at the increasing need for cyber defenders and the skills required.

In this chapter, we shall be exploring cybersecurity defense's future. In the preceding chapters, we have already studied the newest techniques, tools, and methods that enable blue teams to defeat the most sophisticated cyber assaults. This chapter explores the cutting-edge technologies and methods shaping blue teaming, including AI and ML strengthening Zero Trust infrastructures, enhancing threat management, and getting them acquitted with new trends and technologies used.

We can see in the future that defenders are fighting a global digital war. Blue teams will continue to defend digital landscapes against cyberattacks with a proactive approach, unwavering determination, and deep dedication. Join us on this journey into the future of blue teaming and threat management, where you can learn how to remain ahead of the competition.

Structure

This chapter will include the following topics:

- Automation
- Emerging trends and technologies in blue teams
- Role of AI and ML in threat management
- Future of cyber threat intelligence sharing
- Future of blue teaming and threat management
- Skill requirements in the future

Objectives

This chapter aims to give readers a complete awareness of the landscape of evolving cybersecurity defense strategies. Examining new trends, technologies, and best practices will help cybersecurity professionals, aspirant experts, and decision-makers to have the knowledge and insights required to adapt and excel in an increasingly complex digital security environment. By means of an in-depth analysis of subjects including automation, new technologies, the use of artificial intelligence and machine learning in cyber defense, upskilling, and addressing the skills gap, readers will acquire a clear awareness of the transforming powers impacting the future of blue teaming and threat management. The goal is to enable people and companies to actively defend against cyber threats, enhance their security posture, and thereby efficiently reduce risks in a time when cybersecurity resilience is critical. Let us start by diving deeper and exploring how we can leverage automation in the following section.

Automation

A decade ago, cyberattacks often relied on known vulnerabilities, malware, and phishing emails. While some attacks were sophisticated, many followed relatively predictable patterns. Traditional antivirus software dominated endpoint security. Cloud computing was in its infancy, and mobile devices were not as central to daily operations. Security was primarily focused on on-premises infrastructure. Information sharing among organizations and sectors regarding cyber threats was limited. Threat intelligence sharing was not as formalized or widespread. Cybersecurity awareness and training were not as emphasized within organizations. Employees received minimal education on security best practices.

Today, cyber threats have reached unprecedented levels of complexity and sophistication. Nation-state actors, organized cybercrime groups, and even individual hackers leverage advanced tactics such as zero-day exploits, supply chain attacks, and AI-driven malware. Defenders now face adversaries who are highly skilled and well-funded. Endpoint security has evolved into more advanced solutions, incorporating behavioral analysis, ML, and threat intelligence. These modern tools provide proactive protection against both known and unknown threats, reducing the attack surface and improving overall security.

Cloud and mobile security are critical components of the modern cybersecurity landscape. The shift to remote work and cloud-based services has expanded the attack surface. The sharing of threat intelligence has become a cornerstone of cybersecurity defense. Organizations participate in ISACs and exchange real-time threat data to enhance collective security. Organizations prioritize cybersecurity awareness training for employees, recognizing that human error remains a significant risk. Regular training programs, to educate personnel about phishing, social engineering, and safe online behavior, reducing the likelihood of successful attacks, are a must.

All this was possible due to new tools, automation, AI, and ML etc. In the dynamic domain of cybersecurity, automation has emerged as a transformative force, reshaping the strategies and practices employed to safeguard digital assets and its function, practical applications, and optimistic future are of the utmost importance.

Function of automation

Modern defense strategies rely heavily on automation, which plays a multifaceted role in cybersecurity. It enables organizations to respond rapidly to cyber hazards in the first place. Automated systems are designed to detect and respond to threats in real-time or near-real-time, drastically decreasing the amount of time required to identify and mitigate potential security vulnerabilities. This speed is essential for minimizing damage and preventing unauthorized access and data exfiltration.

Endpoint security has become more advanced over the years, with tools like threat intelligence, machine learning, and behavioral analysis being added. These current tools protect you ahead of time from both known and unknown threats, making your security better overall by lowering the number of places an attack could happen. Cloud and mobile security are very important parts of current cybersecurity. The attack area has grown since more people work from home and use cloud-based services. Companies put a lot of effort into teaching their workers about safety since they are aware of the impact and risk that mistakes made by people pose. Regular training programs to teach employees about hacking, social engineering, and how to be safe online make attacks less likely to succeed.

New tools, robotics, **Artificial Intelligence** (**AI**) and **Machine Learning** (**ML**), and other things made this possible. Automation has become a major force in the constantly changing field of cybersecurity, changing the methods and tactics used to protect digital assets.

Applications of automation

There are practical implementations for automation in numerous cybersecurity domains. One of its primary functions is detection and response to threats. Automated systems employ sophisticated techniques such as ML and behavioral analysis to detect anomalies and patterns indicating intrusions. When a threat is detected, these systems can begin automated responses, such as isolating affected systems, blocking malicious network traffic, or launching predefined IR workflows. This capability is essential for mitigating the effects of cyber incidents and drastically decreasing the attacker's time spent within a network.

The automation of IR, a crucial aspect of cybersecurity, is extremely advantageous. Platforms for **security orchestration, automation, and response** (**SOAR**), streamline incident response workflows by automating incident ticketing, evidence collection, and team communication. This streamlined approach guarantees a swift and coordinated response to security incidents, thereby enhancing an organization's capacity to efficiently contain and mitigate threats.

Specialized areas of cybersecurity, such as email security, rely heavily on automation as well. Automated email security solutions thoroughly examine incoming messages to identify phishing attempts and possible malware. Automatic quarantining or blocking suspicious emails reduces the likelihood of employees falling victim to phishing attacks.

Moreover, automated systems are superior at patch administration. They ensure that software vulnerabilities are promptly addressed by deploying security updates automatically. Automation improves an organization's resistance to known exploits by reducing the attack surface.

Security information and event management (**SIEM**) systems utilize automation to collect and analyze security data from multiple sources. Automation facilitates the correlation of security events, the identification of potential threats, and the production of alerts for further investigation.

Future potential for automation

A lot of good things are going to happen in the future of cybersecurity technology. The first change is that AI and ML will collaborate more. This integration will make automated systems more effective by letting them adapt to new threats and act to them in real time.

Predictive analytics will also become more popular, which will help businesses plan in advance and protect themselves against problems before they happen. Automation will use past data, present trends, and the actions of dangerous actors to give businesses useful information about possible future threats, so they can devise ways to enhance their security

As quantum computing technology develops, automation will facilitate the incorporation of quantum-safe encryption algorithms, assuring data security in a post-quantum world. This is crucial because quantum computing poses a threat to conventional encryption techniques.

Moreover, as the IoT and edge computing proliferate, automation will play a crucial role in securing these distributed and frequently resource-constrained environments. It will provide a comprehensive security approach for these ecosystems' interconnected devices and data sources.

Automation will play a significant role in the implementation of zero trust architecture, where trust is never presumed, and continuous verification is the norm. Every user and device that accesses the network must be validated and authenticated by automated systems under this model.

Emerging trends and technologies in blue teams

Cybersecurity is in a constant state of evolution in response to cyber adversaries' constantly evolving tactics. Blue teaming, which entails proactive defense strategies and security operations, must continuously adapt to these emergent trends and technologies to maintain its effectiveness. In this in-depth analysis, we examine the factors that will shape the future of blue teaming and how these trends are transforming the cybersecurity landscape.

Artificial intelligence and machine learning

Blue teaming has AI and ML at the vanguard of emergent technologies since these technologies have the potential to revolutionize cybersecurity by vastly improving threat detection and response capacities. Solutions powered by AI can analyze massive datasets in real-time, identify patterns indicative of cyber threats, and even foretell future attacks based on historical data. Continuously learning from new data, ML algorithms improve their accuracy over time. Blue teams are progressively incorporating AI and ML into their security operations to automate threat hunting, optimize incident response, and identify vulnerabilities proactively.

Quantum computing revolutionizes cybersecurity

Quantum computing, with its ability to perform calculations far beyond the reach of classical computers, presents a paradigm shift in cybersecurity. The advent of quantum computing poses both opportunities and challenges for blue teams. Quantum computers pose a significant threat to currently used *asymmetric* encryption algorithms, such as **Rivest-Shamir-Adleman** (**RSA**) and **Elliptic Curve Cryptography** (**ECC**), which are foundational to securing web traffic and digital signatures. However, symmetric encryption algorithms like **Advanced Encryption Standard** (**AES**) are considered more resistant to quantum attacks, though they may require larger key sizes to maintain their security level.. However, they also pave the way for quantum-safe encryption that can resist quantum attacks. Quantum-safe algorithms are a vital element in the future of cybersecurity strategies. Blue teams must prepare for the post-quantum era by exploring and implementing quantum-safe encryption methods to protect sensitive data from quantum threats.

One of the primary hurdles is the transition to quantum-safe cryptography. Existing cryptographic standards, such as RSA and ECC, are vulnerable to Shor's algorithm, which quantum computers can execute efficiently. Blue teams must therefore identify, test, and implement quantum-resistant algorithms, a process that demands substantial expertise and resources.

Impact of blockchain on cybersecurity

Blockchain, which was initially designed to underpin cryptocurrencies such as Bitcoin, is making significant inroads into cybersecurity. Its fundamental principle of decentralized, tamper-resistant data storage offers promising security applications. Blockchain's capacity to generate a transparent and immutable ledger has the potential to revolutionize several facets of cybersecurity, such as identity administration, secure transactions, and supply chain security. By offering a model of distributed trust, blockchain can reduce reliance on centralized authorities, making it more difficult for assailants to compromise data integrity.

User and entity behavior analytics

Monitoring the behavior of users and entities within an organization's network is the focus of **user and entity behavior analytics (UEBA)**, an emerging trend. UEBA solutions can detect anomalies and deviations that may indicate internal threats or compromised accounts by establishing a baseline of normal behavior. UEBA goes beyond traditional signature-based detection methods, making it a valuable tool for blue teams. It enables proactive threat research by identifying patterns or activities that may be indicative of intrusions or unauthorized access. As UEBA technologies continue to develop, they will play a crucial role in enhancing the defensive capabilities of blue teams.

SIEM/SOAR

SIEM systems are still an important part of blue teams; however, they have been updated to keep up with the needs of the current security landscape. Modern SIEM systems collect and analyze huge amounts of security data from all over an organization's infrastructure, and they are getting better at finding threats and responding to incidents in real time by adding AI and ML features. These advanced features make it easier to spot threats and faster, thereby reacting more quickly. Better processing in SIEM systems also makes it easier to investigate security events. SIEM systems are also connected with other security technologies now more than ever, making a more unified security ecosystem that is better all around.

The progress of SOAR works well with SIEM and makes blue teams even more successful. SOAR platforms make work easier by automating regular tasks like triaging alerts, adding more information to data, and responding to routine incidents. This lets security teams act more quickly and effectively. They use pre-defined, customizable playbooks that are made to fit different attack situations. This makes sure that the response process is consistent and well-organized. Importantly, SOAR works well with other security tools, like SIEM, threat intelligence platforms, and endpoint detection and response. This makes a single location for all security activities. Analysts can focus on more important tasks, like threat hunting, in-depth incident investigations, and constantly improving the organization's overall security posture, when these boring tasks are done automatically by SOAR.

Cybersecurity mesh architecture

Cybersecurity mesh architecture (CSMA) is a new way of thinking about security that provides an autonomous and flexible framework perfect for today's complicated IT settings. CSMA is different from standard perimeter-based models because it does not tie security policy enforcement to specific technical assets. This makes security more flexible and responsive. Identity as the new perimeter is one of the most important ideas behind CSMA. It means putting the safety of usernames and data first, no matter where they are. Traditional perimeter defenses do not work well for companies with hybrid cloud systems and distributed workforces; hence, this method works well for those situations. In addition, CSMA makes security management better by letting stricter security rules be put in place across a complicated and often spread-out IT environment.

Convergence of technologies

The convergence of diverse cybersecurity technologies to produce holistic defense strategies is one of the most compelling trends in blue teaming. AI and ML are integrated with SIEM systems to provide advanced threat detection, and blockchain technology is used to secure data and transactions. Blue teaming's network traffic analysis employs AI and ML to identify peculiar patterns in network traffic that may indicate malicious activity. This convergence of technologies improves not only the precision and rapidity of threat detection but also the capacity to respond effectively to cyber threats. Now, every major cyber security product vendor has an army of high-end tools that work under one ecosystem.

Future of blue teams

The future of blue teaming will depend on how these new tools and trends are used together. AI and ML will continue to be very important because they help blue teams automate routine tasks, find complicated threats, and change their strategies as attacks change. In the age of quantum computing, data will be safe because encryption that is safe for quantum computers will become the rule. The blockchain ledger, which cannot be changed, will be used for safe deals, managing identities, and keeping the supply chain safe. UEBA will change over time to give more detailed information about how users and entities behave, which will make danger detection more accurate. It is expected that SIEM systems will learn more about threats and act on them in real time.

Finally, the future of blue teams depends on how quickly new cybersecurity tools and trends are adopted. If blue teams want to stay ahead of cybercriminals, they need to use AI, ML, quantum-safe encryption, blockchain, UEBA, and advanced SIEM tools. When these technologies come together, they will create a strong defense environment that will help blue teams find, respond to, and stop cyber threats before they happen. Blue teaming will continue to be the best way to protect against new cyber risks as the field of cybersecurity changes.

Role of AI and ML in threat management

The importance of AI and ML in the fight against cyber threats is growing. These revolutionary technologies are revolutionizing the way in which organizations manage and respond to cybersecurity incidents. AI and ML are reshaping how we safeguard digital assets and data, from automating critical duties to augmenting threat detection and analysis.

The following figure shows the difference between AI/ML and traditional threat detection:

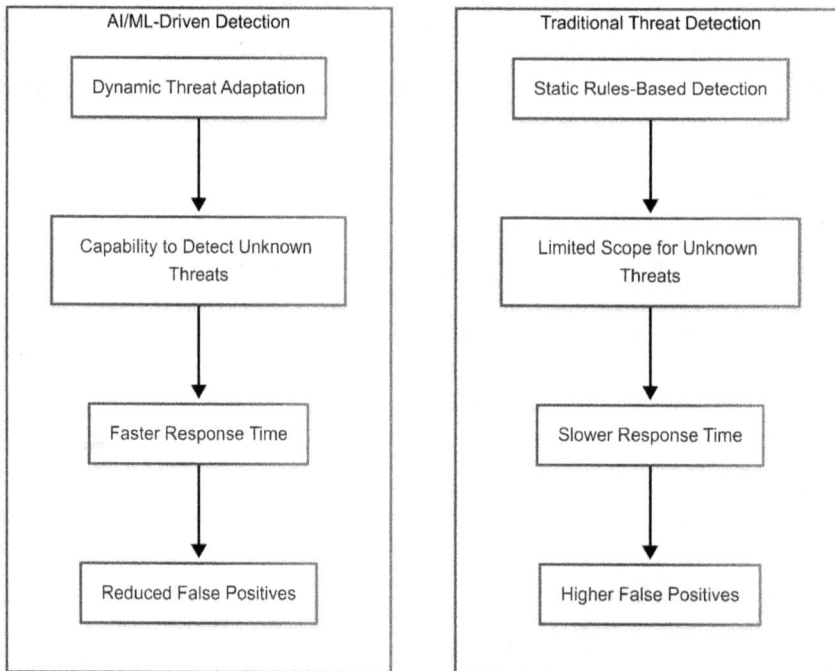

Figure 11.1: AI/ML and traditional threat detection

Automating and improving cybersecurity tasks

AI and ML have ushered in a new period of automation in cybersecurity, enabling businesses to streamline and optimize various crucial duties. For instance, IR is a domain where AI and ML have a significant impact. Historically, cybersecurity professionals were required to manually filter through immense quantities of data to identify and respond to incidents. Not only is this procedure time-consuming, but it is also susceptible to human error. However, AI and ML technologies excel at rapid data analysis. They can swiftly identify patterns and anomalies, enabling incident response to be more effective.

Boosting incident response capacity

AI and ML technologies empower incident response teams by providing them with actionable insights in a timely manner. When a cybersecurity incident occurs, it is crucial to be able to respond quickly and effectively. AI-driven systems can analyze security events in real-time, identifying suspicious activities and correlating data from multiple sources to provide a comprehensive view of the incident. This not only reduces response times but also improves threat identification accuracy. In addition, chatbots and virtual assistants enabled by AI can assist with incident triage and resolution, allowing human analysts to focus on more complex tasks.

Improve malware analysis

Malware analysis is another area where AI and ML algorithms excel. Malware is continuously evolving, with cybercriminals deploying increasingly sophisticated variants to avoid detection. Traditional antivirus solutions based on signatures struggle to keep up with these ever-changing threats. AI and ML, on the other hand, excel at recognizing malware-related patterns and behaviors. They can examine the file's code, behavior, and communication patterns to determine whether it is malicious. This dynamic approach to malware analysis enables organizations to detect threats that have never been seen before.

Network and digital forensics

Digital and network forensics play a crucial role in investigating and identifying the perpetrators of cyber incidents. AI and ML technologies play a crucial role in speeding up these processes. When a security incident occurs, digital forensics specialists must frequently examine a variety of digital artifacts, including logs, system files, and memory dumps. AI can help by automating the initial data triage, labeling potentially relevant evidence, and identifying anomalies that may be indicative of malicious activity. In network forensics, AI-powered tools can analyze network traffic to detect indicators of compromise or data exfiltration, enabling a more focused investigation.

Fraud detection

AI and ML have also proved indispensable in the detection of fraud. Whether it is financial fraud, identity theft, or online schemes, these technologies excel at identifying suspicious patterns and transactions. AI and ML algorithms can detect anomalies that may indicate fraudulent activity by analyzing historical transaction data and user behavior. This proactive approach to fraud detection not only prevents financial losses for businesses but also protects the privacy and safety of individuals and organizations.

Future of cyber threat intelligence sharing

As we step further into the digital age, the future of cybersecurity hinges on the evolution of cyber threat intelligence sharing. This collaborative endeavor is increasingly recognized as a linchpin in the ongoing battle against cyber adversaries. Looking ahead, several key trends and dynamics are shaping the future landscape of threat intelligence sharing, and they promise to usher in a new era of proactive cybersecurity.

The cyber threat map visually represents the ongoing and real-time cyberattacks across the globe. By displaying the origins, targets, and types of cyber threats, it provides an impactful understanding of the scale and scope of cybercrime activities. The map helps organizations, governments, and individuals recognize how interconnected and dynamic the global cybersecurity landscape is. The cyber threat map, as shown in *Figure 11.2*, exemplifies the need for transparency and collaboration in the fight against cybercrime, emphasizing that no single entity can combat these challenges alone; hence the cyber threat intelligence sharing is crucial in the future.

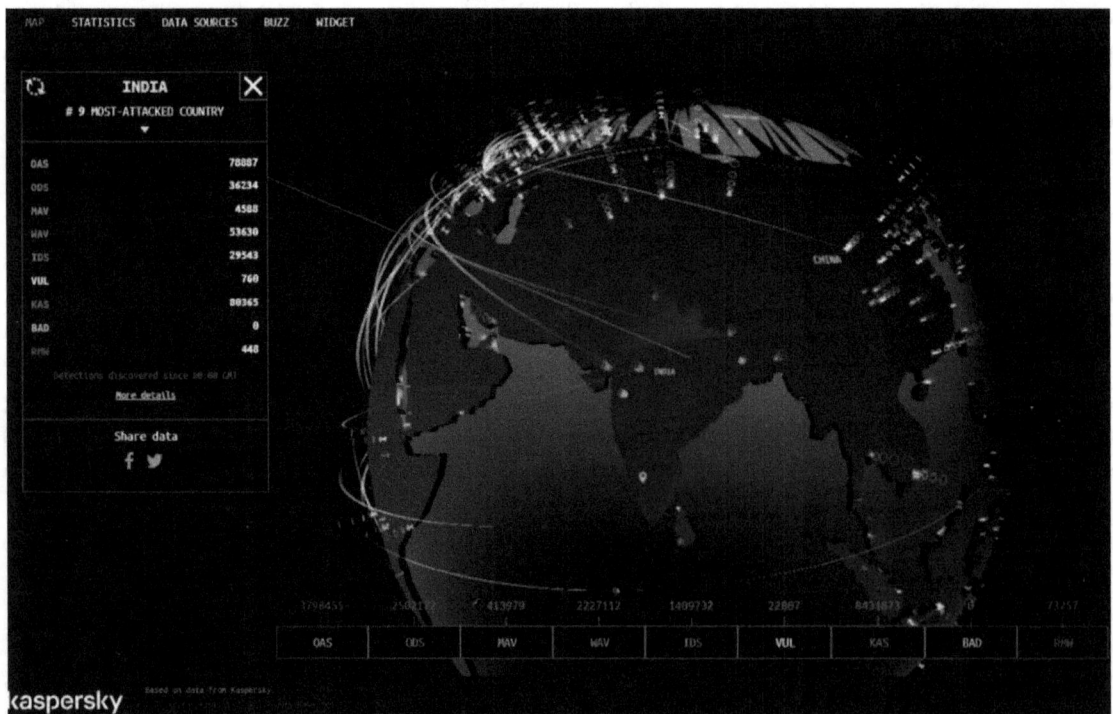

*Figure 11.2: The cyber threat map Kaspersky (**https://cybermap.kaspersky.com/**)*

Power of industry collaboration

Collaboration has long been at the heart of effective cybersecurity, and this trend is set to intensify in the future. Organizations within the same industry are realizing the power of sharing threat intelligence, pooling their resources, and learning from each other's experiences. This industry-specific collaboration allows for the development of tailored threat profiles and defenses that are better suited to the unique challenges and attack vectors of a particular sector.

Proactive measures and prevention of breaches

Threat intelligence sharing is no longer solely a reactive measure taken after a breach. Instead, it is evolving into a proactive approach aimed at preventing breaches altogether. By sharing real-time threat information, organizations can identify emerging threats and vulnerabilities, enabling them to patch weaknesses, fortify defenses, and deploy countermeasures before an attack occurs.

Detection and prevention at scale across industries

The future of threat intelligence sharing envisions a global network of organizations across various industries sharing information seamlessly and on a scale. This cross-industry collaboration allows for a broader perspective on cyber threats, enabling early detection and prevention of attacks that might target multiple sectors simultaneously.

Participation of small and medium businesses

While large enterprises often lead the way in threat intelligence sharing, the future will see increased participation from **small and medium-sized businesses** (**SMBS**). These organizations, which are also prime targets for cybercriminals, will benefit from the collective expertise of the community and, in turn, contribute valuable threat intelligence data to enhance the overall security posture.

Automation and regulation

Thanks to machine learning, AI, and threat intelligence tools, sharing threat intelligence will become a lot more automated in the future. Automated sharing tools like STIX/TAXII will be used more often, which will make exchanging threat info faster and more efficient. To improve national and global cybersecurity, governments and regulatory bodies will probably take a bigger part in standardizing and rewarding the sharing of threat information.

Critical for cybersecurity success

Threat intelligence sharing is increasingly seen as not just a beneficial practice but a critical component of cybersecurity success. As cyber threats continue to grow in complexity and scale, organizations recognize that they cannot defend against these threats in isolation. Collaboration through threat intelligence sharing provides the collective strength needed to confront evolving cyber adversaries.

Sharing threat intelligence data at speed

A lot of different kinds of threat intelligence data will be shared, such as IP names, IP ranges, URLs, file hashes, logs, and more. This fine-grained data lets businesses find and stop malicious behavior at a very specific level, making sure that even the most complex threats can be found and stopped.

In the future, it will be very important for businesses to plan ahead and share danger information quickly. By letting organizations stay ahead of possible threats, this proactive method makes them more resistant to cyber threats. Being able to quickly reply to new threats can mean the difference between a company's defense working well and a costly breach.

Preventing costly downtime and reputation damage

Threat intelligence sharing is not just about protecting data; it is also about safeguarding an organization's operational continuity and reputation. By collectively identifying and mitigating threats, organizations can prevent costly downtime, financial losses, and damage to their brand's reputation, which can be even more detrimental in today's interconnected world.

STIX/TAXII standardization

STIX/TAXII, the standardized protocols for structuring and exchanging threat intelligence, will continue to play a central role in the future of threat intelligence sharing. These protocols ensure that threat data can be shared in a consistent and interoperable manner, regardless of the technology stack used by different organizations.

In conclusion, sharing cyber threat information in the future has a lot of potential to make our defenses stronger against a cyber threat landscape that is always changing. The key to success will be working together across industries, being proactive about prevention, sharing information across sectors, and getting organizations of all kinds to take part. Sharing threat information will get faster and have a bigger effect with the help of automation, rules, and standard protocols. This will make it an important part of modern cybersecurity strategies. Sharing threat information will remain a key part of protecting against cyberattacks as companies continue to adapt to new threats. This will ensure a safer digital future for everyone.

Future of blue teaming and threat management

As the cybersecurity landscape continues to evolve at an unprecedented rate, the future of blue teaming and threat management will likely be characterized by innovation, adaptation, and resiliency. The emergence of sophisticated technologies and the ever-increasing sophistication of cyber threats necessitate a proactive and forward-thinking strategy. In this exploration of the future, we examine the key trends and innovations that will influence the landscape of blue teaming and threat management, ensuring that organizations are prepared to defend against the digital threats of the future.

Automated threat detection and response

The future of blue teaming will see a significant reliance on automated threat detection and response mechanisms. Algorithms for ML and AI will play a crucial role in swiftly identifying hazards and coordinating defensive actions. This automation not only accelerates response times but also reduces the workload of human analysts, allowing them to focus on more intricate duties.

Predictive threat intelligence

Predictive threat intelligence will become a pillar of proactive defense. Through the utilization of historical data, ML, and sophisticated analytics, blue teams will be able to anticipate impending hazards. This foresight permits organizations to implement preventative measures and bolster their security posture. Using predictive analytics, AI will forecast potential attack vectors before they manifest, enabling teams to patch vulnerabilities preemptively.

Behavior-based analytics

Understanding the human element, behavioral analytics will evolve to provide a more in-depth understanding of user and entity behavior. By establishing normal activity baselines, blue teams are able to rapidly detect deviations that may indicate insider threats or compromised accounts. This level of behavioral granularity improves anomaly detection and threat mitigation.

Zero Trust architecture

As organizations move away from traditional perimeter-based security, **Zero Trust architecture** (**ZTA**) will continue to gain popularity. ZTA adheres to the maxim *never trust, always verify*, ensuring that access controls are rigorously enforced based on identity, device, and context. This method is suitable for today's decentralized and hybrid settings.

Zero Trust principles will evolve from best practice to a foundational necessity. In the future, with the help of Dynamic Trust Models, real-time behavioral analytics will continuously assess trustworthiness, revoking access instantly when anomalies are detected. Micro-Segmentation will help networks to dissect into even finer segments, reducing the blast radius of any potential breach

Threat hunting support

Threat detection will become a more integral element of blue team operations. Advanced threat hunting platforms will aid analysts in identifying subtle indicators of compromise and unearthing threats concealed within complex networks. This proactive strategy allows organizations to remain one step advance of their adversaries. Advanced threat hunting will become integral to blue team operations, enabling proactive identification of threats. Future capabilities will include AI-Augmented Hunting, which will leverage machine learning to identify subtle **indicators of compromise (IOCs)** across large datasets. Increase in unified tools for threat hunters to share insights, methodologies, and findings in real time.

Red teaming and threat simulation

Continuous threat simulation and red teaming exercises will be indispensable for evaluating the efficacy of security controls. These simulations enable blue teams to identify weaknesses and vulnerabilities in a controlled environment, allowing them to strengthen their defenses prior to actual attacks. The synergy between blue and red teams will redefine organizational defenses. Red teaming and threat simulation will enhance preparedness as simulated attacks will identify weaknesses before adversaries exploit them. Automated simulations will ensure constant vigilance and adaptive defenses.

Autonomous threat containment

The sophistication of autonomous threat containment systems will increase, enabling organizations to automatically quarantine and neutralize detected threats. This autonomous response reduces the assailants' window of opportunity. The future of threat management will prioritize speed and precision in containing threats. Autonomous systems will isolate threats instantly using AI-driven systems, which will quarantine infected nodes or processes in real time.

Enhanced threats visualization

Advanced threat visualization tools will provide blue teams with intuitive and all-encompassing views of their network and threat landscape. Data visualization will evolve to provide defenders with clear, actionable insights. Future innovations include immersive dashboards, **augmented reality (AR)**, and **virtual reality (VR)** interfaces for intuitive exploration of threat landscapes. Advanced graph-based visualizations to map relationships and uncover hidden patterns in threat data.

Skill requirements in the future

The following table outlines the skills that will be required in the future:

Skill category	Specific skills
Technical skills	• Network security • Cloud security • Thread detection and analysis • Incident detection and analysis • Incident response • Malware analysis • **Identity and access management (IAM)** • Penetration testing • Cryptography • SIEM • Firewall and **intrusion detection/prevention systems (IDS/IPS)**
Programming and scripting	• Python • Bash scripting • PowerShell
Cybersecurity frameworks	• Understanding NIST, ISO 27001, and other industry standards
ML and AI	• Understanding of AI and ML for threat detection and anomaly analysis
Compliance and regulations	• Familiarity with GDPR, HIPAA, and other data protection regulations • Knowledge of industry specific compliance standards
Soft skills	• Communication and collaboration • Problem solving • Analytical thinking • Attention to detail • Continuous learning • Leadership and crisis management skills
Threat intelligence	• Gathering and analyzing threat intelligence • STIX/TAXII frameworks
Cloud platforms	• AWS, Azure, or GCP security knowledge
IoT security	• Securing **Internet of Things (IoT)** devices and networks
Zero Trust security	• Implementing Zero Trust principles

Skill category	Specific skills
Blockchain security	• Understanding blockchain security
DevSecOps integration	• Integrating security into DevOps processes
Incident response coordination	• Leading and coordinating incident response efforts

Table 11.1: Skill requirements

The future of cybersecurity demands professionals who can adapt to emerging technologies and threats while maintaining a general understanding of cybersecurity's role in the broader business environment. Cybersecurity experts will need a blend of technical expertise, strategic thinking, and soft skills to protect organizations effectively in an increasingly interconnected and digitized world.

In recent years, the cybersecurity skills divide has acquired considerable attention as a serious issue. It refers to the gap between the demand for skilled cybersecurity professionals and the supply of qualified workers. This divide has far-reaching consequences for organizations, as it exposes them to cyber threats and compromises their ability to safeguard sensitive data and essential assets.

Conclusion

In this chapter, we learned that the future of blue teaming and threat management is rapidly evolving, driven by technological advancements and the changing threat landscape. Automation, cloud-native security, threat intelligence, and AI are essential tools for blue teams to stay ahead of threats. The role of AI and ML in threat management is becoming increasingly important, enabling more proactive and predictive defense strategies.

The future of cyber threat intelligence sharing is also evolving, with more collaboration and information sharing among organizations and governments. **Threat intelligence platforms (TIPs)** will play a crucial role in aggregating and disseminating threat intelligence, enabling organizations to benefit from collective knowledge.

Other facets of the future of blue teaming and threat management include the use of deception technologies, the development of more sophisticated detection and response capabilities, and the increasing importance of human-machine teaming. We also looked at the skills required in the future. By developing these skills, blue teams can ensure they are well-equipped to defend against the ever-evolving threat landscape and protect their organizations from cyberattacks.

In future sections and chapters, we will explore case studies that provide insights into major cyberattacks, examining how they unfolded and what lessons can be learned. We will also provide a comprehensive list of sites, tools, and references to help readers evolve as proficient blue teamers. Additionally, a detailed glossary of terms related to blue teaming and defensive security will be included to ensure clarity and deepen understanding.

CHAPTER 12

Case Studies

Introduction

This chapter discuss some of the real-world cybersecurity incidents through a series of compelling case studies. Each case study dissects a significant cyberattack, exploring the **tactics, techniques, and procedures (TTPs)** employed by the attackers, the vulnerabilities they exploited, and the responses mounted by the defending organizations.

These case studies are not merely accounts of what went wrong, they are valuable learning opportunities for blue teamers and cybersecurity professionals. By examining these incidents, we can gain critical insights into the evolving threat landscape, identify common security gaps, and develop more effective strategies for defending against future attacks.

Structure

Here, we will discuss the following topics:

- Target breach, 2013
- NotPetya attack, 2017
- Equifax breach, 2017
- Maersk attack, 2017
- SolarWinds attack, 2020

- Colonial Pipeline attack, 2021
- Uber breach, 2022
- Microsoft data breach, 2022

Objectives

This chapter bridges the gap between theoretical cybersecurity concepts and their practical application by examining real-world cyberattack case studies. It aims to enhance your analytical skills, enabling you to recognize common attack vectors and TTPs such as social engineering, malware deployment, and supply chain attacks. By exploring these cases, you will understand the impact security breaches can have on organizations, individuals, and critical infrastructure. The chapter also encourages a proactive security mindset by demonstrating how to apply lessons learned from past incidents to improve your own security posture and mitigate future risks.

Target breach, 2013

In the bustling holiday season of 2013, retail giant Target suffered a massive data breach, exposing the personal and financial information of an estimated 40 million customers. This case study discusses the attack, the vulnerabilities exploited, and the critical lessons learned for the cybersecurity community.

Attack

The attackers did not directly target the Target's robust security infrastructure. Instead, they cleverly exploited a weakness in the company's supply chain. They gained access to Target's network through credentials stolen from Fazio Mechanical Services, a third-party vendor responsible for Target's **heating, ventilation, and air conditioning** (**HVAC**) systems.

Once inside, the attackers moved laterally through the network, installing malware on **point-of-sale** (**POS**) systems. This malware, known as **BlackPOS**, scraped credit and debit card data from customers' cards as they were swiped at checkout terminals.

The attackers operated undetected for weeks, exfiltrating massive amounts of sensitive data, including customer names, addresses, phone numbers, email addresses, and payment card details.

Response

Target's security team eventually detected suspicious activity and launched an investigation. However, the attackers had already established a foothold and exfiltrated a significant amount of data.

The company took steps to contain the breach, remove the malware, and notify affected customers. They also partnered with law enforcement agencies to investigate the attack and identify the perpetrators.

Analysis

The Target breach highlighted several key vulnerabilities, which are as follows:

- **Third-party risk**: The attack demonstrated the risks associated with third-party vendors having access to critical systems.

- **Network segmentation**: Target's network architecture allowed the attackers to move laterally from the HVAC system to the POS network.

- **Lack of strong authentication**: Weak password security at the vendor level facilitated the initial compromise.

Lessons learned and recommendations

The Target breach served as a wake-up call for the retail industry and the broader business community. It underscored the following critical lessons:

- **Secure the supply chain**: Organizations must rigorously assess and manage the security practices of their third-party vendors.

- **Implement strong network segmentation**: Isolate critical systems from less sensitive parts of the network to limit the impact of breaches.

- **Enforce strong authentication**: Implement multi-factor authentication and strong password policies to prevent unauthorized access.

- **Invest in threat detection and response**: Proactive monitoring and rapid response capabilities are crucial for detecting and mitigating attacks.

- **Develop a comprehensive incident response plan**: A well-defined plan helps organizations effectively manage and recover from security incidents.

The Target breach remains a significant case study in the annals of cybersecurity. It highlighted the importance of a holistic approach to security, encompassing not only technical safeguards but also strong vendor management, employee training, and incident response planning. By learning from this incident, organizations can strengthen their defenses and better protect themselves from similar attacks.

NotPetya attack, 2017

In June 2017, a cyberattack disguised as a ransomware campaign wreaked havoc across the globe. Dubbed **NotPetya**, this malware spread rapidly, crippling businesses, disrupting critical infrastructure, and causing billions of dollars in damage. This case study examines the unique nature of NotPetya, its devastating impact, and the crucial lessons it imparted.

Attack

NotPetya initially appeared to be a typical ransomware attack, encrypting files and demanding a ransom for their release. However, its true nature was far more destructive.

The attack began in Ukraine, spreading through a compromised software update for a popular accounting software called **M.E.Doc**. This initial vector allowed NotPetya to quickly infect many Ukrainian organizations, including government agencies, banks, and critical infrastructure providers.

However, NotPetya was designed to spread rapidly beyond its initial targets. It exploited vulnerabilities in Microsoft Windows, leveraging EternalBlue (an exploit developed by the NSA) and Mimikatz (a credential-stealing tool) to propagate across networks.

Unlike typical ransomware, NotPetya's primary goal was not financial gain. It overwrote critical system files, rendering infected computers unusable, even if the ransom was paid. This destructive nature earned it the classification of a **wiper** malware.

Response

The rapid spread and destructive impact of NotPetya caught many organizations off guard. Security teams scrambled to contain the outbreak, isolate infected systems, and restore data from backups.

However, the severity of the damage varied greatly. Some organizations were able to recover relatively quickly, while others suffered significant disruptions and financial losses.

Analysis

The NotPetya attack highlighted several key factors:

- **Destructive intent**: NotPetya demonstrated that not all attacks are motivated by financial gain. Nation-state actors or other malicious entities may deploy malware with the intent to cause disruption and damage.

- **Vulnerability exploitation**: The attack exploited known vulnerabilities in widely used software, emphasizing the importance of timely patching and vulnerability management.

- **Global impact**: NotPetya's rapid spread across borders demonstrated the interconnectedness of global systems and the potential for widespread disruption.

Lessons learned and recommendations

The NotPetya attack provided valuable lessons for the cybersecurity community:

- **Assume the worst**: Organizations should prepare for the possibility of destructive attacks that go beyond traditional ransomware.

- **Prioritize patching**: Timely patching of known vulnerabilities is crucial for preventing the spread of malware.

- **Implement strong backup and recovery strategies**: Regular backups and well-tested recovery plans are essential for mitigating the impact of destructive attacks.

- **Enhance network security**: Network segmentation, intrusion detection and prevention systems, and other security measures can help contain the spread of malware.

- **Improve cybersecurity awareness**: Educating users about the risks of phishing, malicious attachments, and other attack vectors can help prevent initial infections.

The NotPetya attack was a watershed moment in cybersecurity. It exposed the destructive potential of cyberattacks and the vulnerability of critical infrastructure. By understanding the lessons of NotPetya, organizations can strengthen their defenses and better protect themselves against future threats.

Equifax breach, 2017

In 2017, Equifax, one of the three major credit reporting agencies in the United States, suffered a massive data breach that exposed the sensitive personal information of 147.9 million consumers. This case study examines the events leading up to the breach, the vulnerabilities exploited, and the far-reaching consequences for both Equifax and the individuals affected.

Attack

The Equifax breach stemmed from a known vulnerability in the Apache Struts web application framework (CVE-2017-5638). A patch for this vulnerability had been publicly released in March 2017, but Equifax failed to apply it to their systems in a timely manner.

Attackers exploited this vulnerability to gain access to Equifax's network in May 2017. Once inside, they were able to navigate through the network, accessing and exfiltrating a vast trove of sensitive data, including:

- Names, addresses, and dates of birth

- Social Security numbers

- Driver's license numbers

- Credit card information

The attackers operated undetected for months, exfiltrating data until the breach was finally discovered in July 2017.

Response

Equifax's response to the breach was widely criticized as slow and inadequate. The company waited six weeks to publicly disclose the incident, and their initial response efforts were hampered by confusion and misinformation.

Equifax eventually set up a website and call center to provide information to affected consumers and offer credit monitoring and identity theft protection services. However, the website experienced technical difficulties, and the call center was overwhelmed with inquiries.

Analysis

The Equifax breach exposed several critical failures:

- **Vulnerability management**: Equifax failed to implement a robust vulnerability management program, leading to a delay in patching a known vulnerability.

- **Security hygiene**: The company's overall security posture was inadequate, allowing attackers to move laterally within the network and access sensitive data.

- **Incident response**: Equifax's slow and ineffective response to the breach exacerbated the damage and eroded public trust.

Lessons learned and recommendations

The Equifax breach serves as a stark reminder of the importance of cybersecurity fundamentals:

- **Prioritize vulnerability management**: Implement a comprehensive vulnerability management program to identify, assess, and remediate vulnerabilities promptly.

- **Maintain strong security hygiene**: Implement strong security controls, including access controls, network segmentation, and data encryption.

- **Develop a robust incident response plan**: Establish a clear and well-rehearsed incident response plan to ensure a swift and effective response to security incidents.

- **Communicate transparently**: Communicate openly and honestly with affected individuals and the public in the event of a breach.

The Equifax breach had a profound impact on the individuals whose data was compromised and on the company itself. It underscores the critical importance of proactive security measures, timely patching, and effective incident response. By learning from this incident, organizations can strengthen their defenses and better protect themselves from the devastating consequences of data breaches.

Maersk Attack, 2017

In the summer of 2017, A.P. Moller-Maersk, the world's largest container shipping company, found itself at the mercy of the NotPetya cyberattack. This case study explores how the attack crippled Maersk's global operations, the challenges faced in recovery, and the critical lessons learned for businesses of all sizes.

Attack

Maersk, like many other global companies, fell victim to the NotPetya malware, which was initially disguised as ransomware but ultimately revealed itself to be a destructive wiper. The attack vector, as in other cases, was believed to be through a compromised software update for the Ukrainian accounting software M.E.Doc.

On June 27, 2017, Maersk employees began reporting infected systems.

The malware spread rapidly across the company's global network, encrypting data and disrupting critical systems, including:

- **Booking systems**: New shipments could not be booked, and existing bookings were inaccessible.

- **Terminal operating systems**: Loading and unloading of cargo at ports was halted.

- **Communication systems**: Email and internal communication channels were disrupted.

The attack brought Maersk's operations to a standstill, stranding cargo at sea and causing significant disruptions to global supply chains.

Response

Maersk's IT team worked tirelessly to contain the attack and restore systems. However, the scale and severity of the damage were unprecedented. The company was forced to resort to manual processes, using pen and paper to track shipments and communicate with customers.

Recovery was a long and arduous process. It took weeks to rebuild critical systems and restore data from backups. Maersk estimated the total cost of the attack to be between $200 and $300 million.

Analysis

The Maersk attack highlighted several key vulnerabilities, which are as follows:

- **Global interconnectivity**: The attack demonstrated how interconnected global systems can be vulnerable to rapid malware propagation.

- **Critical infrastructure**: The disruption to Maersk's operations underscored the vulnerability of critical infrastructure to cyberattacks.

- **Backup and recovery**: The attack exposed weaknesses in Maersk's backup and recovery strategies, which hampered their ability to restore operations quickly.

Lessons learned and recommendations

The Maersk attack provided valuable lessons for organizations worldwide:

- **Prepare for the worst**: Develop comprehensive disaster recovery plans that account for the possibility of large-scale cyberattacks.

- **Segment networks**: Isolate critical systems to prevent the spread of malware and limit the impact of attacks.

- **Strengthen backup and recovery**: Implement robust backup and recovery strategies to ensure business continuity in the event of an attack.

- **Invest in cybersecurity awareness**: Train employees to recognize and report suspicious activity, such as phishing emails and unusual software updates.

- **Collaborate and share information**: Share threat intelligence and best practices with industry peers to improve collective cybersecurity posture.

The Maersk attack served as a stark reminder of the interconnectedness of global systems and the potential for cyberattacks to disrupt critical infrastructure. By learning from this incident, organizations can strengthen their defenses and better protect themselves from the devastating consequences of cyberattacks.

SolarWinds attack, 2020

The SolarWinds attack, discovered in December 2020, sent shockwaves through the cybersecurity world. This highly sophisticated supply chain attack compromised thousands of organizations, including government agencies and Fortune 500 companies, by exploiting a trusted software update mechanism. This case study discusses the attack's complexity, its far-reaching impact, and the critical lessons it taught about securing the software supply chain.

Attack

The attackers, believed to be affiliated with the Russian government, gained access to SolarWinds' internal systems, likely through a combination of sophisticated phishing and malware techniques. Once inside, they injected malicious code into the Orion network management software, a widely used product with over 30,000 customers.

This malicious code, dubbed **Sunburst**, was then distributed to SolarWinds customers through legitimate software updates. Once installed, Sunburst created a backdoor, allowing the attackers to remotely access compromised systems, steal data, and conduct further malicious activities.

The attackers operated undetected for months, gaining access to a vast network of high-value targets, including the US Treasury Department, the Department of Homeland Security, and Microsoft.

Response

The attack was first discovered by FireEye, a cybersecurity firm, when they noticed unusual activity in their own systems. Further investigation revealed the compromised SolarWinds update and the extent of the attack.

SolarWinds quickly released a security update to remove the malicious code and worked with law enforcement and cybersecurity agencies to investigate the incident. Affected organizations scrambled to identify compromised systems, assess the damage, and implement mitigation measures.

Analysis

The SolarWinds attack highlighted several key vulnerabilities:

- **Supply chain weakness**: The attack demonstrated the vulnerability of software supply chains, where a single compromised vendor can impact a vast network of organizations.

- **Trust exploitation**: The attackers exploited the trust placed in software updates, highlighting the need for enhanced security measures in software development and distribution.

- **Advanced evasion techniques**: The attackers employed sophisticated techniques to evade detection, making the attack difficult to identify and contain.

Lessons learned and recommendations

The SolarWinds attack served as a wake-up call for the cybersecurity community:

- **Secure the software supply chain**: Organizations must implement robust security measures throughout the software development lifecycle, including code reviews, vulnerability scanning, and secure update mechanisms.

- **Adopt a Zero Trust approach**: Verify every user, device, and application before granting access, even within internal networks.

- **Enhance threat detection and response**: Invest in advanced threat detection and response capabilities to identify and mitigate sophisticated attacks.

- **Improve information sharing**: Share threat intelligence and best practices with industry peers to improve collective cybersecurity posture.

The SolarWinds attack was a game-changer in the cybersecurity landscape. It exposed the vulnerability of software supply chains and the need for a more proactive and comprehensive approach to security. By learning from this incident, organizations can strengthen their defenses and better protect themselves from the evolving threat landscape.

Colonial Pipeline attack, 2021

In May 2021, the Colonial Pipeline, a critical infrastructure artery responsible for transporting nearly half of the gasoline, diesel, and jet fuel consumed on the US East Coast, was brought to a standstill by a ransomware attack. This case study examines the attack, its impact on fuel supplies and national security, and the lessons learned about protecting critical infrastructure in a digital age.

Attack

The attack was carried out by DarkSide, a cybercriminal group known for its ransomware-as-a-service operations. They gained access to Colonial Pipeline's network through a compromised VPN account that lacked multi-factor authentication.

Once inside, DarkSide deployed their ransomware, encrypting critical systems and demanding a ransom of 75 Bitcoin (approximately $4.4 million at the time) for the decryption key.

The attack forced Colonial Pipeline to proactively shut down its entire pipeline system to contain the spread of the malware and prevent further damage. This shutdown triggered widespread fuel shortages and panic buying across the East Coast, highlighting the vulnerability of critical infrastructure to cyberattacks.

Response

Colonial Pipeline paid the ransom within hours of the attack, hoping to quickly restore operations and minimize disruption. They also worked with cybersecurity experts and law enforcement agencies, including the FBI, to investigate the incident and recover their systems.

The company received the decryption tool from DarkSide, but the process of restoring systems and resuming operations was slow and complex. It took several days for the pipeline to return to full operational capacity.

Analysis

The Colonial Pipeline attack highlighted several key vulnerabilities:

- **Critical infrastructure risk**: The attack demonstrated the vulnerability of critical infrastructure to cyberattacks and the potential for widespread disruption to essential services.

- **Ransomware threat**: The incident underscored the growing threat of ransomware attacks and the willingness of cybercriminals to target critical infrastructure.

- **Security gaps**: The attack exposed weaknesses in Colonial Pipeline's security posture, including the lack of multi-factor authentication on critical systems.

Lessons learned and recommendations

The Colonial Pipeline attack provided valuable lessons for critical infrastructure operators and organizations worldwide:

- **Strengthen cybersecurity defenses**: Implement robust security measures, including multi-factor authentication, network segmentation, and intrusion detection and prevention systems.

- **Develop incident response plans**: Establish comprehensive incident response plans that address the unique challenges of managing cyberattacks on critical infrastructure.

- **Invest in cybersecurity awareness**: Train employees to recognize and report suspicious activity, such as phishing emails and unusual login attempts.

- **Collaborate with government and industry**: Share threat intelligence and best practices with government agencies and industry peers to improve collective cybersecurity posture.

The Colonial Pipeline attack served as a wake-up call for critical infrastructure operators and policymakers.

It highlighted the urgent need to strengthen cybersecurity defenses and improve resilience against cyberattacks. By learning from this incident, organizations can better protect critical infrastructure and ensure the continued delivery of essential services.

Uber breach, 2022

In September 2022, Uber, the global ride-hailing giant, experienced a significant security breach that exposed internal systems and data. This case study examines how a combination of social engineering, **multi-factor authentication** (MFA) fatigue, and security gaps allowed an attacker to gain extensive access to Uber's network.

Attack

The attacker, reportedly a teenager affiliated with the Lapsus$ hacking group, initiated the attack by targeting an Uber employee with a barrage of MFA push notifications. This tactic, known as **MFA fatigue**, aims to overwhelm the user with requests until they eventually approve one out of sheer annoyance or distraction.

The attacker also employed social engineering techniques, posing as an IT support person and contacting the employee via phone and text message, claiming that the MFA requests were accidental and urging the employee to accept them.

Once the employee approved an MFA request, the attacker gained access to the employee's VPN account. From there, the attacker discovered hard-coded credentials in internal systems, which granted them access to Uber's **Privileged Access Management** (**PAM**) system. This access effectively gave the attacker the **keys to the kingdom**, allowing them to compromise a wide range of Uber's internal tools and services, including:

- Cloud services (AWS, GCP)

- Internal communication platforms (Slack)

- Security tools (SentinelOne)

- Code repositories

The attacker even accessed Uber's bug bounty program on HackerOne and left a message boasting about the breach.

Response

Uber's security team quickly responded to the incident, taking several steps to contain the breach and mitigate the damage:

- They identified and revoked the attacker's access.

- They took down several internal systems to prevent further compromise.

- They launched a comprehensive investigation to determine the scope of the breach and identify any compromised data.

- They notified law enforcement agencies and cooperated with their investigation.

Analysis

The Uber breach highlighted several key vulnerabilities:

- **MFA fatigue**: The attack demonstrated the susceptibility of MFA to social engineering and persistence.

- **Credential management**: Storing hard-coded credentials in internal systems created a significant security risk.

- **Insider threat**: While not malicious, the employee's actions in response to the MFA fatigue and social engineering tactics facilitated the breach.

Lessons learned and recommendations

The Uber breach provided valuable lessons for organizations of all sizes:

- **Strengthen MFA security**: Implement stronger MFA practices, such as number matching, **Time-Based One-Time Passwords** (**TOTP**), and user education on MFA fatigue attacks.

- **Secure credential management**: Implement secure credential storage and management practices, such as password vaults and secrets management solutions.

- **Enhance security awareness training**: Educate employees about social engineering tactics, phishing attacks, and the importance of strong security practices.

- **Implement zero trust principles**: Assume that no user or device can be trusted by default and enforce strict access controls and verification measures.

The Uber breach served as a reminder that even with security measures like MFA in place, human factors and social engineering remain significant threats. By addressing these vulnerabilities and implementing stronger security practices, organizations can better protect themselves from sophisticated attacks.

Microsoft data breach, 2022

In March 2022, Microsoft, one of the world's leading technology companies, became a target of the Lapsus$ hacking group, known for their brazen attacks on high-profile organizations. This case study examines how Lapsus$ gained access to Microsoft's internal systems, the extent of the data they compromised, and the lessons learned about defending against increasingly aggressive cybercriminals.

Attack

Lapsus$ gained initial access to Microsoft's systems by compromising the account of a single employee. While the exact method of compromise remains unclear, it likely involved social engineering or credential theft.

Once inside, Lapsus$ exploited their access to gain deeper access to Microsoft's internal resources, including source code repositories for several products, such as Bing, Cortana, and parts of the Azure DevOps system.

The group publicized their intrusion by posting screenshots on their Telegram channel, showcasing their access to sensitive data and taunting Microsoft. They also claimed to have exfiltrated a significant amount of source code.

Response

Microsoft acknowledged the breach and quickly took steps to contain the incident and mitigate the damage:

- They investigated the compromised account and revoked the attacker's access.

- They reviewed the impacted systems and code repositories to assess the extent of the compromise.

- They implemented additional security measures to prevent further unauthorized access.

- They publicly disclosed the breach and provided updates on their investigation.

Microsoft emphasized that the breach did not impact customer data or the security of their products and services.

Analysis

The Microsoft data breach highlighted several key vulnerabilities:

- **Insider threat**: The compromise of a single employee account allowed Lapsus$ to gain a foothold in Microsoft's network.

- **Privilege escalation**: The attackers were able to leverage their initial access to escalate privileges and gain access to sensitive data and systems.

- **Data security**: While customer data was not impacted, the compromise of source code raised concerns about potential future vulnerabilities.

Lessons learned and recommendations

The Microsoft data breach provided valuable lessons for organizations of all sizes:

- **Strengthen identity and access management**: Implement strong authentication measures, such as multi-factor authentication and passwordless logins, to protect against account compromise.

- **Limit access privileges**: Follow the principle of least privilege, granting employees only the access they need to perform their job duties.

- **Secure source code**: Implement robust security measures to protect source code repositories from unauthorized access and theft.

- **Monitor for suspicious activity**: Employ proactive monitoring and threat detection tools to identify and respond to unusual activity within the network.

The Microsoft data breach served as a reminder that even the most sophisticated organizations can be vulnerable to cyberattacks. By strengthening their security posture, implementing robust access controls, and prioritizing employee security awareness, organizations can better protect themselves from the evolving threat landscape.

Conclusion

The case studies examined in this chapter, from the 2013 Target breach to the 2022 Microsoft data breach, collectively illustrate the persistent and evolving nature of cyber threats. Each incident, including NotPetya, Equifax, Maersk, SolarWinds, Colonial Pipeline, and Uber, exposed distinct vulnerabilities and attack vectors, ranging from third-party compromises and supply chain attacks to failures in patch management and social engineering.

A comparative analysis of these attacks, responses, and lessons learned reveals several recurring themes. Organizations must prioritize proactive security measures, including robust vulnerability management, stringent access controls, and comprehensive security awareness training. Effective incident response capabilities and continuous monitoring are also crucial for minimizing the impact of breaches. Ultimately, these case studies emphasize that cybersecurity is not a static endeavor but an ongoing process of adaptation and improvement in the face of increasingly sophisticated adversaries.

Looking ahead, the next chapter will delve into the essential tools and references that empower defensive security practices and effective threat management. It will explore the resources and technologies that organizations can leverage to bolster their defenses and proactively address emerging cyber threats.

Join our Discord space

Join our Discord workspace for latest updates, offers, tech happenings around the world, new releases, and sessions with the authors:

https://discord.bpbonline.com

CHAPTER 13
Sites, Tools, and References

Introduction

You can access a multitude of resources in this chapter that help improve your security professional efficacy, knowledge, and abilities. The carefully chosen selection of websites, resources, and online forums offered here will be a great help to you as you strive for superior defensive protection and threat management, regardless of your level of experience with cybersecurity.

To make it easier for you to find the materials that are most pertinent to your needs, this section is divided into categories. You will find vital groups where you can interact with other security professionals, strong tools for vulnerability management and incident response, and crucial websites for remaining current on the most recent threats.

Keep in mind that cybersecurity is an ever-evolving field where learning never stops. The resources on this list represent a moment in time and offer a strong basis for you to develop your skills.

Structure

In this chapter, we will cover the following topics:

- General cybersecurity resources

- Platforms and learning sites
- Developing hands-on cybersecurity skills
- OSINT tools
- Sandboxing tools
- Tools for reputation checks and investigations
- Windows tools for system and troubleshooting
- Tools used in phishing attacks
- Phishing emails analysis, tools, and techniques
- Reporting malicious emails, URLs, and IPs
- Threat intelligence and vulnerability management
- Call to action

Objectives

This chapter aims to provide cybersecurity professionals with a carefully selected set of websites, resources, and online forums to aid in defensive security and threat management. It lists important websites, resources, and tools a cybersecurity professional can use, specifically for defensive security and threat management. It is structured to help both new and experienced cybersecurity professionals enhance their knowledge and abilities. The chapter brings all the helpful resources in one place so that the reader can use all these tools and resources for their daily tasks. By providing a strong basis, this chapter intends to equip readers with the essential tools and knowledge to stay current and proficient in the cybersecurity landscape.

General cybersecurity resources

A strong cybersecurity posture relies on a foundation of knowledge and best practices. This section provides essential resources that offer frameworks, guidelines, and authoritative information on a wide range of cybersecurity topics.

General cybersecurity and blue teaming

The following resources can be considered foundational pillars for the cybersecurity community, offering essential guidance. Just as architectural pillars provide crucial support and form the basis of a strong structure, these websites serve as fundamental guides for cybersecurity professionals. Every professional in this industry should bookmark these websites and refer to them regularly:

- **NIST Cybersecurity Framework (CSF): https://www.nist.gov/cyberframework**
- **SANS Institute: https://www.sans.org/**

- NIST SP 800 series: https://csrc.nist.gov/publications/sp800
- Cybersecurity and Infrastructure Security Agency (CISA): https://www.cisa.gov/
- MITRE ATT&CK Framework: https://attack.mitre.org/
- Center for Internet Security (CIS): https://www.cisecurity.org/
- Open Web Application Security Project (OWASP): https://owasp.org/
- The Hacker News: https://thehackernews.com/
- Krebs On Security: https://krebsonsecurity.com/
- Dark Reading: https://www.darkreading.com/
- Security Boulevard: https://securityboulevard.com/
- Threat Post: https://threatpost.com/
- BleepingComputer: https://www.bleepingcomputer.com/
- CSO Online: https://www.csoonline.com/
- SearchSecurity (TechTarget): https://www.techtarget.com/searchsecurity/

Threat and vulnerability management

Proactive identification and mitigation of vulnerabilities are critical components of a robust security strategy. The following resources provide tools and databases to help security professionals discover, assess, and manage vulnerabilities in their systems and applications:

- National Vulnerability Database (NVD): https://nvd.nist.gov/
- Common Vulnerabilities and Exposures (CVE) website: https://cve.mitre.org/
- VulnHub: https://www.vulnhub.com/
- Metasploit Framework: https://www.metasploit.com/
- Nessus Essentials (or Professional): https://www.tenable.com/products/nessus
- OpenVAS: https://www.openvas.org/

Incident response

When security incidents occur, a swift and effective response is crucial to minimize damage and ensure business continuity. Here are the key resources that provide guidance, tools, and support for incident handling and management:

- SANS Institute Incident Response: https://www.sans.org/incident-response/
- NIST SP 800-61 rev. 2: https://csrc.nist.gov/publications/nistpubs/800-61-rev-2
- CERT/CC: https://certcc.github.io/

Platforms and learning sites

Continuous learning is essential in the ever-evolving field of cybersecurity. This section presents a selection of online platforms and learning sites that offer courses, training materials, and opportunities for professional development.

General cybersecurity learning

The following platforms offer a variety of courses and training materials for individuals at different skill levels:

- **Cybrary:** https://www.cybrary.it/
- **Coursera (Auditing Option):** https://www.coursera.org/
- **edX (Auditing Option):** https://www.edx.org/
- **Khan Academy:** https://www.khanacademy.org/computing/computer-programming
- **freeCodeCamp:** https://www.freecodecamp.org/
- **Open Security Training:** https://opensecuritytraining.info/
- **Security Blue Team:** https://securityblue.team/
- **Awesome lists (GitHub):** Search GitHub for **cybersecurity** or **security**. You will find curated lists of free resources, tools, and training materials. These are community-driven and constantly updated.

Vendor specific training

Many technology vendors provide training and resources specific to their products and services. This training can be invaluable for security professionals working with these vendor solutions. Here are a few of them:

- **Microsoft Virtual Academy (older content, still useful)**: While not as actively updated, there is still some valuable free content here. Search for security-related topics.
- **AWS Security Learning**: AWS offers some free training and resources related to security in the AWS cloud.
- **Google Cloud security**: Google Cloud also provides some free resources and training on cloud security.
- **Cisco Networking Academy**: Cisco offers free introductory networking courses, which are fundamental to understanding network security.

Other resources

In addition to general cybersecurity resources and training platforms, many other organizations and initiatives offer valuable guidance and materials for security professionals; some of them are listed as follows:

- **National Cyber Security Centre (NCSC) (UK): https://www.ncsc.gov.uk/**
- **Cyber Aces Online: https://www.cyberacesonline.org/**
- **OWASP: https://owasp.org/**

Note: **Free access can be limited. Some platforms might offer free trials, access to certain modules, or require you to create an account. Not all free training is created equal. Look for reputable sources and check reviews.**

Developing hands-on cybersecurity skills

Theoretical knowledge must be complemented by practical experience to develop proficiency in cybersecurity. This section highlights platforms and resources that provide hands-on labs, simulations, and challenges to build essential cybersecurity skills.

General resources

The following platforms offer hands-on labs and exercises focused on various aspects of defensive security:

- **CyberDefenders: https://cyberdefenders.org/**
- **Blue Team Labs Online: https://blueteamlabs.online/**
- **LetsDefend: https://www.letsdefend.io/**
- **TryHackMe (blue team rooms): https://tryhackme.com/**
- **RangeForce: https://www.rangeforce.com/**
- **ACE Responder: https://www.aceresponder.com/**
- **Malware Traffic Analysis: https://malware-traffic-analysis.net/**
- **KC7 Cyber: https://kc7cyber.com/**
- **Defbox: https://defbox.io/**
- **Security Blue Team CTF: https://ctf.securityblue.team/**

Offensive or red team focus

While this book focuses on defensive security, an understanding of offensive techniques is crucial for building effective defenses. The following resources provide opportunities to develop offensive security skills, such as penetration testing and red teaming:

1. **TryHackMe (Red Team Rooms):** https://tryhackme.com/
2. **Hack The Box:** https://www.hackthebox.com/
3. **OverTheWire Wargames:** http://overthewire.org/wargames/

General or both red and blue

Some platforms offer resources and training for both offensive (red team) and defensive (blue team) security skills, providing a well-rounded learning experience. They are discussed as follows:

- **PentesterLab:** https://pentesterlab.com/
- **PortSwigger Web Security Academy:** https://portswigger.net/web-security

OSINT tools

Open source intelligence (OSINT) plays a vital role in cybersecurity, enabling professionals to gather information about potential threats, targets, and vulnerabilities. This section presents a range of OSINT tools and resources for conducting effective investigations.

Website or domain analysis

Analyzing websites and domains is a crucial aspect of OSINT investigations and also a part of daily work for a security professional. The following tools provide capabilities for gathering information about website infrastructure, technologies, and ownership:

- **Censys:** https://censys.io/
- **Shodan:** https://www.shodan.io/
- **BuiltWith:** https://builtwith.com/
- **DNSDumpster:** https://dnsdumpster.com/
- **ViewDNS.info:** https://viewdns.info/

Social media or people search

Analyzing websites and domains is a crucial aspect of OSINT investigations. The following tools provide capabilities for gathering information about website infrastructure, technologies, and ownership:

- **Creepy:** (No longer actively maintained, but the concept is important. Look for alternatives like SpiderFoot). An OSINT tool for gathering geolocation information from social media. Helped visualize a target's movements and locations.

> Note: **Creepy is no longer actively maintained, so consider alternatives like SpiderFoot or similar geolocational OSINT tools.**

- **Social Analyzer: https://socialanalyzer.net/**
- **IntelTechniques: https://inteltechniques.com/**

Metadata extraction or file analysis

Files and documents often contain valuable metadata that can reveal sensitive information. These tools are used to extract and analyze metadata from various file formats:

- **Metagoofil: https://github.com/codingo/metagoofil**
- **ExifTool: https://exiftool.org/**

Network or infrastructure scanning

Understanding network infrastructure is essential for both offensive and defensive security. These tools enable network scanning, host discovery, and service identification:

- **Nmap: https://nmap.org/**
- **ZMap: https://zmap.io/**

Frameworks and automation

Automation is key to efficient OSINT gathering. These frameworks and tools help streamline the process of collecting and analyzing information from various sources:

- **OSINT framework: https://osintframework.com/**
- **Recon-ng: https://github.com/lanmaster53/recon-ng**
- **SpiderFoot: https://www.spiderfoot.net/**

Web reconnaissance

Web reconnaissance involves gathering information about a target website to understand its structure, content, and potential vulnerabilities. These tools facilitate web crawling, information extraction, and target identification:

- **Photon: https://github.com/s0md3v/Photon**
- **theHarvester: https://github.com/laramies/theHarvester**

Packet analysis

Analyzing network traffic is crucial for incident response, network forensics, and understanding network behavior. Wireshark is a powerful tool for capturing and analyzing network packets: **https://www.wireshark.org/**

Other or specialized tools

In addition to general OSINT tools, several specialized tools and utilities can aid in specific types of investigations and data analysis. A few of them are listed as follows:

- **Hunchly: https://www.hunch.ly/**

- **Maltego: https://www.maltego.com/**

- **CyberChef: https://gchq.github.io/CyberChef/**

Sandboxing tools

Sandboxing is a critical technique for safely analyzing potentially malicious software and isolating untrusted environments. This section provides an overview of various sandboxing tools and technologies.

Malware analysis sandboxes

Malware analysis sandboxes provide isolated environments for detonating and analyzing malware samples to understand their behavior and characteristics. A few of them are listed as follows:

- **Cuckoo Sandbox: https://cuckoosandbox.org/**

- **Joe Sandbox Cloud: https://www.joesecurity.org/**

- **Hybrid Analysis (by CrowdStrike): https://www.hybrid-analysis.com/**

- **ANY.RUN: https://any.run/**

- **VirusTotal (file analysis): https://www.virustotal.com/**

General purpose sandboxes

Sandboxing is not limited to malware analysis. General-purpose sandboxes can be used to isolate applications and browser environments for security purposes. Here are some of them:

- **Sandboxie: https://www.sandboxie.com/**

- **BrowserBox: https://browserbox.io/**

Containerization

Containerization technologies offer a lightweight approach to sandboxing, allowing for the isolation of applications and processes.

- **Docker: https://www.docker.com/**
- **LXC or LXD: https://linuxcontainers.org/**

Virtual machines or traditional sandboxing

Virtual machines provide a more traditional and robust form of sandboxing, allowing for the emulation of entire operating systems. Here are some of them:

- **VirtualBox: https://www.virtualbox.org/**
- **VMware Workstation Player: https://www.vmware.com/products/workstation-player.html**

Other or specialized sandboxes

In addition to general-purpose sandboxing solutions, several specialized sandboxes cater to specific use cases and security requirements. They are listed as follows:

- **AppJail: https://appjail.readthedocs.io/en/latest/**
- **Firejail: https://firejail.org/**
- **gVisor: https://gvisor.dev/**
- **Qubes OS: https://www.qubes-os.org/**

Tools for reputation checks and investigations

Verifying the reputation of IP addresses, URLs, and files is a crucial step in security investigations and threat analysis. This section outlines tools and resources for conducting these reputation checks.

Internet Protocol reputation and analysis

Internet Protocol (IP) address reputation services provide information about the history and potential malicious activity associated with IP addresses. Here are some of them:

- **VirusTotal: https://www.virustotal.com/**
- **AbuseIPDB: https://www.abuseipdb.com/**
- **IPinfo: https://ipinfo.io/**

- **WhatIsMyIPAddress: https://whatismyipaddress.com/**
- **Shodan: https://www.shodan.io/**

URL reputation and analysis

URL reputation services assess the safety and trustworthiness of websites based on various factors, including blacklisting and malware detection. Here are some of them:

- **VirusTotal: https://www.virustotal.com/**
- **URLVoid: https://www.urlvoid.com/**
- **Sucuri SiteCheck: https://sitecheck.sucuri.net/**
- **Google Safe Browsing: https://transparencyreport.google.com/safe-browsing**
- **PhishTank: https://www.phishtank.com/**

SHA reputation and analysis

File hashes, such as SHA-256, can be used to identify known malicious files. The following resources allow you to check the reputation of files based on their hashes:

- **VirusTotal: https://www.virustotal.com/**
- **Hybrid Analysis: https://www.hybrid-analysis.com/**
- **NIST National Software Reference Library (NSRL): https://www.nist.gov/itl/ssd/nsrl**

Windows tools for system and troubleshooting

Microsoft Windows provides a suite of built-in tools for system administration, troubleshooting, and security analysis. This section highlights some of the most useful tools for cybersecurity professionals.

System information and configuration

The following tools provide detailed information about the Windows operating system, hardware, and configuration, aiding in troubleshooting and system analysis:

- **System Information (msinfo32.exe)**: It provides detailed information about hardware, software, and system configuration. Useful for identifying driver versions, system specifications, and other relevant details.

- **Device Manager (devmgmt.msc)**: It allows you to view and manage hardware devices. Useful for troubleshooting driver issues, identifying conflicts, and checking device status.

- **Services (services.msc)**: It enables you to view and manage Windows services. Useful for troubleshooting service-related problems, starting, stopping, or configuring services.

- **Task Manager (taskmgr.exe)**: It provides information about running processes, performance metrics, and resource usage. Useful for identifying resource bottlenecks, unresponsive applications, and potentially malicious processes.

- **Registry Editor (regedit.exe)**: It allows you to view and modify the system registry. Use with caution, as incorrect changes can cause system instability. Useful for investigating configuration settings and troubleshooting registry-related issues.

- **Group Policy Management (gpmc.msc)**: It is used to manage Group Policy settings, which control user and computer configurations. Useful for troubleshooting policy-related issues and ensuring consistent configurations.

- **Local Security Policy (secpol.msc)**: It allows you to configure local security settings, such as user rights, audit policies, and security options. Useful for investigating security-related issues and enforcing security policies.

- **Performance Monitor (perfmon.msc)**: It provides detailed performance information about the system. Useful for identifying performance bottlenecks, analyzing resource usage, and troubleshooting performance issues.

- **Resource Monitor (resmon.exe)**: It provides a real-time overview of resource usage (CPU, memory, disk, network). Useful for identifying which processes are using specific resources.

- **Command Prompt (cmd.exe)**: It is a command-line interpreter for executing commands. Useful for various troubleshooting and administrative tasks.

- **PowerShell**: It is a powerful scripting language and command-line shell. Offers advanced capabilities for automation, system management, and troubleshooting.

Network troubleshooting

Windows includes command-line tools for diagnosing network connectivity issues, analyzing network traffic, and querying DNS information. A few of them are described as follows:

- **ipconfig**: It displays network interface configuration, including IP addresses, subnet masks, and default gateways.

- **ping**: It tests network connectivity by sending ICMP echo requests.

- **tracert (traceroute)**: It traces the route packets take to reach a destination. Useful for identifying network connectivity issues.

- **netstat**: It displays network connections, listening ports, and routing tables.

- **nslookup**: Queries DNS servers for DNS records. Useful for troubleshooting DNS-related issues.

- **pathping**: It combines the functionality of ping and tracert, providing more detailed information about network latency and packet loss.

Event log analysis

The Windows Event Viewer and related command-line utilities are essential for examining system and application logs to identify security events and troubleshooting issues.

- **Event Viewer (eventvwr.msc)**: This graphical interface tool provides a centralized view of system and application logs, recording events related to security, system operations, and application activity. It allows users to examine event details, filter logs, and troubleshoot issues by analyzing event information.

- **Wevtutil.exe**: This command-line utility enables administrators to retrieve information about event logs, manage log files, and query specific events. It offers advanced capabilities for automating log management and analysis tasks, particularly useful in scripting and remote administration.

System file checking and repair

Windows includes tools for verifying the integrity of system files and repairing any corruption that may be present. They are as follows:

- **System File Checker (sfc.exe)**: It scans for and repairs corrupted system files.

- **Deployment Image Servicing and Management (DISM)**: It is used to repair and manage Windows images.

Debugging tools

Windows debugging tools allow for in-depth analysis of software and operating system behavior, which can be valuable for security research and vulnerability analysis. Let us take a look at them:

- **Windows Debugger (WinDbg)**: It is a powerful tool for debugging applications and the operating system.

- **x64dbg**: It is a popular open-source debugger for Windows. It provides a user-friendly interface and powerful features for debugging applications, particularly for reverse engineering and malware analysis

Other utilities

Windows provides various other utilities that can be helpful for system administration, automation, and troubleshooting. They are listed as follows:

- **Msconfig (system configuration)**: It is used to manage startup programs and services.

- **Recovery options**: Windows offers various recovery options, such as System Restore, Startup Repair, and Reset this PC, which can be used to troubleshoot and recover from system issues.

- **Problem Steps Recorder (psr.exe)**: It records the steps a user takes, including screenshots and annotations. Useful for documenting and troubleshooting issues.

- **Windows Performance Recorder (WPR) and Windows Performance Analyzer (WPA)**: Tools for recording and analyzing system performance traces. Used for in-depth performance investigations.

Tools used in phishing attacks

Phishing attacks rely on a variety of tools and techniques to deceive victims and steal sensitive information. Understanding these tools is crucial for developing effective defenses.

Email crafting and sending

Attackers use various tools and techniques to craft and send phishing emails, often spoofing sender addresses and using social engineering tactics. Let us take a look at them:

- **Mail servers (for example, Sendmail, Postfix, Exim)**: Attackers might use their mail servers (or compromised ones) to send phishing emails, bypassing traditional email security measures.

- **Spoofing tools**: These tools allow forging email headers to make it appear as if the email is from a trusted source (for example, a bank or a colleague). This is a core element of many phishing attacks.

- **Email marketing tools (Abused)**: While legitimate email marketing tools are used for bulk email campaigns, they can be abused by phishers to send mass phishing emails.

- **Custom scripts (Python, Perl, etc.):** Attackers often write custom scripts to automate the phishing process, including email sending, tracking, and data collection.

Infrastructure

Phishing attacks require infrastructure to host phishing websites and send emails. Attackers utilize various services and tools to set up and manage this infrastructure. Here are some of them:

- **Hosting services (compromised or dedicated)**: Phishers need web hosting to host phishing landing pages (fake login forms, etc.). They might use compromised servers, bulletproof hosting providers, or free hosting services.

- **Domain registration services**: Attackers register domains that look similar to legitimate ones (typosquatting) to make their phishing sites appear more convincing.

- **URL shorteners**: These services can be used to obfuscate the actual URL of a phishing site, making it harder for victims to identify the malicious link.

- **SSL certificates**: While not always used, some phishers obtain SSL certificates for their phishing sites to make them appear more trustworthy (HTTPS). However, the presence of HTTPS is not a guarantee of legitimacy.

Social engineering and information gathering

Phishing attacks are often more effective when they are personalized and tailored to the victim. Attackers use social engineering and OSINT techniques to gather information about their targets. Some of them are listed as follows:

- **Social media and OSINT**: Attackers use OSINT techniques and social media to gather information about their targets. This information is then used to personalize phishing emails and make them more convincing.

- **Keyloggers and Remote Access Trojans (RATs)**: Once a victim clicks on a phishing link and enters their credentials, attackers might use keyloggers or RATs to steal the information.

- **Phishing kits**: These are pre-made packages containing all the necessary components for a phishing attack, including email templates, landing pages, and scripts. They make it easier for even less technical individuals to launch phishing campaigns.

Other tools

Attackers may employ additional tools to enhance their phishing campaigns, evade detection, and maintain anonymity. Some of them are as follows:

- **Anonymization tools (Tor, VPNs)**: Attackers often use anonymization tools to hide their IP addresses and make it harder to trace them.

- **Virtual machines**: Attackers often use virtual machines to set up their phishing infrastructure, making it easier to manage and harder to trace.

Phishing email analysis, tools, and techniques

Analyzing phishing emails is a critical skill for identifying and mitigating phishing attacks. This section provides an overview of tools and techniques used for email analysis.

Email analysis platforms and services

These platforms and services offer automated analysis of email messages, attachments, and URLs to detect phishing indicators:

- **VirusTotal: https://www.virustotal.com/**

- **Hybrid Analysis (CrowdStrike): https://www.hybrid-analysis.com/**

- **Joe Sandbox Cloud: https://www.joesecurity.org/**

- **ANY.RUN: https://any.run/**

- **Mailchimp's Transactional Email API (for abuse analysis): https://mailchimp.com/features/transactional-email/**

Header analysis tools

Email headers contain valuable information about the sender, routing, and authentication of an email. The following tools help analyze email headers to identify spoofing and other malicious activity:

- **MXToolbox: https://mxtoolbox.com/**

- **Google Admin Toolbox (for G Suite/Workspace Admins): https://toolbox.googleapps.com/apps/main/**

URL analysis and sandboxing

Phishing emails often contain malicious URLs that lead to phishing websites. The following tools and techniques help analyze URLs and safely investigate their destinations:

- **URLVoid: https://www.urlvoid.com/**

- **Sucuri SiteCheck: https://sitecheck.sucuri.net/**

- **BrowserBox: https://browserbox.io/**

Phishing specific tools and resources

In addition to general email and URL analysis tools, several specialized resources and tools are designed specifically for identifying and combating phishing. Some of them are listed as follows:

- **PhishTank: https://www.phishtank.com/**

- **Anti-Phishing Working Group (APWG): https://apwg.org/**

Email client analysis

In some cases, in-depth analysis of email messages within an email client may be necessary for forensic investigations. The following are the email forensics tools widely used for in-depth analysis of email messages, including headers, attachments, and embedded objects:

- **The Sleuth Kit (TSK)**: An open-source forensic toolkit that can be used to analyze disk images and recover email data.

- **Autopsy**: A user-friendly, open-source digital forensics platform that utilizes TSK. It provides a graphical interface for analyzing email data and other artifacts.

- **EnCase**: A commercial digital forensics tool widely used by law enforcement and corporate investigators for email analysis and data recovery.

- **Forensic Toolkit (FTK)**: Another commercial forensic software suite with email analysis capabilities.

Programming and scripting for automation

Programming languages and scripting are often used to automate email analysis and other phishing-related tasks. Refer to the following list, which offers a comprehensive understanding of the same:

- **Python (with libraries like email, imaplib, requests)**: Python can be used to write custom scripts for parsing email messages, extracting information, and automating analysis tasks.

- **Bash**: Bash is a Unix shell and command-line interpreter. It is commonly used for automating system administration tasks, log analysis, and security operations on Linux and macOS systems. Bash scripting is valuable for automating routine security tasks, creating scripts for network analysis

- **PowerShell**: PowerShell is a scripting language developed by Microsoft for task automation and configuration management. It is widely used in Windows environments for, automating system administration tasks, developing scripts for security auditing, log analysis, and incident response on Windows systems.

Other techniques

Manual analysis of email headers and other email components is a fundamental skill for identifying phishing emails. Let us take a look at some more of these techniques:

- **Manual header analysis**: Understanding email header structure and how to interpret **Sender Policy Framework (SPF)**, **DomainKeys Identified Mail (DKIM)**, and **Domain-based Message Authentication Reporting and Conformance (DMARC)** records is a fundamental skill for analyzing phishing emails. No specific tool needed, just knowledge.

Reporting malicious emails, URLs, and IPs

Reporting malicious content is crucial for helping organizations and security vendors identify and block threats. This section provides resources for reporting phishing emails, malicious URLs, and suspicious IP addresses.

Reporting phishing emails

Many organizations have a dedicated email address for reporting phishing attempts targeting their employees or customers. Check the organization's website for its specific reporting address. Listed are the sites where you can report any generic suspicious email:

- **Federal Trade Commission (FTC)**: **https://reportfraud.ftc.gov/**

- **Anti-Phishing Working Group (APWG)**: **https://apwg.org/report-phishing/**

- **Microsoft (for Outlook / Hotmail users)**: Use the **Report Phishing** option within **Outlook.com** or **Hotmail**, or search for Microsoft's phishing reporting page. Report phishing emails received in Microsoft's email services. **https://www.microsoft.com/en-us/wdsi/support/report-unsafe-site-guest**

- **Google (for Gmail users)**: Use the **Report Phishing** option within Gmail. Report phishing emails received in Gmail.

Reporting malicious URLs

The following are the sites where you can report any malicious email:

- **Google Safe Browsing**: **https://www.google.com/safebrowsing/report_phish/**

- **PhishTank**: **https://www.phishtank.com/**

- **URLVoid**: **https://www.urlvoid.com/report-malicious-url/**

Reporting malicious IP addresses

Reporting malicious IP addresses helps block attackers and prevent further malicious activity. Here is the list of websites where we can add IPs to block:

- **AbuseIPDB**: **https://www.abuseipdb.com/report**

- **Team Cymru**: **https://www.team-cymru.com/report-abuse/**

- **Your internet service provider (ISP)**: Report malicious IP addresses originating from your ISP's network to your ISP's abuse department.

Reporting malware

Submitting malware samples to analysis platforms helps improve malware detection and analysis capabilities

- **VirusTotal: https://www.virustotal.com/**

- **Hybrid Analysis: https://www.hybrid-analysis.com/submit**

Reporting scams and fraud

Reporting online scams and fraudulent activity to the appropriate authorities helps protect others from falling victim. Here are some websites where you can report these scams:

- **Federal Trade Commission (FTC): https://reportfraud.ftc.gov/**

- **Internet Crime Complaint Center (IC3): https://www.ic3.gov/**

- **Cybersecurity and Infrastructure Security Agency (CISA): https://www.cisa.gov/ report**

Threat intelligence and vulnerability management

Threat intelligence and vulnerability management are crucial components of a proactive security strategy. This section provides an overview of platforms, tools, and resources for gathering threat intelligence, identifying vulnerabilities, and managing risk.

Threat intelligence platforms

Threat intelligence platforms (TIPs) aggregate, analyze, and disseminate threat data to help organizations make informed security decisions. Some of the platforms are discussed as follows:

- **ThreatConnect: https://www.threatconnect.com/**

- **Recorded future: https://www.recordedfuture.com/**

- **Anomali: https://www.anomali.com/**

- **Malware Information Sharing Platform (MISP): https://www.misp-project.org/**

- **OpenCTI: https://www.opencti.io/**

- **EclecticIQ Threat Intelligence Platform (TIP): https://www.eclecticiq.com/**

Vulnerability scanners

Vulnerability scanners automate the process of identifying security weaknesses in systems, applications, and networks. Here are some of them listed:

- **Nessus (Tenable)**: **https://www.tenable.com/products/nessus**
- **Nmap**: **https://nmap.org/**
- **OpenVAS**: **https://www.openvas.org/**
- **QualysGuard**: **https://www.qualys.com/**
- **Rapid7 Nexpose**: **https://www.rapid7.com/products/nexpose/**
- **Acunetix**: **https://www.acunetix.com/**
- **Burp Suite**: **https://portswigger.net/burp**

Vulnerability management platforms

Vulnerability management platforms help organizations prioritize, remediate, and track vulnerabilities across their environment. Some of them are as follows:

- **Vulcan Cyber**: **https://vulcan.io/**
- **RiskSense**: **https://www.ivanti.com/company/history/risksense**
- **Tenable.io**: **https://www.tenable.com/products/nessus**
- **QualysVM**: **https://www.qualys.com/**

Threat intelligence feeds

Threat intelligence feeds provide a continuous stream of threat data, such as **indicators of compromise** (**IOCs**), to help organizations stay informed about emerging threats. Some of them are discussed as follows:

- **AlienVault Open Threat Exchange (OTX)**: **https://otx.alienvault.com/**
- **SANS ISC Suspicious Domains Feed**: **https://isc.sans.edu/**
- **Malware Information Sharing Platform** (**MISP**): **https://www.misp-project.org/**
- **Commercial threat feeds**: These are numerous research providers like CrowdStrike, FireEye, Recorded Future, and others for their offerings. Pricing and features vary.

Call to action

The cybersecurity landscape is constantly evolving, and the tools and resources available to security professionals are constantly changing. The list provided in this chapter is intended to be a starting point for your exploration. It is crucial to stay updated and continue learning throughout your cybersecurity career.

The following are some ways to stay engaged and continue your cybersecurity journey:

- **Engage with specific communities**:

  o **Open Web Application Security Project (OWASP)**: Join an OWASP chapter, contribute to their projects (e.g., the OWASP Top 10), or participate in their local events. This is an excellent way to specialize in web application security and network with experts.

  o **SANS Institute communities**: Explore SANS community forums and mailing lists focused on specific areas like incident response, forensics, or cloud security. Engage in discussions, ask questions, and share your insights.

  o Participate in relevant cybersecurity subreddits (e.g., r/netsec, r/blueteamsec, r/AskNetsec). These online communities are valuable for staying updated on current events, asking for advice, and learning from diverse perspectives.

- **Contribute to open-source projects**:

  o Contribute to the Metasploit Framework by developing new modules, improving existing ones, or reporting bugs. This is a great way to gain practical experience with penetration testing and vulnerability exploitation (ethically).

  o **Nmap**: Get involved with the Nmap project by submitting bug reports, developing **Nmap Scripting Engine** (NSE) scripts, or helping with documentation. This will deepen your understanding of network scanning and reconnaissance.

  o **Zeek (formerly Bro)**: Contribute to the Zeek network security monitor. This is helpful for people interested in network security monitoring.

- **Seek hands-on opportunities**:

  o **Capture the Flag (CTF) competitions**: Actively participate in CTF competitions, both online and in-person. Platforms like CTF Time list upcoming events and provide valuable learning experiences.

  o **Bug bounty programs**: Explore bug bounty programs offered by companies like HackerOne or Bugcrowd. This provides real-world experience in vulnerability identification and ethical disclosure.

  o **Set up a home lab**: Build a virtualized home lab to practice security tools and techniques in a safe environment. This allows experimentation with different operating systems, network configurations, and security tools.

- **Pursue relevant certifications**:

  - o **CompTIA Security+**: This is an excellent entry-level certification that covers a broad range of security concepts, including network security, compliance and operational security, threats and vulnerabilities, and access control. It provides a strong foundation for anyone entering the cybersecurity field and is often a prerequisite for more specialized certifications.

  - o **Certified Ethical Hacker (CEH)**: While the CEH has an offensive security focus, it can be valuable for blue team professionals to understand attacker methodologies. This knowledge aids in building more effective defenses. However, it is important to note its offensive nature.

  - o **Global Information Assurance Certification (GIAC) Certifications**: SANS Institute offers a wide range of GIAC Certifications covering various cybersecurity domains. These certifications are well-regarded in the industry.

  - o **Certified Information Systems Security Professional (CISSP)**: Although the CISSP is typically geared toward more experienced professionals and security managers, it demonstrates a broad understanding of information security principles. Some of its domains are relevant to blue teaming.

- **Attend conferences and workshops**:

  - o **Black Hat and DEF CON**: Attend major cybersecurity conferences like Black Hat and DEF CON to learn about the latest research, tools, and trends. These events also offer excellent networking opportunities.

  - o **Local security meetups**: Look for local security meetups or groups in your area. These gatherings provide opportunities to connect with other professionals, learn from presentations, and participate in discussions.

Conclusion

This chapter has provided a broad overview of essential resources and tools for cybersecurity professionals, spanning general cybersecurity frameworks and learning platforms to specialized tools for OSINT, vulnerability management, incident response, and phishing analysis. We have emphasized the dynamic nature of the cybersecurity landscape and the ongoing need for professionals to expand their knowledge and practical skills.

In this next and chapter we will learn some of the specialized terminology specifically used in Cybersecurity and Defensive Security. Learning these terms is crucial as these terms are being used in daily use for anyone working in defensive security.

Join our Discord space

Join our Discord workspace for latest updates, offers, tech happenings around the world, new releases, and sessions with the authors:

https://discord.bpbonline.com

CHAPTER 14

Building Your Career in Blue Teaming

Introduction

Mastering the technical tools and defensive concepts in this book is the first step toward a successful cybersecurity career. However, technical skill alone is not enough. A thriving career is built on a strategic approach to continuous learning, hands-on practice, and the development of essential soft skills that transform a good analyst into a great one. This chapter serves as your roadmap to launching and advancing your career in defensive security, moving from theory to real-world application.

In the following sections, we will explore the diverse career paths available within blue teaming, from front-line **Security Operations Center** (**SOC**) analysis to advanced threat hunting. We will provide a step-by-step guide to building a cost-effective home lab, an indispensable tool for gaining practical experience. Furthermore, we will understand the often-overlooked but critical soft skills, such as communication and critical thinking, that distinguish top-tier professionals. Finally, this chapter will offer practical advice on navigating cybersecurity certifications and preparing for interviews to help you successfully demonstrate your skills and defensive mindset.

Structure

In this chapter, we will cover the following topics:

- Blue team career paths

- Building a home lab

- Mastering essential soft skills

- Navigating certifications

- Interview preparation

Objectives

The objective of this chapter is to equip the readers with a practical framework for building and advancing their careers in defensive security. Upon completion, you will be able to identify various blue team career paths and their requirements, construct a hands-on home lab for practical skill development, and recognize the crucial role of soft skills in professional success. You will also learn how to create a strategic plan for pursuing relevant certifications and prepare effectively for technical interviews, enabling you to translate the knowledge gained throughout this book into tangible career opportunities.

Blue team career paths

While the blue team is a diverse ecosystem of interconnected specializations, these defensive roles are not mutually exclusive. Most successful careers are built by mastering a foundational role and then branching out into advanced specializations. This section outlines the common career path and focuses on the specific skills, knowledge, and practice required to prepare for each stage.

Foundational skills for all roles

Before specializing, every blue team professional must have a strong grasp of the fundamentals covered in the preceding chapters of this book. These non-negotiable skills include the following:

- **Networking**: A deep understanding of TCP/IP, DNS, HTTP, and how to analyze network traffic.

- **Operating systems**: Proficiency with both Windows and Linux systems, including their respective command lines, filesystems, and logging mechanisms.

- **Security fundamentals**: A solid understanding of the CIA triad, common attack vectors, and core security concepts.

Preparing for the SOC analyst role

The SOC analyst role is the primary entry point into a blue team career, focused on monitoring, triage, and initial analysis.

The following list outlines the key knowledge areas:

- **Log analysis**: This is the most critical day-one skill. Focus on learning to read and interpret the *big three*: Windows Security Event Logs, firewall logs, and DNS logs.

- **SIEM operations**: Understand the way how a SIEM works. You do not need to be an architect, but you must know how to navigate the interface, understand dashboards, and use the query language to investigate alerts.

- **Basic threat recognition**: Be able to identify the basic indicators of the most common threats, such as phishing emails and common malware behavior.

Refer to the following list to understand the way to practice:

- **Use online platforms**: Websites like *CyberDefenders* and *LetsDefend* provide free, hands-on labs that simulate a real SOC environment where you can analyze alerts using a web-based SIEM.

- **Analyze traffic**: Download real-world malicious **packet captures** (**PCAPs**) from sites like **Malware-Traffic-Analysis.net** and analyze them in your home lab with Wireshark.

- **Certifications**: The **CompTIA Security+** is the industry standard for demonstrating foundational knowledge and getting your first interview. The **CompTIA Cybersecurity Analyst** (**CySA+**) is an excellent follow-up that specifically validates your skills as an analyst.

Advancing to an incident responder

The incident responder role is a high-pressure specialization focused on active crisis management. This is a common next step for an experienced SOC analyst.

The key knowledge areas are as follows:

- **Containment and eradication**: Master the technical steps required to isolate a compromised host from the network, block a malicious **Internet Protocol** (**IP**) address at the firewall, disable a user account in Active Directory, and remove malware persistence mechanisms.

- **Scripting for automation**: Develop proficiency in PowerShell (for Windows environments) or Python to automate response actions, such as scripting the quarantine of multiple hosts.

- **Forensics fundamentals**: Understand the principles of evidence preservation, as it is essential to know the ways to contain a threat without destroying the forensic evidence that will be needed for the investigation.

The following are the ways to practice:

- **IR-focused challenges**: Participate in incident response **Capture the Flag** (**CTF**) events and challenges that test your ability to react to a simulated breach.

- **Read Professional IR Reports**: Study detailed, public breach reports from firms like *Mandiant* or *CrowdStrike*. They provide invaluable insight into how professional teams handle major incidents.

- **Certifications**: The **GIAC Certified Incident Handler (GCIH)** is a highly respected, hands-on certification for incident response professionals.

Specializing in digital forensics

This section offers a deep specialization to investigate the *how* and *why* behind an attack.

The key knowledge areas are as follows:

- **Operating system internals**: Develop an expert-level understanding of filesystems (**NTFS**, **ext4**), the Windows Registry, and how operating systems manage memory.

- **Forensic tooling**: Learn how to use industry-standard open-source tools like **Autopsy** for disk analysis and the **Volatility Framework** for memory analysis.

- **Evidence handling**: Master the process of creating a forensically sound image of a disk or memory and maintaining a flawless *Chain of Custody*.

The following are the ways to practice:

- **Analyze forensic images**: Download freely available disk and memory images from forensic challenge websites (like the *annual SANS DFIR Summit challenges*) and practice analyzing them with your tools.

- **Reconstruct timelines**: Practice building an attack timeline by correlating timestamps from the filesystem, logs, and other artifacts.

- **Certifications**: The **GIAC Certified Forensic Analyst (GCFA)** is a top-tier certification for forensics specialists.

Becoming a threat hunter

This advanced role is for experienced analysts who want to proactively find hidden threats instead of solely responding to alerts.

The key knowledge areas are as follows:

- **Attacker TTPs**: A deep, obsessive understanding of the **MITRE ATT&CK Framework** is mandatory. You need to think like an adversary to know where they might be hiding.

- **Hypothesis-driven investigation**: Master the process of forming a testable hypothesis (e.g., *I believe an attacker is using WMI for lateral movement*) and then using your tools and query skills to find the data that proves or disproves it.

- **Advanced data analysis**: You must be an expert in the query language of your organization's tools (e.g., *Splunk SPL, KQL*) to search for behaviors, not just simple indicators.

Refer to the following list to understand the ways to practice:

- **Hunt in your home lab**: Use your lab to execute specific MITRE ATT&CK techniques and then hunt for the evidence you just created. This builds muscle memory for what different attacks look like in the data.

- **Follow threat hunting blogs**: Follow publications from security firms known for threat hunting (like *Red Canary, SpecterOps*) to learn the latest hunting methodologies.

- **Certifications**: The **GIAC Cyber Threat Intelligence** (**GCTI**) certification can provide a strong analytical foundation for hunting.

Building a home lab

In practice, there is no adequate substitute for **direct, practical experience**. Although theoretical knowledge of security is essential, **true comprehension** materializes when these concepts are actively implemented. We will understand the process of building a home lab. A home lab is the single most important tool for bridging the gap between theory and practice. Think of it as your personal, isolated sandbox. It is a safe place where you will be able to analyze real malware, test security tools, and learn the practical skills you will need on the job. An expensive hardware is not required, just a modern laptop with a decent amount of **random-access memory** (**RAM**) (16GB or more is recommended) is sufficient to begin.

The core components

A functional blue team lab consists of three main components:

- A **hypervisor** to run your virtual machines.

- A **victim machine** where you can detonate malware and observe its effects.

- An **analyst or attacker machine** to launch simulated attacks and monitor the victim.

With an understanding of the necessary components, you can now begin setting up your lab. The following guide breaks down the process into three fundamental stages:

1. **Choose hypervisor**: A hypervisor is a piece of software that allows you to create and run multiple independent **virtual machines** (**VMs**) on a single physical computer. For a cost-effective home lab, you should use one of the excellent free options available:

    - **Oracle virtualbox**: A user-friendly and powerful hypervisor that is completely free and works on *Windows*, *macOS*, and *Linux*. It is an ideal starting point for beginners.

- **VMware workstation player**: It is another excellent, free option for personal use from a leader in virtualization technology.

2. **Assemble virtual machines**: Once your hypervisor is installed, you need to create virtual computers that will live inside your lab. You require at least two, one to act as your target/victim and another to use for analysis and simulated attacks.

   - **The victim (Windows):** A Windows machine is essential, as most enterprise environments are Windows-based and most malware targets it. You can get a free, legal copy for your lab from the *Microsoft Windows Developer* website, which provides evaluation versions of Windows that are perfect for a non-production lab environment.

   - **The analyst and attacker (Linux)**: For your second machine, you have a few options, as follows:

     o **Kali Linux or Parrot OS**: These are Linux distributions that come pre-loaded with penetration testing tools. Using one of these allows you to learn how attackers operate and to launch simulated attacks against your victim VM.

     o **Security Onion**: This is a specialized Linux distribution built for blue teamers. It comes with a full suite of open-source security tools pre-installed and configured, including a SIEM, an IDS, and packet capture tools. It is an incredible all-in-one solution for your lab's monitoring station.

3. **Create a safe, isolated network**: Note that this is the most critical step for your safety. You will be working with live malware samples. You must ensure that your virtual lab is completely isolated from your home network to prevent malware from escaping and infecting your other devices.

   Your hypervisor (*VirtualBox* or *VMware*) allows you to create virtual networks. Do not use the default *Bridged* or *NAT* setting for your victim machine. Instead, create a new network using the *Host-Only* or *Internal Network* setting. This creates a completely private network that only your VMs can access. Your VMs can communicate with each other, but they are sandboxed and cannot reach your home network or the internet, ensuring the malware remains safely contained.

4. **Install your blue team toolkit**: To see what is happening inside your lab, you need to install the following monitoring tools, which can be called a **blue team toolkit**:

   - **Sysmon**: On your Windows victim VM, download and install Sysmon, a free tool from Microsoft. It provides extremely detailed logs on process creation, network connections, and registry changes, giving you the deep visibility you need to hunt for threats.

   - **Wireshark**: Install Wireshark, the industry-standard network protocol analyzer, on your analyst machine. It allows you to capture and inspect every single packet that travels across your virtual lab network, which is essential for analyzing how malware communicates.

5. **Put your lab to work**: With your lab built, you can perform a lot of hands-on practical work. Refer to the following steps to practice:

   a. Navigate to websites like **Malware-Traffic-Analysis.net**, which provide real-world malware samples and their corresponding PCAP files for training purposes.

   b. Download a malware sample and the associated PCAP file.

   c. Execute the malware on your isolated Windows victim VM.

   d. Observe the results:

      i. Watch the alerts fire in real-time in your Security Onion VM.

      ii. Examine the PCAP file in Wireshark to see the malicious network connections the malware tried to make.

      iii. On the Windows VM, dig into the Sysmon logs to see what processes the malware created and what system changes it made.

This cycle of detonating malware in a safe environment and then using your tools to perform a forensic analysis of the aftermath is the appropriate way of building invaluable, job-ready skills.

Mastering essential soft skills

Technical skills will get you the interview, but soft skills will get you the job and make you an invaluable team member. In defensive security, where stakes are high and information is often incomplete, your ability to think, communicate, and collaborate under pressure is just as critical as your ability to analyze a packet capture or read a log file. These skills are not optional extras; they are force multipliers that amplify your technical expertise and distinguish a good analyst from a great one.

Communication

The core of a blue teamer's job is to translate complex technical data into clear, actionable information. This requires mastering the following two distinct forms of communication:

- **Technical communication**: You must be able to articulate detailed findings to your peers with precision. This means clearly explaining the evidence, the methods of your analysis, and your conclusions so that a teammate can understand and build upon your work.

- **Executive and non-technical communication**: You must also be able to brief non-technical stakeholders, like managers or legal teams, on the status and impact of an incident without using confusing jargon. Summarizing a complex attack into a statement of business risk is a crucial and highly valued skill. Clear, concise, and unambiguous incident report writing is non-negotiable.

Collaboration

Security professionals do not work in a vacuum, and a SOC is a fundamentally collaborative environment where the team's success depends on how well they work together. In practice, this means the following:

- **Sharing information**: Actively communicating your findings, even if they seem minor, can provide the missing piece to a puzzle another analyst is working on.

- **Trust and peer review**: Having the humility to ask a teammate for a second opinion on your analysis and trusting their expertise is vital. During a high-stress incident, the team succeeds or fails together.

Critical thinking

Critical thinking is the skill that separates an analyst from a simple alert processor. It is the ability to look at a security event and, instead of just following a checklist, ask probing questions to understand the deeper context.

For example, when seeing a *password spray* alert, a critical thinker does not just note the event. They ask: *Why these specific accounts? Are they all in the same department? Where are the login attempts coming from geographically? What time of day is it happening?* This curiosity and the desire to connect seemingly unrelated data points to see the larger picture is what uncovers a sophisticated, stealthy attack from the noise of everyday alerts.

Problem-solving under pressure

Incident response is inherently stressful. When an active breach is underway, the ability to remain calm and think logically is what defines a senior responder. This skill is not about being emotionless, but rather about being methodical when the pressure is on. It means trusting your training, following the incident response plan, documenting every step you take, and making evidence-based decisions rather than panicked guesses. This is a skill that is best developed through hands-on practice in a home lab and through tabletop exercises, where you can simulate the pressure of an incident in a controlled environment.

Navigating certifications

In the world of cybersecurity, the *alphabet soup* of certifications can be overwhelming. It is crucial to understand that certifications are not a substitute for hands-on skills, but they serve a vital purpose, which is that they validate your knowledge to employers, meet HR filtering requirements for job applications, and demonstrate a commitment to your professional development. Instead of collecting certifications randomly, a strategic, tiered approach will provide the most value for your time and money at each stage of your blue team career.

Foundational certifications

For someone starting their career or looking to formally validate their baseline knowledge, these certifications are the industry standard. They are designed to prove you speak the language of cybersecurity.

- **CompTIA security+**: This is the universal starting point and the most recognized entry-level certification in cybersecurity. It is vendor-neutral and covers a broad range of security concepts, including network security, threats and vulnerabilities, and risk management. Passing the Security+ exam demonstrates to employers that you have a solid grasp of the fundamental principles required for any cybersecurity role.

- **CompTIA Cybersecurity Analyst (CySA+)**: If the Security+ is the foundation, the CySA+ is the first floor built specifically for a defensive role. It moves beyond general concepts and focuses on the practical skills of a security analyst, such as analyzing security data, identifying vulnerabilities, and responding to cyber threats. It is the ideal next step after Security+ for anyone aiming for a SOC Analyst position.

Intermediate certifications/choosing your specialization

Once you have a basic experience of 1-2 years as a SOC Analyst, you can pursue certifications that signal your readiness to specialize in a more advanced field. These certifications are often more hands-on, intensive, and expensive, and are frequently sponsored by employers, details as follows:

- **GIAC certifications (SANS Institute)**: GIAC certifications are among the most respected in the industry because they are tied to rigorous SANS training courses that emphasize deep, practical skills. They are a top choice for specializing:

    o **For incident response**: The **GIAC Certified Incident Handler (GCIH)** is a premier certification that validates your ability to manage and respond to active security incidents.

    o **For forensics**: The **GIAC Certified Forensic Analyst (GCFA)** proves your skills in advanced incident investigation and forensic analysis of compromised systems.

- **Certified Ethical Hacker (CEH)**: This is an offensive-focused certification, but it holds significant value for blue teamers. To build a better defense, you must understand how the offense operates. The CEH demonstrates your knowledge of attacker tools and methodologies, which helps you better anticipate, detect, and counter their moves.

- **Advanced certifications (leadership and strategy)**: After several years of hands-on experience, you may look toward senior, management, or architectural roles. Certifications at this level demonstrate a broad, strategic understanding of security programs.

- **Certified Information Systems Security Professional (CISSP)**: This is widely considered as the gold standard for cybersecurity leadership and management. It is crucial to understand that the CISSP is not a hands-on technical exam; it is a high-level certification covering all eight domains of information security, from risk management to security architecture and governance. It requires at least five years of documented professional experience to even qualify, making it a goal for established professionals.

Interview preparation

An interview for a blue team role is a test of both knowledge and mindset. The interviewer wants to know not just *what* you know, but *how you think*. They are looking for a defensive mindset, a combination of technical curiosity, methodical problem-solving, and a healthy dose of professional skepticism. Your goal is to show them that you are not just a future employee, but a future defender. This section will guide you on how to prepare for common questions and effectively demonstrate that mindset.

Common technical and scenario-based questions

The following questions can be expected to test your foundational knowledge and your ability to respond to a situation. Be prepared to walk through your thought process for scenarios like these:

- *Walk me through the steps you would take to analyze a suspicious email.*

- *A high-priority SIEM alert fires for 'Potential C2 Beaconing' from a user's workstation. What are your first five steps?*

- *Explain the difference between an IDS and an IPS. Where would you place them in a network?*

- *You find a suspicious executable file on a host. How would you determine if it is malicious?*

- *You see a spike in DNS queries for domains that do not exist (NXDOMAIN responses) coming from a single host. What could this indicate?*

The value of practical application

The most impactful way to answer interview questions is to tell a story based on your hands-on experience, and your home lab is the perfect source for these stories. Listing skills on a resume is one thing; describing how you have applied them is far more powerful.

- **Instead of saying**: *I have experience with Wireshark and network analysis.*

- **Say this**: *In my home lab, I analyzed a PCAP of a TrickBot infection. I used Wireshark to filter for HTTP traffic and identified the initial malware download, then I pivoted to the DNS traffic to find the C2 server domains it was trying to contact.*

The second answer proves your capability, demonstrates your passion for learning, and gives the interviewer a concrete example of your skills in action.

Demonstrating the defensive mindset

When faced with a scenario, the most common mistake a junior candidate makes is jumping immediately to a conclusion or a single action. A mature defensive mindset always starts with a search for context.

Your answer to almost every scenario-based question should begin with a variation of this phrase: *My first step would be to gather more context.*

This shows the interviewer that you are methodical, evidence-driven, and not prone to making assumptions.

Example:

- **Interviewer**: *A user reports their computer is running slowly. What do you do?*

    o **Weak answer**: *I would run an antivirus scan. (This is a single action without context)*

    o **Strong answer**: *First, I would gather context. I would ask the user when the slowness started and what they were doing at the time. Simultaneously, I would check our EDR and SIEM for any recent security alerts from that host. I would look at the running processes and network connections to see if any are consuming unusual resources. Based on that initial data, I would form a hypothesis: Is it likely a performance issue, or could it be malware? An antivirus scan would be one part of my investigation, but only after I have some context to guide my actions.*

    This approach demonstrates critical thinking and a structured problem-solving process, which are the most valuable traits in a defensive security professional. An interview is your chance to show them you are not just there to answer questions, but to solve problems. Prepare, be curious, and let your passion for security shine through.

Conclusion

This chapter has provided a roadmap for moving beyond pure technical knowledge to build a successful and sustainable career in defensive security. We have explored the diverse career paths available, from the front lines of the SOC to the proactive world of threat hunting. We have laid out the practical steps for building a home lab to gain invaluable hands-on experience and highlighted the critical soft skills like communication and critical thinking that separate a good analyst from a great one. Finally, we provided a strategic guide to navigating certifications and preparing for interviews, focusing on how to demonstrate a true defensive mindset. Remember that your career is a continuous journey of learning and adaptation; use these tools not as a checklist, but as a framework for your professional growth.

Throughout this book, we have explored the principles of a modern, lean approach to blue teaming and threat management, emphasizing a fundamental shift from a reactive to a proactive defensive posture. From understanding foundational networking concepts and log analysis to leveraging advanced tools like SIEMs and EDRs and adopting strategic frameworks like NIST and MITRE ATT&CK, the goal has been to equip you with a holistic defensive toolkit. We have delved into the methodologies of the SOC, the processes of incident response, and the proactive mindset of the Threat Hunter, all informed by actionable Threat Intelligence. An effective defense is not about having the most tools, but about using the right people, processes, and technology in an intelligent and integrated way. The threat landscape will continue to evolve, but the principles of vigilance, continuous learning, and strategic thinking you have learned here will serve as your constant guide. The ultimate mission of a blue teamer is to be a resilient and adaptable guardian of the digital world.

Join our Discord space

Join our Discord workspace for latest updates, offers, tech happenings around the world, new releases, and sessions with the authors:

https://discord.bpbonline.com

Index

www.ingramcontent.com/pod-product-compliance
Lightning Source LLC
Chambersburg PA
CBHW061744210326
41599CB00034B/6786